THE UNITED NATIONS' TOP JOB

A Close Look At The Work Of The Eight Secretaries-General

BY LUCIA MOUAT

ISBN: 1484806190
ISBN 13: 9781484806197

Library of Congress Control Number: 2013908434
CreateSpace Independent Publishing Platform
North Charleston, South Carolina

CONTENTS

Timeline of the UN Secretaries-General

Trygve Lie	1946–April 1953
Dag Hammarskjöld	May 1953–September 1961
U Thant	November 1961–December 1971
Kurt Waldheim	1972–1981
Javier Pérez de Cuéllar	1982–1991
Boutros Boutros-Ghali	1992–1996
Kofi Annan	1997–2006
Ban Ki-moon	2007–present

PREFACE

Writing this book has been a fascinating journey. I have been keenly interested in the United Nations for as long as I can remember. In my college years, I majored in international relations at the University of Wisconsin and, in my senior year, chaired the committee that organized its regional United Nations conference. Later I received an MA from the Fletcher School of Law and Diplomacy at Tufts University.

Since that time, in closely following UN progress, I have seen that global political gridlock is not so different from its counterpart at the national level. Getting a consensus in the Security Council sometimes means no resolution at all or a mild one that lacks needed punch. Yet those limits on Council action sometimes open the way for a UN secretary-general to make an important diplomatic difference in times of crisis.

As a correspondent for the *Christian Science Monitor*, covering the United Nations for a time, I became increasingly interested in the valuable role—particularly in mediation—that the secretary-general, as the world's top diplomat, has played over the years.

It takes a team of skillful, patient friends and experts to produce a book. I am especially grateful to Jeanne Heller, Ellen Steinberg, Dorothy Dare, Dulcie Leimbach, and Jennifer Murtoff for their steady, talented help in the editing and technical hurdles encountered. Stanley Meisler, Kennette Benedict, and Thomas Weiss helped with needed advice. I am also deeply indebted to the many academic experts who keep close watch on the United Nations and who gave generously of their time and insights in interviews.

I have crafted the book as a journalist, inserting frequent, direct quotes in the interest of keeping the narrative lively and grounded.

To my wonderful family, past and present.
My father had a lifelong special interest in the
United Nations and its future.

CHAPTER ONE

_____

Why a United Nations?

After the failure of the League of Nations to prevent World War II and its horrors, the world was ready in 1945 to try once again to establish a more effective system of collective security.

Right from the start, the role of the United States was crucial. It was President Franklin Delano Roosevelt who began the series of careful steps that led to the unanimous adoption—with a standing ovation by delegates from all fifty nations involved—of the United Nations Charter in San Francisco on June 25, 1945.

Roosevelt knew well the League's shortcomings in both strength and support. For more than 20 years, the Geneva-based world organization had struggled to become an effective tool for international cooperation. It never won United States' ratification and did not succeed in resolving such major conflicts as Japan's 1931 invasion of Manchuria and Italy's 1934 invasion of Ethiopia.

The US President was determined that another attempt be made long before the end of World War II and that, this time, Washington, DC, would ratify the result. At Roosevelt's bidding, US Secretary of State Cordell Hull organized a team in the State Department as early as 1939 to work on the project. The President, who first coined the term *united nations,* worked hard over the next several years to bring his sometimes less-than-enthusiastic wartime allies on board.

The Atlantic Charter, which set several broad peacetime goals, including creation of a new global organization, brought Britain's Winston Churchill into the fold. The two leaders signed the Charter in mid-August 1941 aboard a cruiser off the coast of Newfoundland. On January 1, 1942, representatives of the 26 nations fighting the Axis powers signed the Declaration of the United Nations in Washington. They pledged to continue fighting the Axis powers and to work together to build a permanent system of collective security.

Four of the five governments that were to become permanent representatives on the UN Security Council—the United States, Great Britain, the Soviet Union, and China—signed a declaration in Moscow on October 30, 1943. It called for the early creation of a new organization to maintain global security.

Many refinements and compromises were worked out during the conferences at Dumbarton Oaks in Washington during the fall of 1944, at Yalta in February 1945, and at San Francisco the following June. From the beginning, the use and extent of the Security Council veto was a hotly controversial topic. Ultimately, it was agreed that the veto would apply only to substantive matters. It would not apply to debate on whether an issue was procedural or substantive, as the Soviet Union's Joseph Stalin had hoped. The delegates also agreed that members would abstain from any vote if they were parties to a dispute under discussion.

Mindful of the need for US popular support, Roosevelt, who died just eight weeks before the delegates met in San Francisco, had appointed two US senators to the American delegation. He also launched a major public-relations campaign headed by Adlai Stevenson and Archibald MacLeish.

Harry Truman, who assumed the presidency after Roosevelt's death, energetically carried on the legacy. He kicked off a new, broad-based public-relations effort. He sent envoys to Moscow to persuade Stalin to drop some of his toughest demands. In a speech before the San Francisco delegates, Truman insisted that the United States did not want the United Nations to be another powerless talk shop. It was to have real muscle—but only when the major powers agreed on a course of action.

"We all have to recognize, no matter how great our strength, that we must deny ourselves the license to do always as we please," Truman told the San Francisco conference at its final session. "That is the price which each nation will have to pay for world peace."[1]

It was Truman who personally delivered the UN Charter to the US Senate. This time the United States was the first nation to ratify the document on July 28, 1945.

By October 24, the 111-article UN Charter was in force. It had been ratified by the majority of nations at the San Francisco conference, including all five permanent members of the Security Council.

Next, the new world body needed a permanent home. The UN Preparatory Commission narrowed the choice to Europe (the Europeans largely favored Geneva) or the United States. Most delegations preferred the latter. The Soviet Union's Andrei Gromyko argued that an American location would lie conveniently between Asia and Europe. The Commission agreed—by a slim margin of two votes.

The United Nations began its work in a variety of temporary locations. The first sessions of both the General Assembly (GA) and the Security Council (SC) were held in January 1946 in London. In the fall, the GA moved to New York City to meet, first, in a revamped gymnasium at Hunter College in the Bronx and, later, at a world's fair site in Flushing Meadows, Queens. The SC and Secretariat took up quarters in an unused portion of an arms factory on New York's Long Island.

Several American cities were considered for the United Nations' permanent home. A GA subcommittee recommended Philadelphia or San Francisco. Trygve Lie, who had led Norway's delegation to San Francisco and was elected in February 1946 as the United Nations' first secretary-general, strongly favored New York as the United Nations' permanent home. City officials offered the Flushing Meadows site of reclaimed land, a choice the British ambassador compared to the coastal swamps of southwest Africa.[2]

Lie then asked New York City mayor William O'Dwyer and city planner Robert Moses to come up with a better choice. "He simply said to them, if you want the UN in New York, which you do, you've got to come up with a better offer," recalled Sir Brian Urquhart, who had left the British Army and begun his long UN career with a job at the UN Preparatory Commission.[3] Moses suggested the Turtle Bay area, six blocks of slaughter houses and slums along the East River. He contacted the Rockefeller family.

In a dramatic move in December 1946, John D. Rockefeller Jr. offered the United Nations $8.5 million to buy the Turtle Bay property. The city put up another $26 million, and the United States made a $65 million interest-free loan available. The GA accepted the plan, and the United Nations moved into its new permanent headquarters in 1952.

Sir Brian credits Lie with the major role in that important decision: "The UN wouldn't have settled in New York City if it hadn't been for him. We'd have been wandering around in some rural setting in Westchester County or somewhere.... It was a very important thing for Lie to have done."[4]

Everyone involved in the birth of the organization knew the importance of great-power unanimity. The United States, United Kingdom, France, China, and Russia each had permanent seats and veto power in the SC. As Adlai Stevenson, a US delegate to the San Francisco conference, told the Chicago Bar Association in June 1945, "Everything depends on the active participation, pacific intentions, and good faith of the Big Five."[5]

Yet the need for cooperation of the great powers was far easier to agree on in theory than in practice. Lie writes that even as he prepared for the first UN meetings in New York, he was aware of the depth and danger of a developing East–West split. He still hoped and believed, however, that the spirit of wartime cooperation could be revived.

In his now-famous March 1946 speech in Fulton, Missouri, Winston Churchill spoke of the "iron curtain" that had descended across the heart of Europe and of the massive Russian military presence there. Speaking as a private citizen eight months after leaving office, he urged Western democracies to stand together.

Lie writes in his autobiography that he wished Churchill had coupled that plea for unity with a more positive and conciliatory approach to the Soviet Union. Lie argues that Churchill challenged Russia at a moment when most people were hoping for successful East–West cooperation.[6]

Yet Russia was fast solidifying its hold on Eastern Europe. With the exception of Czechoslovakia, the free elections under joint allied supervision agreed to at Yalta for Eastern Europe were never held. By the 1948 Berlin blockade, the SC machinery for dealing with aggressors was basically inoperative.

As Sir Brian writes in his autobiography, the UN Charter assumed "with a stunning lack of political realism" that the war's victors would "stay united in supervising and, if necessary, enforcing world peace."[7]

Still, the paralysis that quickly developed opened some unexpected opportunities for the job of secretary-general.

This book looks at that role, both as envisioned in the Charter and as it played out.

CHAPTER TWO

The World's Most Impossible Job

While Secretary-General Boutros Boutros-Ghali from Egypt was still in office, a color photo of him appeared on a wall near the press area of the UN headquarters. In handwritten scrawl beside it, someone had written

> The Secretary-General...the most impossible, frustrating, daunting, challenging, rewarding, fascinating, clearly unique job on earth. Chief administrator of the organization. Guardian of the Charter with a global-watching brief. Go-between and honest broker in critical international situations. Articulator of international interests. Guide but not sovereign.

Those who have held the job before and after Boutros-Ghali would doubtless identify with much of this clearly in-awe description.

Technically, the job has little power. The secretary-general heads no government. The people of the world did not elect him. He has no standing military forces at his disposal. He has no intelligence service. His bargaining power is limited. He cannot dictate or enforce UN policy. Delegates and UN staff members often feel far more loyal to their home countries than to the world organization or its head.

Yet in practice the post has evolved into a mix of mediator, administrator, and moral leader. Over the years it has become closely involved with peacekeeping operations, economic and social initiatives, and quiet diplomacy. The secretary-general is, in fact, the only person who represents—and thus can speak for—the organization as a whole.

The US newspaper columnist Walter Lippmann once said that a secretary-general's greatest but least-advertised role is to be "a father-confessor" to member governments—the person to whom they can confide and who knows their "real position" in an international controversy.[1]

What do the secretaries-general themselves have to say?

- In welcoming Dag Hammarskjöld of Sweden as his successor, Trygve Lie, the United Nations' first secretary-general, famously described the post as "the most impossible job on this earth."

- Hammarskjöld himself once half-jokingly compared his role to that of a pope without a church. He explained that he was a trustee of the secrets of all member nations.[2]

- U Thant of Burma embraced Franklin Roosevelt's reported preference during the United Nations' founding days for the term *moderator*. U Thant said, "I know of no better single word to describe my own conception of this office." He also liked the term *mediator,* noting in his memoirs that a secretary-general has to work by persuasion, argument, negotiation, and a constant search for consensus: "I have always felt that the most important political duty of the secretary-general is to concentrate on the harmonizing function of the United Nations." He saw the ability to hold an independent position as vital—implying no disrespect for the wishes or opinions of member governments—but as "an insurance" that the long-term interest in peace of all members would be served.[3]

- The late Kurt Waldheim of Austria, in an interview with the author in Vienna, described the role as mainly diplomatic, requiring "a close working relationship" with all member states. "I think the most important power the secretary-general has is the moral power," he said. "He must convince governments to cooperate, to support his suggestions for peaceful resolution of conflicts."[4]

- In his memoir, Javier Pérez de Cuéllar of Peru argues that the secretary-general serves the organization of governments but must never become their captive. "[He] must be mediator and standard bearer, moderator and guide, conciliator and arbiter, impartial in all."[5] On May 13, 1986, he told an Oxford University audience that to correctly understand the secretary-general's role is to appreciate "the whole mission" of the United Nations itself. He warned against the temptation for any secretary-general to indulge in "extremes"—either that of vanity and wishful thinking or of modestly limiting one's role in hopes of avoiding controversy.

- Boutros Boutros-Ghali of Egypt, who enjoyed describing himself as "the humble servant of the Security Council," calls the post "weak but pivotal" by design. He says the secretary-general has no substantial voice over what goes on but is often "the fulcrum" for cooperative progress.[6] He said that independence most characterizes the role: "the holder of this office must never be seen as acting out of fear, or in an attempt to curry favor with one state or group of states."[7]

- Kofi Annan of Ghana insisted that the secretary-general has only as much power as a united SC decides to give him—as well as the moral authority entrusted to him by the Charter. He must be judged, Annan said, by his fidelity to Charter principles and to his advancement of the ideas behind them.[8]

- Ban Ki-moon of South Korea has described himself as a consensus-builder. He took office with a strong and optimistic pledge to be a listener, make global warming a top priority, move forward on management reform, and try to bridge the gap between the developed and the developing world.

In practice, as head of the UN Secretariat, the secretary-general usually hosts heads of state and governments when they come to the United Nations, sends notes of congratulations or sympathy to high-ranking government leaders, and often plays a prominent role in UN ceremonies and global conferences.

The United Nations' top job has developed far more rapidly than any other UN organ, in the view of Sir Brian Urquhart, the British former UN undersecretary-general who worked under five of the

United Nations' top officials. Sir Brian said in an interview that this growth was due in part to the secretaries-general pushing the limits of the office, the international climate that allowed it, and the start of UN peacekeeping. The latter, he said, gave the secretary-general an operational function that he never really had in the Charter.[9]

Certainly another factor has been the ambiguous nature of many SC resolutions. To avoid a veto, the Council often passes a watered-down measure that implies rather than specifies actions that are needed. The secretary-general, who must implement the orders, has more leeway in interpreting these.

Defining the UN chief's actual role was not a big issue at the founding San Francisco conference. Instead, there was a lively debate about what kind of person was needed, from which country, how that person should be appointed, and for how long. The final decisions were left largely to the UN Preparatory Commission. It decided on a renewable five-year term for the first secretary-general but said the formula need not be set in stone. Still, the custom has held.

Several election options were considered. Small- and medium-sized states wanted the GA, where all UN members were included, to have the sole power to choose the candidate. The larger powers argued that no secretary-general could be effective without their particular vote of confidence. The five permanent members of the SC insisted on veto power, noting that the GA still had the power to reject a candidate it did not want. The Preparatory Commission agreed that the SC should nominate the candidate for the Assembly's yes or no vote, discussions should be private, and the voting kept secret.

Over the years, many have suggested that clearer guidelines and methodical search and screening processes were needed. These have never happened. Rotation among regions has become the practice. The need for consensus takes a certain toll. "Political differences dictate a search for a candidate who will not exert any troubling degree of leadership, commitment, originality, or independence," Sir Brian noted drily in his memoir, *A Life in Peace and War*.[10]

Yet from the start, the hope was to give the secretary-general's position more control and a larger role in peace and security issues than the same post had in the League of Nations.

Inis Claude Jr., a veteran UN analyst and professor emeritus of political science at the University of Virginia, noted in an interview for this book that the UN founders had two models in mind.

One model was Sir Eric Drummond, a British diplomat and secretary-general of the League of Nations for 13 years. He saw himself as the obedient servant of political masters, Claude said. Sir Eric was basically a shy person who preferred anonymity and saw his job as mainly administrative. He made no appeals to public opinion and did not feel he could openly take sides in political disputes.[11] In his book, *The UN Secretary-General from the Cold War to the New Era: A Global and Peace Security Mandate?*, Edward Newman confirmed that role: "This impression was one of quiet behind-the-scenes service."[12]

The second model, more attractive to the framers of the Charter, Claude said, was Albert Thomas, a French citizen who was the director-general of the International Labor Organization (ILO) at the time. The ILO was almost a sister organization of the League of Nations. Thomas, a socialist, saw himself as a dynamic political policy leader.[13]

In the end, the UN Charter says little about the UN chief's role and its limits. The document is definite on one point only: the secretary-general is the chief administrative officer and is to act in that capacity in meetings of the GA, SC, and other UN organs. He is responsible for running the organization, staffing it, and carrying out SC resolutions.

However, at the start, the major powers believed they would run the United Nations together. They thought they needed an office manager rather than a policy maker.

The administrative role is one that no one in the job (with the possible exception of Dag Hammarskjöld) has relished. Waldheim called that responsibility important "but sort of a burden."[14]

Most people in the post have had diplomatic backgrounds. That tends to be their strength.

"Most secretaries-general can barely lead a pack of Boy Scouts to an ice-cream parlor," joked Herbert Okun, former US deputy ambassador to the United Nations, in an interview with the author.[15]

As Inis Claude Jr. said, "Most secretaries-general have seen themselves as potential—or, at worst, frustrated—political leaders. We haven't had any shrinking violets who simply wanted to be anonymous bureaucrats—perhaps not enough so. One might argue that from time to time we ought to have a secretary-general who takes his administrative responsibilities seriously. ...They've too often had their eyes on a more romantic or glamorous political role that they might play—with varying degrees of success."[16]

It is the secretary-general's task to appoint the Secretariat staff. Article 100 stipulates that in performing his duties, the secretary-general and staff must not "seek or receive" instructions from any government or external authority. Article 101 of the UN Charter says the primary recruitment aim should be to seek the highest standards of efficiency, competence, and integrity, and choose from as wide a geographic basis as possible.

That order is like Psalm 100 to any secretary-general in its idea that loyalty must be strictly international, noted Boutros Boutros-Ghali.[17]

Yet in practice these lofty goals have not always been followed. The secretary-general simply lacks the resources to recruit globally on merit. Pressure on staff hiring from member governments is often strong.

Among the secretary-general's few Charter-prescribed duties, he must write an annual report to the GA on the United Nations' work. In practice, the introduction to that report has become a place to voice his personal reflections on the state of the world. The intent is to spur discussion, establish norms and goals, and influence the UN agenda. As Pérez de Cuéllar said in his May 13, 1986, speech at Oxford University, the report allows the secretary-general to both initiate and galvanize.

Claude noted that over the years, secretaries-general have used the introduction to the report as a kind of State of the Union message to lay out suggestions for future action. "That's the bully-pulpit function," he said.[18]

Article 99 of the Charter, adopted in San Francisco with little debate, does give the secretary-general a substantial degree of independence. He "may bring to the attention of the Security Council any matter which in his view may threaten the maintenance of international peace and security."

That Charter clause is the zinger that was never included in the description of the League of Nations' top job. It was a clear attempt to strengthen the UN secretary-general's role, to tap him as an international watchman. Pérez de Cuéllar observed in his 1986 Oxford speech that the word *matter* is not confined to a dispute or situation but leaves the secretary-general free to evaluate independently all issues that, in his view, bear on peace and security.

The UN Preparatory Commission did note that the responsibility requires "exercise of the highest qualities of political judgment, tact, and integrity." Though rarely formally invoked, Article 99 gives the secretary-general a definite political role. Under this article, he can make inquiries and informally mediate any issues he deems a threat to world peace. He becomes, in effect, another member of the SC, though one without a vote.

Referring to Article 99 as one of the wisest "inventions" of the drafters' work, James Sutterlin, a Yale University distinguished fellow and a former director of UN Political Affairs, said in an interview that the article's purpose is to strengthen the organization's ability to maintain peace: "It has given the secretary-general the possibility of really acting as a force for peace on his own."[19]

"There's a strong temptation for a secretary-general to regard himself as kind of the global prime minister," said Claude. "In some ways he is. But he is really in charge of that bureaucratic organization—not the states that form...[its] heart." It is the member states, he says, who are in charge of the muscular, coercive activity.[20]

Actually most secretaries-general have found that they had their hands full just trying to respond to the diplomatic needs of the moment. U Thant once remarked that there had been so many crises during his decade as secretary-general that it was often difficult to recall all of them.[21]

Yet it is also during such crises that the eight people who have held the position have generally made their strongest contributions. With at least some background in diplomacy, most have found the pull to negotiate a very natural part of the job. Indeed, their preoccupation with peace and security issues has intensified over the years.

"Secretaries-general don't have much leverage in mediation," Sutterlin observed. "The main tools they have are the prestige of the UN, their own personal reputation for objectivity, and the possibility that the secretary-general may go public with blaming one party or the other. In that case he loses his value as a mediator."[22]

Nevertheless, there have been numerous mediating successes. Many go largely unnoticed.

"Trying to forestall things that were going to turn sour has been one of the main functions of the secretary-general right from the beginning," Sir Brian said. "There have been many...routine conflict prevention negotiations which nobody's ever going to hear about because nothing happened. I mean, how can you prove something is a success if it wasn't a disaster? It's a catch-22. Yet I think that's a very strong suit of secretaries-general.... People would miss that greatly if [that function] were ever abolished."[23]

Most secretaries-general have traveled extensively. In the process, they have talked with and made speeches to audiences outside the United Nations' inner circle.

"It's terribly wearing but useful," said Leon Gordenker, professor emeritus of politics at Princeton University, in an interview. "For one thing, it gives the national politicians a reason to think their attachment to UN enterprises is taken seriously...and it can sometimes be helpful for the secretary-general's education if he has to confront the agenda that some of these national politicians have. It can help him tailor his notions into something acceptable."[24]

All secretaries-general have made the case for their independence and their right to speak out from an international perspective. All have tried to exert moral leadership—some more successfully than others. Secretaries-general and scholars who study the United Nations generally agree that the challenge is to speak out and act in ways that do not overstep the tolerance levels of member governments, particularly those with veto power. Paul Kennedy, noted in *The Parliament of Man: The Past, Present, and Future of the United Nations*, that "to offend one of the permanent five is usually fatal."[25]

As Hurst Hannum, a professor of international law at the Fletcher School of Law and Diplomacy at Tufts University, observed in an interview, "The secretary-general does set the tone, whether it's very independent or very subservient."[26]

For better or worse, the United Nations' top office holder personifies the organization, which in turn is often judged by his performance. To US diplomat Herbert Okun, the secretary-general is "the meat in the sandwich." His position requires great skill, delicacy, and understanding: "It's a tough job but people run for it, so they must want it," he noted.[27]

Yet the first secretary-general, Trygve Lie, certainly was not seeking or expecting the job to come his way.

CHAPTER THREE

Trygve Lie: A Norwegian Lawyer Accepts an "Awesome Task"[1]

Trygve Halvdan Lie was not the first choice of the UN membership. Few secretaries-general ever have been. Discussion and wrangling are standard procedure. Such well-known names as Dwight D. Eisenhower and Winston Churchill had been mentioned. Washington initially favored Lester Pearson, Canada's ambassador to the United States, for the job.

It was Moscow that first suggested Norway's little-known foreign minister, Lie. The Soviets said the post should go to someone whose country had suffered under Nazi occupation. In 1944, on his last visit to Moscow as Norway's foreign minister, Lie signed an agreement on arrangements for Norway's liberation. More recently he had been Norway's chief delegate to the founding San Francisco conference.

On Christmas Day 1945, he and his wife and three children and another family were staying at his remote cabin high in the Norwegian mountains. They had just returned from an early morning ski run and were sitting down to breakfast when one of the children spied a lone skier heading toward the cabin. It was a farmer who often took care of the property.

He was bringing a telegram forwarded from the United States by the Oslo Foreign Ministry. In it, Adlai Stevenson, the chief American delegate to the UN Preparatory Commission, asked if Lie would accept the presidency of the General Assembly (GA), which was due to convene the next month in London. Stevenson added that he could not comment on Lie's prospects for getting the job, however, because discussions with other delegations had not yet begun.

"My first feeling was almost resentment," recalled Lie, who said he was surprised by the intrusion on the happiness of the family festivities. True, he had been asked in confidence in August about this by Edward Stettinius Jr., the American who had presided over the San Francisco conference. But he had given it little serious thought because it had not been mentioned again.[2]

Lie read the telegram aloud several times for the others in the cabin. A prompt decision had to be made. He described himself as "the most doubtful one present" but said the others argued strongly that he could not refuse. "Yes" was scrawled on a scrap of paper and given the skier to send back to the foreign ministry as Lie's reply.

At that time Lie considered the GA post—later awarded to Paul-Henri Spaak, prime minister of Belgium—preferable to the job of secretary-general. Lie later admitted he saw the secretary-general's job as a "consolation prize."[3]

Yet by late January, the five permanent members of the Security Council (SC), after quietly agreeing that none of their own citizens should ever fill the UN's top post finally settled on Lie for the job. As a veteran trade-union lawyer, Lie had "enough political leaning to the left to be acceptable to Moscow and enough obscurity to pass through American filters."[4] On February 1, 1946, the GA formally elected him to a five-year term.

"There was no consideration of who might be best qualified for the job," recalled Sir Brian Urquhart, who was soon transferred within the UN family to become one of Lie's personal assistants. He felt the choice of Lie illustrated the limits that the increasingly adversarial East–West relationship was placing on UN effectiveness: "The undistinguished choice of Lie was regarded by both sides as politically a safe bet."[5]

Lie had grown up in Norway, the son of a carpenter who died when Lie was quite young. He recalled a difficult life in his youth and an early bond as a teenager with the Norwegian Labor Party. Soon after his graduation from the University of Oslo law school, he took on administrative jobs with the party. He also served as a legal adviser to the Norwegian trade union movement for 13 years, strengthening his skills in mediation and conciliation.

As foreign minister, he often met with top leaders in Moscow, an unusual practice for any noncommunist, according to Lie. Lie had worked for the Norwegian Labor Party in various ministerial positions, eventually becoming foreign minister when the exiled government was based in London during World War II. There he played a major role in saving Norway's merchant fleet from the Germans by ordering it to move to British ports.

A burly man of massive physique, Lie insists in his autobiography that he was both a good tennis player and, once, a good wrestler. Sir Brian described him as having the look of an athlete who had gone to seed in middle age.[6]

Lie was, by all accounts, energetic, enthusiastic, and talkative. Fluent in heavily accented English and German, he usually spoke to others in short, direct sentences. Stephen Schwebel, author of *The Secretary-General of the United Nations: His Political Powers and Practice*, met with Lie on several occasions and noted, "He is at once shrewd and sincere, hardheaded and softhearted. His personality is animated, even emotional; it gives the impression of turbulence, of worry, brightened by a certain unmistakable boyishness."[7]

Lie had developed a taste for the good life, fine cuisine, and wine, but was unsure how to mesh such interests with the respect the new job required. He once made a reservation at a nightclub in Geneva (while there for the closing of the League of Nations) under the assumed name of Rodney Witherspoon. It was a source of great amusement to his staff when they later learned of it during a police inquiry into whether the United Nations was having security problems because the Secretary-General was using an assumed name. "After that, he was always Rodney to us," recalled Sir Brian in his memoir.[8]

How Did Lie View His Role?

Lie spent most of his early weeks in London developing his views on the role he would play and taking the first steps to create a UN Secretariat. Lie wanted the secretary-general's position to be in the forefront of UN efforts to keep peace. He knew, of course, that he had to follow both the Charter and the directions given to him by various UN bodies. Yet his aim was to achieve what he considered "a pragmatic, open-minded approach: I would listen to all my advisers and be directed by none."[9]

In his view, the Charter's Article 99, which he sometimes called "the big gun," gave him a global political responsibility that no individual had ever possessed. This article allows the secretary-general to bring to the attention of the SC any matter that he believes to be a threat to international peace and security. While he knew that many would like to see Article 99 simply gather dust, he was eager to take full advantage of it. He also felt the position carried an important moral responsibility. Lie felt a strong duty to speak up for the United Nations when he believed it was in danger. He often criticized members when he thought they acted against UN interests.

In his memoir, however, he writes that after two years in office he was convinced that it was not his business to assess right or wrong in conflicts between members. He dismissed the view of some that he should be a leader over governments and a kind of "first citizen of the world." He saw that role as having no roots in the UN Charter.

"The concept of a spokesman for the world interest is...far ahead of our times," Lie wrote. "To have gone too far, too fast, might have lost everything. I believe that the influence of the office must be developed slowly and steadily over the years."[10]

Many UN scholars insist that Lie, despite his protests, really did consider himself a spokesman for the world interest. They note he often used his travels and speeches as trial balloons to test public support for different ideas.

On the whole, Lie took a bold approach to his new job. Some of the risks backfired. Yet he was always conscious of those who would follow him in the position and wanted in no way to limit its potential.

Almost immediately, the United Nations was confronted with a series of international crises. The new secretary-general chose to interpret his powers liberally and pushed to expand their investigative limits. Many gains were procedural. Lie strongly insisted, for instance, on his right to gather intelligence in disputes of

UN concern and to take political initiatives without an official invitation.

Soviet Troops in Iran

The first substantive crisis to come before the SC involved Iran. During World War II, Soviet troops had been posted in Iran's northern province of Azerbaijan. British troops were stationed in the south. The aim was to keep transfer routes open and protect the oil-rich nation from Axis occupation. Under a wartime treaty, London and Moscow pledged to withdraw all troops within six months of the war's end—by March 1946. The British troops left early that year, but Soviet intentions remained a question mark.

On January 19, 1946, a few weeks before Lie was appointed to his new post, Iran complained to the SC that the Soviets were interfering in Azerbaijan's internal affairs and were refusing to negotiate. Iran suspected that the Russians were encouraging a separatist movement there.

Moscow hotly denied the charge, calling it a Western-inspired attempt to embarrass the Soviet government. The Soviets insisted they were always ready to negotiate and promptly countercharged that the continued postwar presence of British troops in Greece amounted to interference in its internal affairs. A Ukrainian delegate then charged that British forces were similarly interfering in the newly liberated Dutch East Indies.

"So here we were, right in the middle of a great-power war of maneuver and propaganda in the United Nations before the 'Cold War' had started," Lie noted in his memoir.[11]

Iran, encouraged by the United States, persisted in its demand that the SC address its complaint. In late March, after moving from London to temporary quarters in New York, the SC held several heated debates on the issue. Only a few weeks before, former British Prime Minister Churchill had given his famous Iron Curtain speech in Fulton, Missouri. Clearly the East–West divide was growing.

After the Russian news agency Tass announced on March 25 that Iran and the Soviet Union were close to an agreement and that Soviet troops would withdraw within six weeks, Andrei Gromyko, head of the Soviet UN delegation and ambassador to Washington, repeated a plea to the SC to postpone the date of a formal discussion on Iran's complaint. He lost the vote, picked up his papers, and dramatically left the meeting. Sir Brian, Lie's personal assistant at the time, recalled that the walkout, the first public demonstration of Soviet intransigence, was a "sensation" but later became fairly commonplace.[12]

On March 29, the SC, at the suggestion of US Secretary of State James Byrnes, asked Lie to get more information from Tehran and Moscow about the status of their talks and to nail down Soviet intentions about withdrawing its troops. Lie made inquiries and told the Council that the Russians would completely withdraw by early May.

The troop exit did take place. Byrnes, who had once said the United Nations would "die of inefficiency," called the Russian pullout "proof of the strength and effectiveness of the United Nations in helping those countries which truly desire independence."[13] In his memoir, Lie gave considerable credit to his own behind-the-scenes role.[14]

Gromyko returned to the Council and asked that the issue be removed from the agenda rather than merely postponed. He argued that, legally, it should never have come before the United Nations in the first place.

The Council, with the United States in the lead, refused to take the issue off the table. However, since both Iran and Russia had agreed by then that their dispute was resolved, Lie saw no point in keeping the issue before the Council: "The United Nations, I felt, should aim to settle disputes, not to inflame them."[15] Lie believed that a dangerous precedent was about to be set. So he and his general counsel, Abraham Feller, an American, issued a memo stating that there was no legal justification for keeping the item on the agenda unless the Council began to take some action.

This was Lie's first public intervention in Council proceedings. He tried to hand deliver the legal memo to Council president, Quo Tai-chi of China, just before the group's April 16 meeting. As Lie recalled, the SC president seemed surprised and muttered what may have been a diplomatic version of "What business of yours is this?"[16] Lie then handed the memo to one of the president's aides on his way to a seat.

In Lie's view, he was well within his rights under Article 99. "In fact, I felt that it was the intent of the Charter that the Secretary-General should have not merely the right to submit legal opinions... but that he should be able to address the Council on any question it might consider."[17]

Eventually, the Lie–Feller memo was read aloud at the Council's meeting at the president's request. Washington was convinced that Lie had moved beyond the limits of his job in making his statement. Lie told a Norwegian colleague that the memo "fell like a bombshell."[18]

The Council president ordered the memo submitted to a committee of experts, legal specialists from 11 Council governments. Yet he also called for an immediate vote on whether to keep Iran's complaint on the agenda. Gromyko and the Polish delegate argued that the Secretary-General's view was too important to ignore and that the agenda vote should await the committee report.

The report went against the Lie–Soviet view. It said that a clear vote by the Council is required to remove an item from the agenda. Though it never came up again, the Iran issue remained on the Council agenda for 30 years.

The committee of experts also addressed Lie's right to issue the memo. The US member of the committee insisted that the Charter did not authorize the UN leader to comment on political and substantive issues. However, the committee eventually decided that the secretary-general or his deputy may indeed make oral or written statements to the Council about any issue being considered.[19] The Council redrafted its rules accordingly. Later the GA adopted the same broader interpretation of the secretary-general's rights of intervention.

For Lie, it had been a bitter fight to gain such rights of communication in both major UN bodies. In his memoir, Lie said he was pleased that these rights were secured at such an early stage in the United Nations' development.

James Barros, a Lie biographer, concluded that Lie was biased in favor of direct Tehran–Moscow talks on the dispute and wanted to avoid Council pressure on Moscow that might complicate its troop withdrawal. Lie described himself as a believer in discreet diplomacy rather than "open disagreements, openly arrived at."[20]

The cost of securing his rights in the Iran case was the risk of appearing pro-Soviet in the new cold-war context. At the time, Lie recalled, Washington did not seem inclined to recognize that the UN secretary-general "might in all honor and intelligence take a view of a problem legitimately at variance with that of the United States."[21]

Lie's Muscle Flexing in the Balkans

Ukrainian diplomats had complained to the Council as long ago as September 1946 that Greece was provoking incidents along its border with Albania, threatening the peace and security of the Balkans. After an intense East–West debate, the United States suggested that the Council name a three-person commission to look into the situation.

The still-new Secretary-General told the Council that if the US proposal were rejected, he had powers of his own under Article 99: "I hope the Council will understand that the Secretary-General must reserve his rights to make such enquiries or investigations as he may think necessary...to determine whether or not he should consider bringing any aspect of this matter up to the attention of the Council."[22]

London did not think Lie could or should act on his own initiative. The United States, assuming that Lie's access to the Soviet satellite nations would be denied, argued that his initiative would be inappropriate and unwise since the Council was still examining the issue. At the time Moscow strongly supported Lie in his desire to expand the power of his office, a practice it would later regret. In this case, Lie claimed his right to investigate without actually exercising it.

Later that fall, Greece complained to the Council that Yugoslavia, Albania, and Bulgaria were violating its territorial integrity by helping Greek Communist guerrillas along its border. Moscow and its satellites strongly denied the charge, while accusing Britain of also violating Greece's territorial integrity by the continued presence of its troops there.

On December 19, 1946, the Council unanimously passed a US resolution to establish a Balkan Commission of Investigation to check out border incidents with Greece's Communist neighbors and report its findings.

While the Commission was doing its work, Britain's Labor government decided it could no longer afford to continue major military and economic aid to Greece. Then on March 12, 1947, US President Truman suddenly announced a $400 million program of similar aid (now known as the Truman Doctrine) for both Greece and Turkey. Lie was miffed that Truman had not mentioned his plan in advance to Lie or the Council, which was actively considering Greece's complaint. Lie supported the idea of the Truman Doctrine on its merits but told a colleague it was a "prize example of clumsy diplomacy" that could do the United Nations "utmost harm."[23]

The Council's Balkan Commission finally issued its report in June 1947. It accused Yugoslavia, and, to a lesser extent, Albania and Bulgaria, of supporting guerrilla forces in Greece. It recommended a new commission to establish normal conditions on the northern border of Greece.

Once again in the course of the Council discussions, Lie, privately remarked to Sir Alexander Cadogan, Britain's permanent representative to the United Nations, that the Council's failure to establish a new commission would impel him to claim the right to send out observers to "satisfy himself" on what was happening in northern Greece.[24] Cadogan was skeptical that Lie had such power unless the involved states agreed to accept observers. But Lie never pursued his claim. When Russia vetoed the proposal for a new commission in the Council, the United States moved the issue to the GA, which established a UN Special Committee on the Balkans.

Firm Support for the Partition of Palestine

Lie's involvement in the Palestine issue was important in two major ways. It opened the door for secretaries-general to become active in the peaceful settlement of disputes. It also laid a foundation for later peace-keeping operations—with the secretary-general serving as key recruiter and supervisor.

Lie had been in office a little more than a year when the British government, which held a League of Nations mandate over Palestine since the end of World War I, told him that it wanted the item included in the fall 1947 GA agenda. Relations between Arabs and Jews in the territory were becoming increasingly violent with a large influx of Jewish refugees and growing Arab nationalism. As US President Truman recalled the situation in his memoirs, the British "were determined to wash their hands of the whole matter."[25]

In response to Britain's request, Lie called for a special session of the GA that spring to prepare the groundwork. Members appointed a UN Special Committee on Palestine (UNSCOP) composed of 11 ambassadors to study the issue and suggest a solution. Lie appointed a personal representative, Victor Hoo of China, and supplied more than 50 members of the Secretariat to help. He chose Ralph Bunche as chief secretary for the group. Bunche was a PhD specialist on colonial matters who had participated in the UN founding process and was head of the UN Trusteeship Division.

Within a few months the UNSCOP majority recommended partition: independent Arab and Jewish states that would be linked by an economic union after a two-year transition period.

The GA majority approved the partition plan on November 29, 1947, and established a five-member Palestine Commission to take the necessary administrative steps. However, most Middle Eastern Arabs were adamantly opposed to the idea. Six delegations walked out of the Assembly hall as the vote was being taken.

Britain, concerned that the plan would not work, said it would accept the partition proposal but would not implement it.

Right from the start, Lie admitted he put "the full weight" of his office behind the partition proposal and the creation of the new state of Israel.[26] He saw the issue as a test of UN authority. He recalled that "some Arab spokesmen attacked me openly, but I could not yield."[27] He favored implementation even if it required coercion.

As violence in the region increased, however, the United Nations' right to enforce the partition grew increasingly controversial. At the first meeting in January 1948 of the new Palestine Commission, Lie assured the members that the SC would help them fulfill their mission. Yet many Council members did not think the body had the legal authority to enforce the partition. Lie openly prodded the Council. He said in a press conference at the time that Britain, in effect, had given the United Nations full responsibility and temporary sovereignty over Palestine.

Lie felt strongly that any invasion of the territory after the British mandate expired on May 14, 1948, would amount to outright aggression. He asked Bunche to draft a statement that stressed the need for an emergency UN land force if the moral force of the United Nations were not enough. Lie opted to keep the statement private until he got a clearer sense of the Council's direction.

The Palestine Commission, which had joined with Lie to focus on forming an international force, told the Council in a special report in February 1948 that Arabs inside and outside Palestine were trying to change the UN plan by violence. Only armed assistance by a non-Palestinian force with SC authority, according to the Commission, could assure success when the British left. The report stressed that a dangerous precedent would be set if force were allowed to deter the United Nations' will.

When the Council met later that month to consider the report, the US ambassador to the United Nations, Warren Austin, argued that the Council could take action to maintain international peace but did not have the power to enforce partition or any other political settlement.

Lie, who felt there were special circumstances in this case that justified such action, was very disappointed with the US position. He argued that it "took the heart out of" any Council support that might have been mobilized to enforce peace and maintain the partition decision. The Palestine Commission requested a UN legal opinion. The word came back that the United Nations did indeed have the power to enforce the partition (in this case under Article 24 of the UN Charter). Lie saw to it that the paper was circulated to Council members.[28]

However, as the violence in Palestine continued, Austin, under new instructions, urged the Council on March 19 to establish a temporary trusteeship for Palestine as a way to keep the peace. He proposed that the Palestine Commission halt partition plans.

Arab nations, of course, were delighted. Lie was extremely upset by this "American turnabout" on partition. He termed it a "blow to the United Nations" and said it "showed a profoundly disheartening disregard for [UN] effectiveness and standing." The next day he called on Austin at his suite at the Waldorf-Astoria. Terming the change an "attack on the sincerity of your devotion to the UN cause as well as mine," Lie proposed that both men resign. As Lie recalled the response in his memoirs, Austin, in "his warmhearted, upright Yankee way" gave Lie his "full sympathy" and urged him not to take the reversal personally. Austin insisted he would not himself resign and that it would not change Washington's policy if Lie did so.[29]

The GA debated the issue for almost a month during a special spring session. Yet in the end the trusteeship proposal drew little support.

Shortly after the May 14, 1948, midnight expiration of the British mandate, the provisional Israeli government announced Israel's independence as a Jewish state. US President Truman, knowing that some people in the State Department would try to block his move if he waited, rushed to recognize the new government a mere 11 minutes later.

Within hours, the armed Arab invasion of Palestine began. To justify its role in the action, the Egyptian minister of foreign affairs sent a cable to the United Nations. He insisted that Egyptian troops had entered only to establish security and order. Lie viewed the cable as open defiance of UN authority.

An SC meeting was quickly called for Saturday afternoon, May 15. Lie recalled that the members seemed to be in a "conspiracy of silence." To him, that smacked of appeasement.[30]

Convinced that UN integrity was on the line, Lie called his advisers that night to his home in Forest Hills, Queens. He decided to write a letter to each of the five permanent Council members. In it, he said he felt it was his duty to emphasize that the action marked the first time since acceptance of the UN Charter that any member had openly declared armed intervention outside its borders and inside a territory of special concern to the United Nations. The Council's failure to meet the challenge with armed force, he argued, would adversely affect the prestige of the United Nations and hopes for its future effectiveness.

Over the next several days the Council appealed to the Arabs to end the fighting. Finally, the Council passed a resolution calling for a four-week cease-fire. The terms were to be negotiated and supervised by the tall and elegant Count Folke Bernadotte, a former president of the Swedish Red Cross and a member of the Swedish royal family. The Council had recently appointed Bernadotte as UN mediator at the suggestion of Lie, an old friend who had checked out his willingness to serve in a phone call.

The warring parties agreed to a June 11 cease-fire, and the Council established a team of military observers (the UN Truce Supervision Organization, or UNTSO) to supervise the agreement and act as an intermediary in the dispute.

Bunche was dispatched to serve as Bernadotte's aide and head a team from the UN Secretariat. The team set up its headquarters on the Greek island of Rhodes.

Though early mediation efforts faltered, Bernadotte's continued efforts finally began to work, and real progress toward an armistice got underway. Lie played an active role in these efforts. He conducted intense private discussions aimed at ending the fighting, using members of his staff to get information and make suggestions.[31] Much of his work was done through phone calls and cables. A member of the UN field team in the negotiations said, "If we felt it would be helpful if Lie would in certain instances delegate and apply certain pressure, we would ask him and he would do so.... Lie was constantly carrying on conferences...breaking up logjams."[32]

A major setback occurred, however, when Bernadotte was assassinated in Jerusalem on September 14, 1948, by radical Jewish terrorists. Lie flew to Stockholm for the funeral and delivered a eulogy. He soon appointed Bunche as the Count's replacement. Bunche, a natural leader with a calm and authoritative manner, insisted on keeping the title of acting mediator out of respect for his predecessor.

After months of careful work and occasional cease-fires, Bunche finally persuaded the Israelis and Egyptians to agree to an armistice, signed on February 24, 1949. It became the model for similar Israeli agreements with Lebanon, Jordan, and Syria. It was an accomplishment that earned Bunche the Nobel Peace Prize a year later. In his memoir, Lie said the agreement would not have happened without Bunche's skill and dedication and that the Nobel was a tribute to the man as well as to the United Nations and its Secretariat.[33]

The Enforcement Issue

During the United Nations' dealings on Palestine, Lie remained convinced that the SC should have used coercion to carry out its partition decision and that the United Nations should have some kind of permanent international force at its disposal.[34]

He first proposed establishment of a small UN guard force in a Harvard University commencement speech in June 1948. In his third annual report to the GA that fall, he again broached the idea of a UN force recruited by the secretary-general to help in peaceful settlement of disputes. To many governments at the time, the idea sounded much too radical and difficult to implement.

Though UNTSO was strictly an observation and reporting force, it set a precedent that became a basis of sorts for later UN peacekeeping operations. Lie's argument that recruiting such volunteers should be the responsibility of the secretary-general also prevailed.

The Palestine issue marked Lie's first sustained large-scale effort to influence the outcome of a political problem handed to the United Nations for solution. He admitted that the SC ultimately deserved credit for its efforts to bring peace to Palestine. He argued, though, that by not ensuring that its call for partition was "resolutely upheld," the United Nations failed in its first great test as an international authority.[35]

However, Sir Brian, who served as Lie's private secretary during much of the Palestine drama, questioned whether such enforcement would ever really have been possible:

> It's nice to say, 'Put in an army to enforce it,' but what would have been the orders for firing? In the first place the two key powers then, the US and the British, would never have stood for it. In the second place, who were you going to shoot at? The Arabs? The Jews...I don't think it was ever practical to put in forces.[36]

Lie's staunch support for partition and particularly his later attempts to line up a firm UN response to Arab violence led to suspicions that he was biased in favor of Israel. The charge remains controversial.

"I think Lie just felt that aggression had to be met," said James Sutterlin, retired Yale University UN scholar and a former UN official.[37]

Sir Brian insisted that the tilt was there: "Lie was violently pro-Israel—and anti-Semitic as well, which made it even worse."[38]

In his biography of Lie, James Barros argues that the Secretary-General "disingenuously justified" his stance by pointing to the UNSCOP report that recommended partition. Yet Lie's "lack of knowledge of and sensitivity to the Arab cause were appalling," Barros wrote. He insisted that Lie's position destroyed any chance of his developing an Arab constituency. Instead, the Arab bloc increased in strength and became Lie's "implacable foe."[39]

The Palestine issue has continued to trouble the world and the United Nations in the many decades since the British mandate ended. Israel, bitter that the United Nations did not defend it after the 1948 Arab attack, became increasingly convinced that UN mediation almost inevitably meant giving up battle-won land.[40] As Sir Brian notes in his own memoir, covering his decades of service at the United Nations, the Palestine issue has "twisted the organization's image and fragmented its reputation as no other issue has."[41]

Should Every Nation Be a Member?

Lie was a strong and steady advocate of universal UN membership. In the early talks at Yalta in 1945, only the victors of World War II were to be members. Later, the UN Charter opened the door more broadly to other "peace-loving nations" if "able and willing" to carry out their Charter duties.

Yet it is the SC, where the veto applies, that must first recommend to the GA an applicant's admission. There, a majority vote governs the final outcome. Almost from the start, the Cold War dominated such UN decisions. The Soviet Union cast dozens of Council vetoes against new applicants.

In August 1946, during one of the first intensive Council debates on membership, Lie, using his newly certified right to speak, said that, as Secretary-General, he wanted to support admission of all states applying for membership. He thought the United Nations should represent the maximum number of people and hoped that might calm growing East–West antagonism.

Sir Alexander Cadogan, his good friend, told Lie privately that it was improper for him to support new member proposals. Lie, citing Article 99 and Council rules of procedure, remained resolute, insisting that he was well within his rights to participate in the Council's discussion of any subject. Sir Alexander warned Lie to be very careful and, jokingly, said he would keep a watchful eye out to be sure Lie did not actually vote on such questions.[42]

The most controversial new-member issue, one that would not be settled for more than two decades, concerned the Communist Chinese who took over mainland China in October 1949. Early in 1950, Zhou Enlai, prime minister of the People's Republic of China, cabled Lie and the GA to protest the continued UN seating of Nationalist China and demanded its removal from the SC. During the Council debate that followed, Russia formally proposed expulsion of the Nationalist delegation but lost the vote. The angry Soviet delegation left the table and stayed out of the Council and other UN organs until several weeks after the Korean War broke out that summer.

Once again, Lie sought a legal opinion from his staff and distributed it to the Council. It stated that representation should be based on objective factors, such as whether a government controlled the nation's resources and could direct its people in order to meet Charter membership duties. Though carefully noting that the issue was one for UN members and not the secretary-general to decide, the memo said that recognition by other governments should not be a factor.[43] Lie suggested that the Council conduct an inquiry to see which of the two Chinese governments best met UN criteria. "I was accused of 'surrender' to the Soviets, of being an 'appeaser,' and, of course, of transgressing the limits of my authority as Secretary-General."[44]

During the first half of 1950, Lie repeatedly made the case in speeches that the Chinese people, as original members of the United Nations, should be represented and that ideology should not be a factor. For him, it was a procedural rather than a substantive issue.

Though the outbreak of the Korean War soon took precedence over the issue in the Council, Lie did not change his view. Still, it was not until 1972 that the People's Republic of China was recognized as the sole representative of China in both the SC and the GA. The Assembly vote touched off enthusiastic dancing in the aisles.

Lie's Ambitious Peace Plan

The most dramatic diplomatic initiative of Lie's UN career was his 10-point, 20-year peace plan aimed at encouraging East–West negotiations. He first broached the idea in March 1950 at a national B'nai B'rith convention in Washington.

The plan was extremely broad. Lie's hope was to strengthen the UN system for achieving peace by making key changes in substance and procedure. He wanted the United Nations to resolve at least some of the issues fueling the Cold War. Members were urged to live up to their Charter commitments. Topics ran the gamut—from atomic energy control and decolonization to human rights and the development of international law. The plan called for expanded GA security functions and picked up on Lie's earlier suggestion to establish an international guard force. It included proposals to embrace excluded states and curb use of the veto in the SC.

Lie gave the proposal an enthusiastic global launch that April by taking it to London, Washington, Paris, Prague, and Moscow. He was warmly welcomed in all cities with the exception of Washington. The Chinese representation issue was still hotly controversial in the United States. Many in the West saw some of the suggestions in Lie's plan as much too generous to Moscow.

Lie enjoyed the spike in public interest caused by his trip but defended the secrecy of his talks along the way: "We can't have everything discussed in the press."[45]

In time, Lie distributed the 10 points to all UN delegations and placed the plan on the GA agenda. The Assembly took up the issue on November 19, 1950.

The debate included considerable discussion about the secretary-general's proper role. The GA basically thanked Lie for his initiative and referred parts to other UN organs for further study.

However, the plan got almost nowhere. Few of the ideas were considered new, and most were deemed impractical. The plan's chief value was to serve as a dramatic precedent for Lie's successors to use the office similarly as a bully pulpit to voice their own political views and push for change.

The late Thomas Franck, author of *Nation Against Nation*, viewed Lie's efforts as part of the secretary-general's "lyrical function" in which the UN chief tries to awaken people and nations to face needs when political organizations lack the will and courage to take remedial action.[46]

"I think Lie's salesman trip around the world was very ill advised," said Princeton's Leon Gordenker in an interview. "It was not well prepared. It was very ambitious even to try it, but I don't think it was a wise or very useful thing to do." The plan, in his view, mainly served as a warning that member governments do not necessarily welcome advice on major political issues from the secretary-general.[47]

In any case, it was soon virtually eclipsed by North Korea's invasion of South Korea.

Lie's Stand on Korea Provokes Moscow

The most serious crisis facing the SC in the Lie years was North Korea's June 1950 invasion of South Korea.

Led by Washington, the GA had been trying since 1947 to reunify the divided peninsula and hold national democratic elections. The United States had occupied South Korea since August 1945 and strongly favored national elections under UN auspices. Moscow had occupied North Korea since the war's end and considered UN election efforts illegal, refusing to cooperate.

When the North Koreans suddenly attacked, Lie was alerted by a phone call from US Assistant Secretary of State John Hickerson just before midnight on Saturday, June 24. Lie immediately saw North Korea's move as a clear violation of the UN Charter ban on aggression. He admitted in his memoir that he suspected then that it might have been the start of the next world war.[48] He promptly sent a cable asking for a status report from a UN Commission that had been working on the scene to promote peaceful reunification.

The Commission confirmed the attack and suggested that Lie use his Article 99 powers to call a SC meeting. However, Washington had already requested an emergency session for the next afternoon.

Lie asked to speak first at the Council meeting. Instead of just presenting the report, he chose a bolder course that had a major effect on his UN career. He labeled the North Korean action a definite threat to international peace and said the Council had a clear duty under the Charter to reestablish peace. His firm stance helped spur the Council to take its first collective security action.[49]

"Lie had clearly by now won his battle over the right of a secretary-general to speak his mind to the Security Council," observed Stanley Meisler in *United Nations: The First 50 Years.* "But he also had offended his old Soviet champions, for they did not view the Council as legally competent to deal with the issue."[50]

Despite the Cold War, the Council was in a rare position at that moment. It could act without risking a veto. The Soviet delegation had boycotted sessions since January 1950, six months earlier, because the Council refused to seat the Chinese Communist delegation in place of the Nationalist Chinese. But the United States and others devised a fallback strategy of taking the issue to the GA if the Soviets happened to show up for the Council meeting. Lie had been trying almost daily since the walkout to meet with concerned representatives in hopes of renewing East–West negotiations.[51]

At its emergency session that Sunday afternoon in June, the Council adopted a US-sponsored resolution that called for a ceasefire and withdrawal to the 38th parallel by North Korea. Two days later, the Council, for the first time in its history, authorized collective action to counter international aggression and asked all member states to help South Korea.

On July 7, with the Soviets still absent, the Council officially selected the United States to act as the United Nations' military agent and recommended that member states supply military forces and whatever else they could. Lie, a strong backer of the enforcement effort from the start, quickly cabled every member nation to ask what each could contribute.

Eventually, 16 governments joined the large-scale enforcement mission, but it was Washington that supplied half the ground troops and the bulk of the naval and air forces.[52] "The organization was thus involved by a freak of fate in a collective military action directed almost entirely by a single great power," noted Sir Brian.[53] Lie was concerned about the solo nature of the US role. He had talked to Washington about the desirability of a joint command but without success.

Lie had been warmly welcomed in Moscow that May with his 10-point peace plan, but was now clearly out of favor with Russia. Soviet Ambassador Gromyko angrily insisted that the Americans were the real aggressors in the Korean conflict and that Lie "obsequiously helped [support] a gross violation of the Charter" by the United States and other Council members.[54]

"In Moscow's eyes, I had become the abettor of American aggression, humbly aiding [President Harry] Truman and [Secretary of State Dean] Acheson to wreck the United Nations" Lie recalled. He knew that the Soviets felt that the secretary-general, as spokesman for the interests of the whole United Nations, was obligated to avoid partisan siding with any power or group. Moscow felt he should have tried to mediate the war.[55]

Lie rejected that view: "The secretary-general is not to be 'neutral' above all else, for neutrality implies political abstinence." This stance might, in some cases, keep him from meeting his Charter obligations, he insisted in his memoir. It is not, after all, technically neutral, he argued, to call the Security Council's attention to any threat to the peace under Article 99.[56]

Yet by this time the Soviet Union had begun to realize that its long boycott of the Council was backfiring. To become a player again, it had to return. The Soviet delegate Jacob Malik came back August 1 to serve his rotating one-month term as Council president.

By late September the UN-sponsored troops had fought the North Koreans, who at one point held almost the whole peninsula, back to the 38th parallel. Communist China had warned the United Nations that it would not stand by if UN troops moved north of that line.

On October 7, however, in a US-sponsored resolution, the GA authorized UN troops to pursue the North Korean troops into their own territory and approved steps, including elections, to stabilize and reunify the peninsula.

The United States had long urged passage of its now-famous Uniting for Peace resolution, which authorized the Assembly to take responsibility for dealing with international threats to the peace when the Council is unable to act. Under the measure, finally adopted by the Assembly on November 3, 1950, over strong Soviet objections, an emergency GA session could be called on 24 hours' notice if either seven Council members or a majority of the Assembly requested it.

Lie was delighted with the sidestep. It was a technique that would be used many times in future UN crises.

Yet troops from China soon joined the North Koreans in their fight. At first Beijing (formerly Peking) said its soldiers were there simply as volunteers to protest US aggression and imperialism.

Lie began a brief and ultimately unsuccessful diplomatic effort with Beijing. The Chinese pressed on with the war and held to a firm negotiating stand that included UN recognition of the People's Republic of China (Beijing) as the seat of legitimate Chinese government and the departure of all foreign troops from Korea.

After months of hard fighting, the UN-authorized troops did manage to push the Chinese and North Koreans back to a stalemate near the 38th parallel, where the fighting began.

Lie had just arrived at his summer house on the Oslo Fjord for a brief holiday on June 23, 1951, when he received a cable noting that the Soviet delegate, Jacob Malik, was saying in a series of radio broadcasts from the United Nations that he thought the Korean conflict now could be settled. Malik suggested that the first step should be a cease-fire and an armistice providing for mutual withdrawal from the 38th parallel. Lie phoned UN headquarters to suggest that cease-fire talks begin at the earliest possible date.

The talks began July 10, 1951, but negotiations went on for two more years. It was July 27, 1953, before an armistice was signed.

Lie's vigorous public support for UN action against North Korea's aggression was encouraged by Washington but earned him the everlasting enmity of the Soviet Union.

Despite the criticism, Lie considered his position on Korea "the best justified act of seven years in the service of peace." In his view, the UN "passed the test" and proved that aggression does not pay. He wrote in his memoirs: "The world can never again permit any clear case of international armed attack to pass unchallenged."[57]

"I think Trygve Lie has been underestimated," insisted James Sutterlin, Yale scholar and former UN official:

> [Lie] took very clear positions on the necessity for maintaining the principles of the Charter. That was very clear from the beginning of the Korean War. He felt if aggression were not resisted, there would be more aggression, and the UN would suffer the same fate as the League of Nations. I think he deserves credit for that. He showed courage and leadership [though] he lost the support of the Soviet Union in the process.[58]

The McCarthy Years

Certainly one of Lie's toughest challenges and the focus of some of the sharpest criticism against him concerned the way he handled growing US concern that many American employees in the United Nations were Communist sympathizers who wanted to overthrow the US government. Instigated by Senator Joseph McCarthy, a Republican from Wisconsin, the pressure on Lie was intense.

As the first UN secretary-general, he had been forced to make many appointments very quickly. Since much of the recruiting began after the United Nations moved to New York, an unusually large number of Americans and Canadians were hired. Lie was on record as willing to consult with member governments about which candidates they wanted to propose. Yet he clearly wanted to avoid national pressure on the actual decisions. It was a difficult balancing act.

Lie had not been all that popular with the UN staff even before the McCarthy furor arose. Many did not think that he was making enough of an effort to defend their rights. He had faced a mass employee protest on March 11, 1947, for instance, just over salaries and working conditions.

Lie rejected any suggestion that the United Nations was harboring a nest of spies. He said he agreed with Washington that no American Communist should be working at the United Nations and maintained that he had never knowingly hired one.

The UN compound in New York was considered international territory. For that reason, some critics have never forgiven Lie for letting the US Federal Bureau of Investigation (FBI) set up an office there to interview and fingerprint American employees. Loyalty oaths soon were required of all Americans working at the United Nations.

"I think Lie's great weakness was his failure to stand up to the US," argued Yale's Sutterlin. "He let the FBI into the building. He shouldn't have."[59]

Lie clearly faced a tough choice: "He caved in, and was pushed to do so by the American government which was doing the same thing itself," noted Inis Claude Jr. He said that the only way both Washington and Lie could survive was by giving in to some degree.[60]

Sir Brian, whose good friend Ralph Bunche was a victim of McCarthy's charges, admits to a strong bias on the issue. Yet he said he was not sure that, in the climate of the times, Lie really had much leeway:

> The Russian press had a field day, saying Lie was really an authorized agent of the FBI. But I'm not quite sure what he could do really. McCarthy was a total charlatan who had Washington by the throat. The US was the host country, the main begetter of the UN, and was paying one-third of the budget. If the government of the US wasn't prepared to stand up to McCarthy, how the hell could Lie do it?[61]

Eventually 20 of the United Nations' 2,000 American employees pled the Fifth Amendment of the US Constitution in order to remain silent when called before a Senate subcommittee to testify in 1952. The 20 were later discharged from the Secretariat by Lie's orders. Lie said they had not behaved as international civil servants should.

Princeton's Leon Gordenker conceded that the whole situation posed a severe dilemma for Lie: "There isn't any real reason why the secretary-general of the UN has to defend people who get into political trouble," he said. "This was nasty stuff.... On the one hand you had these people in the Secretariat, you could say, using it [the Fifth] to protect themselves from the trouble they got into in the national sphere. By letting them have this privilege, you're going to get wiped out by the US. Not a good idea. You could take it the other way and say they're being treated unfairly under whatever civilized legal system you have, and that they ought to be held for awhile. In fact, that's what happened. They weren't put out the door right away."[62]

Abraham Feller, the longtime close adviser to Lie and the United Nations' first legal counsel, had to fire some of the Americans who had refused to testify. He once worked with Alger Hiss at the US State Department and had been called himself to testify before a grand jury in New York. He had been a member of a group cited as a Communist front organization by a congressional committee and the US attorney general. Feller denied any sympathy for the Communist Party or its policies.

Yet the strain of it all weighed heavily on Feller. On November 13, 1952, he jumped out of a window in his 12th floor apartment on Central Park West. In his memoir, Lie recalls being overcome by shock and grief on hearing the news. He saw Feller as a victim of the "hysterical assault" on the United Nations at the time.[63]

During the tenure of Lie's successor, some of the firings were deemed unjust by the UN Administrative Tribunal, an independent judicial organ. The tribunal approved the dismissal of 9 temporary employees but overturned it for the 11 others.

Shirley Hazzard, one of the United Nations' sharpest critics and an Australian novelist, argues in one of her nonfiction books, *Defeat of an Ideal*, that the lack of respect for the principle of independence in the McCarthy years violated liberties protected by the United Nations' Declaration of Human Rights and marked the beginning of a long-term decline of UN capacities and operations. In her view, Lie and his staff "made a mockery of the organization itself and of everything that took place there." She writes: "In a time of monumental personal, national, and international cowardice, the United Nations...was pliant to the most evil prevailing forces and bowed to the ground."[64]

Regardless of whether Lie did what he felt he had to do, the repercussions lingered. Support for Lie from the UN staff and from Washington continued to erode. When some UN employees refused to testify at a highly publicized US Congressional subcommittee hearing in New York, the effect was devastating. In the view of US Secretary of State Dean Acheson, the result was a "highly unfavorable opinion of the United Nations in the United States and of the United States in the United Nations."[65]

When he took office later, Dag Hammarskjöld, the Swedish secretary-general, at some political risk, cancelled permission for the FBI to enter UN headquarters. However, he and his successors had to live with US "loyalty" checks of potential American staffers until 1986.

A Second Term?

Both the swift tide of events and a careful rethinking of how he had fared in his first few years on the job made Lie change his mind about how long he was willing to stay on as secretary-general. His term was to end January 31, 1951. As that date drew closer, Lie made it clear that he would resign at the end of his first term. Indeed, as early as December 16, 1949—more than six months before North Korea's attack and Lie's firm stand for a collective UN defense, which so angered Moscow—Lie said at a press conference that he would not be a candidate for a second term. Just three days before, he wrote a letter to his daughter and son-in-law, saying, "It seems to me that I've done my duty, and I'll be completely satisfied if only I can get through this final year with my whole skin."[66]

By the fall of 1950, however, the SC reached an impasse on the issue of who would be the next secretary-general. Moscow, now adamantly opposed to any reelection of Lie, suggested others for the post.

It was a 180-degree turn for the Soviet Union. Lie had been a Soviet favorite at the start. "The Kremlin...often knew which string to pluck and when in order to seduce or to frighten him as he attempted to steer the United Nations," noted the Lie biographer James Barros.[67] Moscow had been pleased with Lie's stand on Azerbaijan and on membership for Communist China. The Soviet Union was the only nation that had supported Lie's claim that he had the right to make inquiries in the Greek frontier situation. Even as late as 1949, the Soviet foreign minister, Andrei Vyshinsky, announced at a dinner for ambassadors that Lie was the only candidate that Moscow could imagine supporting in the next secretary-general election. But that was before the McCarthy challenge and Korea.

The West, of course, did not like Lie's efforts to seat Beijing at the UN table, but it was very enthusiastic about his stand on Korea. Lie had worked hard at keeping a good relationship with important people in the US government, knowing that American support of the United Nations was vital. The United States, Britain, and France felt Lie had done a competent job as secretary-general and favored his reelection. The US ambassador to the United Nations, Warren Austin, threatened to veto any other recommendation.

As Lie recalled in his memoir, "The USSR was determined to throw me out of office, and the US was equally determined to retain me." He wrote to his daughter in Oslo on October 10, 1950, "I'm certain my happiest day will be when I can take Mama in one hand and my suitcase in the other and leave for home. This is like living in a mad-house."[68] When the Council took a formal vote on Lie's reappointment, the Soviet Union cast its 46th veto. The Nationalist Chinese, unhappy with Lie's support for the Beijing government, abstained.

With Washington in the lead, the SC next voted 10 to 1 (Moscow dissented) to send a letter to the GA, saying that it could not agree on a candidate. By that action, the United States and Russia essentially agreed, Gordenker said, that the person in the job was more important than the office itself.[69]

During the GA debate on the issue, the Soviets argued that any unilateral Assembly appointment would violate the Charter's call for a Council recommendation. Moscow said that it and its allies would not deal with Lie if his term were extended. In a press conference on October 30, 1950, Vyshinsky, the Russian foreign minister, said Lie was violating the Charter by not withdrawing after the Soviet veto in the Council and had "done everything possible to cling to his job." He added that Lie's $25,000 annual salary amounted to "quite a bit of money."[70]

Washington took the view that, since the GA had set the secretary-general's five-year term of office in the first place, it had every legal right to extend the time period. Technically, it was not a new term. Finally on November 1, 1950, the GA, by a majority vote of 46 in favor, moved to extend Lie's term for another three years.

By this time, Lie, who had been following the proceedings on television from home, had changed his mind about staying on. He admitted feeling that he couldn't let himself be pushed out as punishment for having done his duty. He did not want his exit to be interpreted by anyone as a defeat for the stand he took on Korea. Yet he had vowed that if he did not get the support of at least 45 members (he did, but barely), he was ready to refuse an extension.

"At that time there was an overwhelming sense of urgency and solidarity among Western member states that Stalin must not get his way regarding Lie in retaliation for what the Charter should expect a secretary-general to do in the face of naked aggression," noted Jeffrey Laurenti, a senior fellow in international affairs at the Century Foundation.[71]

The United States thought it was defending "the UN ideal" by leading the effort to save Lie, but it was really following its own "rather parochial self-interest," insisted Thomas Franck. He said that, otherwise, the United States would not have worked so hard to bend the rules. In Franck's view, Lie had come to suit Washington's own global purposes.[72]

As promised, Moscow would have nothing further to do with Lie. He was not invited to any Soviet bloc social gatherings. All Moscow communications were now directed to the UN Secretariat. Lie's effectiveness was severely curbed, and he knew it. "My hands were tied with respect to governments which controlled or influenced one-third of the population of the world," Lie recalled.[73]

Finally, a little after 3:00 in the afternoon on November 10, 1952, less than two years into his three-year extension, Lie stepped to the podium of the GA where delegates awaited a speech by the prime minister of France. Lie shocked the audience by announcing that he would resign as soon as a successor could be chosen. He explained that he had wanted to retire at the end of his first term but stayed on because of the Korean situation. Now that an armistice was looking more likely, he said, it was time for a successor who would have the strong support of the major powers and other UN members.

The SC did not pick a successor until March 1953. Lie took his official farewell from the United Nations on May 1, an occasion his successor, Dag Hammarskjöld, arranged. Lie recalled that his frequent differences with the staff were forgotten "as my eyes moved along the rows of loyal, familiar faces, and I recalled all the good and bad days we had shared since starting together." He told those assembled, "They say the first seven years are the hardest." He said he hoped, for their sake, that it proved true. He sailed for Norway on May 8, 1953.[74]

How Much Did Lie Accomplish?

Although Lie's actual achievements may appear slim compared to those of most men who followed him, he was the pioneer—the first to really explore the job's potential. He played a key role in locating the UN headquarters in Manhattan. He wanted to expand the secretary-general's role and set important precedents in the process.

However, many of his efforts were limited and often blocked by the East–West rivalry in the intensifying Cold War. The Soviet Union cast no fewer than 58 vetoes during Lie's seven years in office.

"Trygve Lie's period was a disaster," argued Charles "Bill" Maynes, a former US assistant secretary of state for International Organization Affairs, as quoted in a book by Linda Fasulo. "The UN was totally stalemated," said Maynes. "It couldn't do anything but collect Soviet vetoes and American propaganda victories."[75]

"It was a very nasty period, and I don't think he came off with very high marks," agreed Dr. Edward C. Luck, a former president of the United Nations Association of the USA and now dean of the University of San Diego's Joan B. Kroc School of Peace Studies. "It was a time of McCarthyism and US dominance...the beginning of the Cold War. This was not exactly an easy job. It's easy to say he could have been better."[76]

Above all, Lie did not want to do anything to diminish the position that the Charter so vaguely defined. In his view, the sweep of Article 99 included considerable implied powers. He wanted to assert what he felt were the office's prerogatives. Lie thought that his job should be in the forefront of UN peace efforts. He was committed wholeheartedly to the United Nations and its goals. Biographer James Barros wrote that Lie had "a social democratic dedication to the horizontal brotherhood of man."[77]

Lie was a hard worker who could also be highly emotional. Julian Huxley, a former director of the United Nations Educational, Scientific, and Cultural Organization (UNESCO), observed that Lie was badly overstrained to the point of tears streaming down his cheeks when both the Greek and the Palestine issues were before the SC. "I shall never forget his muttering, 'Dr. Huxley, I have had a terrible time, yes, a terrible time....'"[78]

Lie once complained to an interviewer, "Everything is in order as long as I agree with a particular government, but as soon as I don't... 'Aren't we paying you? You are an administrator. Why do you talk?'"[79]

Although few analysts think that Lie raised the prestige of the office, he took several significant procedural steps. He insisted that he had key investigative and preventive responsibilities. He did win the authority—until then confined to member governments—to propose agenda items for UN bodies, make policy suggestions, and take part in their debates. Both the SC and the GA in effect allowed him to make his own invitation to speak. "In a very real sense he gave a voice to his office," wrote Thomas Boudreau in his book *Sheathing the Sword: The UN Secretary-General and the Prevention of International Conflict.*[80]

Lie sent aides on occasional fact-finding missions and helped open the way for secretaries-general to have a role in the peaceful settlement of disputes. One very useful and subtle tool that he used to influence proceedings in the Iran, China representation, and Korea cases was asking his legal advisers to write opinions on the key issues involved.

Though uncomfortable with the press, he was heavily covered by it and well aware of its importance. He held weekly Friday morning press conferences.

While that practice was not followed by his successors, Lie did establish other organizational precedents. He initially proposed, for instance, a system of eight assistant secretaries-general. Five were to be nominated by the permanent members of the SC, according to a private agreement they reached among themselves. The eight met with Lie once a week, concentrating particularly on technical issues and were the nearest thing he had to a cabinet.

According to Sir Brian, who kept the notes as Lie's personal secretary, the personnel selection was "not uniformly impressive" and the meetings, largely dealing with trivial matters, were often disillusioning. "I think Lie found them as irritating as I did," he said.[81]

Yet the pattern largely has held. "The way he organized the UN has more or less endured," noted Sutterlin. "He, of course, dealt with a lot of problems that are still being dealt with."[82]

Lie floated a number of ideas, like a UN police or guard force and changes in how the Council veto is used, which are still being debated. Lie did feel that the gradual move by some nations to abstain rather than cast a veto and the occasional shift of power from the Council to the veto-free Assembly were positive steps. He also argued that, if the Council were ever enlarged, Asia should have priority for stronger representation and India considered as a possible permanent member.

Lie often took risks. "My eyes were open as I pushed my way into each of the many problems that arose," he insisted. In his view, neutrality implied abstinence and that was not for him. He told a press conference on August 7, 1950, well after the Korean War began, that his job was not to be neutral but to give legal effect to decisions of other UN organs.[83]

By most assessments, however, Lie was far from an ideal secretary-general in temperament and follow-through. His lack of experience in running a large organization and not having a broad educational and cultural background, were considered significant flaws.

Lie's first trip to Latin America, for instance, in January 1947, was meant to stimulate government interest and support for the United Nations in the 10 countries he visited. He recalled that the trip actually gave him a "forceful" message. He gained first-hand acquaintance with large-scale poverty. He returned with a new and consuming interest in the work of the UN Economic and Social Council and the UN specialized agencies. Yet Lie's strong feeling on his return that Washington should be doing more economically to help Latin America and nurture democracy there, rather than focusing so heavily on Europe and Asia, was both pedestrian and politically naïve, according to Barros.[84]

As the first secretary-general, Lie relied heavily on what he called his "political nose." Sir Brian insisted that Lie was both jealous of others and nervous about his position. He was apt to leave a public event such as a dinner, for example, if he felt he had not been properly seated. At one dinner for Sir Anthony Eden, the British prime minister at the time, Lie simply surveyed the situation in advance and shifted his place card to a more prominent position.[85]

His hair-trigger temper was legendary. Both diplomats and his staff bore the brunt of his occasional angry outbursts. Urquhart noted that in public life, Lie was naturally suspicious and "apt to go dark red in the face with rage and utter, jowls quivering, complex and ominous Norwegian oaths."[86]

"I think he deserves some credit for having tried to give the secretary-general an activist role," conceded Sir Brian.[87] "But he didn't have the intellectual capacity, the stamina, or the negotiating skill and charisma to take a good idea and make it work."

By Lie's own interpretation of the office and by temperament, he did not approach his job cautiously. He chose a largely public role and sometimes acted or made the wrong decision when doing nothing might have been wiser. Lie did not see that unsolicited initiatives could hurt his relationship with major powers and affect his ability to mediate disputes.

He learned slowly that the most productive initiatives and those least likely to be criticized tended to be private ones that usually required great patience and self-control, not Lie's special strengths.[88] Lie was the "wrong man in the wrong job at the wrong time," according to Barros.[89]

"Lie was an unpleasant character," Gordenker added. "He could be awfully stupid at times.... Yet if you look back at what he did, there was a certain boldness there, a certain willingness to get into it. He did after all get the Secretariat organized."[90]

In reflecting on his years in office back at his Norwegian hunting lodge, Lie wrote that he was proudest of the fact that world peace was preserved during his tenure: "I probably made many errors as Secretary-General," he conceded. "I felt morally and legally compelled to take what I saw as the 'United Nations view.' I did everything in my power to keep the UN from sinking or running aground."[91]

Yet in the aftermath of Lie's service, many nations were clearly ready for a change in the pace and style of UN leadership. Lie's style had been blundering and assertive, and the SC members wanted a more passive successor.[92]

It did not happen.

CHAPTER FOUR

Dag Hammarskjöld: A Swede Takes the Role a Step Further

Like Lie, Hammarskjöld was not particularly well-known internationally. Similarly, he was not seeking the United Nations' top job. Like Lie, he was surprised to be tapped for it and eventually also incurred the wrath of the Soviet Union while doing it.

Yet his approach to the task was far more cautious and nuanced than Lie's. In retrospect, Hammarskjöld is widely considered the most effective, innovative, and admired of all UN secretaries-general.

Lie, who had strongly opposed Hammarskjöld's appointment, nonetheless welcomed him at Idlewild [now Kennedy International] Airport on April 9, 1953, just two days after the General Assembly (GA) confirmed him. He wished his successor the best of luck and happiness in "the most impossible job on earth." Lie later wrote in his 1954 memoir, "He will be the target of criticism from right, left, and center."[1]

The throng of reporters and photographers at the airport that day wanted Hammarskjöld's views on everything from the job itself to the global climate but got very little from him. As the new Secretary-General later told a friend, "I was hoping I could get out...alive."[2] He told the press he wanted to do the job and not talk about it since his views were still those of a private man, not yet those of an international civil servant. But he made a point of saying that he did not consider his new role a passive one. He said he intended to listen and hoped to be "an instrument, a catalyst, perhaps an inspirer."[3]

How did the United Nations' top job happen to come to the 47-year-old Hammarskjöld?

He grew up in Sweden in an aristocratic Lutheran family, the youngest of four brothers. His father, said to be austere and disciplined, was the governor of the province of Uppland in Uppsala for several years. The official family residence was a 16th-century castle. In 1914 his father became prime minister and is credited with helping to keep Sweden neutral during World War I.

As a child, Hammarskjöld collected butterflies and beetles to the point where his mother Agnes, with whom he was very close, was sure that he would one day become a scientist.[4] He was also an active bicyclist and mountain climber, serving for several years as president of the Swedish Alpinist Club.[5]

Fluent in French, German, and Spanish, he was considered a brilliant student. He earned a degree in law at the University of Uppsala and a PhD in economics at the University of Stockholm. He later became chairman of the board of the Swedish National Bank and undersecretary of the Swedish Ministry of Finance. After World War II, he shifted to the foreign ministry where he was, in effect, the second in command.

Hammarskjöld attended several meetings at the United Nations in the 1950s but apparently first came to the attention of both Britain and France for his administrative talents in helping create and operate the Marshall Plan agencies in Western Europe that coordinated postwar aid and reconstruction. The late British diplomat, Paul Gore-Booth, a longtime friend of Hammarskjöld's, credits him with having done more than anyone at the time to bring the Swedes back into the European family. Sweden was the only northern European country untouched by the war and, according to Gore-Booth, had developed a certain "shyness" about its European connections.[6]

After Lie announced his intention to resign, the five permanent members of the Security Council (SC) held talks—largely in secret—over the next several months. Agreeing on a successor was no easy task. Washington at first championed Carlos Rómulo of the Philippines. He had been nominated in 1951 by the Soviet Union although Moscow no longer favored him. Europe's choice was Lester Pearson of Canada, who was vetoed by Moscow.

The Western members of the Council finally put forward four names that they hoped were veto proof. Three were swiftly rejected, but Sweden's relatively obscure deputy foreign minister was formally accepted by the Council on March 31, 1953. When rumor of that choice had first surfaced, Hammarskjöld thought it speculation. He reportedly told a Swedish delegate to the United Nations that he was "amused but uninterested." When informed in Stockholm of the actual Council vote by its president, he cabled back, "With a strong sense of personal insufficiency, I hesitate to accept...but I do not feel I could refuse the task imposed upon me..."[7]

At the time, he was considered a safe, soft-spoken, nonpolitical technocrat by most who voted for him. These people knew him as a skilled administrator, which, after all, was the only specific duty of the secretary-general actually spelled out in the Charter. In time, it was their turn to be surprised. As Seymour Finger, a former director of the Ralph Bunche Institute for International Studies at the City University of New York, noted, Hammarskjöld "turned out to be a man of deep convictions, daring, and with a messianic belief in the need for an effective UN."[8]

Though there was a certain crisis of confidence in the United Nations at the time, partly because of the McCarthy situation, Hammarskjöld inherited a somewhat better global climate than did Lie. Sir Brian, who worked for Hammarskjöld for eight years and has written the most extensive and authoritative of the several biographies on him, said the new Secretary-General was "lucky" since Stalin died in March and a new US administration led by President Eisenhower had taken hold in Washington. Later that summer the United States would be able to negotiate an armistice in Korea, something the Truman administration had been unable to do. "There was kind of a thaw in East–West relations," Sir Brian said.[9]

Hammarskjöld proved to be a disciplined, energetic, and enthusiastic worker. He was neat (never more than a few papers on his desk), ambitious, and focused. He was kind to his staff though he kept them working long hours. "I have never worked with anyone who seemed so impervious to fatigue—or human weakness," noted Lester Pearson in the *Montreal Star* after Hammarskjöld's death.[10] Once, on his return from a long trip during which he slept little during the previous three nights, the Secretary-General was asked if he felt tired. "That would be frivolous," he promptly replied.[11]

To most onlookers he appeared to have a healthy degree of modesty and humility. Sir Brian mentioned a certain "childlike purity and innocence."[12] Yet Leon Gordenker, professor emeritus of international relations at Princeton, argued, "He was a very sophisticated man who had a certain arrogance and a certain righteousness that didn't always show."[13]

Hammarskjöld did not delegate a great deal of work to others, preferring to keep control. He would subject issues before the United Nations to rigorous intellectual analysis. He could be angry and impatient when colleagues did not measure up to his own high standards.

"In truth, he had a lightning capacity for gathering and appraisal of facts, for the making and implementation of decisions," said Andrew Cordier, his executive assistant. "I never had the impression that he worried himself into decisions." Nor, he said, after they were made. "He frequently indulged in a reasoned self-confidence that the decision taken was the right one."[14]

Hammarskjöld was not particularly influenced by emotion, pride, or sentiment, in Pearson's view, "but by a cold, yes, cold, intellectual search for a solution.... [He was] never willing to give up."[15]

During his first years on the job, Hammarskjöld gave several public speeches to make his views known and to improve the United Nations' image. He was not an impressive public speaker. Sir Brian wrote that he had a "flat unemphatic voice" and spoke with a "tubular Swedish intonation."[16] Yet he was a strong believer in the importance of public understanding and support for the United Nations.

As time went by, Hammarskjöld increasingly wrote many speeches himself and did not rely heavily on notes or references. In 1959, he gave a long extemporaneous speech in Mexico. When the foreign minister asked him afterward for a copy of the text, he dictated it on his return to New York—exactly as he had given it. Similarly one Sunday afternoon, he dictated the 8,000-word introduction to his last annual report to the GA without notes or a pause.[17]

"I had a good friend in the Secretariat who happened to be in Geneva for a conference when Dag came, I think, to open the conference with a formal speech," recalled Inis Claude Jr., professor emeritus of political science at the University of Virginia. "My friend, a good bureaucrat, wrote a brief speech, met him at the airport, and handed it to him, suggesting he might like a text for his remarks. Hammarskjöld looked at him with great disdain and said, 'What kind of a man do you think I am?' He shoved it back at him. He didn't want a ghost writer."[18]

Most descriptions of Hammarskjöld paint him as reserved and a loner. Friends and colleagues say that is only somewhat true.

"He was a deep thinker," recalled Indar Rikhye, a former major general in the Indian Army and a key military adviser to Hammarskjöld, in an interview. "He used to go for long walks late at night, often in Central Park, to relax and think about issues. On weekends he never saw anyone. He had a house near Brewster, New York, and the only person he talked to was the security officer who had gone with him."[19]

Nevertheless Hammarskjöld was very close to his family and had a number of good friends. "He was a great conversationalist," said Rikhye. "He loved talking when he had the time, over a meal or in the evening.... He was also a damn good listener. He had an incredible knack for getting to the core of issues. He'd pick your brain. He'd ask, 'Well, what do you think about this?' and he'd wait for you to give him your opinion. Then he would say right then and there, 'OK, we'll do this.' Of course if he had questions, he'd raise them and argue, but, more often than not, he'd tell you to draw up the draft and bring it back."[20]

Hammarskjöld, who had a Swedish housekeeper/cook, often had small dinner parties at his East 73rd Street apartment. Close aides such as Ralph Bunche and Andrew Cordier would come. Honored occasional guests included his fellow Swede Greta Garbo, as well as Pablo Casals, James Michener, and Leonard Bernstein.[21]

The new Secretary-General also had a great appreciation for New York's rich offerings in music, literature, and art. His taste was varied, and he didn't want to be categorized. "I would prefer...to be known as an admirer of both Thomas Wolfe and Virginia Woolf," he once said.[22]

He borrowed paintings by such artists as Georges Braque and Pablo Picasso from the Museum of Modern Art to hang in his 38th-floor office. He took an active role in deciding where art donations from governments and individuals should be placed. He planned the design for the UN Meditation Room off the first-floor lobby and commissioned works of art for it, such as stained-glass windows by Marc Chagall.

He was also an admirer and friend of the British sculptor Barbara Hepworth, whom he got to know shortly before his death. She created a wooden sculpture for him, which he viewed at a London exhibit in 1961 and brought back for his office. He wrote Hepworth that it is "a strong and exacting companion but at the same time one of deep quiet and timeless perspective in inner space."[23]

After his death, thanks to the generosity of philanthropist Jacob Blaustein, another abstract sculpture of Hepworth's—"Single Form"— was installed at the UN Secretariat entrance as a memorial.

Sir Brian says that Hammarskjöld carefully guarded his privacy and tended to keep people at a "dignified distance."[24]

Though rumors still persist that Hammarskjöld was gay, Sir Brian said he never saw anything in his years of working with the Secretary-General that would provide the slightest justification for the claim. He added that no one who worked closely with him or knew him well thought it true either. Hammarskjöld himself was painfully aware of such gossip and once said that if there had been any truth to it, given the prevailing public opinion at the time, he would never have accepted the UN job.[25]

Sir Brian surmised that the rumors were spread by those who didn't know him, resented him, and wanted to demean him: "Many find the concept of a man totally dedicated to his work, to intellectual and aesthetic interests and to the spiritual experience a difficult concept to accept."[26] There has never been any question of his deep commitment to the United Nations and its goals.

Ralph Bunche, who was transferred to Hammarskjöld's office as one of two new undersecretaries-general without portfolio, described Hammarskjöld as a supranationalist who wanted to make the United Nations a dynamic force for peace and human advancement.[27]

Hammarskjöld got that message across in a way few others have succeeded in doing. He had a commanding personality and presence that earned him respect.

"He was a shy, quite awkward intellectual who was spectacularly bad at dealing with people," recalled Sir Brian. "But the most amazing thing about him was that you could go to Rio, New Delhi, or Cape Town, and the taxi driver would have heard of him and have an astonishingly clear idea of what he was trying to do. That's charisma. I don't understand it, and I don't think it is true of any other secretary-general."[28]

Certainly Hammarskjöld lacked some of the outward signs of great leadership. Yet his confidence and strength gave others the comforting feeling that in any situation he knew what to do and how to do it, where he wanted to go and how to get there, according to Sir Brian.[29]

An Enthusiastic Administrator—At First

In a way no other secretary-general has, Hammarskjöld took on the Charter-designated role of chief administrator with energy and enthusiasm. He listened and analyzed. And he acted.

"The Secretariat under Lie had gotten completely out of control—it was hopeless," recalled Sir Brian. "Hammarskjöld really loved administration, and he was very good at it. He spent the first year going around to every single office in the Secretariat and looking at it. He came up with a complete reorganization. He cut the staff [through attrition], cut the budget, and rewrote staff rules and regulations. He produced a totally different line of authority."[30]

The new Secretary-General, who inherited a staff of 5,700 from 67 nations, insisted on an independent civil service.[31] He wanted uniform standards for recruiting staff. He assured member governments that they were free to suggest individuals for UN jobs but made it clear that he would make the final decisions on hiring and firing. In his view, an independent international civil service was vital to the United Nations' vibrancy and credibility.[32]

His May 30, 1961, Oxford University lecture on the importance and character of the United Nations' international civil service is still considered a model.

"I don't know if he wrote every word but it was certainly his voice," Leon Gordenker said. "Every time there was an occasion when he could formulate something as a policy or a law, he did it. Then it was a 'take it or leave it.' Since nobody else had done it, it was usually a 'take it.'"[33]

Hammarskjöld also stood up for his staff by insisting that the FBI office at UN headquarters, opened at the height of the McCarthy scare, must close. Though he refused to reinstate a number of staff members who had been discharged at the time and had won an appeal to a UN tribunal, he deftly sidestepped American opposition to paying those employees fair compensation.

The US Congress had stipulated that no part of Washington's dues could be used to pay such "traitors." Instead, Hammarskjöld used a portion of the tax equalization fund collected from all UN staffers (except US citizens) in lieu of their paying national taxes. Though loyalty screening and advisory bulletins from Washington continued for many years, Hammarskjöld insisted he was not bound by them.

In time, he reorganized the top staff at the United Nations. Lie had eight assistant secretaries-general who were geographically representative and politically chosen. They enjoyed considerable freedom in their activities and helped coordinate UN business with their own governments. Hammarskjöld reshuffled the lineup to create two new undersecretary-general positions, one from the United States and one from Russia. Ralph Bunche, who had been transferred to Hammarskjöld's office as a top assistant, was tapped for the US position. Though Anatoli Dobrynin held the other job for a time, Moscow rotated the post among others every year or two. Hammarskjöld brought those two jobs as well as the top personnel, financial, and legal officials under the direct supervision of his office.

By the time Hammarskjöld arrived at the United Nations, many governments had established permanent missions at the UN headquarters. Frequent direct contact between member nations and the Secretary-General was therefore easy. He viewed this as a sort of continuous diplomatic conference and suggested in his annual report to the 1959 GA that the results of these informal contacts might become the most important "common law" development so far in the Charter's framework.[34]

As part of his reorganization efforts, he suggested that some of the UN research and training work could be taken on by universities and that the United Nations could easily reduce the number of its own publications. He personally wrote many of the reports issued during his tenure. He also persuaded the SC on several occasions to write specific instructions for him to follow exactly as he wanted them to read. Sir Brian noted that Hammarskjöld put major time and effort into making sure that Council resolutions were practical—"so that it was actually possible to do something with them."[35]

Through all his initiatives, Hammarskjöld brought a large swath of UN work under his immediate, personal direction. He saw administrative activities as a stepping stone to greater influence.[36] He argued that the Secretariat must be able to respond swiftly to new developments and needs. Some nations were skeptical that a centralized shift was wise. Yet the result, by and large, was a sharp improvement in the attitude of the staff and in the renewed respect with which governments and observers began to treat the United Nations.[37]

As time went on, however, Hammarskjöld became more interested in the political and diplomatic demands of his job and was ready to delegate many of the administrative details to others.

The First Diplomatic Challenge

The first public test of Hammarskjöld's diplomatic skills arose in late 1954. His unique response added a new dimension to the secretary-general's role.

In late November, Peking Radio announced that 11 US Air Force personnel and two US civilians had been convicted of espionage. Captured during the Korean War, all were described as Central Intelligence Agency (CIA) agents. Their sentences were to range from four years to life.

Washington, which had been demanding their release for many months, hotly denied the charges. In US eyes, the men were prisoners of war, not spies, and should be repatriated. The Republican Senate leader, William Knowland of California, was pushing for a naval blockade of mainland China until freedom was granted. A few of his colleagues were calling for nuclear strikes. President Eisenhower urged patience. He insisted that the United Nations had a special responsibility to free the men since they had been doing their jobs under UN command.

The United States took the issue to the GA, asking for condemnation of China's refusal to free the men. By this time, Beijing had four other American jet pilots also in custody. The US ambassador to the United Nations, Henry Cabot Lodge, consulted on Assembly action with 15 other governments who had sent troops to Korea.

The resulting Resolution 906 of December 10, 1954, sharply criticized China and passed against objections from Moscow and its allies. The Assembly contended that the detention, trials, and convictions all violated the Korean armistice agreement and asked the Secretary-General to make "continuing and unremitting efforts" to secure the Americans' release. Hammarskjöld, who had taken part in the discussions, argued without success against condemning Beijing but managed to include wording that he would represent the United Nations in this situation and that the means were to be of his choosing.

The risks for the Secretary-General were considerable, and he knew it. The Beijing government was not a member of the United Nations and was angered by the Assembly resolution. Washington had no diplomatic ties with the People's Republic of China, and tensions were high. Hammarskjöld knew that a direct approach risked a rebuff without results. He knew that Lie, in trying to end the Korean War, had met with a Chinese envoy who would discuss only US aggression and who left for the airport in the middle of the talks.

Still, Hammarskjöld reasoned that only a bold move had a realistic chance of success. He knew that Beijing wanted international recognition and UN membership. Unlike Lie, who had warmly embraced the SC stance on the Korean War, the new Secretary-General opted for a more independent role.

He cabled China's foreign minister Zhou Enlai, saying that the GA had asked him to seek release of the Americans (he did not include the resolution's text) and that he had a special responsibility under the UN Charter as a representative of the international community to do so. The Charter, not the Assembly, would be the basis for his visit. Would the foreign minister set a date on which the Secretary-General might personally visit him?

In his reply, Zhou Enlai called the Assembly resolution "absurd" and insisted that Beijing had a sovereign right to convict American "spies." However, within a week China's foreign minister agreed to see Hammarskjöld in January in the interests of peace and relaxed global tension.

Hammarskjöld flew to Beijing with several advisers but no press representatives on January 5, 1955. He held four working sessions with Zhou which totaled 13 hours. The Secretary-General did not put Beijing on the defensive or question the legality of its action. He later wrote to a Swedish friend that "[Zhou Enlai] to me appears as the most superior brain I have so far met in the field of foreign politics."[38]

The Secretary-General's attempt to distance himself from the Assembly's judgmental resolution and play a more independent role became known as the now-famous Peking Formula. The aim was to find a neutral avenue by which Hammarskjöld could satisfy the Assembly but not humiliate Zhou Enlai.

"Occasionally, it is useful to have the secretary-general in his role as the impartial man in the middle—technician, negotiator—deal with a problem on the basis of his inherent powers," George Sherry, a former UN assistant secretary-general for special political affairs, noted in an interview. "This notion of impartiality is extremely useful. Everybody knows it's sort of stretching the language but it is very convenient. And as long as everybody accepts it, perhaps with a wink of the eye...."[39]

"This was an important breakthrough—a very big deal," Sir Brian agreed. "The US, to everyone's credit, realized that an impartial, objective secretary-general was greatly to their advantage, even if you didn't always agree with him."[40]

On January 21, 1955, Peking Radio announced that the Chinese foreign minister was offering family visits to the prisoners. Although Hammarskjöld embraced the idea, the US State Department discouraged it. The Secretary-General sent a note to the US secretary of state, John Foster Dulles, to say that US handling of the situation might jeopardize the possible release of the prisoners.

More United Nations–China talks through intermediaries followed. Actual release of the prisoners took several more months. The four jet pilots finally were freed on May 30, and the 11 who had been part of a B29 crew were released on August 1, a few days after Washington said it was willing to hold talks with Beijing at the ambassador level. The two American civilians were not freed until the early 1970s.

Hammarskjöld enormously enjoyed the challenge of the task, according to Sir Brian. The work stimulated in the Secretary-General a new taste and new ideas for using his office to tackle difficult problems. Noting that the UN leader was "zealous" in not permitting others to share the limelight, Sir Brian said it was not a question of ego but of ensuring that the credit went to and strengthened the office of the secretary-general.[41]

The Suez Canal Crisis

Despite a strong penchant for preventive diplomacy, Hammarskjöld was unable to avert the Suez Canal crisis of 1956. Yet he did much to turn the event into a major victory for the United Nations and his office and to keep the turmoil from evolving into a wider war.

The UN intervention "helped the big powers involved in the Cold War to stand back and avoid the temptation to be brought in competitively," observed Inis Claude Jr.[42]

"The Great Powers wanted to find some way to insulate themselves against the risks of confrontation arising from that conflict," agreed Lawrence S. Finkelstein, a UN scholar who attended the organization's founding conference in San Francisco and helped draft the UN Charter, in an interview. "Hammarskjöld was in a sense the epitome of the secretary-general as leader in the role of peace manager."[43]

Once again, as with the Korean War, the UN action eventually shifted from the veto-prone Council to the GA. The first formal UN peacekeeping force was launched.

The 1949 Mideast armistice agreements had not brought peace. Arab–Israeli tensions were rising. In early 1955, the Israelis, long subject to terrorist raids, began retaliating against Egyptian-trained Palestinian soldiers in the Gaza Strip and Sinai. Palestinian *fedayeen* fought back. No Arab nation would claim responsibility.

Yet Israel's massive reprisals were clearly identifiable and thus sharply condemned by the SC as violations of the armistice agreements. Though the United Nations essentially had presided over the birth of Israel, Israel was becoming increasingly skeptical of the United Nations' claim to impartiality.

On April 4, 1956, in a unanimous resolution, the Council handed Hammarskjöld the job of working with the Arabs and Israelis to find a way to reduce tensions. He left two days later for a month's tour of the Middle East and managed to secure new cease-fire assurances between Israel and Egypt, Jordan, Lebanon, and Syria.

After the first agreement with Egypt was announced, Henry Cabot Lodge, the US ambassador and president of the SC at the time, said, "We can all be thankful...that the position of the secretary-general of the United Nations exists and that it is filled by such a capable individual as Mr. Hammarskjöld, when we think of how much we all want to avoid war."[44]

Meanwhile, Egypt's president Gamal Abdel Nasser was relying more and more on Moscow for support and arms purchases and was increasingly friendly with the Communist Chinese government, which Cairo formally recognized in May 1956. Though the United

States and Britain had offered grants to Nasser for his Aswan Dam project on the Nile, he balked at certain conditions they attached, arguing that the West was trying to control his economy. In mid-July, both Washington and London abruptly withdrew their offers. The World Bank, which had offered a loan premised on the grants, followed suit.

On July 26, Nasser responded by nationalizing the Suez Canal Company. The British and French governments strongly protested. Britain in particular depended heavily on use of the canal to import its oil and was the largest shareholder in the canal company. Along with Washington, the West Europeans called for a conference to take up the matter. In London, some 22 canal users soon began discussing a plan to internationalize the waterway. Nasser refused to accept their proposal. He insisted he was well within his rights under international law in choosing to nationalize foreign assets on Egyptian territory.

In early October 1956, Britain and France, once reluctant to bring the issue to the United Nations, called for a Council meeting. They proposed resolutions to condemn Egypt for its unilateral action and to endorse their plan for international supervision of the canal. Their proposal clearly was headed for a Soviet veto. Hammarskjöld quickly proposed a series of private meetings with Egypt, France, and Britain to be held at the foreign-minister level in his 38th floor office. In the process, he drafted and got tentative agreement to six principles, including open transit through the canal, respect for Egypt's sovereignty, and arbitration of any disputes.

In negotiating, Hammarskjöld committed little of the prestige of his office, according to Gordenker. "He always tried to claim that he was merely assisting delegates to see their own somewhat obscured agreements."[45]

On October 29, just as private talks were set to resume, Israeli troops suddenly attacked Egypt's Sinai Peninsula with the stated aim of eliminating guerrilla bases and more terrorist attacks.

At a SC meeting the next morning, the United States, with Soviet support, called for an immediate Israeli–Egyptian cease-fire and withdrawal of all foreign troops from Egyptian territory. This time, the British and French vetoed the proposals and issued an ultimatum to Egypt and Israel to withdraw at least 10 miles from each side of the canal within 12 hours. Israel agreed. Egypt did not.

One day later, under a prearranged plan with Israel, France and Britain began bombing Cairo and the Suez Canal zone as the first step to an invasion. Neither Washington nor the United Nations had been warned beforehand. Hammarskjöld felt doubly betrayed. He thought his diplomatic talks with the parties had been making progress. He had also looked to London and Paris as the longtime standard-bearers of Western civilization.[46]

The British and French vetoes and the increasing danger of the new situation prompted the SC's Yugoslav delegation to invoke the Uniting for Peace resolution. On a procedural vote, requiring only a majority, the Council shifted further UN consideration of the Suez crisis to the GA.

The Assembly met a few hours later in an emergency session that lasted until 4:20 the next morning. US Secretary of State Dulles proposed a resolution calling for an immediate cease-fire and withdrawal of all forces from the canal. During the debate, Canada's minister of foreign affairs, Lester Pearson, suggested that a UN military force take over the French and British positions. There was no specific provision for this in the Charter, and Hammarskjöld initially was doubtful it could work.[47]

Still, on November 4, 1956, the Assembly formally asked him to submit a plan. It was to be a temporary emergency international force, operating with the consent of the concerned nations, to seek and supervise a cease-fire.

Hammarskjöld asked for and got 48 hours in which to draw up the plan. He completed the outline for it the very next day. The force was to be more than an observer but less than a military occupier. He sent the text to the British and French governments. Replacement of their troops by UN forces was their condition for agreeing to a cease-fire.

Hammarskjöld later flew to Cairo and worked with Nasser to create an acceptable framework for the UN force.

"Those negotiations with Nasser were very difficult, particularly [defining] the conditions for stationing the forces on Egyptian territory and for how long," noted Yale's James Sutterlin. "Hammarskjöld and his staff did in fact develop the outline and procedures and almost the constitutional basis [for peacekeeping], and these did not really change much until the end of the Cold War."[48]

Hammarskjöld later called peacekeeping "Chapter Six-and-One-Half" of the Charter, halfway between pacific settlement of disputes described in Chapter 6 and enforcement allowed under certain conditions in Chapter 7.[49]

"The original notion of peacekeeping was that troops would be there by consent [of the involved government], be impartial, be helpful to all sides, and not get in the way of anybody who wants to fight," confirmed Inis Claude Jr.[50]

Sir Brian, who worked on the plans with Ralph Bunche and other UN staff, described the Hammarskjöld peacekeeping strategy as "a conceptual masterpiece in a completely new field—the blueprint for a nonviolent, international military operation."[51]

Nations with troops available soon met on the 38th floor of UN headquarters while two US officials coordinated the airlift and logistical details. There were more than enough volunteers. Ralph Bunche called it "the most popular army in history...[one] which everyone fights to get into."[52] It was agreed that some distinguishable sign of UN command, such as the blue beret, was needed. Yet since getting those would take weeks, organizers opted to have American helmet liners, plentiful in Europe at the time, spray painted blue.[53]

The UN Emergency Force (UNEF) was on the job by November 14 and remained for more than 10 years—until Nasser demanded its departure in 1967. At one point, UNEF had 6,000 troops from 10 nations. It was stationed on the Egyptian side of the canal and became a major factor in preventing more terrorist raids on Israel.

Because UNEF was to take responsibility for canal security, the West Europeans could say their aim was achieved. British and French troops withdrew by the end of 1956. The Israeli troops lingered on for three more months. Hammarskjöld had arranged earlier for a fleet of salvage vessels to clear the canal, and Egypt announced its reopening in April 1957.

As a face-saving device, UNEF more than proved its worth. In a function it has since fulfilled many times, the UN was able to serve as "a smokescreen behind which losers could appear undefeated and altruistic," noted Thomas Franck in *Nation Against Nation*.[54]

Hammarskjöld's skill in setting up UNEF drew widespread praise both for him and the office.

Sir Brian called UNEF an "unexpected success" that marked a "great victory for common sense, innovation, hard work, and intelligent leadership."[55]

"There was a good deal of feeling in the [US] State Department that we had a staunch individual there who would stand for what was right and to whom we could turn to get out of difficult situations," noted Francis Wilcox, US assistant secretary of state for International Organization Affairs, 1955–61.[56]

Yet Hammarskjöld, ever reserved, kept his sense of perspective. In 1958, he was asked to report to the GA on the UNEF experience. Enthusiasm for establishing a standby UN peacekeeping force was at an all-time high. Sir Brian prepared the first draft of that report without knowing what Hammarskjöld really had in mind. The draft was received in "polite silence" by the Secretary-General, who then wrote his own analysis. The overall message was that it would be wise to avoid the degree of improvisation necessary in creating UNEF but that "strictest respect for the rules of the Charter" must be followed. "In other words, no standing peacekeeping force," Sir Brian said.[57]

In many ways, the Suez crisis is viewed as a turning point. Stanley Meisler, the former *Los Angeles Times* reporter who wrote a history of the United Nations' first 50 years, called the United Nations' handling of the Suez crisis a "defining moment" for the organization. Arguing that the United Nations proved strong enough to "bend and almost break two tired old imperialist powers," Meisler argued that the British and French empires "died at Suez" and that the crisis marked the end of traditional imperialism. [58]

The Challenge of Hungary

Hammarskjöld's best efforts did not always succeed, and he seemed to sense when a solution really was possible and when it was not.

Hungarian students staged a major revolt against Soviet repression in their country in October 1956. They issued no less than 16 demands, including withdrawal of Soviet troops and more political rights.

Like the Suez crisis, it was again a situation of major powers (though in this case only one—Moscow) hoping to preserve the threatened status quo. Unlike the Middle East threat to the peace, however, the two superpowers, the United States and the Soviet Union, were not of one mind in this case, making its resolution far more difficult. The United Nations could act against aggressors only if the two major powers agreed or if one were indifferent. The United Nations thus did not dare to do more than try to persuade Moscow to back off, and the Soviets knew it. [59]

In SC meetings in late October and early November that year, Moscow did not budge from its insistence that the issue was strictly internal and no business of the United Nations. When the United States sponsored a resolution to condemn the Soviet invasion as a violation of the Charter and hit an easily predicted Soviet veto, the Council voted to move the issue to the GA. There, a similar resolution passed on November 4. Hammarskjöld was asked to investigate and report on the situation.

By November 8, 1956, however, the Soviets already had crushed the Hungarian rebellion. Hammarskjöld, who had been busy drawing up UNEF plans under a 48-hour order from the SC when he was handed the Assembly mandate on Hungary, had not rushed to act. Though the United States' anger had helped to force a reversal by France and Britain in the Suez case, the Soviet Union seemed to have little regard for US opposition or international public opinion. The Western powers knew that any use of force risked a possible nuclear conflict, a risk they clearly were unwilling to take.

On December 12, the GA again asked Hammarskjöld to take any initiative he thought would help. He suggested sending a team of observers to Hungary, but the new pro-Soviet regime there would have none of it. His request to personally visit Budapest also received a negative response. The Secretary-General himself even refused to meet a Hungarian representative in Rome on grounds that it might severely compromise UN prestige.[60]

Sir Brian noted that all the Secretary-General's efforts were rebuffed until it was too late to do anything useful: "The UN was the ideal dumping ground for such an unmanageable problem, and the Secretary-General the perfect scapegoat for the international community's inability to act."[61]

The Assembly, in taking no meaningful action on Hungary, showed "all the firmness of a creampuff in a heat wave," wrote Roscoe Drummond in his column in the *Washington Post*.[62]

Hammarskjöld, strongly criticized by the West for his failure to act more forcefully, was resigned to dealing only with the humanitarian side of the situation. Budapest would accept aid. The Secretary-General asked the UN High Commissioner for Refugees to coordinate the UN response. Some 200,000 Hungarian refugees had fled, largely to Austria, during the fighting. In the first successful repatriation program of its kind, the United Nations helped to return close to 20,000 Hungarians to their homeland.

Of his overall efforts in the Hungarian and Suez crises, Hammarskjöld stressed that the Suez situation had a higher priority on his time. As he later admitted during a February 6, 1958, press conference, "I did what I could, and it did not yield the results I was hoping for."[63]

A Second Term?

Hammarskjöld had long made it clear that he would not serve a second five-year term unless he was reelected unanimously. When his candidacy came to a vote in the GA on September 26, 1957, a year after the Suez–Hungarian crises, approval was quick, quiet, and unanimous.

As he later wrote to his close friend Per Lind, a former colleague at the Swedish Foreign Office, "What created unanimity was the fact that, whatever the national grudges, everybody felt that they could not afford to run into a conflict over this issue." He also confided to Lind that he might be considered "mad to continue" in the job but that he felt no more "free" about refusing it than when first elected. He added that, "You well know that I would never hesitate to put the UN first."[64]

In his acceptance speech to the Assembly, he said that no one could accept the job, knowing what it involves, except from a sense of duty. Still, he said the post was also deeply rewarding.

He stressed that, as Secretary-General, he must act on the basis of the Charter principles or the wishes of the UN organs but that he should also be free to act without such guidance if needed to fill any "vacuum" in the system.

Gordenker called Hammarskjöld's description "the full flowering" of a far-reaching concept of the office.[65] Paul Kennedy, author and Yale scholar, termed it "an acute self-assessment of the office, and no one, not even the Soviets, protested despite their increasing unhappiness at his roles."[66]

Lebanon and the Need to Act

One such "vacuum" in the UN system occurred a few months into Hammarskjöld's second term. Cold-war friction again led him to seize the moment to act independently. Somewhat curiously, his move met no protest.

In the spring of 1958, the word was out in Lebanon that President Camille Chamoun wanted a constitutional amendment that would allow him to seek a second term. The news stirred strong and increasing opposition to his government.

On May 22, Chamoun asked for an urgent meeting of the SC. He complained that the newly formed United Arab Republic (UAR), then composed of Egypt and Syria, was interfering in Lebanon's domestic affairs. By moving weapons and fighters into Lebanon, he said, the UAR was trying to overthrow his government. The UAR scoffed at the charges, insisting that it was all an internal matter related to Chamoun's reelection plan.

After a delay to see if the Arab League could settle the matter, the Council took up the issue in June. It adopted a resolution, crafted in part by Hammarskjöld, that gave him the authority to set up a UN Observation Group in Lebanon (UNOGIL) to investigate the claims and prevent foreign involvement. He was to decide on the size, composition, and deployment details.[67] Hammarskjöld attended the group's first meeting in Beirut in late June and held talks in Jordan, Israel, and Egypt. He specifically warned Nasser that continuing UAR infiltration into Lebanon could erode the UN consensus still supporting UNEF in Egypt.

However, UNOGIL's first report to the Council on July 4 said that it had found no evidence of "mass infiltration" by the UAR in support of Lebanese rebels.

Chamoun's government, which had already quietly approached the United States before the UN involvement, again appealed to Washington for help. The United States initially resisted. However, an unrelated Iraqi coup on July 14, 1958, fueled American concerns that a Communist-inspired Arab takeover of the Middle East might be in the planning stage. Hammarskjöld tried in vain to dissuade Washington from any action that might prompt a Soviet countermove.

On July 16, some 10,000 US troops landed on a Beirut beach. US President Eisenhower said the aim was to protect American lives and preserve Lebanese independence. Henry Cabot Lodge, US Ambassador to the United Nations, told Hammarskjöld that Washington saw the action as strictly in line with Article 51 of the Charter (guaranteeing the inherent right of individual or collective self-defense if an armed attack occurs against a UN member). Lodge recalled that Hammarskjöld's anger, on learning that the troops had landed, was "indeed memorable."[68]

Two days later Moscow proposed a SC resolution, asking US troops to leave immediately. The proposal was defeated.

Hammarskjöld then recommended an expansion of UNOGIL as a replacement force for US troops. He reasoned that it would allow the American troops to make a face-saving exit. Moscow promptly vetoed it.

The Council was stymied. On July 22, Hammarskjöld announced that he would take immediate action to expand UNOGIL to prevent further deterioration of the situation. He said he had a duty under the Charter to fill such a "vacuum" in the interests of world peace. However, he said, if the Council disapproved, he would bow to its judgment.

The Council adjourned without taking action. Hammarskjöld played a prominent role in the diplomatic efforts that followed in the Assembly. Soon he expanded the UN force of a few dozen men to include some 600 more military observers.

He effectively transformed UNOGIL into the very peacekeeping force that Moscow had vetoed. He established for the secretary-general's office a "stand-by power" to initiate peacekeeping in the face of the Council's failure to act.[69] Hammarskjöld himself called UNOGIL a classic case of preventive diplomacy.[70]

"Part of how he got away with that is that he was only the second secretary-general," said Gordenker, "but I think he also had enough political experience to know that he had to take some chances like that—and he picked those spots well."[71]

Hammarskjöld's job turned into a rescue operation as Washington realized the risk and irrelevance of its action.[72] Eventually the situation stabilized. The last US marine left Lebanon on October 25. UNOGIL's job officially ended in December 1958 after it submitted a final report that all was calm along the Syrian–Lebanese border.

Mediating a Cambodian–Thai Dispute

During that same autumn of 1958, Hammarskjöld began a quiet, successful mediation effort in a dispute between Thailand and Cambodia.

Each was accusing the other of aggression and border violations. Negotiations on several issues, including ownership of the Buddhist temple of Preah Vihear, had broken down.

In late November, Cambodia complained to Hammarskjöld that Thailand was threatening international peace by stationing troops and military equipment on their common border and occupying the temple which, Cambodia insisted, was on its soil. Thailand claimed the temple was inside its own territory and that it had no troops—just police reinforcement—at its border to prevent armed raids.

Thailand, being pro-West, and Cambodia, on its way to becoming a Soviet ally, wanted to take the dispute to the SC, but Hammarskjöld tried to convince the two nations that their dispute could easily get bogged down there in public meetings and debates. He persuaded them that a simpler and more useful route would be to resolve the issue with the help of one of his personal representatives. Though Paris and Moscow were not pleased with this maneuvering, Cambodia and Thailand agreed.

Hammarskjöld tapped the veteran Swedish diplomat Johan Beck-Friis, who flew to the area on January 20, 1959. By early February, the two nations agreed to resume diplomatic relations. Cambodia released all Thai prisoners, and the border was reopened. Hammarskjöld called the method one of "adjusting the procedures."[73]

However, the initial issue—which nation had sovereignty over the temple—was not resolved for another three years. Thailand took it to the International Court of Justice, which ruled in June 1962 that the temple was indeed in Cambodian territory and that Thailand must withdraw its forces stationed in or around the temple.

Laos Asks for Help

By late summer 1959, the government of Laos asked Hammarskjöld for UN help in an increasingly divisive civil war. The government had been shifting from a neutral to a more pro-Western stance. It argued that armed foreigners, presumably from North Vietnam, were aggressively helping local communist Pathet Lao rebels fight the government.

In early September, the Laos foreign minister sent Hammarskjöld a letter, asking for a UN emergency force. It was widely assumed that the Pathet Lao would never accept such a force, but the matter was clearly a SC responsibility. Hammarskjöld was aware of the paradox. He lacked the facts to make an intelligent decision but had a duty to process a serious request.[74] He took a calculated political risk. He did not rely on his Article 99 powers to call a Council meeting, in which case his right to speak at the meeting could be refused. Instead, he asked the Council's Italian president to call the meeting. The Secretary-General was invited to be the first speaker.

At the September 7 session, Hammarskjöld read aloud the letter he had received. After what was widely described as a torturous debate, the United States, France, and Britain proposed sending a subcommittee to investigate the situation and report back. Moscow vetoed the measure. The Council president ruled, however, that the issue was procedural, rather than substantive, so that the veto did not apply.

In early November, the subcommittee reported back that it had found no clear evidence of North Vietnamese aggression or involvement. Given the rugged nature of the terrain and the Pathet Lao's unwillingness to cooperate, the finding was "hardly surprising," according to Seymour Finger, who served in the US Embassy in Laos in 1955–56.[75]

Shortly after the report was made, Hammarskjöld suggested that he personally make a trip to Laos. He soon received an official invitation. In the face of Soviet threats to veto the visit if he put it to a Council vote, he flew to Laos for a week in mid-November without specific UN authorization. He wrote each Council member to explain that he needed to assess the situation as part of his own duty as secretary-general. He said he would probably also station a personal representative in Vientiane, the administrative capital.[76]

This was yet another of Hammarskjöld's "crisis mediation efforts," noted Hammarskjöld biographer Peter Heller.[77] The Secretary-General encouraged the Laotian government to form a less pro-Western and more neutral coalition. Months later, when asked whether Laotian policies were moving to the left or to the right, he diplomatically replied, "Forward."[78]

He also named a Finnish diplomat as his personal representative in Laos to assess economic and social needs and to manage a program of UN aid. Hammarskjöld viewed the aid effort as a further way of providing good offices.[79] Moscow charged that he was using the UN name to disguise what was really further Western interference in Laotian domestic affairs.

Yet Hammarskjöld defended the UN presence in Laos and his own role. At a meeting of the GA's Fifth Committee in October 1960, he said that a secretary-general sometimes "has to find out for himself, and that may mean, as in the case of the [Soviet-] criticized journey to Laos last November, that he has to go himself." He added that some countries may wish to have the independent help of the United Nations without the "stormy weather of a major, international political debate."[80]

The civil war in Laos continued as the Pathet Lao rebels steadily took over more territory. A 1962 Geneva conference agreed to by the superpowers essentially took the issue out of UN hands. After several more coups, the Pathet Lao took over the country in 1975.

The Belgian Congo: Hammarskjöld's Last Major Challenge

The Belgian Congo crisis of 1960–61 was the toughest challenge of Hammarskjöld's UN career. As secretary-general, he had taken major initiatives. Yet, in the Congo case, he worked hard to keep the United Nations from getting involved in the nation's volatile internal politics. Still, the way he approached the situation often drew sharp criticism—not just from the Soviet Union and its allies, but at times from Western Europe and even Washington.

In many ways, though, this was also Hammarskjöld's finest hour. In the end, the UN Congo operation achieved virtually all its objectives.

"Talk about a power vacuum—that really was one," said Sir Brian, who was closely involved in the UN effort from start to finish. "The Congo had everything. It was decolonization. It was also a major East–West threat because both the United States and the Soviet Union regarded it as a key strategic territory...the US because it had NATO bombing bases there and Moscow because it was an enormously important source of minerals. The situation really was very dangerous."[81]

Early in 1960, Belgium announced that its longtime colony would become independent on June 30. Hammarskjöld, who visited Africa that January to gather some political background, suspected that the transition could be difficult. The Congolese had held no major administrative or military posts in the Belgian colony. There was to be no preparatory period of self-rule. The nation had fewer than 20 university graduates out of a population of close to four million.

In May, Hammarskjöld sent Ralph Bunche, the undersecretary-general for political affairs and the man who had drafted the chapters on decolonization in the UN Charter, as his Special Representative to the Congo during the independence ceremonies. Bunche's reports were not encouraging. He commented on the condescending and paternalistic attitude among Belgian officials. He also noticed that Prime Minister Patrice Lumumba and President Joseph Kasavubu, men from rival tribes who had agreed shortly before the Congo's independence to share power, were already bickering with each other.[82]

After the independence ceremonies, at which Lumumba lashed out in resentment at the Belgian leadership, the situation deteriorated at record speed. The poorly paid black army troops (*Force Publique*) soon rebelled against their white officers amid rumors that the Belgians intended to disarm them. The mutiny spread and led to large-scale rioting, looting, and even reports of rape and murder of Belgian citizens. Many of the 100,000 remaining Belgians, who had expected to keep their jobs in business and administration, panicked and fled.

In response, Brussels sent paratroopers to restore order and protect the remaining Belgians and their property. Many Congolese, however, assumed the aim was to reassert colonial control. Public services broke down, and the situation became desperate.

On top of that, on July 11, Moise Tshombe, the elected president of the copper-rich Katanga Province, announced that Katanga would secede from the central Congo government in Léopoldville.

Lumumba and Kasavubu quickly cabled Hammarskjöld for UN military help. They spoke of Belgian troop aggression and wanted protection and a return to order. The Secretary-General saw the situation as a clear threat to international peace and security, and formally invoked the UN Charter's Article 99 to call an emergency session of the SC for the evening of July 13. At 3:25 the next morning, the Council voted to ask Belgium to withdraw its troops and authorized Hammarskjöld to draft plans to replace them. The United Nations was to supply military and technical aid until Congolese troops were up to the job. Force was to be used only in self-defense.

Hammarskjöld, who essentially designed the resolution that gave him the power to act, worked fast with his immediate staff to organize and deploy UN forces. "It was the high point of Hammarskjöld's, and perhaps any secretary-general's, powers of initiation," noted Thomas Franck.[83]

The first four nations to supply troops were lined up within hours, and the United States and the Soviet Union agreed to fly in troops and supplies. The first 3,000 forces of the UN Operation in the Congo (ONUC) were on the ground within three days.

Hammarskjöld thought a swift and highly visible UN intervention was the only hope of getting the Belgian troops out and restoring order.[84]

The previous UNEF force in the Sinai served as a basic model. "The manual, the design for peacekeeping, was already there," noted Lawrence S. Finkelstein, author of several books and articles on the United Nations. "When the time came for ONUC, they just pulled it out of the file drawer, so to speak."[85]

Still, the Congo case was markedly different from others. The scope of UN troop duties was far broader. This was no classic case of patrolling a cease-fire among willing belligerents, as UN troops had done in the Sinai. Here the situation involved a mutinous national army, returning troops from the former colonial power, a rich breakaway province, and a new government with very little experience. Few in the Congo seemed to know much about the United Nations, and ONUC troops were often mistaken for Belgians.

The United Nations, in this case, also organized a large civilian task force (drawing on its special agencies) to run essential services. The world organization helped with everything from air-traffic controllers and police to doctors and communication workers.

"It was really a very broad-based nation-building exercise," said Edward C. Luck, a former head of the United Nations Association of the USA."[86]

Meanwhile the Katanga situation was worsening. Tshombe, the president, had hired Belgian troops and foreign mercenaries to keep Congolese troops from taking back the province. On July 30, the Congolese government demanded that UN troops go into Katanga immediately to end the secession. Strong Katanga opposition, however, managed to force postponement of the planned UN military intervention. Hammarskjöld felt he needed fresh authorization from the SC. In a move again designed and championed by the Secretary-General himself, the Council voted on August 9, 1960, to ask Belgian troops and officials to leave Katanga and ordered UN troops in to replace them.[87]

At this point, praise for Hammarskjöld was still running high. For example, in a column published that same day in the *New York Times*, James Reston observed, "This remarkable man is proving to be one of the great natural resources in the world today."[88]

Three days later, the Secretary-General took a major risk by personally leading the first UN troops into Katanga. Lumumba was not told until after the fact. ONUC's aim was to provide the basis for the Belgian troop withdrawal, a feat already accomplished in the rest of the Congo. Hammarskjöld pledged not to interfere in the Congo's internal disputes. Although the Council action had clarified his position, he was not authorized to end the secession by force.

Lumumba, the Congo's mercurial prime minister, was puzzled by the UN stance. He insisted that the United Nations must take the side of the Congo government, support reunification, and remove Tshombe. Lumumba bitterly resented his not having been told about and included in the trip to Katanga. He appealed to Moscow for military help and sent units of the national Congolese army (now *L'Armée Nationale Congolaise,* or ANC), though untrained and leaderless, into Katanga, He sharply criticized Hammarskjöld and demanded that the United Nations leave the Congo at once. His relations with the United Nations were never the same. He sent insulting letters to the Secretary-General and would not speak with him, even when Hammarskjöld came to Léopoldville. Soon Moscow began echoing Lumumba's charges against the United Nations.[89]

Meanwhile tension between the liberal and hot-tempered Lumumba and the more conservative and calm Kasavubu was intensifying. On September 5, Kasavubu dismissed Lumumba from the Congo government for acting arbitrarily and taking the nation into a civil war. A mere 30 minutes later, Lumumba issued an emotional radio broadcast in which he declared that Kasavubu was no longer president and called on the public to rise up in rebellion and join him (Lumumba) in establishing a caretaker government.

Less than 10 days later—on September 14—Joseph Mobutu, a former journalist and military official in Lumumba's government, announced by radio from the Congo capital the first of a series of coups d'état. He said he would ask young technicians to run the country while he tried to get the two leaders to cooperate. Lumumba was furious, refused to recognize Mobutu and announced that Soviet troops would come in to expel UN forces. To avoid a full-scale civil war, the United Nations closed the major airports and radio stations.

Hammarskjöld's efforts to resolve the Congo and Katanga crises were becoming increasingly controversial. The Soviets had begun to help Lumumba and thought the United Nations was not aggressive enough in helping him unite the country. They attacked the United Nations for allowing the dismissal of Lumumba and Mobuto's expulsion of Soviet bloc embassies from Léopoldville. The United States, France, and Britain, on the other hand, favored Lumumba's exit and thought the United Nations should be more supportive of Mobutu and Kasavubu. Western Europe had strong financial ties to Katanga and favored secession. Many in the West considered Tshombe a hero.

U Thant, who would later succeed Hammarskjöld in the top UN post, wrote in his autobiography that the Secretary-General once told him that he had never received as much hate mail on any issue as he had with regard to the UN's role in the Congo.[90]

Sir Brian insisted that the Secretary-General's main aim throughout was to keep the Cold War out of the Congo: "[Hammarskjöld] had cabled Bunche July 23: 'If the Cold War settles in the Congo, our whole effort is lost.'"[91]

On September 23, 1960, at the opening annual session of the GA, Soviet leader Nikita Khrushchev called it "deplorable" that colonial powers have been "doing their dirty work in the Congo" through the Secretary-General and his staff. Khrushchev said the secretary-general "alone" directs the staff and interprets and executes Council decisions. The post, he said, should be abolished and replaced by a three-person executive group that would represent the West, the Socialist countries, and the nonaligned nations.

Hammarskjöld was sure that this troika proposal would lead to an ineffective executive and kill any idea of an independent international civil service. He announced to the Assembly three days later that he would rather see his office "break on strict adherence to the principle of independence, impartiality, and objectivity than drift on the basis of compromise." Compromise, he added, was a choice he faced daily as secretary-general.

"His view was that he was being impartial—not necessarily neutral," noted Leon Gordenker. "When attacked by Khrushchev, he [essentially] said, 'Look, I have to carry out the Charter. I'm not neutral on that point.' No one objected to his saying that at the time except Khrushchev."[92]

"A secretary-general can be impartial, but he can't be neutral," argued Sir Brian. "He's got to take a stand when something is clearly outrageous."[93]

Yet Khrushchev did not let up. On the morning of October 3, 1960, he told the Assembly that Hammarskjöld should have the "courage" to resign, "There is no room for a man who has violated the elementary principles of justice in such an important post as that of secretary-general," he said.

"Khrushchev hated Hammarskjöld because the Russians knew he was independent and would act on his own judgment of what was right and wrong," Sir Brian said.[94]

In an Assembly reply that same afternoon, Hammarskjöld said that it would be easy to resign and less easy to stay on. However, he felt a responsibility to all UN members (other than the major powers) who really needed the United Nations for their protection. By stepping down, he would be replaced by a troika, he said, which could not be an effective executive post. "By resigning, I would, at the present difficult and dangerous juncture, throw the organization to the winds," he said. "I have no right to do so." With the exception of the Soviet bloc, the Assembly rose to its feet with a roar of approval and applause that lasted several minutes.

The Secretary-General had carefully cultivated the support of numerous newly independent African and Asian nations. James Jonah, a former UN undersecretary-general for political affairs, insists that developing nations "saved the day" by siding with Hammarskjöld despite Khrushchev's efforts to win them over.[95]

Before Khrushchev left for home after the fall GA session, he delivered a farewell speech in which he slightly softened his criticism of Hammarskjöld. He still was promoting the idea of a troika and described the secretary-general as a representative of "big capital." He then recalled having rowed Hammarskjöld in a boat on the Black Sea, noting that the Secretary-General had not yet paid off that "debt." Hammarskjöld said that his promise to reply in kind still held but noted that Khrushchev would then discover, "I know how to row—following only my own compass."[96]

While all this was going on at UN headquarters in New York, the friction between Mobutu and Lumumba in the Congo was growing.

Congolese troops loyal to Lumumba were conducting a spirited rebellion against the Kasavubu-Mobuto troops and, on November 12, 1960, took back control of Stanleyville, Lumumba's longtime political and tribal base in the northeast.

Though UN troops were sticking to their mandate of noninterference in internal politics, the GA voted on November 22 to seat the Kasavubu–Mobutu regime rather than the Lumumba supporters.

Mobutu's Congolese troops were working hard to find the elusive Lumumba. They finally arrested him on December 1, 1960. He was charged with inciting the Congolese army to rebellion. Moscow called for his immediate release and the restoration of the pro-Lumumba Congolese Parliament. Hammarskjöld urged that Lumumba be treated with respect and given due process of law. It did not happen, and neither the United Nations nor the Red Cross was allowed to visit him.

In mid-January 1961, Lumumba, who had steadily protested against Katanga's secession, was transferred from a military prison in the Congo to one in Katanga. Care was taken not to tell the United Nations in advance. Lumumba arrived blindfolded and was brutally beaten. On February 12, he was murdered.

On hearing the news, the Soviet Union promptly demanded that Hammarskjöld be dismissed for "complicity" with Belgium in the assassination. Moscow said ONUC troops must withdraw within a month.[97]

Hammarskjöld insisted that he would not resign and that he had done only what his UN mandate allowed him to do. Sir Brian noted that the Secretary-General was extremely upset by Lumumba's death: "His normal Olympian control and demeanor at times lapsed into shrill indignation."[98]

The SC was galvanized to take stronger action in the Congo now. It voted on February 21 (with France and the Russia abstaining) to direct ONUC to take immediate steps to end the Congo civil war, using force if necessary as a last resort. The resolution also asked ONUC to remove all mercenaries and Belgian officers from Katanga and called for an investigation into Lumumba's death.

Efforts to reunify the Congo and bring all ANC units under a central control made some progress over the next several months. It soon became apparent, however, that for further progress, all foreign personnel in the Katanga military would have to go. The foreign fighters had been encouraging Tshombe to resist integration with the Congo. At Hammarskjöld's suggestion, Kasavubu ordered their immediate expulsion. His request was seconded by Cyrille Adoula, the Congo's newly elected premier, who asked ONUC to enforce the order.[99]

ONUC finally abandoned the pretense of neutrality. The Irish diplomat Conor Cruise O'Brien, tapped by Hammarskjöld as his new personal representative in Katanga, started several intensive efforts to round up foreign personnel. Though many were arrested and deported, the fighting was bloody and the losses were heavy.

Tshombe promised to cooperate and rid his army of foreigners but failed to follow through. O'Brien once said that no contradiction or detected lie caused Tshombe the slightest embarrassment. At one point during an intensive UN attack when Tshombe phoned him, O'Brien guaranteed his personal safety but asked him to issue a radio broadcast saying that the secession had ended and that he had ordered a cease-fire. Tshombe agreed but then fled to northern Rhodesia without making the broadcast.[100]

Anxious to negotiate with Tshombe a clear end to Katanga's secession, Hammarskjöld took off in a DC-6 from Léopoldville for Ndola in northern Rhodesia on September 17, 1961. It was to be his final trip. The plane, with wheels lowered, passed low, about 2,000 feet, over the Ndola airport just after midnight, but crashed on a tree-covered hill about nine miles away. The wreckage was found about 15 hours later. The Secretary-General, seven staff members, and the Swedish crew all died.

Rumors still swirl as to whether some kind of plot was involved, but no credible evidence has surfaced. Most UN officials dismiss the crash as a horrible accident. It took time to get over the shock of it all. Sir Brian wrote that Hammarskjöld held a "unique place in our lives, thoughts, and affections" because of his character and leadership: "For a long time it was hard to think of him without tears, not least because one would never see his like again"[101]

The Philadelphia Orchestra was brought into the UN headquarters in New York to play a memorial concert in the GA Hall where Hammarskjöld had enjoyed arranging annual UN concerts.

A little over a month after his death, on October 23, 1961, he was posthumously awarded the Nobel Peace Prize.

At the time of his death, the UN operation in the Congo was widely viewed as a disaster. It began as an operation designed to ease the transition from colony to independence. However, the United

Nations soon found itself embroiled in a violent civil war that raised difficult questions about both UN partiality and effectiveness.

Yet in retrospect, the Congo crisis is widely viewed now as a major plus for the United Nations and for peacekeeping. ONUC managed to disarm some Congolese units, and UN troops replaced Belgian soldiers. The Congo's territorial integrity was preserved—though at a steep price. Katanga did rejoin the Congo but not until 1962. Public services were maintained and some sense of law and order reestablished. Despite the heated rhetoric, no major East–West confrontation occurred.

"We now realize what a success [the UN Congo effort] was," said George Sherry, a former UN assistant secretary-general for special political affairs. "It achieved virtually all its purposes."[102]

"Actually I think the Congo was the most successful operation the UN ever did," insisted Sir Brian. "It was the only one where the UN did everything it was asked to do."[103]

Edward Luck agreed: "The UN really took over running the Congo. It ran the government and the administration."[104]

Yet the Congo experience also threw a spotlight on the limits of peacekeeping. For most of the next three decades, the United Nations stayed away from any other major military engagement. Peacekeepers afterwards were sent in only when there was support from all sides involved. Instead of open-ended mandates, as with UNEF and ONUC, the SC began periodic reviews of peacekeeping operations and exercised more formal control over secretaries-general in troop composition and command.[105]

In his Congo role, Hammarskjöld showed how Article 99 could be effectively used. He had strengthened the independent and political aspects of his post. As only the second secretary-general, he was able to take initiatives that others who followed could not.

The Secretary-General from Sweden may well represent a "high point" in terms of great-power trust in UN management of global events, argued Thomas Boudreau in *Sheathing the Sword*.

Yet, the author added, that, for all his courage, intelligence, and skill, Hammarskjöld ran into the same strong Soviet opposition that Trygve Lie encountered a few years earlier, as well as a debilitating Soviet boycott.[106]

Hammarskjöld strongly defended his active role as secretary-general, while conceding that he sometimes lacked clear guidance from UN organs. In the introduction to his 1961 annual report to the GA, he said that anyone in his post was obligated to seek guidance to every possible extent from the main UN organs. However, he added, when such guidance is not forthcoming, sometimes a secretary-general has to take responsibility for limited political functions in line with the spirit of Article 99, as long as these are legally based on the decisions of UN bodies.

"One of the real difficulties—and it limits the secretary-general—is that he's dealing with governments, and it's hard to move them," noted Leon Gordenker. "It takes time and consistent political effort."[107]

"I think Hammarskjöld in the end went to somewhat unrealistic lengths in making the UN an autonomous organization that was not dependent on any state or group of states," said Harold Jacobson, a former University of Michigan political scientist, in an interview. "It's very difficult for a secretary-general, if he annoys someone, as Hammarskjöld did...to go as far as he tried to go."[108]

In his last major speech, given at Oxford University on May 30, 1961, Hammarskjöld again stressed the importance of an independent secretary-general. Sensitive to charges that he had taken sides in the Congo crisis, he said, "The international official cannot be accused of lack of neutrality simply for taking a stand on a controversial issue when this is his duty and cannot be avoided." He stressed that his job was protected by the Charter and that one must check oneself "like a judge" to keep personal views from influencing actions.[109]

"He explained his view as to when a secretary-general should act on his own as he had to do in the Congo when neither the Council nor the Assembly could act on instructions and guidance," said James Sutterlin. "He rationalized it in this public speech."[110]

"There's an ambiguity about the nature of the role the secretary-general is supposed to play," noted Inis Claude Jr. "Each has a way of coming around to the view that they really ought to be the political leaders of the whole organization, the prime minister of the world. Hammarskjöld above all tried to play an active political role, taking a lot of initiatives, asserting his own views. He was always making one major power or another upset with his political assertiveness. I remember lots of people saying before he was killed that he was a dead duck as secretary-general. His physical death was almost an aftereffect because he had overplayed his hand. He proved the possibilities but he also ran up against the limits of the job."[111]

The Hammarskjöld Record

"The only value of a life is its content—for others," Hammarskjöld wrote on July 29, 1958. "Apart from any value for others it may have, my life is worse than death."[112]

The second UN Secretary-General jotted down many such private thoughts in *Markings*, the diary he kept during his UN years, published after his death.

He clearly felt a strong sense of mission in the United Nations' work. For him, his eight-year job was a heavy responsibility but one that he largely relished. Most of those who voted him into office expected a quiet technician. That he was not. He often acted boldly, stretching his role to its outer limits. He felt his independence and that of the Secretariat were crucial. His successes relate to a combination of his pragmatic intelligence and skills, and, of course, to global circumstances.

The Cold War was undergoing a slight thaw. Stalin was dead. The new Eisenhower administration in Washington at last negotiated an end to the Korean War. European colonialism was on its way out. By the end of 1960, the United Nations had 100 members, almost double the original 51. Until the mid-1950s when the Warsaw Pact was formed, a pro-West majority still dominated the GA.

"Hammarskjöld was lucky," insisted Sir Brian. "He had a much better climate than Lie had. But he wouldn't have been any good if he hadn't also been a remarkable person. It's very unusual to get both."[113]

While Trygve Lie struggled just to assert his right to speak before the Council, Hammarskjöld often spoke at such meetings. He also fought hard for his right to gather information in potential conflict situations.[114] Lie sometimes intervened in Council proceedings with legal memos. Hammarskjöld often wrote his own instructions that the Council passed and reported back as his own mandates required.

He wanted the United Nations to be as effective as it possibly could. He spoke often of the value of quiet mediation and preventive diplomacy. He tried to keep the superpowers from intervening in regional conflicts like the Congo civil war. He saw his own efforts at good offices as one way to contain the Cold War and keep regional issues off the Council agenda where they might be vetoed into inaction. In his view, it was all a matter of filling a "vacuum." If the UN offered parties a face-saving way out of disputes in the process, so much the better.

"He was very clear that he did not require SC authority to conduct a good-offices mission when the states directly concerned wanted it," said Lawrence Finkelstein.[115]

The Peking Formula is considered Hammarskjöld's invention. He used it very successfully in rescuing the US airmen held in Beijing. He separated himself from a GA resolution, highly critical of China, to stress that he was talking and negotiating in his independent capacity under the Charter as head of a separate UN organ. He felt the Charter was an expression of moral purpose on which all members agreed.[116]

He also used the Peking Formula in visiting Pretoria after the Sharpeville Massacre of March 1960. The SC had often discussed South Africa's apartheid policy and asked the Secretary-General in a vaguely worded resolution to consult with the government. Such frequent Council requests became known as the "leave it to Dag" syndrome. South Africa saw the United Nations as having no competence to deal with what it regarded as a strictly domestic affair. However, Hammarskjöld, who had to delay a visit until January 1961 because of the Congo situation, stressed that he would come in his independent capacity.

Though it would be another 33 years before South Africa held its first multiracial elections, the Secretary-General's visit had an impact.

His plane was forced to shift its landing to a military base to avoid the throngs that had gathered at the commercial airport to greet him.[117]

"Hammarskjöld had this extraordinary conversation of three days with [Prime Minister Henrik] Verwoerd," recalled Sir Brian. The two men discussed everything from racial issues to human rights policies. "Verwoerd wasn't in the Middle Ages—he was in the Dark Ages," said Sir Brian. He added that the Peking Formula, which made the visit possible, remains "an important principle which has never been challenged."[118]

"The secretary-general usually finds it helpful to say, 'I am here because the SC has given me a mandate...to go out and negotiate a settlement'—but occasionally that's not the case," explained longtime UN official George Sherry. "This notion of impartiality [with the Peking Formula] is so important. It's the same thing, writ large, that you have in peacekeeping and good-office missions.... [They're] not fighting one of the parties [but] seeking to be friends to both, not trying to impose settlements but helping the parties obtain a *modus vivendi*."[119]

Hammarskjöld and Pearson of Canada are widely credited with inventing peacekeeping together. The theory is that the multinational troops will be impartial, arrive only with the consent of the parties involved, and be lightly armed for use only in self-defense.

General Indar Rikhye, who was military adviser to Hammarskjöld's Congo peacekeeping group, recalled that if anything crucial arose in their daily meetings, the Secretary-General would want to take action right away by phone or in person.

"He was very good at getting things to happen," General Rikhye said. "He was quick, very quick."[120]

Preventive diplomacy is exactly what Hammarskjöld had in mind with peacekeeping operations, in Inis Claude Jr.'s view. It was the Secretary-General's answer to how the United Nations could be directly relevant in the East–West struggle.[121]

"I think his invention of the peacekeeping role was responsible in large part for his prominence," Claude said. "He may have been the only sort of person who could have invented it and made it work. He had to get the consent of a lot of people to pull it off."[122]

However, as UN peacekeeping operations expanded in the 1950s and early 1960s, UN costs shot up. A perennial financial crisis began, lasting through the 1980s and 1990s. Many nations, including the United States and the Soviet Union, failed to pay enough and on time.

The secretary-general's "bully pulpit" role in which he speaks out as a world leader also began during the Hammarskjöld years.

"I think it really starts with him," suggested Thomas Franck. "He would use fairly highbrow occasions to deliver some very thoughtful pieces on what UN priorities should be and on what the office of the secretary-general should and should not do."[123]

Franck added that it was not a part of the job that the Secretary-General particularly liked but that he used it to extraordinary effect.[124] Indeed, Hammarskjöld once joked that his job was a bit like being "a secular Pope."[125]

He also tried, whenever he could, to package his ideas as policy statements, according to Gordenker. "With the Suez situation, for instance, he went out of his way to draft a report on what could be done," he said. "It wasn't a history at all. It was a definition of the principles of peacekeeping. He did this consistently. It was smart."[126]

Hammarskjöld also began what became a tradition by using the introduction of the annual report to the GA as a kind of "personal testament," Claude said. "It's an important document—really a 'state of the union' message and part of the 'bully pulpit' function."[127]

In his annual report of 1959, for instance, the Secretary-General claimed the right to carry on diplomatic efforts and travel as a way to inform himself so that he could competently alert the Council (under Article 99) of any threat to international peace.[128]

Hammarskjöld now receives almost universally high praise for his special talents and the skillful way he played his role.

Sir Brian described him as "the most unusual and striking personality I ever encountered in public life."[129] He says the Secretary-General had a special talent for suggesting effective solutions to conflicts that also happened to be acceptable.[130] He developed an almost "evangelical" passion for his work that grew over the years as he identified more with the objectives of the UN Charter, according to Sir Brian.[131] He observed that the Secretary-General rarely spoke of his faith but had a Christian sense of sacrifice in service to others.[132]

Hammarskjöld was the perfect person for the job, in the view of Paul Kennedy, author of *The Parliament of Man*. He was firm, politic, an innovator, and a practical idealist. Even in his first relatively quiet years, he developed a special place in discreet diplomacy. Kennedy argued that Trygve Lie proclaimed the good-offices role "a little too publicly." In contrast, Hammarskjöld just performed it.[133]

"If one wanted to make a list of UN heroes, Dag would have to be up at the top," Claude insisted. "He made a splash that nobody else has. He brought a unique ability and dignity to the job, and he served at just the right time: when nobody could do anything except the secretary-general. The opportunity was right for him, but he was the person for it too."[134]

"He was an international civil servant of such rare sensibility and catholic interests, of such stubborn principle and exquisite tact... that he seems to belong far more in a Herman Melville novel than in an account of the travails of an international organization," argued Stanley Meisler in his book on the history of the United Nations.[135]

"Hammarskjöld was really the ideal secretary-general," agreed Seymour Finger. "He was very careful about public statements but very bold about action and working with governments. He used the job to its full potential. He was kind of like Theodore Roosevelt in the [US] presidency."[136]

Gordenker said:

It's normal for secretaries-general to try to extend the reach of the office. They do it. I think they should. Hammarskjöld did it quite spectacularly in 1956 [with the

Suez situation]. Did you ever hear of the appointment of anybody to high office where it's said, 'Our expectation is that you're going to fade into the gray woodwork'?[137]

Still, Hammarskjöld seems to be far more revered now than he was while in office.

"Of course—in public—everyone says he was the greatest, terrific fellow," Sir Brian observed. "I worked for him for eight years. But at the time he was very unpopular. He was independent, couldn't be pushed around. He had very strong views and was quite often right. Some of his initiatives and his activist concept of the UN were seen with misgivings by many governments. When he was safely dead, everyone thought he was wonderful."[138]

"He was a very shrewd, farsighted calculator in estimating the effects his moves would have and in getting support," Gordenker noted.[139]

Hammarskjöld's effort to be both independent and impartial often angered both the Soviet Union and the West.

In a Council meeting on October 31, 1956, he was clearly impatient (and said so) at the superpowers' reluctance to negotiate on nuclear arms control. When he was attacked for acting too independently, he reminded the Council that in addition to being its servant, he also had a duty under the Charter and that its aims must ultimately determine for him what is right and wrong.[140]

He had no qualms about taking a firm stand against Washington when he felt it was necessary. During the McCarthy flap over UN personnel, Hammarskjöld insisted that the hiring and firing were his decisions alone.

In the summer of 1954, when US-backed forces from Honduras were trying to overthrow the leftist government in Guatemala, the United States insisted that Guatemala must first seek a remedy in the Organization of American States (OAS) before its complaint could come before the SC. Hammarskjöld promptly sought and got a legal opinion that flatly rejected the US claim.[141]

"Hammarskjöld was very clear," Sir Brian recalled. "He said he couldn't believe that a permanent member, a guardian of the Charter, would be doing that. He was very good at that."[142]

Washington, of course, was not pleased. However, soon after that, Hammarskjöld set out on his successful mission to Beijing to negotiate the release of the captured American airmen.

"The United States then realized that an impartial, objective secretary-general was greatly to their advantage, even if they didn't always agree with him," Sir Brian said. "It was a very important breakthrough."[143]

When Moscow complained that too many political questions were being transferred to Hammarskjöld and that he was grabbing too much authority, he replied that he was the only member of the UN administration chosen by election to take political responsibility and that it could not be delegated.[144] The Soviet anger with Hammarskjöld, however, was such that Moscow eventually refused to recognize him or pay its UN assessments. The Russians wanted a troika leadership and pressed the point many times.

"He operated in the Cold-War context and did it amazingly well," said Jeffrey Laurenti, a senior fellow at the Century Foundation, "but his doing it came close to tearing the organization apart. You had a rogue superpower that was furious that Hammarskjöld would not just shut up and do what he was told."[145]

Edward Luck agreed: "He was in many ways a very impressive secretary-general, but he almost brought the end of the organization."[146]

"If he hadn't lost his life," said George Sherry, "one might ask if he would have survived in the job very long."[147]

Yet Hammarskjöld's singular talents, his reach for the boundaries of the job, and his varied, intense interests leave a lasting legacy—even at UN headquarters itself.

It was he, for instance, who planned the Ford Foundation–financed UN library at the southern end of the New York complex. It bears his name as a memorial.

He also planned the design and ordered the art work for the United Nations' Meditation Room, where those of any faith may sit and pray. Andrew Cordier, his longtime executive assistant, noted that Hammarskjöld's interest in the room was "deeply personal" and that he went there often to sit and think. At the entrance is a plaque with his words: "This is a room of quiet where only thoughts should speak."

In a poetic tribute in the *Saturday Review* of October 21, 1961, shortly after Hammarskjöld's death, Cordier wrote, "Sometimes he had the charm and quality of a symphony, sometimes the decisive abruptness of the hammer or anvil, but they [his words and behavior] were always calculated to gain the high ends of which he never lost sight.... His deep inner stillness was a mainspring of his strength—a fortress so strong that disappointments, failures, setbacks, and even personal attacks couldn't weaken his will or compromise his resolution to carry on his great task."

CHAPTER FIVE

U Thant: A Modest
Man from Burma Becomes
a Risk Taker

"I was stunned with shock and disbelief," recalled U Thant when he heard the news of Hammarskjöld's sudden death in mid-September 1961.[1]

Thant had been Burma's ambassador to the United Nations for the previous four years. Only a few days before the announcement, he received a letter from Hammarskjöld, sharing his thoughts on a one-act play written by U Nu, Burma's prime minister and a good friend of Thant's. A few weeks before, Hammarskjöld tapped Thant to chair the second Conciliation Commission for the Congo. Thant had been a strong supporter of Hammarskjöld when he was personally attacked by Moscow and firmly backed the use of UN power to restore order in the Congo.

The annual fall session of the UN General Assembly was about to convene. Thant notes in his memoir that the news of Hammarskjöld's passing cast a notable pall of sorrow and confusion over the proceedings.[2]

Moscow, still angry over what it saw as Hammarskjöld's bias toward the West in the Congo conflict, seized the opportunity to give one more hard push to its proposed troika—three leaders at the helm to balance political interests rather than one. Just that spring, the Soviet premier, Nikita Khrushchev, told the newspaper columnist Walter Lippmann that he thought there could be neutral countries but not neutral men: "We can't have another Hammarskjöld, no matter where he comes from among the neutral countries."[3]

Though Hammarskjöld's term still had one and a half years to go, in 1961 Moscow essentially had the power to refuse to accept a successor or any concept except a troika. Yet there was little enthusiasm for a troika either in the West or among the nonaligned countries.[4]

The developing nations, almost one-fifth of the UN membership, wanted a non-European UN leader. Hammarskjöld had once spoken of two possible successors: Burma's U Thant or Tunisia's Mongi Slim who had worked closely with Hammarskjöld in developing UN Congo policy. Moscow viewed Slim as too pro-West, however, and Israel thought him too friendly with its enemies. Thant was less controversial. Still, Arab nations were skeptical because Burma had diplomatic ties with Israel. France was similarly unenthusiastic because Thant had chaired the Afro-Asia Committee on Algerian Independence and had been critical of French policy.

U Thant insisted he never sought the top UN post and told all who asked that he had no interest in the job. Yet he recalled in his memoir that, while France was considering him for the post, he heard that a French diplomat remarked disparagingly to a reporter that Thant was a short man and did not even speak French (the United Nations' second official language). Thant noted with humor that, at 5 feet 7 inches, he was certainly taller than Napoleon, who did not even speak English.[5]

Washington and Moscow began private talks that October about Hammarskjöld's successor. Though the United States wanted someone for a full five-year term, the two finally agreed on the concept of an interim neutral leader who would cooperate with a cabinet of advisers spanning a broad ideological spectrum.

The Security Council met in closed session and recommended Thant. On November 3, 1961, the General Assembly, by secret ballot, unanimously elected him as acting secretary-general to fill the rest of Hammarskjöld's term. Adlai Stevenson, the US ambassador to the United Nations, told the Assembly two days before the election that there would be no troika and no veto. He praised Thant as a man of the highest character and ability.[6] Once elected, Thant was described by Stevenson as "the only human being out there out of a hundred nations represented at the UN who was acceptable to everybody."[7]

In his acceptance speech, Thant noted that most of his UN colleagues knew him personally. Stressing that Burma had long followed a policy of nonalignment, he pledged to continue that same objective attitude in a spirit of universal friendship.[8]

At 52, Thant was the first Asian and the first from a developing nation to fill the United Nations' top job. The moment was important in UN history. The Cold War was still going strong. Moscow had recently erected the Berlin Wall and decided to resume nuclear testing. The Congo situation was still unresolved. The secretary-general's authority to take independent action was widely viewed with increased skepticism. The third world was emerging as a major new force. The United Nations had almost doubled its membership since its founding, and many of the most recent members were newly independent states.

Just before his election, Thant took part in a conference in Belgrade attended by 28 nations that strongly endorsed an end to colonialism and essentially launched the nonaligned movement. Growing up in a country that had been occupied by the Japanese and colonized by the British, the new Secretary-General now wanted to expand and update the UN agenda. He thought the Cold War would be a passing phenomenon and that the North–South conflict between developing and developed nations would soon become the focus of world politics. He saw development as a top UN concern.[9]

"[My] conception of the United Nations was primarily from the vantage point of the third world," Thant recalled.[10] He was convinced that the global gap between rich and poor was far more important and potentially explosive than any ideological split.[11] "I...had first-hand experience of colonialism at work," he recalled. "I know what hunger, poverty, disease, illiteracy, and human suffering really mean." It was difficult for him to shake off unhappy memories of servitude. He said he would never forget that even the highest officeholders in Burma could never become members of Rangoon's three most prestigious clubs simply because they were not European.[12]

As a young man, Thant hoped to become a journalist. However, the death of his father when Thant was only 14, and the successful effort of a relative to wrest away his mother's inheritance, changed the plan.

He enrolled at Rangoon University where he became active in the debating society and wrote letters to local newspapers that were often critical of Burma's British colonial government. It was there he met and became friends with U Nu, a fellow student who was increasingly active in Burma's independence movement. After two years in Rangoon, Thant returned to his hometown of Pantanaw to teach in the high school and later become its headmaster. When the job of school superintendent opened up there, he urged U Nu to take the job. Later, Thant took on the post himself when U Nu decided to return to law school.

In 1947, when Burma had already made clear its intent to become independent, Thant moved back to Rangoon to publish a new magazine. When U Nu became premier of the newly independent government a year later, he soon drew Thant into a variety of government jobs from deputy information secretary to director of broadcasting. In 1952 Thant moved to New York as a member of Burma's UN delegation, and in 1957 was named its UN ambassador.

By the time he was elected to the United Nations' top job, he was a familiar figure to most delegates with his round face, dark brown eyes, tailored suits, and ever-present cigar. He was known as a good storyteller and listener. The *London Observer* described him as a typically cool civil servant, a charmer, a man of infinite discretion, and the embodiment of nonalignment.[13]

The new Secretary-General was a devout Buddhist who set aside time for meditation at the start of every day. He often thought deeply about the "oneness of the human community."[14] Some colleagues referred to him as the "Bronze Buddha."

"I was trained to be tolerant of everything except intolerance," he said. His aim was to cherish such qualities as modesty and compassion and to develop a certain degree of emotional equilibrium: "I must say that I am not easily excited or excitable."[15]

He worked hard to develop that sense of balance. Yet he was not without empathy. C. V. Narasimhan, Thant's cabinet chief, recalls the most uncomfortable moment in his own life on May 21, 1962—when he had to tell the Secretary-General that Thant's son, Tim Maung, had been killed in a fall from a bus. He recalled that Thant's first words were: "My poor wife." The couple had already lost an infant son to illness. Thant went home immediately to be with his wife but was back at the office the next day. He bitterly regretted that the press of work did not allow him to attend the funeral in Rangoon.[16]

Yet by all accounts Thant was very much a family man and relished quiet time in the Thants' ivy-covered house in Riverdale in the Bronx. He rarely traveled and avoided most UN social functions. He was an avid reader of newspapers and books. Though he often appeared somewhat detached and inscrutable to colleagues, his wife and daughter insisted that he was easy to beat at poker.[17]

In a TV interview before his election, he told Adlai Stevenson that it was important for a secretary-general to be impartial but not necessarily neutral. He added that even impartial people cannot avoid judging the guilt or innocence of parties to a conflict.[18] He strongly favored quiet diplomacy as having the greatest potential for success.

"He had Asian values and a great deal of patience," recalled Indar Rikhye, the Indian general who served as Thant's military adviser. "He probably had the most political sense I have seen in any secretary-general other than Pérez de Cuéllar.... Thant also had his human side. He enjoyed a daiquiri and liked light jokes."[19]

Thant drafted most of his own political speeches and reports. Yet he met regularly with his eight undersecretaries-general, including Hammarskjöld holdover Ralph Bunche, and delegated much of the work of his office, even having aides choose his office paintings.

"He trusts us so much that we feel a greater responsibility, and we work twice as hard as we would if he were constantly checking on us," recalled Constantin Stavropoulos, an undersecretary-general.[20]

Like most in the job, Thant did not rate high marks as an administrator. His tenure marked the beginning of the perennial UN debt crisis. Philip Klutznik, a former US ambassador to the United Nations, recalled Thant showing little interest in or understanding of UN finances.[21]

In the course of UN history, Thant is often dismissed as the forgotten secretary-general. Does he deserve better than that? A careful look at his record suggests that he does. He was a definite risk taker. First, he had to do something about the Congo crisis.

Congo: The Secession That Would Not End

Hammarskjöld was killed while on his way to negotiate a cease-fire with Moise Tshombe, the premier of the breakaway Congo province of Katanga. When that trip was abruptly halted, it looked, for a time, as if there were no hope for a unified Congolese peace. No one knew that a communications gaffe would largely resolve the problem more than a year later.

The fighting had continued hot and heavy despite an October cease-fire. Finally, on November 24, 1961, just three weeks after Thant's election, the Security Council passed a resolution opposing the Katanga secession and, for the first time, authorized the Acting Secretary-General to "take vigorous action" to apprehend all military and paramilitary personnel and political advisers in Katanga who were not under UN command.

Even so, it took three major UN offensives against Katanga and several agreements later to bring Tshombe to accept Congolese rule.

Tshombe was "a master of procrastination and of the misinterpretation of agreements," recalled Sir Brian.[22] Thant agreed in his memoir that the Katanga leader "*always* went back on his promises, assurances, and declarations."[23] At his very first press conference December 1, 1961, Thant referred to Tshombe as "a very unstable man."[24]

The signs were numerous. By the end of 1961, a peace agreement was reached between Congolese Prime Minister Cyrille Adoula and Tshombe. However, after Tshombe's return to Katanga, he denied that the pact was final and said he needed the consent of his cabinet before it could take effect. The cabinet insisted that Katanga's National Assembly must also give its approval. Finally, in mid-February 1962, the National Assembly ratified the agreement—but as a basis for further discussion only.[25]

Talks continued for the next several months, ultimately breaking down in June. At a press conference in Helsinki on July 20, Thant referred to Tshombe and his colleagues as a "bunch of clowns." He said they were not to be taken seriously in their negotiations with either the Congolese government or the United Nations.[26]

Two months later, Thant, by now very familiar with Congo personalities and issues, laid out a national reconciliation plan. It called for a federal system in the Congo, integration of the armed forces, and a 50–50 split of revenue with the federal government from Katanga's natural resources.

The Congolese government quickly accepted the plan. So did Tshombe several days later. Yet the discussions still dragged on. The Katangese leader thought only a loose confederation of Congolese states would allow his province to keep the stability it needed for its mining operations.[27] Sir Brian recalled that trying to get Tshombe to follow up on the plan was "like trying to get an eel into a bottle."[28]

Thant was rapidly losing patience. In September he threatened economic sanctions against Katanga, but Britain and France were not supportive. In late December 1962, for no apparent reason, Tshombe's troops fired on UN forces in Elizabethville and other Katangese towns for four straight days and shot down a UN helicopter.

Thant authorized one more major UN military offensive in response, dubbed Operation Grandslam.

Tshombe threatened to destroy all mining installations in Katanga if the raid were carried out. The British and Belgian governments, worried about the threat, told Thant that they had heard that if UN troops crossed the Lufira River to Jadotville, a key Katangese mining center on the river's west bank, they would meet heavy resistance. Washington, too, was hesitant about the wisdom of an all-out attack.

Thant, now convinced of the need for greater caution, repeated the warnings in a cable to the UN force commander in Katanga. The Secretary-General urged no more moves against Tshombe's forces unless the Katanga leader reneged on his threats.

However, leaders of the UN Operation in the Congo (ONUC) did not receive the cable soon enough to change the previous plan of action. Thant got word back on January 3 that UN troops had already crossed the river and had been met by widespread cheering and no destruction of resources. It was, Thant recalled, "a most pleasant surprise." The success, in his view, was due to a winning combination of speed, surprise, bravery, and skill.[29]

The secession was over. The Katangese leader surrendered in Elizabethville. On January 14, 1963, Tshombe, who fully accepted the reconciliation plan, voluntarily declared that he would no longer engage in secessionist moves.[30] UN troops left the Congo on June 30, 1964.

The UN Congo operation, costly in both manpower and money, remained controversial for a long time. It was often cited as an example of what the United Nations should try to avoid in the future.

"It was widely regarded at the time as a disaster," Sir Brian recalled. Still, he said, the nation's relative stability and prosperity for years afterward actually compared favorably to that of many other newly independent African nations. Had the United Nations not intervened, he said, the Congo might well have broken up or become an East–West battleground.[31]

"Thant had the guts to take the necessary measures, including military ones, to complete the operation and prevent the Congo's breakup," confirmed George Sherry.[32]

"Thant's greatest contribution to the Congo situation was the reconciliation plan," insisted Rikhye, Thant's military adviser. "The plan was worked out by the United Nations, but he was very much in it. He has said—he was really a political animal—that he grasped it, understood it, and determinedly pursued it. He did not allow nitty-gritty details, the daily incidents, to worry him. He truly was operating at the highest strategic level."[33]

Rikhye added that Thant took the view that the UN military action was based on self-defense. "Buddhist or not, he felt that if they [the Katanga forces] kept fighting, the only way was to defend yourself—that it's not enough to sit down in front of them and pray. You handle them in a civilized way, using minimum force. You stop when they surrender."[34]

As a Buddhist, Thant always insisted he abhorred violence. He said that, to him, all war is "folly and insanity." He described the UN operation in the Congo as a battle for peace, rather than a war and UN troops as soldiers for peace.[35]

Thant also stressed in his memoir that the people of Katanga themselves opposed secession, that the Elizabethville government never had effective control over the northern half of the province, and that no nation ever recognized Katanga's independence.[36]

Throughout the crisis, Thant continued his practice of delegating work, a move Rikhye strongly applauded. General Rikhye said that Thant admired Hammarskjöld greatly but thought the former Secretary-General became overly involved in the Congo crisis at the cost of neglecting other important duties. As time went by, Thant let Bunche do more and more of the work and planning. "Thant was very cautious about taking complete charge," Rikhye said.[37]

Despite the United Nations' eventual success in the expensive Congo operation, France and the Soviet Union opposed that UN venture and refused to pay their share of the peacekeeping budget.

To help fund the rapidly rising costs of UN peacekeeping, Thant, soon after taking office, had endorsed a US proposal to sell bonds to UN members. Philip Klutznik, the former US ambassador to the United Nations, recalled a conversation in which Thant asked him when the United States would present the bond plan. Told that Stevenson would ask the Secretary-General to suggest the idea to the General Assembly, Thant protested that the United States should propose the plan. "We don't have that much credibility, and you're on your honeymoon," Klutznik responded. "It's a logical moment."[38]

Thant did win the Assembly's approval (despite the opposition of France and Belgium, and 11 Soviet bloc nations) to issue $200 million worth of bonds for sale to member states. Within two years, members had purchased $154.7 million, a figure widely considered generous.[39]

The Secretary-General was soon facing a new major challenge: the US–Soviet standoff over nuclear weapons in Cuba.

Missiles in Cuba: To the Brink and Back

Few who followed the tense exchange of threats between Moscow and Washington in October 1962 will ever forget it. The possibility of a nuclear war seemed to hang on each response to the blustery rhetoric coming from each side.

U Thant later wrote that the United Nations had never faced a moment of "graver responsibility and grimmer challenge."[40] He opted to do what he could to restore calm and balance to the situation.

Many say he played only a minor role in easing the standoff. Others insist that his courage and persistence made a crucial contribution. What exactly did he do?

US–Soviet tension over Cuba had been heating up for many months. For the United States, it had been a year and a half since the embarrassment and failure of the Bay of Pigs episode in April 1961. CIA-trained Cuban exiles had landed in Cuba to try to overthrow the two-year-old Castro government and were defeated in less than three days.

For Havana, the memories lingered. Cuba often complained to the UN Security Council that Washington was planning ever more aggressive moves against it.

On September 11, 1962, Moscow warned the United States that an attack on Cuba, or on Soviet ships carrying supplies there, could lead to a nuclear war. The Americans and the Soviets had not agreed during the previous summer on any plan for a nuclear test ban.

It was, however, more than a month later—October 16, 1962— before US President John Kennedy saw the actual photos, taken by a U-2 spy plane that confirmed that the Soviets indeed were building ballistic missile launchers in Cuba and shipping nuclear-armed missiles there.

Many of Kennedy's closest advisers urged a swift response with US airstrikes. The President, less sure that such strikes were wise, went on television Monday evening, October 22, to alert the American public to the situation. Despite Soviet promises to the contrary, he said, Moscow was building offensive missile and bomber bases in Cuba. He said the evidence was unmistakable and deliberately provocative. Thus the United States was imposing a naval and air quarantine of the island to stop further shipments of offensive military equipment from Moscow.

Washington, Kennedy said, would ask for an emergency UN Security Council meeting to demand removal of all offensive weapons from Cuba. He warned that any attack on any country in the Western Hemisphere would require a full retaliatory strike on the Soviet Union.

U Thant, who watched the speech on TV in his 38th-floor UN office, recalled that he could scarcely believe his eyes and ears. He realized that Washington felt ready and able to act alone. He was puzzled as to why Kennedy would not have discussed the matter privately with Khrushchev rather than try to corner him publicly. Thant said he was "more deeply troubled than I ever have been in my life."[41]

That same evening, the Secretary-General received official requests from both Washington and Moscow for an emergency Security Council meeting the next day. The Soviet UN ambassador, Valerian Zorin, who happened to be the Council president that month, asked for an immediate probe into whether the US threat and planned action violated the UN Charter. Several strong resolutions were proposed in the Council, but none passed.

Convinced that negotiation and compromise were the only route to peace and prodded to seek a solution by several neutral nations, Thant decided to intervene directly. On October 24, he sent identical notes to Kennedy and Khrushchev, urging them to have the good sense to negotiate. He proposed a halt to further shipments to Cuba by Russia and a temporary suspension of the quarantine until a compromise could be worked out.

On October 25, Thant got word that Moscow had accepted his proposal. That allowed the Soviets to stop shipments and save face in the process. Washington, however, wanted not only a halt to more missiles but also removal of those already in Cuba. The Kennedy administration said only that it was open to further discussion. The quarantine was not lifted.

Thant again sent messages to the two leaders. He urged Moscow to keep its ships away from the quarantine area and Washington to do all that it could to prevent any confrontation. To this, both sides agreed.

Yet the crisis did not end there. It was well known that Washington was ready to bomb the Cuban bases if Moscow did not dismantle and take back its missiles.[42]

The now-famous dramatic confrontation between the Soviet ambassador, Valerian Zorin, and the US ambassador, Adlai Stevenson, took place at the next Security Council meeting on October 26. Stevenson, pressing a cagey Zorin as to whether Moscow actually was placing missiles in Cuba, said he could wait for the answer "until hell freezes over." Stevenson then wheeled in enlarged US aerial photos of Soviet missiles in Cuba that, in effect, answered the question. Stevenson, in Sir Brian's description later, "shone as the prosecuting attorney."[43]

On that same day, Thant sent a message to Cuba's prime minister Fidel Castro, telling him of the positive answers to his US–Soviet appeals. Thant asked that any further construction of major military installations in Cuba be suspended while talks were in progress. He reminded Castro that the Cuban president, Osvaldo Dorticos, told the General Assembly just two weeks earlier that if Cuba had proof that the United States would not invade, Soviet weapons would be unnecessary.

Castro replied that he would do all he could to resolve the crisis. He said, however, that he viewed both the blockade and the US assumption of its right to dictate what kind of arms were appropriate for Cuba's defense as violations of the island's sovereignty. He invited Thant to visit Havana for more discussion.[44]

Meanwhile Khrushchev sent a private emotional letter to Kennedy, offering to withdraw the missiles in return for a US pledge not to invade Cuba. Before he answered, Kennedy received a second message from the Soviet leader, suggesting a trade. Moscow would withdraw its missiles from Cuba if Washington would withdraw its Jupiter missiles from Turkey, its North Atlantic Treaty Organization (NATO) ally. The Jupiter missiles were largely obsolete, but Kennedy chose to respond for the moment only to Khrushchev's first message, accepting the conditional no-invasion pledge. The Soviet leader announced the agreement publicly on October 28.[45]

Still the question of verification remained. Moscow would accept oversight of the missile withdrawals by the United Nations or the International Committee of the Red Cross (ICRC). Yet Cuba's approval was also needed and not forthcoming. Thant, with General Rikhye and a few other staff members, picked up on Castro's invitation and flew to Cuba on October 30 to discuss the inspection issue. Thant was hopeful, but the trip's main aim was not achieved.

Castro, though crediting Thant with a noble mission, remained firm in opposing any system of international inspection as a violation of Cuba's sovereignty. If the Soviets were amenable to international inspection, he said, that was Moscow's business and would need to be conducted on the high seas.[46]

Yet the Soviet ambassador to Cuba and the general in charge of the missiles assured the UN visitors that the missile dismantling had begun and would be finished by November 2. Rikhye told Thant that their visit to the island was worthwhile for that information alone.[47]

"The president [of Cuba] and Castro had been sort of saying no to everything," General Rikhye recalled. "We knew the whole thing was a joke because everything [between Moscow and Washington] was already negotiated—the stuff was already going out." Noting that the Soviets had sent in thousands of troops and civilians to the island, the general added that the Cuban government had been kept largely out of the negotiations. He also said he learned later from another ambassador that even Raul Castro, Cuba's minister of defense at the time, had been refused entrance to the Russian camp there. Rikhye said he told Thant that Fidel Castro was in no position to discuss anything with the United Nations when he didn't really know what was going on.[48]

In the end, Washington relied on low-flying American reconnaissance planes to satisfy itself that the agreed bargain had been met. Although Cuba had shot down one U-2 plane on October 27, killing the American pilot, Castro quietly allowed the US aerial inspection.

The related question of a deal involving the Jupiter missiles was made public years after the incident. The US attorney general, Robert Kennedy, had met secretly at the time with Anatoli Dobrynin, Soviet ambassador to Washington, to assure him that the US missiles in Turkey would be withdrawn in due course but only if Moscow did not make that link public.

If the Russians did not back down and accept that condition, the United States was prepared, as a face-saving device, to ask Thant to propose publicly a simultaneous US–Soviet missile withdrawal.[49] That shift to the UN never proved necessary.

The Soviet missiles and bombers were fully withdrawn by mid-December 1962.

Looking Back at the 13-Day Cuba Crisis

The danger if the two leaders were not able to find a way to retreat from the threats and counterthreats was very real. In Thant's recollection, the East–West confrontation brought the world "to the edge of a nuclear holocaust."[50]

President Kennedy's aim in taking the issue early on to the United Nations was not to get authorization or intervention but to put the Soviets on the diplomatic defensive. In that, it largely succeeded, said Theodore Sorenson, Kennedy's special counsel and a member of the National Security Council executive committee.[51]

Certainly the Security Council could not agree on any action. Yet the debates there rallied public support for an alternative to war. In the view of most analysts, Thant's good offices role helped to cool the rhetoric and pave the way to an acceptable compromise. In early January 1963, Thant received letters from both the American ambassador and the Soviet ambassador thanking him for his efforts to resolve the crisis.

Yet some scholars, such as Thomas Franck, a leading expert on international law, give Thant little credit: "He tried to make himself central to the Cuban missile crisis and totally failed. He didn't really play any role except to antagonize both sides...telling them what they ought to do."[52]

Lawrence Finkelstein said that at the time he, too, thought the UN role was largely irrelevant. However, more recent revelations such as the Jupiter missile trade-off, he says, convinced him that the United Nations really was an important part of the solution.[53]

The decision certainly was up to Washington and Moscow. Their communication, or sometimes the lack of it, was vital. US military superiority surely played a key role as well. However, Thant's willingness to serve as an intermediary by making proposals, sending private notes to the two leaders, and relaying information helped to provide breathing space and an acceptable exit strategy.

Thant's chief contribution was to buy time for the two sides to cool down, said Seymour Finger, a former US ambassador to the United Nations: "He gave both the Soviets and the US a pretext...for not taking immediate rash action."[54]

Thomas Weiss, director of the Ralph Bunche Institute for International Studies at the City College of New York, agreed: "The vehicle of having him [Thant] around to talk to, hold meetings with... certainly didn't hurt."[55]

"U Thant provided the ladder down which both the Soviet Union and the United States descended when they agreed to call things off," noted Sir Brian. "He was the only one who went to Cuba during the missile crisis. It was a good start because Castro was chewing up the carpet—the only one who wanted to fight the US."[56]

Biographer June Bingham noted that at one point Thant had members of the US mission in his conference room and those of the Soviet mission in the next door office. He commuted between them with his own analysis of each proposal.[57]

Bernard J. Firestone, another Thant biographer, credited him with "scrupulous evenhandedness" even though Thant personally saw the US quarantine effort as politically very dangerous and legally questionable.[58]

Thant's overall role in the crisis is often underrated in the view of Edward Newman, the author of *The UN Secretary-General from the Cold War to the New Era: A Global Peace and Security Mandate?* Through his requests to the Security Council and by helping to move the process forward, Thant, in Newman's view, did make a significant contribution.[59]

The precedent was set for UN involvement in a nuclear crisis, and the range of the UN chief's future role was expanded, in the view of Thomas Boudreau, author of *Sheathing the Sword*. He wrote that Moscow and Washington not only allowed but also made full use of Thant's move to inject his office directly into the superpower dispute.[60] Kennedy himself later acknowledged that the world was in Thant's debt for the important role he played.

Thant suggested in the introduction to his autobiography that the public did not know how much it owed to the United Nations for its involvement in that "decisive" moment:

> Not only was the United Nations the only spot on the globe in which the three contestants could and did literally face each other without a resulting catastrophe. The man in the street...did not realize how much his survival depended on what the United Nations *did* to help the rival factions gain the time they both needed to effect the compromise that eventually came about.[61]

In a unanimous Assembly vote on November 30, 1962, Thant was elected to a full first term, to expire in November 1966. He was to face several more major challenges—unrest in the Middle East, the India–Pakistan War, and the long Vietnam War, for which his bold efforts at resolution were largely unwelcome.

The Vietnam Debacle

It was Thant's own choice to get involved in trying to end the war in Vietnam. Washington was not asking him for help, nor was Hanoi or Saigon.

He felt a personal and moral obligation to act. He insisted in his memoir that he was less concerned with whether US political goals were right or wrong than with the escalation of the war itself. In his view, modern war was "nothing less than mass murder."[62]

As early as April 29, 1964, the Secretary-General told a news conference that military might would not defeat the Vietnamese communists.[63] A month later, he described Barry Goldwater, the Republican US senator from Arizona, as "out of his mind" for suggesting use of nuclear weapons in Vietnam.[64]

Throughout the crisis, Thant made full use of his good offices as well as his "bully pulpit" position. He was outspoken in his criticism of the United States, a practice that nettled US President Lyndon Johnson and most of his administration.

In early August 1964, after two US destroyers were attacked by the North Vietnamese in international waters in the Gulf of Tonkin, US Navy planes retaliated by bombing North Vietnam. The US Congress quickly passed a resolution supporting the President's decision.

Thant's mediation efforts essentially began on August 6, the day the White House held an evening reception in the Secretary-General's honor. He attended a working lunch at the State Department that day where he urged US Secretary of State Dean Rusk to begin direct negotiations with Hanoi. Thant said he was sure he could arrange such a meeting with North Vietnam's Ho Chi Minh.

Although US officials were noncommittal, Thant left Washington believing that he had been encouraged by the administration, to approach Hanoi. He made the contact through the Soviet undersecretary-general at the United Nations and insisted that the negotiations be secret and held in Rangoon, the capital of Burma. Three weeks later, he got word that Hanoi agreed. He told the US ambassador to the United Nations, Adlai Stevenson, who was sympathetic to Thant's efforts and said he would pass the word along.

Yet the Secretary-General waited a long time for any answer from Washington.

Thant insisted that an independent, noncommunist South Vietnam could be arranged by negotiation. US officials were skeptical that Hanoi would accept anything short of total victory. The United States also had a contact of its own at work. Washington had asked a Canadian diplomat, Blair Seaborn, a member of the International Control Commission established in Geneva after the French withdrawal from Indochina, to find out Hanoi's conditions for talks. The word back was not encouraging: if Washington wanted an end to the war, it must withdraw from South Vietnam and allow the National Liberation Front (Vietcong) to take over.[65]

Finally, in mid-January 1965, Stevenson told Thant that Washington had decided against any talks with Hanoi. The United States, he said, did not think negotiations could be kept secret and thought any leak might demoralize South Vietnam and lead to its downfall.[66]

Peace prospects steadily worsened. Washington began bombing North Vietnam in February. Thant did not buy Washington's domino theory or the idea that South Vietnam was strategically vital to Western security.[67] He became increasingly outspoken in his criticism of US policy.

At a news conference on February 24, he passionately argued once again for negotiation. He said it was the only route for a graceful US withdrawal. "I am sure that the great American people, if only they knew the true facts and the background to the developments in South Vietnam, will agree with me that further bloodshed is unnecessary...As you know in time of war...the first casualty is truth."[68]

The Johnson administration was furious.

"Whatever his motives, we felt U Thant had grossly misrepresented the situation," recalled Dean Rusk in his autobiography. "Frankly I thought he had lied like a sailor. I never had much respect for U Thant's integrity.... The fallout from U Thant's misrepresentation damaged US prestige and added to our so-called credibility gap."[69]

Stevenson, on orders from his superiors, met with Thant. He strongly criticized the Secretary-General's comments. Thant apologized but noted that most Asian leaders thought the chances for a Communist victory in Vietnam would only improve as the war intensified.[70]

By the next summer, Thant said he became convinced that President Johnson had never even known about the UN leader's peace initiative.

Both Thant and President Johnson gave speeches at the San Francisco Opera House in honor of the United Nations' 20th anniversary on June 25, 1965. In Thant's view, Johnson was in a "sour" mood in a face-to-face chat afterward. The President said he wanted to tell the world at the White House reception the year before that Thant was a man of peace, but that he was too distressed at the Secretary-General's continued criticism of his Vietnam policy.

Thant mentioned his peace initiative of the previous fall, noting that Washington rejected it. The US President indicated no surprise, but Thant had the distinct impression that Johnson first learned of the offer only when the media reported it after Thant's February press conference, when he urged negotiations. Thant told Johnson that Hanoi now refused to talk at all unless the United States stopped the bombing and included the Vietcong in the discussions.[71]

Dean Rusk later wrote in his memoir that the United States had been given no proof that Hanoi was willing in 1964 to meet secretly with Washington officials, as Thant said. Rusk said the United States had nothing in writing on which to make a judgment and that he suspected that Thant's communication channel to Hanoi worked for the KGB, the Soviet intelligence agency. Rusk charged that Thant probably knew he never had a message from North Vietnam that truly pointed toward peace. Still, Rusk insisted that he did indeed brief Johnson about Thant's Rangoon initiative despite the Secretary-General's suspicion that Johnson only learned much later of the proposal.[72]

Thant was persistent. Aware that his usefulness was limited, he suggested a three-step peace proposal in March 1965. It included a halt to the bombing of North Vietnam, deescalation of all military activities in South Vietnam, and participation of all those fighting in the South in any negotiations. Washington rejected the ideas of both a bombing halt and the call for broader participation in any talks.

Two years later, Thant proposed a revision of his earlier plan after meeting in Rangoon with a top North Vietnamese official. Yet he soon concluded that even that was not acceptable to either side.

In 1968, after President Johnson announced an end to much of the US bombing in the North, the way opened for all parties to agree to peace talks in Paris. The process dragged on until 1975.

The jury is still out on how wise Thant's peace efforts were.

Rusk conceded that Thant might have been trying to find a way for Washington to save face through his initiative. Yet Rusk argued that the United States was not trying to save face but to save South Vietnam.[73]

"If Dean Rusk hadn't been so obstinate, I think U Thant would have produced the end of the Vietnam War—which Kissinger finally did later [at the Paris talks]," said Sir Brian. "It was exactly the same plan—a cease-fire in place, talks about talks, and then a general negotiation on the whole problem.... When Thant gave this plan, he had the North Vietnamese, the Vietcong, and everybody else on board."[74]

"I've always thought Thant's involvement was kind of foolhardy, but, on the other hand, what do you think about Don Quixote?" asked Lawrence Finkelstein. "In a sense Thant was following the Hammarskjöld tradition of staking out an independent role. It was a moral and decent thing to wish to do."[75]

"I think Johnson absolutely hated his guts," noted Indar Rikhye, "but Thant knew what he was doing, and he was prepared to pay the price."[76] Sir Brian agreed: "He was courageous. He thought this was an immoral war for a number of reasons and that he really ought to stop it."[77]

By the mid-1960s, Thant was a victim of his own optimism, in the view of Thomas Franck. By then, the Communists knew they could win, and any talk of compromise became a tactic for dividing and demoralizing the enemy, according to Franck. Thant's experience showed that a secretary-general, if inclined, can make himself a powerful force in domestic politics. Thant's comments helped create a perception of the US government as untruthful and belligerent, an essential ingredient in the success of the antiwar movement. Still, Franck said, Thant's reasoning in this case was "dead wrong." Hanoi was not after a neutral political solution in the South—but a unified communist state.[78]

The Kashmir Crisis

Even while the Vietnam War continued, U Thant tried to resolve other global crises as they arose.

One of his most vigorous but also discouraging efforts was his attempt in 1965 to stop the fighting over Kashmir by India and Pakistan.

Their first battle over the disputed province was in 1948. A cease-fire of sorts, watched over by a UN military observer group (UNMOGIP), has been in place ever since.

Violations of the truce increased sharply in August 1965. By September, both sides had captured new territory and conducted intensive airstrikes. Thant sent urgent messages to both nations' leaders, advocating respect for the old cease-fire agreement.[79] He asked the United States, then presiding over the Security Council, to call a meeting to discuss the situation. China's close ties with Pakistan and Russia's ties with India added to the sense of urgency.

The Council met twice in the next few days. Each time it issued a unanimous call for a new cease-fire. At the second meeting on

September 6, the Council also asked Thant to make every effort to secure that goal.

In response, the Secretary-General set off the next evening with a small group of aides for nine days of talks with Pakistani and Indian leaders. Thant told the press that he had no illusions about the success of his venture since Kashmir had posed a "baffling problem" for the United Nations for 17 years.[80]

Sir Brian, who accompanied Thant on the trip, recalled that at one point along the route, someone from a Burmese embassy, aware of Thant's wife's fondness for mango jam, stashed some aboard one of the flights. When one case began to "hiss and tick," the unaware pilot declared a bomb emergency. When the source of the noise was finally diagnosed as spoiling food, all the jam had to be thrown out.[81]

The Secretary-General was given a courteous reception by both India and Pakistan. However, the cease-fire conditions promptly raised by each side were, he felt, beyond his range of authority. His goal was to stop the fighting and withdraw troops to pre–August 5 positions by a certain date. Pakistan wanted a link with some assurance of an overall political settlement. India, which held a larger chunk of predominantly Muslim Kashmir, did not favor new elections and wanted to be sure that a cease-fire would also include out-of-uniform infiltrators from Pakistan. Thant issued urgent appeals to both sides, but there was no give.

"From the beginning of this crisis to its end, practically every attempt I made to mediate it was frustrated by the recalcitrance of either or both parties," he recalled.[82]

When he flew back to Kennedy Airport, he was surprised to be greeted, in an unprecedented show of support, by all UN Security Council ambassadors, including the US ambassador, Arthur J. Goldberg, who was the Council president.

"I was overwhelmed and at a loss for words," noted Thant. Yet he sadly reported to the Council that the situation was deadlocked. "I had now played all my cards."[83] He suggested that the Council order the two nations to stop fighting or face UN sanctions.[84]

As the fighting again intensified, the Council issued one more call for a cease-fire to take effect on September 22, 1965, with a troop withdrawal. Both sides accepted.

Thant then strengthened UNMOGIP forces and, despite a Soviet challenge to his authority, set up a new observer group—the UN India–Pakistan Observer Mission (UNIPOM)—to patrol new cease-fire lines between India and West Pakistan.

Despite the pledges from both sides, the new cease-fire did not hold. Ultimately, it was an offer by the Soviet premier, Alexei Kosygin, later that year that led to the January 1966 signing by India and Pakistan of the Declaration of Tashkent. That agreement led to a cease-fire that lasted for a time and the withdrawal of troops from Kashmir. Thant readily credited Kosygin, rather than the Council or the United Nations, as "mainly responsible" for the outcome. Thant described him as a courteous man of quiet dignity and an able and persistent mediator.[85]

Sir Brian said that the Secretary-General also deserved some of the credit. "I think he did a very good job of...gradually getting things calmed down," he stated. "This was a very dangerous situation that threatened to bring in both China and the Soviet Union."[86]

The Soviet leadership was becoming increasingly critical of Thant's independent efforts. Moscow had expected him to be more compliant than Hammarskjöld but ultimately found him just as hard to control. As one Russian diplomat described the challenge, "Convincing Mr. Thant is like fighting your way through a room full of mashed potatoes."[87]

A Second Term?

By fall 1966, the Council had to decide whether to reelect U Thant to a second five-year term or appoint a new secretary-general. Thant was reluctant and had long evaded a direct answer to the question. In September 1966, he announced that he would not seek a second term. He also made it clear that, from the start, he had never wanted to be "just" a chief administrative officer or "glorified clerk."[88]

Certainly, the continuing tragedy of Vietnam, the frustrations of the Cuban missile crisis and the Kashmir problem, as well as an ongoing UN financial crisis, were factors in his reluctance to serve again.

Yet, despite his reservations, Thant ultimately agreed to accept one more term. On December 2, 1966, the Council unanimously reelected him. It noted, at Thant's urging, that it fully respected his position and action in bringing basic issues to the Council's attention.[89] The General Assembly unanimously confirmed the choice that same day.

U Thant's War?

That's what his critics called it when war erupted between Israelis and Arabs in June 1967. The six-day battle had enormous consequences. Israel captured the West Bank of the Jordan River, a large portion of the Sinai Peninsula, East Jerusalem, and the Gaza Strip from Egypt, Jordan, and Syria.

Still debated years later is the question of how much choice the Secretary-General really had in the matter and the wisdom of his decision to withdraw UN peacekeepers from Egypt.

Egypt had been well aware of Soviet rumors that Israel planned to attack Syria, Egypt's partner in the United Arab Republic (UAR) at the time. Cairo had put its forces on alert and was demanding the immediate removal of UN troops, for their own security, from positions just inside the Egyptian border. The UN Emergency Force (UNEF) had been posted on Egyptian land along the Sinai and Gaza borders with Israel since the end of the Suez Canal conflict more than a decade before.

Egypt's new request for a UN troop withdrawal came in a letter signed by an Egyptian general and handed in the late evening of May 16, 1967, to General Rikhye, the UNEF commander on the scene. Rikhye had no power to make such a decision and said he would refer it to the Secretary-General for instructions. Rikhye was both surprised and worried by Egypt's demand: "It was a shattering blow to me...[w]ith UNEF's withdrawal, war would be inevitable."[90]

By May 17, Egyptian troops moved into UNEF positions along the Israeli border. After receiving the message in New York from General Rikhye, Thant called Egypt's UN ambassador to his office. He made it very clear that Cairo's demand should have come directly to him. He said that any request for temporary withdrawal or a move of UN troops to less sensitive positions was not acceptable. UNEF, after all, was there to prevent renewed fighting, not to witness it. However, Thant told the ambassador that if the UAR wanted the troops to totally withdraw, it could take back the consent it gave to the UNEF posting in 1956.[91]

"The Secretary-General's reply was really...disastrous," General Rikhye recalled. "It was the first time the word *withdraw* was used." Rikyhe said that Thant told him that he had consulted many experts about his decision. Yet Thant's stance was essentially "a legal position in a political situation," the general added. "I'm absolutely a strong believer that they [Egypt] were prepared for us to negotiate. That's the way they work. But we didn't do that."[92]

As Thant saw it, he had little choice. He felt obliged legally to comply with what he saw as Cairo's cancellation of its consent to base UN peacekeepers on Egyptian soil.

UNEF had been authorized under the Uniting for Peace Resolution by the General Assembly in 1956. Hammarskjöld and Egypt's president, Gamal Abdul Nasser, had spent seven hours in Cairo hammering out the details of the UN operation.

In Thant's opinion, it would have been pointless to take the issue to the Council again. The SC had been previously paralyzed by British and French vetoes on the issue. Thant also doubted that it was possible to get the two-thirds majority that was required to put the issue on the agenda of the Assembly. It was well known that most member states agreed with Egypt's view that it was legally within its rights in requesting UNEF's withdrawal. Indeed, Pakistan, Yugoslavia, and India had made it clear they would pull their UNEF troops out once Cairo's request was officially in hand.[93]

When Thant consulted with the advisory committee to UNEF, a group that included UNEF contributors, the members were divided on the wisdom of his decision. Yet they could not agree on another strategy. As Sir Brian put it, "They wrung their hands and were deeply disturbed, but no one was able to suggest a way out."[94]

Still, the Secretary-General did not give up on efforts to prevent war. On May 18, 1967, the day he received Cairo's official request, he asked Israel to reconsider posting the UN troops inside its own borders rather than inside those of Egypt. The answer from Israel, which had already refused a UNEF posting on its soil in 1957, was *no* once again. In his memoir, Thant argues that a positive answer at that point, even if temporary, could have made all the difference.[95]

Sir Brian and Ralph Bunche prepared an appeal to Nasser. They said there was no evidence of Israeli troop concentrations near Syria and stressed the danger if UN troops were to leave. They urged Egypt to reconsider its decision. But their appeal was never sent. Nasser had made it clear that any such effort would be rebuffed.[96]

Thant decided on his own to fly to Cairo on May 22 to talk with Nasser in a last-minute effort to stop hostilities. While he was en route, however, Nasser publicly announced the closing of the Straits of Tiran. That waterway, in the Gulf of Aqaba, allowed access to Israel's southern port of Eilat. Israel had long said that any shutdown of the strait would be a cause for war. The talks with Nasser made no progress. Thant returned to New York empty handed.

The Secretary-General had earlier suggested that the Security Council call for a breathing spell resolution to give time for Thant to go to Cairo and persuade Nasser to change his mind. "We picked up on that," recalled Seymour Finger, former US ambassador to the United Nations. "We were working like mad, that month of May, on a 'breathing spell' resolution.... We had [one] ready to present on June 4 with nine votes assured. By June 5 it became irrelevant."[97]

The war began that day. Israeli planes promptly destroyed 400 Egyptian, Syrian, Jordanian, and Iraqi aircraft, which were largely sitting on tarmacs.[98] When the brief but intense war ended on June 11, Israel had captured virtually all the Arab territory that is still in dispute.

In an interview in February 1970, Nasser told *Le Monde* that he never intended to start the 1967 war or to close off the gulf. He said that he had only asked Thant to withdraw UNEF from part of the border area but that the Secretary-General, on Bunche's advice, decided to remove the entire force.[99] Thus, Nasser argued, he had no choice but to act as he did: "We fell into the trap that was set for us."[100]

Western nations, especially the United States, were sharply critical of Thant and his decision. President Johnson was reportedly "dismayed." Illinois Senator Everett Dirkson charged that Thant had acted "like a thief in the night." C. L. Sulzberger wrote in his column in the *New York Times* that the Secretary-General had "used his international prestige with the objectivity of a spurned lover and the dynamism of a noodle." The *Spectator of London* editorially proclaimed it "U Thant's War."[101]

Some analysts contend that the moment marked an important turning point in Washington's relations with the United Nations, throwing a needed spotlight on the limits of the UN chief's powers.

"He [Thant] is not an independent actor in the sense of being formally free to choose his own policies," charged Alan James, professor emeritus at Britain's Keele University, in an essay. He described Thant's action as probably the most independent administrative act ever of any secretary-general. He said the deed underscored the need to take "great care not to upset ...[one's] sensitive political masters.... Particularly with respect to political issues, he [the secretary-general] is a man under authority."[102]

Many analysts argue that Thant should have done more to explore his options and should not have acted so speedily.

Thant could have sent an immediate message to Cairo, saying, "Hold everything: am already en route to see you," argued Paul Gore-Booth, the respected British diplomat, in his autobiography. Still, Gore-Booth readily admitted that such a move could have put both the Secretary-General's dignity and the United Nations' authority at risk.[103]

The Secretary-General should have called for a meeting of the Council under his Article 99 authority in sensing a threat to the peace, suggested former assistant secretary-general George Sherry.

"There would have been much more of a possibility [then] of reaching some sort of compromise," he said. "Thant assumed a burden he didn't have to assume."[104]

Thant could have postponed his decision, in the view of Thomas Franck. He might first have asked the advisory committee to UNEF to either support the view that the task was not yet completed or to explore other options, such as asking the General Assembly to advise or mediate the dispute. Indeed, Franck noted that Ernest Gross, a former US ambassador to the United Nations who was involved in the original 1956 UNEF negotiations, said that Nasser and Hammarskjöld had an understanding at the time that the actual interpretation of just when UNEF's job was completed would be left to the General Assembly.[105]

Some analysts say, however, that Thant had little choice.

"I've always thought that his pullout of UNEF in 1967 was an act of courage and integrity and shrewdness," insisted Inis Claude Jr., professor emeritus of political science at the University of Virginia. "I think he saved peacekeeping.... [The UN troops] went there with the consent of the parties [who] needed, wanted, and were willing to accept their help. If the parties decide to have a war, the peacekeepers are supposed to get out of the way and go home.... This is not a fighting force. I've always credited the Secretary-General with doing the right thing for good reasons."[106]

In his book, *The UN Secretary-General from the Cold War to the New Era*, Edward Newman agreed that international law and the emerging principles of peacekeeping demanded the compliance of Egypt, which the UN no longer had.[107]

By his quick decision, Thant actually chose to become a convenient scapegoat rather than pass the blame on to others, in Sir Brian's view. "The Cold War was really responsible." he said. In his view, UN members could not have reached a consensus in either the Council or the Assembly. The Israelis, he added, having been given an opportunity they were unlikely to get again, "were not going to be stopped very easily."[108]

In Sir Brian's view, Thant tried as hard as he could to avert a war. Noting that the Secretary-General was the only one who went to Cairo, where he tried to persuade Nasser to reverse his decision, Urquhart said that Thant "got no support whatsoever from the Russians, the Americans, or the British. None!" He added, "There is no episode in my entire career that made me angrier than that."[109]

If Thant had flown to Cairo immediately after getting Nasser's request, things might have turned out differently, but by the time he went it was too late, according to General Rikhye. Yet Rikhye does not consider the Secretary-General responsible for the war: "In the end, to put the blame on U Thant is grossly unfair," said Rikhye. "The fact is, he was the boss.... But there were so many wise heads who always thought they knew better than he did, and they did not give him the proper advice."[110]

Kurt Waldheim, who succeeded Thant in the top UN job, said in an interview in Vienna that he knew his predecessor quite well and talked with him about that painful decision. While it is imperative to involve the Council in peacekeeping matters, Waldheim said he did not blame Thant. "Sometimes the situation is so urgent that an immediate decision has to be made in order to avoid a greater disaster," he explained.[111]

On November 22, 1967, the Council took a major step forward. After two months of wrestling with the wording and tone, it unanimously passed its now-famous Resolution 242, which called for Israeli withdrawal from captured territories in exchange for peace. It also asked for acknowledgment of the sovereignty, territorial integrity, and political independence of all states in the region and of their right to live in peace with secure and recognized boundaries.[112]

In response to the Council's specific request that the Secretary-General choose a special representative to keep in contact with the states in the region and promote an agreement, Thant tapped Gunnar Jarring, Sweden's former UN ambassador. Another cease-fire was reached but remained unsteady.

In Summary

As Thant has said, there were so many crises during his more than two terms in the job, he could scarcely remember them all. He dealt with some more successfully than others. In the process, he definitely took risks.

In the Cuban missile flare-up, he felt his efforts helped significantly to reduce tension.[113] He suggested forward moves that the superpowers eventually followed. He also acted as a messenger, passing crucial information from one side to the other.

"One of the things to use a secretary-general for is to drop hints... [as in] 'we are ready to settle this nonsense,'" confirmed Leon Gordenker.[114]

Thant felt he made a similarly positive contribution to the India–Pakistan face-off over Kashmir in 1965. He also thought his quiet mediation efforts were helpful in both the Netherlands–Indonesia friction over the status of West New Guinea and the Saudi–UAR dispute over Yemen.

After its independence from the Netherlands in 1949, Indonesia continued to lay claim to West Irian (also called West New Guinea), which was still administered by the Dutch. In the early 1960s, sporadic fighting broke out between the two independent nations. Thant made several appeals to both governments to talk. They did so during the winter and spring of 1962.

Veteran American diplomat Ellsworth Bunker was serving as Thant's special envoy. However, Thant had to intervene several times himself to keep the talks going. In August 1962, a compromise was reached. The Dutch agreed to turn over temporary administration of the disputed territory to the United Nations, a first for the world body. The agreement called for a transfer of authority back to Indonesia in May 1963, after which a plebiscite would be held on whether ties to Jakarta should be kept or cut.

Also early on in his new job, Thant encountered a crisis in the former British colony of Yemen. After a September 1962 coup there, which sparked a growing civil war, the UAR threw its support behind the new government, while Saudi Arabia and Jordan favored the deposed leadership. The neighbors sent troops and aid to help their chosen sides. In Thant's view, it was a problem that threatened to split the Arab world.[115]

On his own authority (but sanctioned well afterward by the Security Council) Thant proposed a demilitarized zone with UN observers on both sides of the Yemeni–Saudi border to prevent infiltration. The warring parties accepted the plan in April 1963 and agreed to share expenses. Thant borrowed troops from the Mideast's UNEF group and the Royal Canadian Air Force. After an agreed-upon timeline, the Secretary-General withdrew the troops and urged the UAR and the Saudis to settle "their needless and now senseless disputes."[116] A peace agreement was signed in August 1965.

As Sir Brian described the UN–Yemen experience later to a group of correspondents, "It was so successful that nobody ever heard of it.... Prevention sounds wonderful when making lectures and speeches, but it's very difficult to do. Human beings don't like to be prevented from doing disastrous things until it's too late."[117]

In addition to Thant's ultimately successful efforts in these disputes, some analysts believe that one of his most important but least heralded preventive efforts involved Bahrain, an archipelago of 30 islands in the Persian Gulf.

In 1970, Britain and Iran were at odds over the future of Bahrain. Iran claimed the archipelago as part of its territory and said that British interference kept it from exercising its legitimate rights there. Britain countered that Bahrain was a sovereign Arab state with which it had a special treaty relationship. Thant and Ralph Bunche discussed the matter with the respective ambassadors over many weeks. In March, Iran formally asked Thant to exercise his good offices in the dispute. Britain agreed.

Thant chose an undersecretary-general, Vittorio Winspeare Guicciardi of Italy, as his special representative to sound out the will of Bahrain's residents. The virtually unanimous result was that residents wanted Iran's claim removed. A decision to grant Bahrain independence was soon accepted by both sides and the Security Council.

Thant noted in his memoir that "the dispute was settled before it broke into armed conflict." For the first time in UN history, the parties to a dispute gave an *a priori* pledge to accept the United Nations' proposal as long as the Council also approved.[118]

Britain's ambassador to the United Nations, Lord Caradon, was so delighted that he broke into verse at the Council session:

> The play is over. Witness now
> The actors come to make their bow.
> Praise first the Shah; what joy to see
> Imperial magnanimity.
> Cheer next U Thant who never tires
> In harmonizing our desires.
> Next the Italian wins applause
> For Roman justice is his cause.
> In gratitude we cry, "Long live
> The Special Representative."
> The people made their wishes plain,
> Their independence they retain.
> Good luck, God Speed to Bahrain.[119]

The Cyprus situation, unresolved after many decades, stands as a decidedly mixed victory for Thant and the United Nations. In March 1964, after violence broke out between Greek and Turkish Cypriots, the Security Council authorized a peacekeeping operation there—the United Nations Force in Cyprus (UNFICYP). Size and composition details were left to the Secretary-General. Thant put together a multi-national force of 7,000 troops. But, in his view, the very presence of the troops—although it stopped the fighting—effectively delayed any resolution of the dispute.[120]

He readily admitted that relations did not improve between Israel and its Arab neighbors and among most African states during his tenure.[121] Moscow's successful invasion of Czechoslovakia also occurred on his watch. No UN organ managed to stop it.

Though certainly most widely criticized for his solo decision to pull UN troops out of Egypt in 1967—considered the crucial spur for the war that followed—he felt he had no choice. In his view, Egypt initially gave its consent and had a right to take it back.

Thant was keenly aware that he had profoundly irritated the Johnson administration in Washington both by his failure to prevent the 1967 war and by his several efforts to intercede in the Vietnam conflict. In a sarcastic public speech, Dean Rusk, then US secretary of state, implied that Thant's real goal, in trying to resolve the Vietnam situation, was to win the Nobel Peace Prize.[122]

"Everyone thought he would roll over on that issue, but he took a strong position," noted Bhaskar Menon, the former editor of *UNDiplomatic Times* and veteran UN correspondent.[123]

"It doesn't hurt to try," Thomas Weiss, codirector of the United Nations Intellectual History Project, said of Thant's Vietnam efforts, "[but] the ability to influence major powers is always less than your ability to influence minor powers."[124]

At least early on, the Secretary-General's relationship with Moscow tended to be warmer, both diplomatically and personally, than with Washington.

Thant tells of his first meeting with the Soviet chairman Khrushchev on August 22, 1962, at the Soviet leader's country home near Yalta. After a relaxed lunch with the Soviet leader's large family, Thant said Khrushchev invited him to take a swim in the Black Sea. When Thant protested that it might cause indigestion, Khrushchev countered that a swim right after lunch is very good for digestion.

The Soviet leader lent the slender UN chief a pair of trunks "that would have fit a Japanese heavyweight Sumo wrestler with a 50-inch waist," according to the Secretary-General. Thant somehow managed the challenge. Noting that neither man spoke the other's language, Thant said, "Those 30 minutes in the Black Sea were the most memorable and at the same time the most boring I had ever spent with a head of state." Khrushchev, he recalled, spent the time humming what sounded like a Russian tune.[125]

Many analysts credit Thant for significantly broadening the United Nations' agenda. "He'll be remembered as the secretary-general who turned the organization more toward third world concerns," said Inis Claude Jr.[126] Thant saw narrowing the gap between rich and poor as a crucial part of the United Nations' role to keep the peace.

During the 1960s, while Thant was in office, the UN Conference on Trade and Development (UNCTAD), the UN Development Program, the World Food Program, the UN Industrial Development Organization, and the UN Population Fund all were launched. The UN Environment Program, an initiative he personally nurtured, was started shortly after he retired.

Though it is not well known, Thant is also credited with the founding of the United Nations University in Tokyo, an institution offering postgraduate degrees. In 1969 Thant suggested that the United Nations needed an institution to focus on its Charter objectives of peace and progress. The General Assembly agreed to the concept and the university began operations in the mid-1970s.

Thant also started the first large-scale UN relief program for civilians who were caught in war. With no specific UN authorization, he started the UN East Pakistan Relief Operation (UNEPRO) in 1971, responding to a huge need in the wake of the civil war that had broken out between East and West Pakistan. This eventually led to the formation of Bangladesh in the East. Millions of refugees poured into India. In time, India was involved in the war as well, but neither India nor Pakistan wanted UN involvement. They both insisted that the conflict was strictly an internal matter.[127]

The Secretary-General took the view that the Charter authorized him to take humanitarian action, if needed to save lives, without a specific enabling resolution. His UNEPRO initiative was later endorsed unanimously by the Assembly.[128] In a press conference near the end of his second term, he told reporters that he sometimes thought the UN Charter's drafters were "overly obsessed" with political and military conflict. He suggested adding a new provision to Article 99 of the Charter that would authorize a secretary-general to alert UN members to global threats to human well-being as well as to the standard peace and security concerns.[129]

Thant said he felt obliged to take a firm stand to support every UN Security Council or Assembly resolution regardless of his own personal views.[130] Yet he also took the initiative many times in extending his good offices. He saw his job primarily as that of a bridge builder.[131]

As he tells it, "Great problems usually come to the United Nations because governments have been unable to think of anything else to do about them. The United Nations is a last-ditch, last-resort affair." As such, he argued, it is not surprising that the world organization is often blamed for failing to solve those problems.[132]

To his colleagues, Thant often appeared unemotional. By his own telling, he usually avoided open arguments with delegates. Reportedly, he never lost his temper. When unusually stressed, he was known to tap his foot rhythmically.[133] Thant biographer June Bingham insisted that deceit was the only thing that would arouse his "open anger."[134]

Although he tended to use mild language in discussions, he could be very frank when he felt strongly about something—particularly when a moral issue was involved. As he put it in his memoir, "I am not a believer in honeyed words."[135]

In a commencement speech at Williams College in 1962, he told his listeners that in the past the primary motive of colonial powers in developing natural resources was their own commercial profit.[136] He told another audience in February 1964 that he thought racial prejudice was a serious form of mental illness and no justification for violence or revenge.[137] In a press conference on July 6, 1966, he told reporters that unresolved economic problems tended to be even more explosive than political problems.[138]

Sir Brian, who worked closely with Thant over the years, is a strong defender: "His stewardship had none of the flair or high personal style of Hammarskjöld but his undertakings were just as courageous."[139] Thant's strong personal effort in 1964 and 1965 to stop the Vietnam War before it really escalated did not succeed. Yet his approach, essentially the same one that the United States later proposed, was taken up five years afterward, noted Sir Brian. Then all parties agreed to the plan.[140]

Thant had little apparent interest in getting credit for any achievement. "Thant always took the blame if anything went wrong and never took credit if anything went right," insisted Sir Brian.[141]

When the two men flew to India and Pakistan in 1965 during the tense situation there, Thant did not show much interest in his staff's concerns for his security. "Everybody said, 'Oh, Christ, he'll get shot down,'" recalled Sir Brian."Everybody was rushing around, trying to take security precautions. U Thant wasn't interested. He said, 'I'm not worried. If I get shot down, that's it. All I'm interested in is getting there and [talking] to these people.' He was wonderful, very refreshing."[142]

"U Thant really hasn't been given sufficient credit," agreed George Sherry. "He was a very decent, honest man. He gave a great deal of latitude to his staff. And he had a very strongly developed moral sense.... He knew what was right."[143]

Thant described the job to his friend and biographer Bingham as "lonely and difficult" in terms of responsibilities.[144] He admitted that serving the United Nations as ambassador from Burma in his younger days was definitely "more relaxed and fun" than being in the United Nations' top job.[145]

The role of the UN secretary-general took few major leaps forward under Thant. Yet his efforts clearly kept the momentum going. Thant did much of his work in private and, like Hammarskjöld, took many independent political initiatives, often later approved by other UN organs.[146] The United Nations' humanitarian agenda also grew tremendously during his years.

CHAPTER SIX

Kurt Waldheim: An Austrian Eagerly Pursues the Job

The all-important first step—his selection by the Security Council—occurred on December 21, 1971, an unusually late date for such an important decision and a day that happened to coincide with Kurt Waldheim's 53rd birthday. The vote followed several rounds of secret ballots and vetoes. Communist China, which had displaced the Taiwan Nationalist government in the key UN China seat just that September, finally backed away from its two previous vetoes to abstain.

Waldheim, "convinced that I could no longer influence the [Council] decision," had opted for a stroll in Central Park that day. He got the news on his return to the UN Mission of Austria where he was the ambassador. The General Assembly's unanimous stamp of approval the next day swept away his worries and doubts about the job's possible pitfalls.[1]

He was also, however, acutely aware of the scope of his new responsibility. As he later recalled, somewhat incredulously, "I had just become...a spokesman for humanity."[2]

It was the first time in UN history that candidates had openly campaigned for the secretary-general's job. Waldheim's chief rival was Max Jakobson, Finland's permanent representative at the United Nations.

Waldheim had recently taken a six-month leave from his ambassador's post to run for Austria's presidency but had lost. On the day after his return to New York, he was surprised to see a *New York Times* editorial that strongly supported Jakobson. Since the Finnish ambassador was a good friend, Waldheim arranged to have lunch with him. Jakobson, as Waldheim recounted it, noted that the Austrian had also been mentioned for the top job. Was he seriously interested?[3]

"Obviously I was interested; for any diplomat...the post...is the utmost aim of a successful career," Waldheim recalled. Though he knew geographic representation played a role, he was convinced that "personal competence and reputation...figure decisively in the choice."[4]

The United States, though preoccupied with tending to its relations with China and the Soviet Union during a period of relative détente, favored Jakobson. Russia, which was supporting Gunnar Jarring, Sweden's ambassador to Moscow, was less keen. Moscow reportedly spread the word that Jakobson's Jewish ancestry would work against any Arab support for him.[5]

During two secret Council ballots, involving nine candidates and several vetoes, Waldheim emerged with the largest majority of supporters and no veto. Austria had been neutral in the Cold War, a point Waldheim often stressed in courting votes. "The deciding factor was not who was best qualified for the post, but who could avoid a veto," according to Waldheim biographer Seymour Finger.[6]

"I think the main reason the Soviets supported Waldheim was that they thought he would not be a strong secretary-general," Finger explained in an interview. "As my book title suggests, he would 'bend with the winds,' and he did. Max Jakobson, on the other hand, would have been a strong figure, and they [the Soviets] didn't want that. They saw Waldheim as more... predictable. We [the US] supported Jakobson but shifted to having 'no objection' to Waldheim. We knew his weaknesses, and I'm reasonably sure the CIA knew about his war record."[7]

That record, which never came up in the UN vetting process, has been a matter of contentious debate for many years. Detailed records of his service in the German Army in World War II did not really become public until 1986 when he was again running for president of Austria.

There is no question that he glossed over the length and depth of his wartime experience with the German Army in his two memoirs. After receiving and being treated for a serious thigh wound on the Russian front early in the war, Waldheim claimed to have returned to academic studies. He did for a time. However, he also returned to wartime service as a lieutenant with a German unit in the Balkans that was responsible for the deportation to Auschwitz of thousands of Jews from Greece and for the deaths of thousands of innocent civilians in Greece and Yugoslavia as reprisals for attacks by resistance fighters.

Yet there is no sure evidence that he was personally involved in Nazi crimes. He was an intelligence officer who prepared situation reports used by the war criminals in planning attacks against the resistance fighters. Though charges were filed against him with the UN War Crimes Commission in London, no trial was held. The commission was abolished in 1948.

Robert Edwin Herzstein, the University of South Carolina historian who made an in-depth research study of the issue in his 1988 book, *Waldheim: The Missing Years*, concluded that the former UN Secretary-General did not "order, incite, or personally commit" war crimes. But in Herzstein's view, that finding did not necessarily mean innocence: "The fact that Waldheim played a significant role in military units that unquestionably committed war crimes makes him at the very least morally complicit."[8]

Stanley Meisler insisted that "by sweeping this [mention of his later service with the German Army] out of his biography, Waldheim lived a lie for more than 40 years."[9]

In choosing Waldheim for the United Nations' top job, member governments apparently did not know the extent to which he had concealed his wartime record. When Finger later asked William Rogers, the US secretary of state, about the omission, Rogers told him "somewhat ingenuously" that he had assumed that the United Nations would have done a background check.[10]

Ambitious Quest

Waldheim was the grandson of a blacksmith and the son of a Czech teacher and school superintendent in the rural Austrian town of Tulln. Waldheim's father, Walter, had been a soldier in World War I and was strongly anti-Nazi. After Germany annexed Austria in the

Anschluss of March 1938, Walter was twice arrested by the Gestapo. He was released each time but later dismissed from his job.

Though Walter's son, Kurt, was a member of an anti-Nazi organization in his teenage years, the younger Waldheim became a member of the National Socialist (Nazi) German Students League shortly after Germany took over Austria. In November 1938, he was drafted and joined a cavalry unit of the German storm troopers or brownshirts. Confronted with these affiliations years later, Waldheim at first scoffed at their importance and then insisted that his involvement with these groups and his eventual wartime service were all a matter of survival for him: he did what he had to do.

Right from the start he had his eye on a diplomatic career. In 1937, he had enrolled in the University of Vienna Law School and the Vienna Consular Academy. Though he left to serve time in the German Army, he eventually completed his studies. During one of his army leaves, he selected the topic for his law dissertation and married Elizabeth (Cissy) Ritschel, a 21-year-old fellow law student.

After the war ended, the United States held Waldheim in a prisoner-of-war (POW) camp for a few weeks but released him for lack of evidence of his involvement in war crimes.

He soon entered Austria's diplomatic service, beginning as a personal assistant to the new foreign minister and rising slowly through the ranks. After his country regained its sovereignty in 1955, Waldheim went to New York as a member of Austria's first delegation to the United Nations. Though he later became ambassador to Canada (1958–60) and was named foreign minister of Austria in 1968, he frequently returned to the United Nations as a member of Austria's delegation.

Though clearly impressed with the prestige of his new 1972 job as UN Secretary-General, Waldheim also well knew he would be taking on a formidable list of problems.

The United Nations at the time had three times as many members as it had when the organization was founded. Western powers no longer dominated General Assembly decisions. Colonial and racial controversies and social and economic demands competed for UN attention. Waldheim had already seen much of the daily routine. He knew that UN operations were "cumbersome, often ineffectual, and sometimes even mind-numbing."[11]

Dealing with the Nuts and Bolts

The most pressing challenge was financial. Waldheim called it his top priority in his first address to the Assembly. Debt and a cash shortfall were threatening to bankrupt the organization. France and Russia, the second- and third-largest contributors to the UN budget (after the United States), had refused to put up money for peacekeeping in the Mideast and the Congo. They had never approved either operation.

Waldheim quickly announced a freeze on recruitment and $6 million worth of staff cuts. Staff salaries accounted for three-fourths of the budget total. He also encouraged more advance payments on member contributions and greater fiscal restraint—fewer meetings, conferences, and documents.

In his view, the Assembly agenda was much too long and repetitive. But, when moving an item to the next session was suggested, the steering committee would begin a long discussion, and interest groups would lobby to keep the item in. "Each year we had the same extensive and acrimonious debate on issues such as the Middle East, South Africa, and similar problems without making any progress," Waldheim recalled.[12]

Waldheim's varied efforts to streamline operations and trim the budget put the United Nations on a more stable footing for a couple of years.[13] Unfortunately, the impact did not last. Expenses grew. The GA kept voting in higher and higher budgets. Yet the new Secretary-General fared better at fiscal reform than in his attempts to restructure and improve the UN Secretariat.

During his tenure, the number of high level positions jumped by 25 percent. His appointments followed political lines, reflecting the strength of the major powers and voting blocs.[14] Jacob Malik, the Soviet ambassador to the United Nations, once even told Waldheim that he would never be reelected unless Moscow was awarded certain jobs.[15]

Other governments pressed Waldheim hard for a wider geographic spread among lower staff positions. He complained of the pressure but also often gave in to it. He knew the pleas from newer members had merit. Three-fourths of the staff had been hired for permanent posts in the early years of the United Nations. Most were from the United Nations' first member nations.[16]

Waldheim tended to use the hiring process as a way of ingratiating himself with governments—"like a politician earning support by patronage," Finger said.[17] A City University of New York (CUNY) study during Waldheim's first term confirmed the increasing member pressure for jobs and criticized the effect as lower-quality hires and the demoralization of veteran staffers.[18]

"Administration is important but sort of a burden," Waldheim told this author later in Vienna. "The secretary-general's job is a diplomatic one. The real challenge...is to make his contribution to peace and international understanding.... It is necessary to have the goodwill of the member states to solve the problems.... If they don't accept him, he has no chance to make his contribution."[19]

Waldheim could be polite, even at times obsequious, toward governments. Yet he could also be cold and arrogant toward the UN staff. One respected mediator said in 40 years of labor negotiations, he had never seen such an authoritarian attitude toward employees.[20]

Bhaskar Menon, who wrote many of Waldheim's speeches, said that the Secretary-General did nothing as the inflation of the 1970s lowered the value of UN staff salaries and some more affluent governments awarded bonuses to their nationals. Nor did the UN chief protest when UN staff members were among the thousands who disappeared in Latin right-wing dictatorships that were guilty of human rights violations. Menon charged that Waldheim had "an amazing lack of fixed principles and showed it as an administrator."[21]

Menon, who in 1990 became an independent journalist covering the United Nations, recalled attending a reception hosted by the

Secretary-General for about 20 people. When Waldheim entered, Menon shook his hand and introduced himself as one of his speech writers. Waldheim "went around the room totally like a dead fish with no expression." Menon recalled. "He shook hands with me on the way back to his office as if we had never met before."[22]

Clovis Maksoud, a former Arab League Ambassador to the United Nations and the United States, confirmed the characterization, saying, "Waldheim was something of a mix between an aristocrat and an autocrat."[23]

Working with Waldheim

Senior staff members who worked with the new secretary-general on a day-to-day basis said he was conscientious and hard working. Waldheim has described himself as a workaholic.[24]

Sir Brian Urquhart, who ran Waldheim's Special Political Affairs Office until appointed an undersecretary-general in 1974, admitted that, at first, he questioned whether his "unknown and untried boss" was right for the job. Yet Sir Brian says he soon came to respect Waldheim's receptivity to new ideas and suggestions and the wholehearted effort he was making.[25]

Waldheim was a detail man. Sir Brian said the Secretary-General went over and over the smallest details. He rarely liked to come down firmly on one side or another in a dispute. Once when Sir Brian insisted that a decision of some kind must be made quickly, Waldheim shot back with, "There will be no decision.... That IS a decision."[26]

From the start Waldheim knew that his powers were limited. "All I have is moral power," he noted. "I have not got the power to force anyone to do anything."[27]

"The public feels that the secretary-general has the power of a head of state and can give orders to member states," noted Waldheim. "He can't. What he can do is try to mediate, to convince the parties in a conflict to do something positive to solve a problem. As long as he is able to convince the parties that he's objective, not biased, he can work successfully."[28]

During the Christmas season of 1972, the US ambassador to the United Nations, George H. W. Bush, sent the new secretary-general a small kit of hand tools in a yellow box. Bush said he hoped the kit would help the UN chief to solve the world's problems. Waldheim saw it as a "thoughtful and touching gesture."[29]

He was often critical of Security Council resolutions so watered down for acceptance that they became almost meaningless. He delivered stern lectures now and then on the dangers of such a lack of social and political willpower.[30]

"Governments sitting on the Council sometimes purposely don't want to make a clear statement on difficult matters," he explained in the Vienna interview, "because they know very well they will then be attacked by one of the other parties."[31]

Yet if asked for his help by the Council or the parties to a dispute, Waldheim himself could be similarly cautious. He tried not to make public statements that could be easily distorted or considered biased.

"This is the gift which a secretary-general must have," he said. "He must judge how far he can go in criticizing another country...in order to be helpful. It doesn't really solve a problem if you don't get the necessary cooperation"[32]

"The secretary-general needs a lot of—what we call in our language *fingerspitzengafu*—feeling in the depths of the fingers," he insisted. "How far can I go in making this or that statement to maintain the negotiating process....You have to be careful but also clear enough so you are understood and seen to be sticking fully to the Charter of the UN."[33]

Relief Challenge in Southeast Asia

A month before his election—in November 1971—a civil war between East and West Pakistan had evolved into a brief but much larger battle involving India on the side of the Bengali insurgents in East Pakistan. Neither India nor Pakistan wanted UN involvement. Security Council efforts to send a peacekeeping force were deadlocked. A General Assembly call for a cease-fire was ignored.

By mid-December India was victorious. East Pakistan declared its independence as Bangladesh. However, the devastation and misery were widespread. Roads, bridges, and river channels had been thoroughly destroyed. Bangladesh's two main ports were silted and blocked, and its 75 million inhabitants were facing a serious threat of famine. Several million others who had fled to India were trying to return home.

Before he left office, U Thant had begun a UN East Pakistan relief operation. Waldheim promptly picked up the ball, urging all member states to contribute as much as they could. Within a year, he received pledges of $1.3 billion. Waldheim appointed top people such as Sir Robert Jackson of Australia and the UN High Commissioner for Refugees, Prince Sadruddin Aga Kahn, to coordinate the effort. Every possible UN agency was brought in to help. Soviet teams cleared harbors while the United States concentrated on reconstruction efforts in Dacca. European nations and international relief groups were also hard at work. Aid was supplied on a scale never before achieved.[34]

Waldheim, who paid a personal visit to all three capitals a year later, termed the UN relief operation a "resounding success."[35]

Terrorism in Munich

Waldheim attended the Munich Olympics in September 1972, where 11 Israeli athletes were murdered by Palestine Liberation Organization (PLO) terrorists.

Security Council efforts to condemn the terrorists were blocked by vetoes. Determined that the United Nations could not remain "a mute spectator" to terrorism, Waldheim, despite opposition from the Arab bloc, managed to shift the item to the General Assembly agenda as an urgent matter. To assuage Arab concerns, the topic eventually was broadened to include discussion of the underlying causes of terrorism.[36]

Yet the problem was seen as chiefly a Western concern. Because he had raised the issue, Waldheim's image was tarnished in the eyes of the third world, according to biographer James D. Ryan. The problem was raising and spotlighting a cause that showed UN impotence and alienated many of the nonaligned countries.[37]

Though little progress was made at the time, Waldheim defended his move as a beginning.[38] The Assembly established an ad hoc committee on terrorism, and, in 1977, the GA took another step forward by adopting a German proposal against the hijacking of civilian aircraft.

Namibia: A Strong UN Push for Independence

The Namibia case is considered unique in UN history in terms of the depth and nature of the organization's involvement. It was the first time the United Nations became a direct party in a decolonization dispute and actually supervised the transition to independence.[39]

More than half of all Security Council meetings between January 1971 and October 1972 dealt with colonialism in Africa. Actual independence for Namibia did not come on Waldheim's watch. However, he and both the General Assembly and the Security Council all worked energetically together during long hours toward that goal.[40]

The former German colony, long known as South West Africa, had been mandated to South Africa by the League of Nations after World War I. In 1946, South Africa petitioned the United Nations for the right to annex the territory but was refused. Still, South Africa managed to keep a firm grip on its mandate despite repeated attempts by the Council, the Assembly, and the International Court of Justice during the 1960s and 70s to declare its hold illegal and order its withdrawal.

At a special series of Council meetings in Addis Ababa early in 1972, members asked Waldheim to make contacts in South Africa to help move Namibia toward independence. The GA had voted in 1968 to change the territory's name to Namibia. The Council also condemned South Africa once again for failing to heed past UN decisions and, once more, ordered its withdrawal from Namibia and the transfer of its administrative responsibilities there to the United Nations. All such demands were defiantly resisted.

Waldheim visited South Africa (and briefly northern Namibia) to meet with top officials in March. There was no breakthrough. But by midsummer, South Africa agreed to receive a special representative of the Secretary-General.

"We had used all our moral power," recalled Waldheim. He saw that act of acceptance as an important, if small, step forward. "Don't forget, it was sanctions, embargoes, and all those concrete measures adopted by the international community against the policy of apartheid in South Africa and against its policy of keeping Namibia under South Africa's power [that were at work]."[41]

Yet South Africa turned down several nominees before accepting Waldheim's bid of Alfred Martin Escher of Switzerland as his special representative. After a trip to Namibia of several weeks in the fall of 1972, Escher reported that the overwhelming majority of the non-white population favored independence. South Africa again rejected that conclusion.[42]

It was another four years before the Security Council adopted a UN plan for elections and independence which became the basis for the eventual settlement. However, it would be another 13 years before South Africa actually withdrew and elections were held.

As Sir Brian, who helped develop the UN plan for Namibia, put it, "Nowhere has the South African talent for delay and obfuscation been deployed with such skill."[43]

The Mideast Erupts Again

It should have come as no surprise when Egypt attacked the east bank of the Suez Canal on October 6, 1973. After all, Cairo had been holding forth at numerous Council meetings over the summer on the need for Israeli withdrawal from the Occupied Territories. Egypt even hinted that it might resort to other means if the Council did not resolve the issue. Still, most members were not aware of just how determined Cairo was to pursue that goal.

Once the Yom Kipper War started, the Council was powerless for the first few weeks to end the fighting. Syrian troops had also opened fire along the Golan Heights. Several Council meetings produced no results.

When Egyptian forces were making progress, Cairo and its supporters, including Moscow, wanted no cease-fire unless Israel agreed to withdraw from all territories seized in the 1967 war. When Israel began to make strong forward strides, helped by a massive mid-October airlift of supplies from the United States, Washington and its allies preferred a delay on any call for a cease-fire.

Waldheim had visited Syria, Egypt, and Israel briefly in August 1973. He described the results as "anything but reassuring."[44] Egypt's President Anwar Sadat was sharply critical of the United Nations' ability to get a broad Middle East settlement. Syria's President Hafiz al-Assad told the Secretary-General that there could be no peace without a full Israeli withdrawal from the Sinai and the Golan Heights.

During a luncheon discussion in Israel, Prime Minister Golda Meir reproached Waldheim for describing the Middle East situation as "highly explosive." She confidently insisted, "The Arabs will get used to our existence and in a few years, they will recognize us, and we shall have peace."[45]

It was on this same trip, at an informal dinner in the Jerusalem home of Israel's foreign minister, Abba Eban, that Waldheim responded to a welcoming toast with his well-known faux pas, "I am happy to be in your beautiful capital." Though the event was presumably off-the-record, it led the news on the BBC the next morning.[46]

Waldheim was frustrated by the Council's inability to act despite the "appalling human losses." He said the Council was neglecting its primary duty to maintain peace and security.[47] He also appealed to the combatants in a television message to shift their goals and halt this "war of attrition."[48] In addition, he wrote personal letters to the Soviet and US leaders. Aware that cynics might dismiss such efforts as "drops of water falling on a stone," Waldheim said he nonetheless felt obliged as a "global spokesman" to speak out.[49]

Soon US Secretary of State Henry Kissinger flew to Moscow for talks with Leonid Brezhnev, the Soviet general secretary. Together they crafted a cease-fire proposal and a call for immediate negotiations. On his way home, Kissinger stopped in Israel to warn Golda

Meir that any further shipments of US arms depended on Israel's acceptance of the cease-fire.

Though the Council approved the US–Soviet call for a cease-fire on October 22, the fighting continued. At one point, the Israelis completely encircled one Egyptian army unit.

"It was really a very critical situation," Waldheim recalled. "If they [the Israelis] had destroyed the Egyptian Army, the whole psychological climate would have been so bad that negotiations would probably not have taken place.... Kissinger convinced the Israelis that it was important to solve the problem peacefully.... This is a classic example of how good cooperation between the parties concerned and the secretary-general can solve the problem." The United Nations did manage to deliver desperately needed water and food.[50]

On October 24, 1973, President Sadat urged Washington and Moscow to send troops to enforce the UN cease-fire. The Soviets were receptive. The United States was not. President Richard Nixon, after receiving what Kissinger described as a "menacing" telegram from Brezhnev, put US military forces on alert. Washington urged Sadat to withdraw his troop invitation, and he did. The United States made it clear that it would send no troops to the front and would veto any Council move to authorize sending any Russian troops.[51] US–Soviet relations remained tense.

Waldheim had phoned Kissinger to suggest sending UN peacekeeping troops to the scene instead. Finally, in a move sponsored by eight nonaligned nations, on October 25 the Council repeated its call for a cease-fire and asked the Secretary-General to prepare plans for an emergency UN peacekeeping force. It was, at Washington's insistence, to include no troops from the so-called Permanent 5 Council members, though US and Soviet personnel would be sent to an expanded UN Truce Supervision Organization (UNTSO) observer force. Waldheim was to report back within 24 hours with a plan on the financing, composition, and command.

His report marked a major breakthrough in defining the somewhat foggy line between the role of the Council and that of the secretary-general in peacekeeping operations. A special General Assembly committee had been discussing the issue since 1964 without much success.[52]

Some 900 UN troops were promptly transferred to Middle East service from their duties in Cyprus. The speed of that move was widely regarded as a major UN accomplishment.[53] The operation was to be known as UNEF (United Nations Emergency Force) II, the sequel to UNEF I established in 1956. The new force was to operate for renewable six-month stints and be financed by regular member assessments. Council approval would be crucial for any early withdrawal. The Secretary-General was to keep the Council fully informed and let it decide all matters that might affect the nature or operation of the force.

Though the Council makes the basic decision to send UN troops, Waldheim insisted that a secretary-general has "great responsibility and freedom of action—as long as it works." However, if he makes a "mistake," he said, laughing, "as in choosing the wrong country for a certain operation, it falls on his head." He gets the blame.[54]

Waldheim said the secretary-general himself can decide which countries to contact for troops but that he has to be careful. "In the Middle East, it is always a problem to find the right nationalities," he said. "I remember once, in regard to the Golan Heights, I had to contact the president of Syria and the government of Israel to find out whether the nationalities I had in mind to send were agreeable."[55]

UNEF II was in many respects a model for future UN forces. Its work led to a cease-fire that held and paved the way to an eventual peace treaty.

On November 11, 1973, Egypt and Israel at last signed a cease-fire agreement in a tent along the Cairo–Suez road.

With that agreement in place and largely observed, a peace conference was scheduled for December 23 in Geneva to tackle disengagement and withdrawal issues. Waldheim was to convene the conference and preside over the first phase, but Washington and Moscow were to act as co-chairs. Israel, keenly aware of third world criticism against it in the United Nations, much preferred the United

States to the United Nations as negotiator. The formal invitations to the conference stressed that the United Nations was convening but not running the conference.[56]

"Waldheim insisted on being part of the conference...that the Russians promoted and the Americans reluctantly went to," noted the international legal scholar Thomas Franck. "I think it was a real blunder. They told him from the beginning, 'You don't have any role in this.' You can't be taken seriously if you're prepared to waste your time that way."[57]

A key challenge at the conference concerned seating arrangements to keep everyone happy. Arab states did not want to sit next to the Israeli delegates. Moscow finally was persuaded to sit next to the Israelis. The Soviet foreign minister, Andrei Gromyko, however, demanded that he must be personally asked first by Kissinger himself. Compared to the seating drama, the results of the conference were somewhat anticlimactic.[58]

Still, Waldheim considered the gathering an important step on the road to regional peace. Though never formally reconvened because of disagreement over Palestinian representation, the conference provided a framework in which the nations could talk without losing face and remained the basic umbrella for talks until 1977 when Sadat made his surprise visit to Jerusalem.[59]

The conference also opened the way to a series of military disengagement agreements. The first of those, negotiated by Kissinger, was signed by Egypt and Israel on January 18, 1974. It called for the separation of the troops, enforced by UNEF II, and the reopening of the Suez Canal.[60] Another agreement, also negotiated by Kissinger, was signed in September 1975. Through it, the Israelis gave up the oil fields in the Red Sea and two passes (Giddi and Mitla) in the Sinai.[61]

Both UNEF II, assigned to the Sinai, and later the UN Disengagement Observer Force (UNDOF), assigned to the Golan Heights, were important as guarantors. Kissinger did a marathon five-week shuttle between Damascus and Jerusalem to get an agreement on an observer force for the Golan Heights. Sir Brian called it "an extraordinary feat of ingenuity, endurance, and persistence on

Kissinger's part."[62] The Council approved the UNDOF plan on May 31, 1974. Egypt and Israel signed the agreement that same day in Geneva and asked Waldheim to set up the new force.[63]

One key provision of support for peacekeeping operations that had been lost in the 1960s was reestablished in the process. In his report to the Council, Waldheim included a clause stipulating that expenses of UNEF II should be considered those of the whole organization, not dependent on voluntary contributions.[64]

Besides enforcing the needed separation of Arab and Israeli forces in the 1973 war, the United Nations is widely credited with defusing a potentially dangerous Washington–Moscow confrontation in the region. Waldheim considered the war in many ways a turning point in Arab–Israeli relations. He credited Henry Kissinger, who became more supportive of the UN after this episode, with the crucial diplomatic role. "He never lost his *sangfroid* or his sense of humor," noted Waldheim.[65]

More Mideast Trouble

Waldheim was in no way finished with handling flare-ups in the Middle East. They would, as he put it, "dog my entire term of office."[66]

Israel had already been dealt a major blow after the 1967 Six-Day War. The Council passed Resolution 242, calling on Israel to withdraw its armed forces "from territories occupied in the recent conflict." The wording had been very carefully crafted.

"Israelis told me, and it was also their public position, that the resolution did not say from 'all' occupied territories," Waldheim explained in the interview. "The English version leaves out the word 'the'.... The Palestinians said, 'This [the Israeli position] is not acceptable to us—either they withdraw [from all] or there is no withdrawal."[67]

"The poor man who is secretary-general," Waldheim continued, "will be asked by one side to make sure Israeli forces withdraw from ALL occupied territories. At the same time he will be accused of being biased by the other side if he requests it.... I suffered again and again under the accusation that I supported either the Palestinians or the Israelis."[68]

UN pressure on Israel continued in several ways.

In 1974 the Assembly majority recognized the PLO as the representative of the Palestinian people and invited it to participate in its business. The Assembly also asked the Council to establish contacts with the PLO on relevant matters.

On November 10, 1975, the Assembly majority passed its "Zionism is racism" resolution. With strong PLO support, the Assembly held that Zionism was a form of racism and racial discrimination.

In their defense, the sponsors, including the Soviet Union and 21 Muslim nations, called the resolution a symbol of third-world solidarity. They insisted it was not aimed at eliminating Israel or increasing Soviet influence.[69] The United States saw it differently. Pat Moynihan, the feisty new US ambassador to the United Nations, said that "grave and perhaps irreparable harm will be done to the cause of human rights."[70]

Waldheim did not speak out publicly against the resolution. It had been passed by a major UN organ of sovereign states. He did not feel it was his role to condemn it, even if he personally believed it to be wrong.[71]

"He could have criticized it and he didn't," explained Finger. "He probably didn't because it was adopted by a majority, and he wanted to please everybody."[72]

Finger added that he did not think Waldheim's reticence had to do with any feeling of support for the measure. Finger noted that Waldheim's lawyer and doctor and the ghost writers of his three books were all Jewish.

> "I don't think he had a gut hatred of Jews," he said. "On the other hand, he was an opportunist.... Once Hitler came in, and he had to join Nazi groups to get ahead, he did."[73]

Cyprus: A Thankless and Frustrating Task

When asked by the Council to provide his good offices in the ongoing Greek–Turk dispute over Cyprus, Waldheim noted that the parties at first could not even agree on a location for talks. It was a harbinger of just how insoluble the problem would continue to be.[74]

Cyprus gained its independence from Britain in 1960. Britain, Greece, and Turkey were to be the treaty's guarantor powers. From 1964 on, the UN Force in Cyprus (UNFICYP) patrolled the island to try to keep conflict from erupting between the Greek and Turk communities there. Years of talks under UN auspices had made little progress.

The situation took a major turn on Waldheim's watch in 1974. On July 15, in a plot organized by the military junta in Athens, eager to unite the island with Greece, Cyprus President Archbishop Makarios, was overthrown in a coup. Waldheim alerted the Council and called on Greeks and Turks to show restraint.

The next major challenge came at dawn five days later. Turk army troops began a major air and sea invasion on the island's north coast. They claimed to be acting to protect Turk Cypriots as guarantor parties to the 1960 independence treaty. Greek Cypriots did not see it that way.

"I told the Council that the situation was...extremely dangerous and appealed to the parties to halt the battle...and cooperate with UNFICYP," Waldheim recalled.[75]

The Council called for an immediate cease-fire, but violations occurred in several areas within a few days. As the Turk troops neared the Nicosia International Airport, UNFICYP forces were moved in, as a precaution, to replace the Cypriot National Guard, a group led by Greek army personnel.

On July 24, 1974, while in Washington talking with US Secretary of State Kissinger, Waldheim and Sir Brian had a call from George Sherry, Sir Brian's assistant who was keeping watch on the Cyprus situation at UN headquarters. The message was that UNFICYP forces had been warned by the Turk army commander to withdraw from the airport by the next day or face an attack.

The Secretary-General told Sherry that UN forces must be told to hold their ground. He then quickly telephoned Turkey's prime minister, Bulent Ecevit.

"I couldn't afford to lose time—it was a decisive action I had to take," Waldheim recalled. "It was a very dangerous threat. I told [the prime minister] that if our forces were attacked, it will not just risk war. There will be bloodshed."[76]

Waldheim explained that the largely Greek Cypriot National Guard had turned the airport over to the United Nations on his assurance that it would not fall into Turkish hands. Ecevit seemed surprised, according to Waldheim, and said he would look into it. Within hours Ecevit reported that the issue was now settled and that UNFICYP would continue to hold the airport.[77]

Waldheim felt that the United Nations then became, by default, the custodian of Cyprus—"its orphan child."[78] Over the next several weeks he held talks with a number of Western ambassadors as well as Cypriot leaders about needed next steps.

Though Turkey's advance continued, Western powers were unwilling to pressure Turkey to stop its army.[79] Waldheim felt it was clear that the Turks were willing to use force to achieve their aim of two autonomous regions on Cyprus and that UNFICYP had too narrow a mandate to halt the advance.[80]

Indeed, in February 1975 the Turk Cypriots announced formation of a separate Turkish Federated State of Cyprus and elected Rauf Denktash as their president. By this time the Turks held 40 percent of the island in the north, a region that included 20 percent of Cyprus' population.[81]

The next month, after numerous calls for cease-fires and talks, the Council proposed new negotiations under the Secretary-General's personal auspices.

That started the process that Waldheim said took more of his time and attention than any other crisis during his term of office.[82] "For 10 years I labored for innumerable hours and with all the energy at my command to bring about a Cyprus settlement," he recalled.[83] When he made one of his numerous trips to the island in February 1977, the warring parties could not even agree on whether his plane should land in the ethnic Greek sector at Lanarca or in the

UN buffer zone at the Nicosia airport. So he landed in one and took off from the other.[84]

Certainly one factor in the continuing lack of willingness to compromise by either side was that little if any East–West pressure was being exerted. Cyprus was not high on the US–Soviet political docket as a major concern. Still, that gap gave Waldheim wider room to maneuver.[85]

A 10-point agreement was signed May 19, 1979, by Spyros Kyprianou, the Greek president of Cyprus, and Rauf Denktash, the Turkish Cypriot leader. The document outlined the basis for resuming talks. However, the negotiations ended abruptly a month later.[86]

Asked if Cyprus would go on forever as an unresolved issue, Waldheim said, "It should not, but it's a very tough question....We had a number of very reasonable proposals—like rotation of the presidency every two years and internationalizing institutions like the Nicosia Airport—but it's a psychological question. There's so much mistrust between the two sides."[87]

Sir Brian, who took part with Waldheim in many of the Cyprus-related trips and talks, said each negotiator felt the betrayals of the past, an almost certain formula for deadlock. He described the discussions as frustrating but, like a ship stabilizer, producing a certain balance even if they go round and round rather than forward.[88]

Waldheim also took a certain satisfaction in just keeping the parties talking and the fighting down. He viewed the United Nations as the essential catalyst in both efforts. Yet the question was always whether Cyprus should be a single state or a confederation of two substantially independent states.[89]

"The UN Cyprus operation is a holding operation," explained George Sherry. "It doesn't pretend to solve the problem. It seeks to control the situation and prevent escalation while efforts to find a solution go on."[90]

A New Term—Determined Quest

Waldheim announced his candidacy for a second term on October 12, 1976. It was an easy win some eight weeks later. The prevailing climate of East–West détente in the 1970s surely helped. So did Waldheim's careful cultivation of the nonaligned movement from the early days of his UN career.

Still, the emergence of other candidates and China's apparent wish that a viable third-world candidate would emerge spurred Waldheim to court the press and governments aggressively. "He seemed to be a man without real substance, quality, or character, swept along by an insatiable thirst for public office," recalled Sir Brian.[91]

The Secretary-General had little to worry about. China vetoed the first Council ballot but abstained on the second on December 7. On his last visit to the United Nations as US secretary of state (after the Democrat Jimmy Carter was elected US president), Kissinger, a Republican, told Waldheim, "Well, Kurt, you certainly manage your elections here much better than we manage ours in Washington."[92]

Rescuing Hostages in Africa

Before his reelection in 1976, Waldheim had experienced one hostage rescue in Guinea. He would soon have another in the Western Sahara.

The German government had asked him in March 1974 to intercede on behalf of three German development experts imprisoned in Guinea in West Africa. They were charged with taking part in a plot, albeit an unsuccessful one, to overthrow the government.

Guinea's Marxist President Sekou Toure met Waldheim at the airport and personally drove him to a stadium to see displays and a procession. Along the way, the President, one hand on the wheel, waved a white handkerchief in the other hand to the thousands lining the streets. Waldheim assumed the people were acting under instructions. At the stadium, the Secretary-General reported that he was appalled when the President pointed to a performer. He said she was dancing to show her gratitude for the fact that Toure had executed her husband, a traitor denounced by his own family.[93]

When the two men got to the topic of the German prisoners, Toure insisted that the three were guilty. He was not inclined to let them go.

He finally agreed on one condition: that the German government must send a letter accepting responsibility for the aborted coup.

Waldheim knew that delicate negotiations and far more ambiguous wording would be needed. He left behind his French press spokesman and career diplomat, Andre Lewin, asking him to find an acceptable formula. Lewin did so and later managed a similar exercise on behalf of 18 French citizens being held in Guinea under similar charges.[94]

While all of this was certainly a victory for UN mediation, Waldheim was even more pleased with his successful effort eventually to gain the release of eight French hostages in the Western Sahara in late 1977. Largely engineers, they had been working in Mauritania when they were seized by the Polisario Front, the Algerian-backed liberation movement, during fighting in the Western Sahara.[95]

Morocco and Mauritania, Western Sahara's neighbors to the north and south, had occupied the territory in 1975 after Spain ceded its former colony. The two nations wanted to divide and annex the nearby halves of Western Sahara. The General Assembly, however, affirmed the Saharan residents' right to self-determination and asked Waldheim to make the arrangements. Spain preferred a UN-run referendum and asked the Council that October to start talks among all parties.

Waldheim shuttled for a time among the various capitals, trying to resolve the political dispute, but the talks soon broke down, and he publicly bowed out. Thomas Franck, the international law scholar, termed it the correct response. "The Secretary-General is not a fire department, obliged to answer every alarm," he observed. Part of the job, in Franck's view, is to know "when to hoard and when to spend one's effectiveness."[96]

On February 27, 1976, the Polisario Front announced the territory's independence as the new Saharan Arab Democratic Republic. It was promptly recognized by Algeria.

Later the next year, after the eight French workers were seized, France asked the Secretary-General to help rescue them. Their capture had been aimed at pressuring France not to sell fighter planes to Morocco.[97]

Waldheim did not request or receive any UN authorization for his intervention in this hostage rescue effort.[98] He contended his authority to act was based on humanitarian grounds. Waldheim and a Polisario leader held a long series of negotiations in New York over many months. Agreement finally was reached that the hostages would be released personally to Waldheim. He flew to Algiers to pick them up, and they all flew off together on Christmas Eve to Paris where the anxious families were waiting.

"I will never forget the relatives who came to the airport," he said. "I saw those parents, tears in their eyes, receive their sons who were completely innocent but accused of sabotage. This was one of the most moving experiences in my life as Secretary-General."[99]

The Challenge in Lebanon, 1978

For more than 20 years the Israeli–Lebanese border had been relatively quiet. Inside Lebanon, a delicate balance between Muslims and Maronite Christians prevailed.

However, in 1970 the PLO had moved its headquarters and thousands of refugees from Jordan to Lebanon. In time, the PLO gained de facto control of the south. Border complaints from both Israel and Lebanon about raids by one side or the other led to several Security Council meetings in the early 1970s. These resulted in a few more UN observers being sent to the scene but little else. When a civil war broke out inside Lebanon in the mid-1970s, it was soon largely stopped by an Arab League force.

Meanwhile, Waldheim was trying to find ways to revive the Geneva peace talks on the Mideast. He made a personal visit to the region to press the point in February 1977. Yet the question of PLO participation remained a major stumbling block. Arab nations insisted the PLO must be represented. Israel was interested only if the PLO first publicly recognized Israel's right to exist.[100] Yasser Arafat, the PLO leader, ignored the request. He said he needed to know the agenda before agreeing to more talks.[101]

Finally, in a bold move on March 11, 1978, that would lead to much greater UN involvement in Lebanon, the PLO launched a major raid on the Israeli coast north of Tel Aviv. Two buses were hijacked, and 37 Israelis were killed.[102]

The Israeli response was massive. On March 14 its forces seized most of southern Lebanon below the Litani River. Only a small pocket near Tyre remained under PLO control.

The Council swung into action. Within a few days, it approved a US call for a cease-fire and immediate withdrawal of Israeli troops. President Carter was eager to avoid any possible upset to future Israeli–Egyptian peace talks. The Council also asked Waldheim to assemble a UN peacekeeping force of 4,000 to supervise the cease-fire and help restore Lebanon's sovereignty in the south. Like its two predecessors in the region, the UN Interim Force in Lebanon (UNIFIL) was to use force in self-defense only.

The task was not easy. Recruiting the troops was not the problem, according to Waldheim. The challenge was the vagueness of the mandate and the fact that this was not a fight between two states. Different armed groups held enclaves in southern Lebanon. There was no clear definition of UNIFIL's area of operation. Israel regarded the guerilla forces of the PLO as terrorists and was in no way eager to withdraw.[103]

Indeed, Israel never really accepted the UN mission, and UNIFIL did not prove effective.[104] In the end, UNIFIL suffered more casualties than any UN peacekeeping operation since the United Nations had intervened in the Congo.[105]

During the first week in April, Israel finally announced a two-step plan for withdrawal, making it clear that it did not yet feel that UN troops could protect Israeli forces. Waldheim condemned the delay and noted that the Council had called for an "immediate" Israeli withdrawal.[106] Yet he admitted that no air-tight protection guarantee to satisfy Tel Aviv was possible.[107]

To step up the pressure and clarify the situation, Waldheim made one more trip to the region in mid-April. He arranged to speak with the governments of Lebanon and Israel as well as with Arafat and UN troops. As he made the rounds, Israel insisted it was not yet safe for it to withdraw, and Arafat hinted that he could not control certain extremist elements within the PLO.[108]

As Waldheim approached the Palestinian refugee camp of Rachideye, en route to the UNIFIL base, a large protest against Israel was underway. Some young men immediately jumped onto Waldheim's car, beating their fists on the roof and doors and displaying undetonated grenades that looked like green golf balls.[109]

"It was an instructive and moving experience to have witnessed the bitter despair and the violence prevailing among the people," the Secretary-General recalled. "It is also sobering to see the quality and quantity of the weapons with which almost all of the men and women lining the road were armed."[110]

Waldheim and Sir Brian, who was traveling with him, were forced to take a helicopter to the UNIFIL barracks. When the plane picked them up for the trip, another angry crowd gathered, making threatening gestures. Guerillas fired shots from the ground as the UN team took off. "Fortunately there were no hits," Waldheim recalled.[111]

Arafat later told a UN employee that he was astounded at the security decision to allow Waldheim to go into the area. Arafat explained that an extremist Palestinian group had planned to kill Waldheim in an effort to discredit the PLO leader.[112]

In June, the Israelis withdrew from southern Lebanon. However, they turned over some of the land they had occupied to Christian militia groups who were opponents of the United Nations rather than directly to UNIFIL. Israel insisted the Christian groups were legitimate representatives of the Lebanese government.[113]

Cross-border attacks continued off and on for the next few years. UNIFIL, though bolstered by 2,000 more troops in May 1978, had difficulty stopping the attacks. Waldheim noted that many people in the Secretariat increasingly felt the force should be dubbed Mission Impossible. Even so, he argued, the UN troops prevented hundreds of infiltrations across the Israeli border and discouraged the outbreak of more general fighting.[114]

Meanwhile, in a much more positive vein, the long-planned peace talks between Israel and Egypt managed to make significant progress under US auspices. Negotiations began in the fall of 1978, and a peace treaty was signed in March 1979.

To Tehran and Back: "They Almost Killed Me There"[115]

Waldheim fully understood the challenge he faced in dealing with the US hostage crisis in Tehran. He took the risk anyway.

On November 4, 1979, an angry crowd seized the American Embassy in Iran and held 52 employees and diplomats hostage. Waldheim sent an immediate appeal to Ayatollah Khomeini, Iran's supreme ruler and the man with the final say on foreign policy. The Secretary-General urged him to order the hostages' quick release in accord with international law. There was no response.[116]

Within a few days, the Security Council formally condemned the seizure and demanded the hostages' release as well. Iran refused.

Waldheim then sent a message to the Council president on November 25 under his Article 99 authority to alert the Council to threats to global peace. He said the gravity of the US–Iran situation could have "disastrous consequences" for the entire world and requested a new Council meeting.[117]

On December 4, after a delay for "holy days" at Iran's request, the Council repeated its demand that the hostages be released and asked Waldheim to take "all appropriate measures" to implement its resolution.[118]

US ambassador to the United Nations Donald McHenry first broached the idea to Waldheim of a personal visit as the next positive step. The Secretary-General recalled, "It was a daunting prospect...indeed, I was full of foreboding. The mood in Tehran was clearly hysterical, with unpleasant undertones of ungovernable violence."[119]

Still, it was a "question of conscience" for him. He thought it was important to show the Iranian people that, as secretary-general, he was ready to make every effort to save the lives of the hostages.[120]

Waldheim met secretly several times with US Secretary of State Cyrus Vance to try to work out a plan that might prove acceptable to all sides. The Iranian revolution had unleashed citizen resentment against the United States for its decades of support for the shah, Mohammad Reza Pahlavi. More recently, President Carter had allowed the ailing shah to come to the United States for medical treatment. The Tehran government was adamant that he be returned to Iran for trial. Iran also insisted that the shah's property and assets be turned over to the government before any release of hostages could even be discussed.

Washington decided to hold off on its call for sanctions until after Waldheim's visit. On December 31 the Security Council approved the Secretary-General's mission. Like Hammarskjöld in the rescue of the American airmen in China, Waldheim made it known through a spokesman that his trip was based on the authority of his own office and not on that of any other UN organ.[121] He wanted to separate himself from the threat of sanctions that the Council had discussed. Though Iran tended to view the Council as a tool of the Americans, there was no sign that Tehran appreciated or was persuaded by Waldheim's careful distinction.[122, 123]

He boarded a plane that same day, stopping overnight in Paris. Just before midnight he phoned his daughter, Liselotte, who worked for the United Nations in Geneva. She said he sounded troubled. "Indeed, I was," he recalled.[124]

When he arrived at the Tehran airport on New Year's Day, 1980, he was met by Iran's foreign minister, Sadegh Ghotbzadeh, the man who had somewhat grudgingly told Waldheim over the phone two days before to visit Iran if he really wished to do so. Yet after Waldheim's arrival at the Iranian airport, Ghotbzadeh urged him to return to New York right away. He told Waldheim there was a group in Iran that was against his mission and that government security forces were not adequate to protect him. Waldheim said he was not going back.[125]

Ghotbzadeh, whom Waldheim described as depressed and almost embarrassed, warned the Secretary-General to stress publicly that he had come on a fact-finding rather than a negotiating mission.[126]

It was not an auspicious beginning. Mobs, angry at the United States and the United Nations were everywhere. On Waldheim's arrival, old news photos appeared of him, kissing the hand of the shah's twin sister, Ashraf, during a previous official visit. Split TV screens featured photos of Waldheim on one side and citizens suffering under the shah's brutality on the other.

The Secretary-General held several talks with Ghotbzadeh, but little progress was made. Waldheim was carrying a four-point proposal that Washington was willing to accept: a commission of inquiry to look into human rights violations and other illegalities under the shah, a willingness to let Iran work to recover the shah's assets through American courts in exchange for previous or simultaneous release of the hostages, and Iran's recognition of normal diplomatic immunity. The only item of major interest proved to be the commission.[127]

Waldheim's request to meet with Ayatollah Khomeini was never granted. The ayatollah had been quoted as saying of Waldheim, "I do not trust this man."[128] The Secretary-General was also never allowed to meet the hostages as a group, though he did meet privately with three separately detained diplomats.

Iran had its own agenda for Waldheim. First he was to visit a cemetery and lay a wreath on the graves of the "martyrs" who were victims of the shah's brutality. Though Ghotbzadeh again warned of rumors of an assassination plot by "foreign agents," Waldheim said he had not come to spend the time in a hotel.

They flew by helicopter and switched to a car to get to the burial sites. Within seconds, according to the Secretary-General, angry crowds there surrounded the car, jumped and pounded on the roof, and shouted. The driver swiftly reversed the car, and he and his aides managed to make it safely back to the helicopter, "by the skin of our teeth," Waldheim said.[129]

The next part of the visit was to a former officers' club, to meet some of those attacked and abused by the shah's secret police. Waldheim stayed an hour in the packed room amid, as he put it, "the crippled and blind and those missing arms or legs. They shouted, wept, and chanted as if on command as each in turn recounted his sufferings.... It was a shocking and distressing spectacle."[130]

His last ordeal was to meet with the Revolutionary Council of the Islamic Republic of Iran. He was driven at night to a Tehran park where a crowd of rough-looking men with submachine guns escorted him up the darkened stairs of a building that looked like an abandoned fortress. Ten members of the Revolutionary Council were sitting around three sides of a rectangular table. The atmosphere was that of a court. "They wanted us to be the accused, pleading our defense," Waldheim recalled.[131]

After stressing that the demonstrations he saw were not against the Secretary-General but against the United States, the chairman of the Revolutionary Council launched a tirade of familiar arguments, Waldheim recalled. The chairman insisted that the shah's extradition had to be part of the package and that the "students" guarding the hostages at the US Embassy had the full support of the Iranian people.[132]

Waldheim said he would convey the message to the Security Council. To bring the meeting to a close, he asked once again—without success—if he could see the ayatollah. Waldheim then left the Revolutionary Council and was surrounded by yet another angry mob.[133]

Throughout his visit, he felt there had been an orchestrated campaign to cast the United Nations as the servant of the Iranian royal family and an institution that ignored the suffering of the Iranian people.[134]

Waldheim returned to New York the next day, noting, "I'm glad to be back, especially alive."[135] At the time, he felt he had come back empty handed, except for Iran's interest in a commission of inquiry. He reported on his visit to the Security Council and briefed President Carter at the White House.

"If there was one experience in all my years at the top of the UN which proved the limits and frustrations of this job, it was that trip to Tehran," he recalled in *In the Eye of the Storm*, his memoir. "The Secretary-General...has no executive power," he wrote, adding that, "all his efforts...and the principles of international law are of little help if member governments disregard them."[136]

During that winter of 1979–80, a UN commission did collect information about Iran's grievances and alleged US misdeeds. A broadcast in Khomeini's name then demanded that the commission issue a statement on the shah's crimes and the history of US intervention in Iranian affairs. The broadcast stipulated that, after the Iranian people approved the information, it might be possible for the commission to visit the hostages. The commission decided, however, that it could do no more and returned to New York on March 12, 1980. Waldheim told the commission not to bother preparing a report. He said the enormous expense and effort involved had come to nothing.[137]

In desperation, the United States broke off diplomatic relations with Iran. President Carter launched his ill-fated helicopter rescue effort in April. US Secretary of State Vance immediately resigned. Three months later, the shah died in the United States.

Eventually, of course, the hostages were freed when Iran was ready to do so. Carter, no favorite of Tehran, lost his reelection to Ronald Reagan in Washington and the transition was about to occur. Muslim Algeria had kept a line of communication open to the Khomeini government and was chosen by Iran to mediate terms of the release. On January 18, 1981, Washington agreed to unfreeze Iranian assets in the United States and return them to Iran in exchange for the hostages.

The Americans were freed on January 20, 1981, 444 days after the hostages were seized. It was the day of Reagan's inauguration as the new president.

What made the crucial difference?

Certainly Iraq's invasion of Iran in September 1980 was a factor. Iran's new prime minister, Mohammed Ali Rajai, came to the United Nations that October to urge condemnation of Iraq for the invasion. Instead of invoking sympathy for Iran, widely seen as defying international law, he was greeted with reprimands and criticism.[138]

Waldheim felt that the UN visit, in light of Iran's more recent troubles, was an important turning point. He reported that Iran's prime minister was visibly shocked by the lukewarm reception he got from the West and the developing world. The Secretary-General concluded that Rajai then was apparently able to convince those in power in Tehran that the time had come to negotiate in earnest. "In two days of long talks with him," Waldheim recalled, "I made it clear that as long as Iran held hostages in the face of universal condemnation, he couldn't expect much support."[139]

Although readily conceding that his own trip was not successful, Waldheim insisted that it marked the beginning—particularly with the UN commission of inquiry—of the long negotiating process. "I conveyed to the Iranians for the first time the suggestions of the Americans," he said in the interview. "If you fail, you are always criticized [he laughed], but the main task is to save lives. This has priority."[140]

"I think Waldheim did something quite spectacular in going to Tehran," observed Leon Gordenker. "The mission wasn't well prepared. It was stupid in a lot of ways. But it was certainly one of those ways to push the secretary-general's role farther out. It's normal to try to extend the reach of the office."[141]

Certainly the media coverage stressed the fear factor.

"Waldheim was treated very badly," Sir Brian said. "He started off in a kind of Marx Brothers situation. Indeed, there was every indication they were going to humiliate him.... He did it [the trip] to try to help the United States. The United States needed to show that something was being done."[142]

Sir Brian added that one advantage of the United Nations in normal times is to provide a face-saving role that allows governments to shift positions. Yet, in his view, the United Nations in this case was dealing with a militant theocracy that did not see face saving as necessary.[143]

Trying to Stop the Iran–Iraq War

United Nations members had provided a needed wake-up call for Iran on the hostage crisis. Yet neither the organization nor Waldheim had much success early on in bringing the new war between Baghdad and Tehran to a close.

Iran and Iraq had long disagreed over their border lines and navigation routes in the Shatt al-Arab River. It was Iraq's only outlet to the open sea. The 1975 Algiers Accord, negotiated by the United Nations and accepted by both nations at the time, gave them joint sovereignty over the entire waterway.

However, Iraq later renounced the treaty. On September 22, 1980, when Iran's revolutionary fervor was at an all-time high, Iraq's president, Saddam Hussein, decided the time was right for an attack to reassert his own border claims. The invasion was widely seen as a clear violation of Iran's sovereignty. Yet no nation in the Security Council made a move to criticize Iraq or try to stop the war.

"It was impossible to avoid the conclusion that members of the Security Council, under strong Iraqi pressure, were sitting on their hands, hoping that the Iraqi victory would be quick and total," noted Sir Brian.[144]

Ayatollah Khomeini vowed full-scale resistance against Iraq. Iraq said it would accept a cease-fire and talks but that its territorial claims must be met.[145]

Waldheim, who offered his good offices almost immediately, urged the Council to hold informal consultations, a practice that had become more frequent in recent years than formal public meetings.[146] After the talks, the Council president issued a relatively bland statement supporting Waldheim's good-offices effort and urging both governments to solve their dispute peacefully.

Finally, six days after Iraq's invasion, the Council unanimously called for a cease-fire in place. But the Council did not condemn Iraq for its action nor demand its withdrawal. Iran vehemently rejected the resolution as biased toward Iraq and refused to deal with the Council again during the next eight years while the war continued.[147]

Over the next few weeks, Waldheim tried to get both sides to agree to let foreign ships depart that had been trapped on the river during the fighting. The two nations agreed to free 63 such ships and exchange prisoners of war.[148]

Other mediation efforts, however, made little progress. Waldheim favored a cease-fire followed by troop withdrawal and negotiations. Iran insisted that Iraqi troops must withdraw before any talks could be held.

The two nations were at an impasse. Olaf Palme, a former Swedish prime minister appointed by Waldheim as his special representative in the dispute, made several trips to the region from 1980 to 1982. Though several other nations and the Conference of Islamic states also tried to mediate, they had even less success than the United Nations.[149]

Timing played a role. Waldheim's effort to bring the parties together under Palme was both too late and too early, argued international law scholar Thomas Franck. The fighting was already well underway, he said, and the parties were not exhausted enough to stop.[150]

"The fact was that no negotiating process could curb a war in which the egos and mutual hatreds of the two leaders were decisive factors," noted Sir Brian.[151]

The Council did not take the Iraq–Iran issue up again until 1982 when Javier Pérez de Cuéllar had replaced Waldheim.

Helping Refugees

Waldheim had somewhat more success in his efforts to protect the human rights of Vietnam War refugees during the last days of his second term.

Years of fighting on the Indo-Chinese Peninsula had taken an extreme toll in the exodus of refugees to neighboring countries whose capacity to absorb them was diminishing. British Prime Minister Margaret Thatcher urged Waldheim to get involved. He resisted at first, reasoning that he did not have the authority. Yet he soon decided to cut through the red tape.[152]

In a major personal initiative, Waldheim convened a 65-nation pledging conference in Geneva on Vietnamese refugees on July 20 and 21, 1979. It was very successful. He got a doubling of placement offers and some $190 million in new funds for resettlement centers.[153] He also negotiated an agreement with Hanoi that stopped forced departures of the so-called "boat people," largely ethnic Chinese. They were fleeing at the rate of about 70,000 a month. Many were drowned, robbed, or killed in the hectic rush. Under the new, more orderly and humane procedures worked out, the monthly exodus fell to about 10,000 refugees a month with far fewer casualties.[154]

That same year, the General Assembly asked Waldheim to use his good offices to negotiate Vietnam's withdrawal from Cambodia and promote democracy there. He made little progress. Thomas Franck noted that such turning to the secretary-general's mediating role, without careful thought, can diminish his effectiveness.[155]

Still, the plight of refugees—this time from Cambodia—was once again an area where Waldheim could make a solid contribution. The refugees were fleeing by the hundreds of thousands into Thailand. Relief organizations were not handling them in a well-coordinated way. This time, Rosalynn Carter, the first lady of the United States, who was just back from a visit to a Thai refugee camp, made a personal appeal to Waldheim to act. He appointed Sir Robert Jackson, a UN official from Australia, to set up a headquarters in Bangkok as his representative, a move that led to a dramatic improvement.[156]

Waldheim also organized a successful pledging conference on behalf of the Cambodian refugees. A former UN ambassador from Singapore, T. T. B. Koh said that "if the Cambodian nation has survived, it is due in no small part to the humanitarian relief operation started by" Waldheim.[157]

The refugee problem was also increasingly serious on the African continent. Political instability in newly independent nations, as well as tribal warfare and famine, were all fueling the problem. By 1981 there were an estimated five million displaced people in 18 countries. Waldheim again was asked to help organize a major aid effort. He asked the Assembly to authorize another conference in Geneva in April 1981. More than $550 million in aid was pledged.[158]

Hoping for a Third Term

The Soviet invasion of Afghanistan in late December 1979 heavily overshadowed the work of the last two years of Waldheim's second term.

On January 7, 1980, a Council call for a withdrawal of all foreign troops from Afghanistan was promptly vetoed by Moscow. The Council then passed the issue, by a majority procedural vote, over to the Assembly for consideration.

The Assembly asked Waldheim to find a solution that would preserve Afghanistan's sovereignty and political independence. He held a number of discussions with top leaders in the region, tapping the Peruvian diplomat, Javier Pérez de Cuéllar, as his personal representative on the issue in 1981. The choice not only eventually solved the problem of the Soviet withdrawal from Afghanistan but also that of finding Waldheim's successor.[159]

Waldheim definitely was eager to serve a third term as secretary-general. His extensive travel program in 1981 left no doubt that he was "hell bent" on winning one more term, according to Sir Brian. Waldheim's performance, as he "buttonholed, cajoled and wheedled everyone in sight," became a something of a joke in UN corridors. Ministers and diplomats came to dread the familiar grasp of the Secretary-General's hand on their elbows. Such blind ambition, in Sir Brian's opinion, showed a lack of both self-respect and concern for the United Nations' reputation.[160]

Waldheim was very conscious of the need to court Washington and Moscow. The two were quite ready to back him for a third term.[161] Rumors had surfaced by this time regarding his wartime record, but the United States and others made no effort to examine his files.[162]

China, though not dissatisfied with Waldheim, was ready to veto his selection in favor of a third-world candidate. The Secretary-General's chief opponent, as in the 1976 campaign, was Salim Ahmed Salim, the foreign minister of Tanzania. He had openly celebrated the defeat of the United States' two-China policy with Taiwan's ouster in 1971. Jeane Kirkpatrick, the US ambassador, was ready to veto him if he got the needed nine votes.[163]

Waldheim surmised later that China would have accepted a compromise in which the two men would split the five-year term.[164] However, both candidates were eventually persuaded to withdraw. The Council president at the time, Olara Otunnu of Uganda, conducted a straw poll to see which candidates had a real possibility of election without a veto. That list was led by Pérez de Cuéllar, a former ambassador to Moscow and Waldheim's special representative for Afghanistan.

A Mixed Record

Waldheim is largely remembered for his varied efforts to free hostages and to end the 1973 Middle East War.

When asked what he felt best about during his 10 years in the United Nations' highest post, he singled out the successful rescue of the hostages in the Western Sahara and the launch of Namibia on its road to independence. He said he also took great satisfaction in South

Africa's ultimate decision to abandon its apartheid policy. He said he was convinced that years of almost daily UN condemnation of the policy played a major role.[165]

In Namibia he and his colleagues were closely involved in working out what he said was still called "the Waldheim plan" for UN-supervised elections that led to independence.

"Of course it took many years and developed in phases," he said, "but the UN policy was very clear: colonialism was a thing of the past and has no place in our time."[166]

Academic analysts generally give Waldheim his highest marks for starting new Middle East peacekeeping efforts—particularly UNEF II on the Sinai Peninsula and UNDOF in the Golan Heights—which helped solidify the truce between Israel and Syria.

"Those two operations were the most important things he did," insisted Waldheim biographer Seymour Finger in an interview. "He provided an outline of how he proposed to proceed, and the Security Council accepted it.... It was done skillfully." A key reason, he said, was that records of the debate in the decade-old GA Committee on Peacekeeping Operations were carefully studied to see what the tolerance limits were of various delegations, including Washington and Moscow.[167]

"The Soviets were willing to accept things in practice that they wouldn't have accepted in principle—like the designation of a commander and giving him authority," Finger explained. "The United States accepted Polish troops [in the mix], marking the first use of East European troops [in UN peacekeeping]."[168]

Finger said that the UN research and the organization's proposed plan defused potential US–Soviet confrontation and established peacekeeping guidelines that helped pave the way for the peace agreement between Egypt and Israel.[169]

Waldheim is generally credited for his work in helping refugees in Bangladesh, Southeast Asia, and Africa. He was well aware of the conflict between the Charter's protection of national sovereignty and the United Nations' moral commitment to protect human rights. His view was that when a human rights issue reaches the "threshold of world conscience," a secretary-general has a right to intervene.[170]

Waldheim readily admitted to many ups and downs during his years in office, including several in the human rights realm. "I am very aware—much to my regret—that our endeavors merely scratched the surface, while the rule of injustice and terror still holds sway."[171]

Certainly his efforts on the Iran hostage crisis were a major disappointment to him.

"I thought it was extremely foolish of him to go," Sir Brian noted. "You're dealing with a bunch of loonies, and there was every indication they were going to humiliate him."[172]

Waldheim saw his chief role as mediator. He felt a secretary-general should always offer, but never force, intervention in a dispute. Successful mediation, he argued, must be wanted by all parties.[173]

"He tried to use his office to best effect, but there really weren't many possibilities," suggested James Sutterlin.[174]

"It's been said that Waldheim was a very ineffective secretary-general," observed veteran UN analyst and author Lawrence S. Finkelstein. Yet, "he used the secretary-general's right of intervention without Council authority.... He didn't abandon that concept of the secretary-general [role]."[175]

The multilateral approach of the United Nations was largely marginalized in the 1970s. Some analysts see it as a caretaker period. It was a time of numerous civil wars. US–Soviet relations were tense. Washington was skeptical and sometimes scornful of the United Nations.[176] The major powers preferred dealing with foreign policy issues outside the United Nations.

By 1975, in a radical shift in the balance of power, developing nations accounted for the majority of UN members. They wanted to see an end to South Africa's apartheid policy, more economic justice, and recognition of Palestinian rights. The anti-Western rhetoric in the Assembly heated up accordingly. The GA was no longer a safe refuge from a Council veto.

One consequence was the Assembly's passage of the "Zionism is racism" resolution. Israel and its defense had become a staple of US foreign policy. The resolution was deemed an attack on both the United States and Israel.

"It simply wiped out with one sweep one of the strongest elements of support for the UN—the Jewish elite on the [US] Eastern seaboard," Sutterlin said.[177]

Though the GA rescinded the resolution in 1991 and Israel never opposed his reelection, Waldheim was widely criticized for not working harder at the time of its passage to stop it. Some analysts feel he did the best he could to sidetrack it but just didn't have the needed diplomatic muscle. Stanley Meisler, in his book on the history of the United Nations, argued that maybe a smarter secretary-general with less World War II baggage might have dissuaded the Assembly but that "we will never know."[178]

Waldheim mostly supported the economic and political goals of developing nations. He was particularly pleased that, shortly before his 1971 election, Communist China replaced Taiwan in China's UN seat. He worked hard to cultivate third-world nations and often spoke of his native Austria as nonaligned and neutral. Waldheim, according to biographer James D. Ryan, was particularly proud of defining what came to be called North–South polarity.[179] The Secretary-General publicly deplored the growing gap between rich and poor.

Yet Waldheim wanted no enemies—particularly among the major powers.

"He didn't want to antagonize anyone because his main goal was to be reelected," Finger said. "He was an opportunist."[180]

William Schaufele Jr., a former deputy US representative to the United Nations from 1973–75, said, "We saw him sometimes as bending over backwards to submit to pressures he didn't have to. He probably thought he was establishing his credibility and had to take all views into account."[181]

In his book, *The UN Secretary-General from Cold War to the New Era*, Edward Newman wrote, "Waldheim did try to avoid confrontation and make friends. That contributed to his reputation of being vacuous and a sycophant."[182]

The Secretary-General was not considered an innovator or a particularly inspiring leader. However, those who worked with him say he was a man of great physical and mental stamina. He was energetic and tenacious in trying to resolve problems. Sir Brian recalled that traveling with Waldheim, as he often did, meant late nights, overcrowded schedules, and frequent last-minute dashes to the airport at dangerous speeds.[183]

"One of the very good things about him was that he was always ready to do difficult things, such as to make disagreeable telephone calls," Sir Brian said. "He was always prepared to give it a go."[184]

Waldheim also was a delegator, a practice his staff generally applauded.

"He would delegate and let you get on with it," Sir Brian added. "If what one did was right, he got the credit. If it was wrong, I got the blame."[185]

Finger said, "He did like the limelight. One of his frustrations was that he didn't get featured enough in the media."[186]

Waldheim made every effort to court the press and was often sensitive to media criticism. Yet as Secretary-General, he was always limited in what he could say.

"He seemed to believe that a good proposal or performance had no validity unless it was publicly reported," recalled Sir Brian, who said he urged the Secretary-General to just let his initiatives grow quietly. Waldheim's constant need for public recognition deprived his office of both dignity and mystery—two "essential" qualities, according to Sir

Brian. He said he once told Waldheim that if the Loch Ness monster came ashore and gave a press conference, it would never be heard of again. The Secretary-General did not get the point, Urquhart said.[187]

"He tried too hard with too little to say," Sir Brian added. "He had to resort to bland statements and clichés which bored the press.... He had a tendency to make off-the-cuff statements that he would later try to change."[188]

Waldheim clearly did enjoy the prestige of his office.

"Throughout his career, protocol was a refuge and when he reached the top, he expected full deference to his position," noted biographer Ryan.[189]

In July 1972, his first summer on the job, he accepted the donation of an elegant mansion near the United Nations as the secretary-general's permanent residence. He brought in expensive furnishings, silver and porcelain, and gifts from heads of state.[190]

Waldheim also felt that personally knowing another leader could make a crucial difference in how issues are resolved. "I was convinced that personal contacts were indispensable to success," he argued in *In the Eye of the Storm*.[191]

"He took that from Carlyle who said that history is the story of great men—that personalities are important," noted Finger.[192]

In talking about his various hostage rescue efforts, Waldheim cited a much later example while he was president of Austria after leaving the United Nations. Some 95 Austrians and Swiss, serving in a mix of jobs from secretaries to engineers, were taken hostage in Iraq before the 1990 war started. Their relatives, fearing the hostages would be used as human shields, appealed to him for help. They even came to his summer home, where he had just started a vacation.

"I was so deeply touched that I concluded I had to do something," he recalled. He had previously met Saddam Hussein. "I knew him, and he knew me.... I took the risk and flew to Iraq. We had long, endless negotiations, and I was able to rescue them from Saddam, who let them go free. I mention this only to give an example of how important personal knowledge is."[193]

All things considered, Waldheim felt that both he and the United Nations were somewhat sidelined during the 1970s. He thought most nations viewed his role as largely ceremonial. As an example, he cited being asked to give opening remarks at a 1975 Helsinki conference on European security, yet having no seat reserved for him during the meeting so that he might play a meaningful role.[194]

"I think he pretty keenly felt it [this period] was sort of a historic failure," Finger said. "Of course, it's a matter not wholly or even primarily in the secretary-general's control. It's a matter of circumstances."[195]

Edward Luck, a former president of United Nations Association of the United States of America (UNA-USA), said, "Waldheim was in many ways a Cold-War product. Austria itself was. I think he saw himself as caught in the middle and always recognized the relatively narrow channel within which to navigate.... He was really very skillful in playing the game of politics."[196]

Speaking of his frustration, Waldheim said, "The big powers have the veto and use it when it comes to their own interests. Kissinger has said with his usual bluntness that foreign policy is about national interests.... I can support that statement because I went through it again and again. As secretary-general, one of your tasks is to convince the parties in a conflict to take into account also, most of all, the interest of the international community in order to maintain peace."[197]

Waldheim almost made it to a third term.

The fact that he was a former officer in Hitler's army did not become public until 1986 during his run for Austria's presidency. It is a fact that still puzzles onlookers and grates on many who worked with him. For Sir Brian, it was "mortifying" to discover that he had spent a decade working intensively with and publicly defending a man who "deliberately" told lies about his past.[198]

"When he was being considered for an appointment, he should have said that he served in a subordinate capacity, and nobody would have given it further thought," suggested George Sherry. "He didn't go around killing people or shoving them into gas chambers. But he was involved, and he lied."[199]

Waldheim later admitted that he had been no hero and simply wanted to survive. He told Finger that he knew of an Austrian hanged from a tree by the Nazis simply for listening to the British Broadcasting Corporation (BBC).[200]

After leaving UN headquarters, Waldheim accepted an offer from Georgetown University to become a research professor of diplomacy and a counselor of its program in business diplomacy. During his time in Washington he also organized his files and worked on his memoirs. In 1983, he returned to Vienna and was elected president of Austria three years later.

Trygve Lie, August 1, 1949. UN Photo

Dag Hammarskjöld, June 1, 1959. UN Photo

U Thant, June 16, 1965. UN Photo/Yutaka Nagata

Kurt Waldheim, November 25, 1979. UN Photo/Milton Grant

Javier Pérez de Cuéllar, January 21, 1982. UN
Photo/Yutaka Nagata

Boutros Boutros-Ghali, December 11, 1996. UN
Photo/Evan Schneider

Kofi Annan, January 23, 2004.
UN Photo/Sergey Bermeniev

SECRETAIRE GENERAL

Ban Ki-moon, July 4, 2009. UN Photo/Mark Garten

CHAPTER SEVEN

Javier Pérez de Cuéllar: A Low-Key Peruvian Becomes an Effective Mediator

The ever-calm Javier Pérez de Cuéllar knew he was being considered as the United Nations' fifth secretary-general. However, he had made a firm decision not to campaign for the job. He wanted no part of the debts and commitments that could be involved.

He got the news of his election in a phone call after returning from an isolated beach house near Lima where he had gone with his wife, Marcella, for rest and reading.

He was clearly a compromise choice. The Security Council had been deadlocked on the issue for more than six weeks. In the process, some 16 vetoes had been cast. Finally, in a secret straw poll of several possible choices, Pérez de Cuéllar emerged as the only one who would not be vetoed by one of the five permanent members.

The Council elected him on December 11, 1981, and the General Assembly unanimously approved the choice four days later. The new Secretary-General noted in his memoir that his election was greeted with widespread relief, an outcome he attributed partly to exhaustion and partly to members' desire to adjourn for Christmas.[1]

Pérez de Cuéllar was widely viewed as capable and polite but a man with zero charisma. "I was not considered...an exciting choice for the job," he admitted.[2]

One of his biographers insisted that he had a gray personality and a speaking style that lulled audiences to sleep.[3] Some UN members even wondered if he were tough enough for the job. They worried that, like Waldheim, he might be more concerned with the pomp of the post rather than with its potential power.[4]

Yet in many ways, Pérez de Cuéllar was born to the job. His ties with the UN dated back to 1946 when he was a Peruvian delegate to the UN Preparatory Commission in London. "I sensed the spirit of hope that pervaded the Commission meetings," he recalled.[5]

He was a lawyer and longtime diplomat. He was also a man from the developing world who happened to be sophisticated, cultured, and multilingual. French was his second language, and he had a special fondness for French literature. "Maybe in an earlier existence I was a Frenchman—a musician or an artist," he wrote in his memoir. He also enjoyed reading Spanish and Latin American authors. He said he learned English from a Polish speaker, whom he blamed for his pronunciation problems.[6]

He was only four years old when his father, a prominent Lima businessman, died, and he was brought up with two cousins by relatives in a comfortable, conservative family. He had access to superior schools, studying both law and literature.

In a sense, Pérez de Cuéllar began his diplomatic career while still in law school, serving as a $50-a-month clerk in Peru's Ministry of Foreign Affairs. After earning his law degree in 1944, he joined the diplomatic service as a third secretary in Peru's embassy in Paris. It was there that he acquired his well-known taste for French cuisine and fine wines. In time, he served as ambassador to Switzerland, the Soviet Union, Poland, and Venezuela.

While Peru's ambassador to the United Nations from 1971 to 1975, he served twice as the rotating president of the Security Council. It was here that his mediating skills came to the attention of Kurt Waldheim, the secretary-general at the time, who tapped him in 1975 as his Special Representative to Cyprus. Pérez de Cuéllar recalled in his memoir that it was his first experience as an international civil servant. He later realized he would be dealing with that island issue for the next 17 years—"not without considerable frustration."[7]

In February 1979, Waldheim raised Pérez de Cuéllar's status to undersecretary-general for special political affairs. Waldheim often invited him to his office at the end of the day for a quiet discussion of current problems.[8] Then in April 1981, Pérez de Cuéllar became Waldheim's personal representative in Afghanistan. His mission, to see if the United Nations could negotiate a Soviet withdrawal, resulted in no breakthrough at that point. However, George J. Lankevich argued in his biography of the Secretary-General that the experience helped earn the Peruvian the respect that eventually elevated him to the United Nations' top job.[9]

Sir Brian Urquhart, who knew the new Secretary-General well, noted that he was generally quiet but had "excellent ideas of his own and no inhibitions about sticking his neck out." He also had a preference for short, decisive conversations and was uninterested in his public image, according to Sir Brian.[10]

The new Secretary-General was liked and respected by both the Secretariat and UN diplomats. Jeane Kirkpatrick, a former US ambassador to the United Nations, usually sparse in her praise of anyone, described him as "a man of great intelligence, high integrity...an unusually fair, reasonable, decent man."[11]

Managing and leading the Secretariat was an important part of the new post. Yet the Secretary-General was well aware that his administrative experience was limited. "He was most hesitant about that part of the job," confirmed James Sutterlin, a former senior aide.[12]

Before leaving the Lima airport for the United States on December 17, 1981, the newly elected Secretary-General told reporters that his first goal was to restore the morale of the UN bureaucracy, by then a group of about 15,000.

Though he later admitted to feeling political pressure to make certain appointments, he wrote in his memoir that the Secretariat was often unjustly criticized as lazy, overpaid, and even corrupt. On the contrary, in his view, most staff members were gifted, committed, and impartial hard workers who were sometimes overqualified for their tasks.[13]

When the new Secretary-General arrived in New York, he lived for several weeks at the Waldorf-Astoria until, as Sir Brian put it, Waldheim "reluctantly" moved out of the official UN residence on Sutton Place.[14] When Pérez de Cuéllar did move in, he brought with him his continuing love of music, art, and literature. Sutterlin described him as a man of "enormous esthetic sensitivity" who "reacted very strongly to beautiful things."[15]

William Luers, a former American ambassador and president of the United Nations Association of the United States of America (UNA-USA), said, "There was a well-educated, intellectual European approach to his appreciation." The men met each other when they were ambassadors to Venezuela.[16]

The Secretary-General liked doing his UN paperwork in the book-lined fourth-floor study of the townhouse where he could listen to recordings of Beethoven string quartets.[17] He kept three classical music stations on automatic dial on his radio, noting he had always been "surrounded by music."[18]

In his new official capacity, he found he had some 31 senior officials reporting to him, a situation Urquhart described as "hopeless." The Secretariat, he argued, had become "fat and flabby," and its civil service standards, so carefully guarded at the start, had eroded.[19]

The Secretary-General himself noted that the Soviet Union, like other Communist nations of the time, required its nationals serving in the Secretariat—all on temporary assignment—to turn over major portions of their salaries to the Soviet government. During the Cold War, their first loyalty clearly was to Moscow.[20]

In time, Pérez de Cuéllar developed a comfortable working relationship with a group of about 10 staffers and met regularly with them.

"He depended very heavily on a small but influential staff who, generally speaking, developed positions to be taken in mediation—and in many cases carried them out," recalled James Sutterlin.[21]

Unlike his predecessors, Pérez de Cuéllar began to make a regular habit of attending Security Council sessions and consultations.

"He always had time to go to meetings and receive less important members of the Security Council," noted Sutterlin. "He really extended himself to do that...and was able to maintain [member] confidence. Publicly, he appeared to be a very cautious person, and he was. On the other hand, when crises arose...he was able to bring Council members quietly around.... They liked him— partly because he'd been a permanent representative [to the UN] before."[22]

"He was going all the time," recalled Giandomenico Picco, the Italian UN staff member who served as a close aide. "His strength [in informal Council sessions] was that he was making proposals all the time—on substance.... If nobody knew how to react, he'd say, 'O.K., I take it that it's fine.' He did that all the time. That's the way we [the staff] would go right ahead [with what he'd proposed]."[23]

Joe Sills, a former spokesman for the Secretary-General said in an interview: "Pérez is a very sharp person. He was quiet and had sort of a laid-back manner. He would never be confrontational.... He really did take very seriously [the concept] that he was the servant of the member states."[24]

Indeed, in his memoir, *Pilgrimage for Peace*, Pérez de Cuéllar was firmly against any "kiss and tell" approach. "Anytime I wrote any- thing critical," said Sutterlin, who wrote much of the book's draft, "he took it out—even though I knew he felt that way."[25]

The Climate of the 1980s

Pérez de Cuéllar took on his new job during the coldest days of the Cold War when the United Nations was discredited and widely attacked. The Council was unable to respond effectively to threats to peace and seemed to lack a clear sense of direction.

In Washington, the new Reagan administration was eager to reduce US multilateral commitments. Some in Congress, in Pérez de Cuéllar's view, acted as if the UN headquarters served mainly as an outpost for the Soviet KGB. The United States put strict travel limits on Soviet members of the Secretariat.[26]

"When Reagan came in, conservative think tanks began to have an influence on United States foreign policy," noted Fred Eckhard, a former spokesman for several UN secretaries-general. "Ironically, the United Nations was raised to a level of significance it hadn't had previously [Washington had largely ignored the organization in the Waldheim years].... Conservatives would say, 'We have to decide whether to get the US out of the UN or get the UN out of the US.'"[27]

In a speech to the Council on Foreign Relations a few weeks after Pérez de Cuéllar took office, Jeane Kirkpatrick called the UN an important organization but not the one that its founders had hoped for. She said the UN process "breeds polarization."[28]

The new Secretary-General found the critical attitude of the US government and some of the media "profoundly disturbing," since he viewed the United States as the most important member of the United Nations and its support and leadership as crucial. He said the real problem was that Washington was consistently in the minority on such high-profile issues as the Middle East and the US military invasions in Panama and Grenada, as well as on the budget. Indeed, the most "virulent" effect of the US criticism, in his view, was on the UN budget.[29]

Washington withheld major portions of its assessment. Later, the United States held back some of its peacekeeping obligations and deferred all payments until the last quarter of the UN fiscal year.

Yet few anti-UN barbs were aimed at the Secretary-General himself. His previous experience, for instance, as Peru's ambassador to Moscow, seemed to have left a favorable and lasting impression on Soviet diplomats. He mentioned in his memoir that he was always warmly received by Soviet leaders, even when a controversial topic of discussion such as Afghanistan was not of their choosing.[30]

Immediately after his election, Pérez de Cuéllar began to compile a survey of conflicts and points of tension and an assessment of the global economic and social situation. The Iran–Iraq War was in its second year, the Soviet Union was occupying Afghanistan, Israel and the Palestinian Liberation Organization (PLO) were in a virtual state of war, and US–Soviet relations were at a major low point.

The combination of Cold-War antagonism and the cumbersome mechanics of Council and Assembly proceedings took a certain toll on the Secretary-General's own mediation efforts. The prevailing climate made it difficult for him to establish a sense of credibility and play a substantive role in peace efforts.

Edward Newman, Director of Studies on Conflict and Security at the United Nations University in Tokyo and prolific author on UN issues, has noted that many of the conflicts that arose during Pérez de Cuéllar's first term were tied to outside historical trends. Essentially, Newman argued, the Secretary-General had to wait until there were changes in the "external dynamics."[31]

Pérez de Cuéllar's many frustrations erupted in a remarkably candid first annual report to the Assembly in September 1982. Pointing to an "alarming succession of international crises and stalemates," he said the Council was too often powerless to act decisively. Even when resolutions were unanimous, he said, they were often defied or ignored. The report noted that most countries with conflicts didn't even bother to take their troubles to the Council. Thus, he argued, the secretary-general must take a stronger preventive role. He warned that the world was dangerously near a "new international anarchy."[32]

Later, he admitted that *anarchy* was really an overstatement since most governments were beginning to face the need for better joint planning in such areas of common interest as population, environment, and development.[33]

In that first annual report to the Assembly, he argued that the Council must play a more forthright role and urged a thorough study of why some nations were so reluctant to use UN machinery in conflicts.[34] The report and his suggestions for strengthening the United Nations were discussed for more than two years without much effect. In Sir Brian's view, only a complete change of heart among the five permanent members or a devastating international crisis could change Council ways.[35]

Crisis in the Falklands

The first new international challenge on Pérez de Cuéllar's watch concerned Argentina's claim of sovereignty over the Falkland (Malvina) Islands.

Though these 200 treeless islands were once widely recognized as Argentine, they had been seized by the British in 1833. Argentina periodically challenged the British claim. Argentine protests became increasingly vigorous after 1965 when the General Assembly first considered the issue and urged its peaceful resolution.

A few months after Pérez de Cuéllar took office, the junta then ruling Argentina decided to stake its claim militarily. On April 2, 1982, some 5,000 Argentine troops, more than twice the number of the islands' inhabitants, invaded the Falklands at dawn and quickly took over.

Sir Anthony Parsons, Britain's ambassador to the United Nations, promptly introduced a resolution in the Council, calling on Argentina to withdraw immediately and begin negotiations. The resolution passed by a narrow margin. Argentina ignored it, insisting that its longtime claim to sovereignty was legitimate.

US Secretary of State Alexander Haig opted to act as mediator and launched four rounds of shuttle diplomacy between Buenos Aires and London. However, Argentina rejected his proposals. He cancelled his efforts after a few weeks. Washington then began to publicly support the British position and offered intelligence and technical aid to British troops. By April 30, the British had imposed a blockade on the Falklands.

Pérez de Cuéllar, watching the varied efforts discreetly from the sidelines, moved into the diplomatic vacuum. Though he had no specific authorization from the Council, in early April he established a Falklands crisis team in the Secretariat to consider UN options.[36]

In his 38th floor office at the United Nations, he conducted some 30 negotiating sessions with the British ambassador to the United Nations and Argentina's deputy foreign minister. Meetings were often held twice a day, including weekends.[37] The Secretary-General, cautiously optimistic, proposed a plan that would include an interim UN administration on the islands. However, both sides had developed vocal popular support by this time, making any retreat from their stated positions extremely difficult. By May 20, the Secretary-General announced that his negotiating effort was at an end.

The very next day Britain invaded the islands. Argentina finally surrendered on June 14. The humiliation forced the military junta in Buenos Aires to resign. The Organization of American States (OAS) condemned the British assault. A similar resolution in the Council was vetoed by Washington and London.

The war had been costly and its value questionable. Legally, Britain could claim that it had been a victim of aggression and had simply resorted to self-defense under Article 51 of the UN Charter. Indeed, many UN members supported that view, since Argentina was the first to use force.[38]

Noting that the dispute had been aptly described as "two bald men fighting over a comb," Sir Brian insisted that it was a mere "white elephant" gain for Britain. In his view, the war should never have been fought.[39]

Some close observers, including Pérez de Cuéllar himself, argued that if only he had become involved earlier in the dispute, the war might have been averted. In his memoir, he wrote, "The shortness of time was a fatal enemy." He said he had no criticism of Haig's tactics but did have reservations about the time those mediation efforts took and Haig's failure to keep him informed of their progress.[40]

Still, the Secretary-General generally earned praise for the skill and persistence of his mediation efforts during the Falklands episode.

"I actually think this was the Secretary-General at his best...his finest hour," James Sutterlin said. He noted that Pérez de Cuéllar wisely kept the Council informed but did not involve it in the process, assuming that would not be helpful. Sutterlin argued that both nations changed their views of the Secretary-General during the negotiations. The British government's initial wariness of having a Latin American do the mediating evolved into genuine respect for the UN leader. Argentina, on the other hand, began to view him as "overly neutral."[41]

In his memoir, Pérez de Cuéllar called the Argentine invasion "a tragic and misguided act of an inept military government."[42]

Though he intervened at the last minute, his determined efforts almost succeeded, in the view of Thomas Boudreau, author of *Sheathing the Sword*, a book focused on the preventive role of UN secretaries-general. Boudreau noted that a UN diplomat told him in confidence that the British government stiffened its bargaining position late in the game and that Argentina viewed this "final position" as a "stab in the back."[43]

Was a diplomatic solution ever really possible? Certainly the dispute was not embroiled in the Cold War. Patriotic fervor, however, was high. The initial military battle on the high seas had led to a heavy loss of life, particularly for Argentina.

Some observers argued that both sides may simply have been seeking diplomatic cover to save face. As it was, the Secretary-General could offer few, if any, carrots or pressures to induce a compromise. Both sides seemed firmly locked into their positions.

Álvaro de Soto, a fellow Peruvian and one of Pérez de Cuéllar's senior colleagues, said that the Argentine junta's need to take unanimous decisions—involving perhaps 80 to 100 people with no clear leader—was the crux of the problem. "They had to agree in consultations with the people below them," he said. "The dynamics of demagoguery and patriotism were completely out of control. The die was cast."[44]

After the war, the Assembly asked the Secretary-General to resume his good-offices role in the dispute. Yet Argentina and Britain eventually reestablished diplomatic relations. The Secretary-General dropped his effort to remain involved.

New Tension along the Israeli–Lebanese Border

It was virtually a no-win situation for the United Nations and Pérez de Cuéllar right from the start.

The Camp David accords and the 1979 Israeli–Egyptian peace treaty had fueled a certain amount of optimism in the region. However, rising friction and back-and-forth attacks between Israel and the PLO, then well-entrenched in southern Lebanon, posed an increasingly serious challenge.

In early June 1982, just six months into Pérez de Cuéllar's term, the situation exploded with a fresh intensity. On June 3, Israel's ambassador to Britain was seriously wounded in a PLO assassination attempt. The next day, Lebanon's ambassador to the United Nations told the Council that the Israelis had launched nine successive bombing raids on Beirut.[45] The PLO sent rockets and artillery fire in return.

Though the UN Interim Force in Lebanon (UNIFIL) was stationed in the south, it was largely ignored during the border battles. Its only weapons were the neutrality of its presence and its efforts to defuse tensions. As Urquhart, former head of UN peacekeeping operations, noted, "A peacekeeping operation is not intended to fight the army of a member state, and it is neither equipped nor authorized to do so."[46]

On June 6, Israel invaded Lebanon in force, despite a public appeal for a cease-fire made the day before by the Secretary-General. In a unanimous vote on the day of the invasion, the Council urged an immediate end to all fighting and an unconditional withdrawal of all fighting forces.

It was not to be—at least for some time. Within days the Israelis had taken over several PLO strongholds and moved into central Beirut.

Pérez de Cuéllar wrote to Israel's prime minister, Menachem Begin, urging him to do all he could to end hostilities. On August 1, the Council passed Resolution 516, demanding a cease-fire and authorizing Pérez de Cuéllar—if Lebanon requested—to send UN observers to monitor the situation around Beirut. Lebanon and the PLO agreed.

However, the small UN observer group was unable to get through Israeli lines to Beirut's center. Though from the start the UN officials tried to persuade both sides that they were better off with a UN than a non-UN presence, Israel strongly preferred a non-UN multinational force to do any monitoring.

Finally, on August 6, the PLO agreed to leave Beirut peacefully. The United States drew up a plan for assistance and monitoring by a non-UN force of Americans, British, French, and Italians. By September 1, some 10,000 PLO (and 3,500 Syrian) soldiers had left Beirut.[47]

Still, the war did not end. Lebanon's president, Bachir Gemayel, was assassinated on September 14, just weeks after taking office. In retaliation, the Christian militia, which he had headed and which was closely allied with Israel, launched a number of fierce attacks on unprotected Palestinian refugee camps in Beirut's southern suburbs. The Council strongly condemned the attacks and called for an increase in the size of the small UN observer group.

Washington helped to work out a May 1983 Lebanese–Israeli agreement on force withdrawals and a continued Israeli security role in south Lebanon. However, the agreement depended on a withdrawal of Syrian troops as well, and Syria rejected it. Attacks continued against the Lebanese government, Israel, and the multinational forces viewed as supporters of Lebanon's pro-Western government.[48] That fall, some 241 US Marines stationed in Beirut were killed in a suicide bomb attack.

The General Assembly in December 1983 called for a global peace conference on the Middle East, saying the PLO must be invited and authorizing the Secretary-General to make arrangements. Pérez de Cuéllar said he knew that Israel would not accept the proposal, and it did not.[49] Nonetheless, in June 1984, he set out on a five-capital tour of the region, reminding leaders of the importance of a settlement and offering UN help.[50] For the time being, there were no takers.

It was a discouraging time both for the Secretary-General and the Secretariat. The Cold-War alliances had been clearly drawn. Both Washington and Moscow had worked to protect their respective allies—Israel and the PLO—against any UN actions they deemed unfair. Pérez de Cuéllar wrote that at the beginning of his first term, he felt that developments in the Middle East, more than anywhere else, could threaten world peace because the opponents were so closely linked to Moscow and Washington.[51]

"I was continuously involved and personally determined, from a humanitarian as well as a political point of view, to do everything possible to end the horror," he said. Noting that he met all of the "protagonists," he wrote that he was appalled by their "dubious judgment" and shocked by the "disregard for human life" shown in their actions.[52]

The Secretary-General was generally credited for his persistence and diplomatic skill and for keeping a low political profile. Yet his influence was mostly confined to managing UN peacekeepers and providing relief programs for Palestinian refugees.[53] The United Nations and its top official largely had to watch from the sidelines.

"Impartiality Is...the Heart and Soul of the Office of the Secretary-General"[54]

Although Pérez de Cuéllar's first term was nearing an end without significant accomplishments, he clearly understood the importance of his role and his mission. In a widely quoted speech at Oxford University on May 13, 1986, he spoke frankly about the loneliness and occasional helplessness he felt in the job, the pressures on his office, and about the careful balancing act required of him.

In warning the Council of potential threats to world peace, he said that his obligation under Article 99 is, first, to assess whether raising the issue might aggravate the situation if the Council chose to do nothing about it. He said he must also weigh just how far the issue could be insulated from great-power rivalries. To do that task properly, he said, requires a better system of getting timely information.

In his own good-offices work, the Secretary-General said that, unlike traditional diplomacy, where stability and speed are often aims, his quiet multilateral diplomacy must be geared to getting a just and lasting settlement. The fears of each party must be addressed with empathy and imagination, he said. The secretary-general must avoid judging the moral worth of each party's stance by what leaders or the media of one nation say about the position of the other. The need, he said, is to remain flexible and exercise "unlimited patience and an unfailing sense of justice and humanity." Each secretary-general must develop a sense of belonging to every nation or culture "because all world problems are his problems," he said. The Charter's principles are "his moral creed."

He noted that, at the time of the Oxford lecture, he was the only channel of communication between the parties in the Afghanistan conflict, the continuing Iran–Iraq War, and in the Cyprus and South Lebanon situations. With the exception of Lebanon, the other conflicts persisted into his second term.

Though Pérez de Cuéllar insisted that his administrative role was as important as his political role, he said his powers in that area had steadily eroded. He noted in particular government pressures on Secretariat appointments, adding that it would be a "refreshing change" if governments gave him needed flexibility.

Beyond his political and administrative responsibilities, the United Nations' top official should do what he could to help bring relief to victims of oppression and disaster, he said. He mentioned that at the end of his first year in office in December 1982, he was asked by the new president of Bolivia to use his good offices to mobilize global financial support to ease that nation's serious inherited financial and social problems. He appointed a Special Representative to Bolivia, convened several special UN meetings, and helped establish a special emergency fund.

Pérez de Cuéllar told his Oxford audience that the secretary-general's role should enhance rather than reduce the role of the Council. He said the Council had the primary responsibility to maintain world peace and that his efforts must not become an "alibi" for Council inaction. "The secretary-general is, after all, a collaborator of the Security Council, not its competitor," he said.

He urged those who saw the United Nations as a safety net to push for a much more vigorous defense of the organization: "The UN needs its champions. They must speak more boldly and knowledgeably."

With a clearer sense of the breadth of his role, he agreed to a request several weeks later to arbitrate a dispute in the case of the *Rainbow Warrior.*

Arbitrating a Sunken-Ship Dispute

France and New Zealand had been in a war of words for almost a year after two French agents planted explosives on the Greenpeace ship, *Rainbow Warrior*, and sunk it in July 1985 in an Auckland, New Zealand, harbor.

Greenpeace had planned to use the ship to demonstrate against French nuclear testing in the Pacific. France's defense minister was forced to resign over the incident. New Zealand arrested the French agents and sentenced them to 10-year prison terms. Paris was insisting that the agents be released and threatened to tighten quotas on New Zealand's agricultural exports to the European Community.

A Dutch photographer was killed in the incident, and the Dutch government finally suggested that the two nations ask the UN Secretary-General to arbitrate the differences between them. They did so on June 19, 1986, and agreed that his decision would be binding.

The two nations outlined in writing what parts of the problem they had resolved and listed the points still in dispute. Pérez de Cuéllar sent written questions to both parties and produced specific proposals to which they agreed on July 6, 1986.

His decision as arbiter called for a formal apology by France for the sinking and asked for compensation of $7 million dollars to New Zealand. The ruling also called for release of the two French agents and their assignment for three years to the isolated French island of Hao in Polynesia. In turn, France agreed not to try to restrict New Zealand's trade with the European Community.

In fact, despite agreement that the ruling would be binding, not all parts were implemented. The French agents, for instance, were allowed to return home before the three-year island stay expired.

Still, the Secretary-General's intervention allowed both sides to save face. Although there were critics of the settlement in both countries, the agreement proved more acceptable in the view of international legal scholar Thomas Franck, "precisely because of its unimpeachable source" than if they had continued to try to agree on their own. This way, neither government could be accused of yielding to the other.[55]

A First Term Plagued by the Cold War

Cold-War tensions were at an all-time high during the Secretary-General's first term. US President Reagan blasted the Soviet Union as "the evil empire." The United States also sharply denounced the Russians in the Council in 1983 for shooting down a civilian Korean airliner that mistakenly flew too near to a Soviet submarine base. All aboard were killed, including 69 Americans, but Moscow refused to admit the error. President Reagan called it an act of barbarism by a society that had no respect for human life.[56]

The Soviets were equally combative on other issues. With respect to the United Nations, Moscow insisted that Washington was failing in its responsibilities as host nation. Charles Lichtenstein, a member of the US delegation to the United Nations, said during a UN committee meeting that if the United Nations chose to leave New York City, the US mission to the United Nations would be at the dock to wave farewell as it sailed into the sunset.

Under the circumstances, some analysts saw the Secretary-General's role as coming out ahead of the other organs in the internal UN power struggle. The General Assembly could make more noise and the Security Council could get TV attention, but to the extent that the United Nations was having "any salutary effect on the real world," according to Thomas Franck, it was largely because of tasks performed by the Secretary-General.[57]

Certainly Pérez de Cuéllar himself was discouraged at this midpoint in his UN service. He said both in his memoir and in his 1986 annual Assembly report that he could not point to one conflict that the United Nations had successfully resolved during his first five years.[58]

"My impression is that his role during the Cold War was almost more internal," suggested Hurst Hannum, an international law scholar at the Fletcher School of Law and Diplomacy at Tufts University. "He was more of an administrator because there wasn't much else that he could do, unless very quietly."[59]

One thing the Secretary-General clearly hoped to do was play a stronger preventive role in potential conflicts. Near the end of his first term, he established on his own initiative the Office for Research and the Collection of Information (ORCI). The aim was to strengthen staff analysis of current issues to give him a more effective early warning system by which to alert the Council. Though the office was not managed well and was later dissolved by his successor, it was considered a major reform at the time.[60]

By the end of his first term, the Secretary-General felt he had learned much about the United Nations' inner workings and the organization's potential. He concluded that the United Nations was probably of most value to smaller nations, especially former colonies for whom membership was a stamp of legitimacy.[61] Yet he also urged third-world nations to put their own economic houses in order before asking the rest of the world for help.[62]

By the mid-1980s, the UN was facing a major economic crisis of its own. Even though the Secretary-General had cut expenses by about $30 million a year, the United Nations was literally on the brink of bankruptcy by the end of 1986.[63]

Based on a percentage of national income, the seven richest nations had been paying some 70 percent of UN general expenses. When the two-year UN regular budget for 1982–83 had been drawn up, Washington, London, and Moscow strongly protested to the Secretary-General that total expenses were too high. By the 1984–85 budget, 25 members withheld part of their assessments.

As the wealthiest member, the United States was paying 25 percent of the UN budget. Many in Congress were strong critics of the United Nations and felt the US share was too high and that the third-world majority had too much power in deciding how the money should be spent. In 1985, a US Senator, Nancy Kassebaum, a Republican from

Kansas, introduced an amendment to the State Department funding bill that became law. Terming the United Nations no longer a "sacred cow," she called for a cap of 20 percent on US contributions to international organizations.

In response to the continuing budget crisis, the General Assembly established a high-level panel of expert government representatives in 1986. It was known as the Group of 18 and included the five permanent Security Council members. They met 67 times. The report they issued advised a major cut in staff positions, particularly at upper levels, more consolidation of departments, and a ban on rehiring retired staff as consultants.[64]

By 1988, well after Pérez de Cuéllar's election to a second term, the US debt from unpaid UN treaty obligations reached $500 million. While Washington was in default, some other UN members managed to pay up old debts.

The Secretary-General addressed the Assembly twice on the emergency and met personally with President Reagan on the issue in 1988.[65] Stressing that full payment was a treaty obligation, the Secretary-General asked, "Will it be said that one legacy of the Reagan administration will be the destruction of that which Roosevelt started?"[66]

The whole experience weighed heavily on Pérez de Cuéllar. He wrote, "This financial problem was to plague me for the rest of my tenure as secretary-general."[67]

The Iran–Iraq War: The Battle That Would Not End

Iraq's massive invasion of Iran by air and ground forces began in September 1980, well before Pérez de Cuéllar took on the United Nations' top job. In the end, however, he played a key role—along with the Cold-War thaw—in ultimately ending the conflict.

Despite a 1975 agreement to share sovereignty of the 120-mile Shatt al-Arab waterway, Iraq's only outlet to the Persian Gulf, Baghdad renounced the treaty and sought full control of the river.

Other factors also figured in Iraq's aggressive move. Iran underwent a major revolution in 1979, installing a fundamentalist Muslim Shi'ite government. Many analysts are convinced that Iraq's president, Saddam Hussein, wanted to establish Baghdad as leader of the region and the Arab world.[68] Iraq's Sunni government was also wary of possible close ties developing between its own Shi'ite majority population and the new government in Tehran. Iran's president, after all, had urged Iraqi Shi'ites to rise up and establish an Islamic regime.

At first, neither Iran nor Iraq wanted any UN involvement. Even so, during the long fight, the Council passed at least six cease-fire resolutions. Few had much effect. One early resolution called for a cease-fire while Iraqi troops were still very much inside Iran. In those early days, the Council did not scold or blame Iraq for the initial invasion. As time went by, Iran and Iraq often attached conditions that the other would not accept. Both nations wanted a military win and thought they could get it.[69]

Iran was convinced that the Council had a strong tilt toward Iraq. Certainly US–Iran relations were strained after the shah's fall from power and Tehran's recent seizure of American hostages. Iraq was receiving intelligence and weapons from the West. The Soviet Union, which also once had a close relationship with Iraq, seemed to quietly agree with the United States that wisdom called for avoiding direct intervention or any shift in the regional balance of power.[70]

Pérez de Cuéllar was well aware that neither major power was eager to use its influence to end the war. As for the warring parties, he thought that Iran was basically unwilling to negotiate with Hussein, hoping instead to overthrow his regime and establish an Islamic government there. Iran wanted massive war reparations as well. "While I had always blamed Iraq for starting the war, by the summer of 1985, I had reached the point of blaming Iran for continuing it," the Secretary-General noted in his memoir.[71]

In May 1982, Pérez de Cuéllar wrote to both governments to offer his good offices, a proposal that went nowhere.[72] Yet eventually, he earned the respect of both nations and became virtually the only channel of communication between them. "It soon became evident that my role would become central since [ultimately] only I was accepted as impartial by the two parties," the Secretary-General recalled.[73]

In the early years of the war, the only apparent progress lay in his humanitarian efforts to limit the effects of the fighting. In 1983, at the request or Iran, later seconded by Iraq, Pérez de Cuéllar sent a small mission to both countries to assess the damage to civilians in city attacks. In the aftermath, he got both sides to agree not to bomb urban civilian areas. Though the agreement did not last, the two nations set an important precedent in humanitarian cooperation.[74]

A year later, Iran accused Iraq of using chemical weapons and again asked the Secretary-General to investigate. He told the Council he would do so.

"That was a pretty courageous thing to say," recalled Pérez de Cuéllar's senior aide Giandomenico Picco. "Could the Council have stopped him? Of course. But if you say something like this openly, it is difficult to stop you openly."[75]

Though the Secretary-General dutifully kept trying to get a reciprocal agreement from Iraq, he followed through on Iran's request. He sent a team of medical and military specialists in March 1984. Its unanimous conclusion was that chemical weapons had been used against Iranian civilians and soldiers in defiance of the 1925 Geneva Protocol that barred the use of poisonous gases in warfare. In reaction, the Council expressed its "grave concern."[76]

Pérez de Cuéllar received new reports that same year of more attacks against civilians in cities of both nations. He asked both Tehran and Baghdad for assurance that such attacks would stop. He told the Council that he intended to send observation teams to ensure compliance. Later, at Iraq's request, he sent a team to examine conditions of prisoners of war in both countries.

"Through these initiatives, the Secretary-General created, in effect, a humanitarian regime in the midst of a savage and bloody war," concluded Thomas Boudreau, who wrote an early report on the need for civilian protection in the war for the former Council on Religion and International Affairs.[77]

In 1985, Pérez de Cuéllar produced an eight-point plan for ending the war. He presented it to the Council and separately to Iraq and Iran. Both sides agreed that the plan could become the basis for further discussions, but there was no rush to action.

Iran's top concern was that the aggressor in the war be held liable. The Secretary-General spoke with several leaders including Hashemi Rafsanjani, then the speaker of Iran's parliament, who argued strongly that the aggressor and the victim must not be treated as equals.

After speaking with Iraq's President Hussein, the Secretary-General noted later that the leader was not particularly charismatic or a good listener and seemed eager to preach his own perception of the truth to others.[78]

It had long been clear to Pérez de Cuéllar that his mediation efforts would not be enough. The leverage of the Council was necessary for a final solution. By fall 1986, US and Soviet warships were present in the Persian Gulf, adding to his concern that the regional war could expand.

Yet a notable Soviet shift was also underway. Mikhail Gorbachev came to power in Moscow and was slowly revamping his nation's foreign policy. More than any of his predecessors, he seemed ready to use the United Nations to resolve conflicts. The sense of a common stake in everything from economic development to human rights issues was growing.

At the start of his second term in 1987, Pérez de Cuéllar had an idea that he broached publicly in answer to a question during a press conference on January 13. He suggested that the Security Council meet at the foreign minister level to work on a new initiative to end the long Iran–Iraq conflict.

Two days later, he invited the ambassadors of the Council's five permanent member nations and its president to meet with him the next day at his residence to discuss new steps to end the war. At that meeting he suggested that a working group might investigate which country had responsibility for starting the war. He also suggested that the group find ways to protect freedom of navigation in the Gulf and the possibility of shutting off arms supplies to both sides. The ambassadors' reaction was "muted but positive," he recalled.[79]

The joint consultations went on for more than six months. When the 10 other Council members protested the secrecy of the meetings, the permanent members met privately with them and accepted some of their amendments.[80]

The history-making result was Security Council Resolution 598. Meeting at the foreign-minister level, the Council passed the measure on July 20, 1987. US Secretary of State George Shultz, never one to hastily praise the United Nations, heralded the unanimous vote as a first in UN history "on an issue of real importance and difficulty."[81]

The resolution called for an immediate cease-fire, backed by possible enforcement measures under Chapter 7 of the Charter. An exchange of prisoners of war and troop withdrawals were to follow. The Secretary-General was asked to send an observer team to supervise the cease-fire and withdrawals. In a bow to Iran, he was also asked to set up an impartial team to look into who was responsible for starting the war. The resolution made no mention of the waterway.

Iraq promptly accepted the resolution on July 23 and temporarily suspended its air attacks on Iran's ships. Yet Tehran was in no hurry to comply. Iran refused to discuss the waterway until Iraq reaffirmed its support for the joint sovereignty provision of the 1975 Algiers Accord. Iran also wanted a verdict on responsibility for starting the war before agreeing to any cease-fire.

It took more than a year of negotiations and changes in the global climate before Iran consented to the resolution.

At one point, in March 1988, Iran said it would accept the resolution but not while the Council was debating a possible arms embargo. The Council had clarified that such a move against both nations was a possible second step if Resolution 598 did not take hold. China and Russia had long opposed such a move, but in December 1987, Moscow had said it would no longer do so.

In spring 1988, Iraq began a new offensive, leading to more charges of chemical weapons use. Finally on July 18, Iran accepted Resolution 598. The formal letter from its president Ali Khamenei was delivered to Pérez de Cuéllar at his residence just after midnight that day. Iran blamed its reluctant decision both on a recent accidental shooting of an Iranian commercial airliner, killing all 290 on board, by the US cruiser *Vincennes* in the Gulf and on Iraq's continued use of chemical weapons.

Certainly the military situation for Iran was fast deteriorating. Iraq, being superior in weaponry, had attacked Iran's oil terminals and blocked its tanker traffic. The threat of a wider war was growing, and the possibility of an arms embargo still loomed. In the Secretary-General's view, Iran was finally realizing that its war goals could not be achieved and that the cost of the fighting was becoming too high.[82]

Pérez de Cuéllar had to choose the actual date for the cease-fire. He picked August 20, 1988. "Announcing the date for a cease-fire in this seemingly endless war gave me a greater sense of fulfillment than any other action during my 10 years as secretary-general," he recalled.[83] Soon the 350-person UN Iran–Iraq Military Observer Group (UNIIMOG) was on the ground to monitor compliance along the 1,400 kilometer border.[84]

Still, the negotiations that followed were often frustrating for Pérez de Cuéllar. Both Iran and Iraq were highly suspicious of each other's willingness to follow through on their pledges. The Secretary-General admitted that he was constantly afraid the cease-fire would collapse, particularly when Iraq accused Iran of encouraging the Kurdish rebellion in Iraq.[85]

A breakthrough occurred on August 15, 1990, some two weeks after Iraq's invasion of Kuwait, a move that triggered a strong reaction from the Council. Iraq's ambassador to the United Nations told Pérez de Cuéllar that Hussein had sent a letter to Iran's president that confirmed Iraq's recognition of the Algiers Accord regarding the waterway. As a result Hussein would begin to withdraw its troops and would agree to a POW exchange.[86] UNIIMOG later confirmed that all soldiers on both sides had fully withdrawn by February 20, 1991.

Still, Iran kept up the pressure on the question of blame for the war. Pérez de Cuéllar asked both governments for their detailed views and gave a report to the Council on December 9, 1991. It confirmed that Iraq's attack against Iran was started in violation of international law.[87]

"The Iranians wanted that report that placed the blame, and that was something which the Secretary-General could do," said James Sutterlin. "He didn't do it until the very end. That was a kind of carrot he had to offer which the Iraqis still resent."[88]

Both sides also were tired of fighting. The loss of Iran's civilian airliner gave Tehran the necessary opening to announce compliance with the cease-fire.

"They [both nations] wanted an end," confirmed Princeton's Leon Gordenker. "One technique...they use is time wasting as an instrument. That's exactly what happened here. Things change. Now we're ready to talk."[89]

"Readiness was really the key ingredient [in ending the war]," insisted University of Virginia professor emeritus Inis Claude Jr. "Any mediator has a possibly useful role to play if and when all parties decide they would rather have peace than war.... It can't be imposed on them or forced down their throats."[90]

Pérez de Cuéllar played a crucial role as chief mediator and impartial broker. Looking back, he argued that the war brought no gains to either nation but did significantly strengthen the United Nations. The early Council resolutions were "essentially unhelpful" because they did not tackle the question of which party started the war. Yet eventually, Resolution 598 was accepted, and the office of the secretary-general took on added credibility.[91]

Indeed, for many years, the Soviet position was that the UN chief should limit his activities to following instructions from the Assembly and the Council. However, in October 1988, Vladimir Petrovsky, the Soviet Union's deputy minister of foreign affairs, told the Assembly that the secretary-general should take on an "ever greater" role in maintaining international peace and stability.[92]

A major contribution of the Secretary-General in this case was a shift in procedure. During most of the war, Iran would not deal with the Council but was willing to meet with him. Then in 1987, Pérez de Cuéllar also began to meet separately with the five permanent Council members. He gave them an early draft of what was to become Resolution 598. That change proved to be vital for the cooperative work of the Council.[93]

At the beginning of the war, Moscow blocked Washington's efforts to bring UN sanctions against Iran as pressure to release the American hostages held at the US embassy in Tehran. Yet as the Cold-War thaw took hold and the Secretary-General brought the two nations together in consultations, they began to put a higher value on their bilateral relationship. Cameron Hume, a US diplomat who took part in many of the negotiating sessions, argued that the most important development that led to Resolution 598 was the fact that the Council's permanent members kept on talking.[94]

Afghanistan: Stepping In for a Partial Victory

The lengthy Moscow–Washington proxy war in Afghanistan called out for some kind of UN involvement. Eventually, the office of the secretary-general would perform a key role. In late 1979, the Soviet Union sent troops into Afghanistan to support Babrak Karmal's Marxist government against the challenge of a persistent Islamic resistance. That government was viewed by its critics as an anti-Islamic Soviet puppet. The Carter administration in Washington had begun to send nonlethal aid to the Afghan *mujahideen* months earlier. Direct arms supplies soon followed.

On New Year's Eve, the government of China complained in a statement to Kurt Waldheim, secretary-general at the time, that the Soviet invasion amounted to interference in Afghanistan's internal affairs. The Council promptly took up the issue, but Moscow vetoed a resolution calling for the immediate and unconditional withdrawal of all foreign troops from Afghanistan.

Under the procedural Uniting for Peace resolution, adopted during the Korean War and requiring only a majority vote, the Council shifted the issue to the Assembly, which asked Waldheim to use his good offices. By an overwhelming majority, the Assembly repeated the call for a Soviet troop pullout. Well aware that no Assembly demand was mandatory, the Soviets ignored the request.

Some were already calling the situation "Russia's Vietnam."

"Everybody thought it was the beginning of a never-ending war for the Russians," recalled the United Nations' Giandomenico Picco.[95]

In 1981 Pérez de Cuéllar, then a UN undersecretary-general, was tapped by Waldheim as his personal representative in Afghanistan. That designation, as Pérez de Cuéllar recounted in his memoir, allowed Moscow to "pretend" that the job was unrelated to the Assembly resolutions that were repeated year after year.[96]

He persuaded Afghanistan and Pakistan, which did not recognize the Kabul government and was receiving US and Saudi aid, to agree that year on an agenda for talks. However, the Afghan government insisted that a format be agreed on first. That proved more difficult than agreeing on an agenda. As the Secretary-General noted, "The procedural process would impede the negotiating process until the very end."[97]

Shortly after becoming Secretary-General, Pérez de Cuéllar chose Diego Cordovez of Ecuador, a UN undersecretary-general for political affairs, as his personal envoy to conduct proximity talks between Pakistan and Afghanistan. The Secretary-General noted diplomatically in his memoir that Cordovez had a tendency "to keep matters in his own hands."[98]

Cordovez was not necessarily the man most trusted by Pérez de Cuéllar, according to James Sutterlin, but was chosen because he was known to have "real ability."[99] Since Pakistan did not recognize the Kabul government, Cordovez had to meet separately with the two governments in New York and Geneva—often after the other party left the building. Neither side was in a rush to settle.

The Secretary-General himself carried on another set of talks with Moscow and Washington. At one point, Soviet leader Yuri Andropov told Pérez de Cuéllar that his country did not want to be in Afghanistan but would not leave unless others stopped interfering in its internal affairs. Andropov said he suspected that Washington liked having Afghanistan as a stick with which to beat the Soviet Union.[100]

The two sets of talks made little progress until 1985, when Gorbachev arrived on the scene. He invited Pérez de Cuéllar to meet with him at the funeral of his predecessor, Konstantin Chernenko. Though Afghanistan was not discussed, Gorbachev spoke with conviction of Moscow's support for the United Nations and for the Secretary-General's efforts. Noting that the Soviet leader glanced only occasionally at his notes and smiled (but "not excessively"), Pérez de Cuéllar said he sensed that Gorbachev's comments "were not mere platitudes but represented something new in Soviet policy."[101]

In 1986, Moscow brought in Mohammad Najibullah to replace Babrak Karmal as the Afghan president. Pakistan still refused to deal with the successor government. Yet the situation was slowly changing. Washington began publicly to support the UN efforts of Cordovez. Gorbachev started talking about a possible withdrawal timetable and a UN monitoring framework in exchange for US–Pakistan pledges to stop aiding the *mujahideen*.[102]

Yet the Afghan resistance continued to be strong. Finally, in April 1988, Pakistan and Afghanistan signed an agreement in Geneva with Pérez de Cuéllar looking on. The two nations promised to establish mutual relations, not interfere in each other's affairs, and return each other's refugees voluntarily.

Foreign troops were to return home. Moscow withdrew its troops within nine months of the effective May 15 treaty date. Moscow and Washington were to serve as co-guarantors of the treaty. That was a "first" for an agreement negotiated under a UN secretary-general's auspices, as Pérez de Cuéllar noted in his 1988 annual report to the Assembly.

He knew the moment was historic. He termed it the first Soviet withdrawal from an occupied country since 1946.[103] However, he also knew that the Afghan situation was far from resolved. Though the government had not totally collapsed, as many in the West expected, Afghan internal politics remained in turmoil.

The rebel *mujahideen* still thought they could win. The fighting and continued supply of arms showed no signs of stopping. Indeed, US Secretary of State George Shultz said when the accords were signed that the United States felt it had a right to continue supplying arms to the "legitimate representatives" of the Afghan people until Russia also stopped sending arms to Kabul.[104]

Meanwhile, some kind of monitoring system was needed to ensure that the new treaty would be obeyed. Instead of the usual Security Council call for a peacekeeping force, widely considered unacceptable in this case, Pérez de Cuéllar wrote a letter that he cleared with all parties. It proposed that the Council ask him to send a new UN Good-Offices Mission in Afghanistan and Pakistan (UNGOMAP). It was to have 50 men from 10 nations. In his memoir, he termed the innovative proposal "a notable example of diplomatic circumlocution."[105]

While in New York in December 1988, Gorbachev told Pérez de Cuéllar that he did not think either the Afghan government or the *mujahideen* were strong enough to win. He also said he did not like the US insistence that the Najibullah government be dissolved before elections were held. Gorbachev said he wanted to see an independent and neutral Afghanistan and suggested an international conference on the subject, with a simultaneous cease-fire. Washington, however, wanted a broad-based government established before any cease-fire.[106]

Though internal politics are normally off limits to the United Nations, the Secretary-General reluctantly concluded that the United Nations had no choice in this case but to further involve itself. He announced that he was taking personal charge of efforts to find a political settlement. An Assembly resolution asking him to do so followed. To replace Cordovez, the Secretary-General appointed Benon Sevan, another senior member of the Secretariat and a Cypriot. The major question was how elections should be conducted and whether Najibullah should resign before or after them. When the Secretary-General met with the Afghan leader in September 1990, Najibullah accepted the need for elections and a transition period. He suggested that the United Nations oversee the process.

Though Washington and Moscow agreed to stop arms shipments to their Afghan proxies, Pérez de Cuéllar's second term was rapidly ending with no real Afghan solution in sight. He finally stopped his decade-long effort to resolve the situation in October 1991. He noted that the imminent halt in arms shipments and the emerging political consensus at the time might actually have inspired the *mujahideen* to step up their fighting and to eliminate the Najibullah regime. Indeed, that is what happened.[107]

Although the Secretary-General had achieved only a partial victory, the United Nations had helped both Moscow and Washington to save face. Pérez de Cuéllar told a *Le Monde* journalist that the United Nations had been "used by the superpowers." In his view, the UN role was essential but not decisive. He said it was not UN negotiating skill but the "invincible resistance" of the *mujahideen* and the arms they got from the United States and Pakistan, as well as support from Iran and Saudi Arabia, that ultimately persuaded Moscow to withdraw its troops.[108]

"The great success was to get the Russians out," observed James Sutterlin. "But Pérez himself recognized very clearly that the Afghan problem...was in many ways worse than before. He blamed both the Russians and the United States for that because, while they had solved their problem...and had done what they needed to do, they then got out, leaving the country in a disastrous situation."[109]

Though Pérez de Cuéllar and his emissaries managed for many years to keep alive the potential for a negotiated settlement, their experience in the Afghan case shows that a secretary-general cannot impose his good offices where the parties involved are neither supportive nor that interested.[110]

Those Hostages in Lebanon

Pérez de Cuéllar always considered hostage taking one of the cruelest forms of terrorism.[111] So when the systematic seizure of Western hostages began in the mid-1980s in Lebanon, he took on the problem personally, as a humanitarian crusade. It took many years of persistent effort—shuttle diplomacy, with shifting demands from both Israel and radical Shi'ite groups—before most hostages were released in late 1991.

By the time Pérez de Cuéllar was elected to the United Nations' top job, Israel and the Arab states had already fought four wars. Yet in December 1983, the radical Shi'ite group al-Dawa launched a series of attacks in Kuwait, which appeared to spur Hezbollah and its allies in Lebanon to begin kidnapping Western hostages. The hope was to put Western pressure on Kuwait for the release of 17 Shi'ites sentenced to life in prison for the attacks.[112]

By 1988, when the Secretary-General started to focus on the kidnappings as a key concern, two UN workers were among the abducted. The first, seized in March 1985, was Alec Collett, a British journalist who was writing articles in Lebanon for the UN Relief and Works Agency (UNRWA). He was labeled a British spy and executed a year later. The second, captured three years after that, was Colonel William R. Higgins, the American head of the UN military observer force in Lebanon. He had been driving the last Jeep in a convoy returning from a courtesy call on an official of a mainline Shi'ite group in Tyre.

In all, 23 Westerners, including journalists, academics, and government officials, were kidnapped. Several national efforts to free them did not succeed.

Pérez de Cuéllar had no direct authorization from the Assembly or the Council to do what he decided to do. He knew that each side had strong interests for which it might be willing to bargain. Israel wanted the return of seven nationals—alive or dead—held by different groups in Lebanon. Israel also especially wanted information on the whereabouts of Ron Arad, a navigator captured by Palestinians. It pressed for that information for years during the talks.

The other side knew that Israel was holding close to 400 Shi'ites. The Lebanese kidnappers particularly wanted the release of Sheik Abdel Karim Obeid, a prominent fundamentalist Shi'ite leader seized by Israeli agents in Lebanon in July 1989. Colonel Higgins was killed in retaliation the day after Obeid's capture.

The negotiations evolved into a delicate, lengthy balancing act involving Iran, Syria (which had a large presence in Lebanon), the United States, Britain, and Israel.

Certainly it helped that the Secretary-General had already established a good working relationship with Hashemi Rafsanjani, Iran's president, during the Iran–Iraq War. Iran had a strong influence on Hezbollah, and thus to some degree on its shadowy offshoots, but said it had no direct control over any group linked to the kidnappers.

Pérez de Cuéllar also spoke frequently with Uri Lubrani, Israel's chief hostage negotiator. The Secretary-General tried to get Washington, largely through his contacts with the national security adviser, Brent Scowcroft, to use its influence with Israel. The United States, usually noncommittal in its response to such urgings, insisted it would make no deals with the kidnappers.

Little progress was made for almost two more years. Each side wanted offers first from the other side. At times, a breakthrough looked likely but did not come.

The Secretary-General finally tapped his trusted colleague, Giandomenico Picco, as his chief emissary. Picco had worked with Pérez de Cuéllar on the Cyprus problem during the Waldheim years and had helped negotiate and oversee the cease-fire and end of the Iran–Iraq War. Pérez de Cuéllar knew that Picco had the initiative and discretion for the job.

"Picco was ideally suited for the challenge of lengthy and devious negotiations in which pride and hatred, faith and distrust were intermingled," the Secretary-General wrote in the long chapter in his memoir devoted to the Lebanese hostage situation. "He gained and retained the confidence of all the parties in this secret game."[113]

At one point in August 1989, Picco told Rafsanjani in Tehran that Pérez de Cuéllar knew President George H. W. Bush well and thought he would like to improve US–Iran relations. At the Secretary-General's suggestion, Picco said that the United States might free up frozen Iranian assets if the hostages in Lebanon were released. Iran's response was not helpful. He was told that Iran had no relations with those holding the hostages and that those groups would not discuss anything until Sheik Obeid was freed. Rafsanjani said that Washington needed to stop its "unreasonable animosity" toward Iran.[114]

Picco later said he felt, during his many days of secret talks, as if he were in the middle of a vicious circle.

"One side says, 'I agree if they agree' and the other, 'I agree if they agree,' so what do you do?" he asked. "It was really a tug of war." Picco thought he knew what each side wanted and chose at times to say more than he had actually been promised by the other side to get some forward motion.[115]

In March 1991, Iran finally agreed to help Picco make contact with the hostage holders in Lebanon. At 8:30 a.m. on April 13, he was picked up for the first of several meetings with the masked kidnappers. He traveled alone and was often blindfolded. At one point, he was asked why he should be trusted. Picco responded, "I put my life in your hands to come here and talk to you.... If you have half the guts I have shown, the least you can do is trust me."[116]

As Picco recalled, "There was never, ever a moment when I was prepared to fail. I said to myself...this thing has got to work.... I kept going like a train."[117]

The Secretary-General also remained deeply involved in the effort. In his view, the situation took an important turn that spring in 1991. He had concluded that no further progress was likely until Iran decided to be helpful. Iran was no longer stressing the importance of freeing its frozen assets in the United States. But Tehran insisted that, in addition to the release of imprisoned Shi'ites, Iran must be removed from the US State Department terrorist list and blame must clearly be established for the launch of the Iran–Iraq War. Iran also wanted a formal visit by the Secretary-General. The UN chief considered that bid as an effort to show Iran's acceptance by the international community and visited Tehran that September.[118]

Iran's regional position had much improved after the Iran–Iraq War and the brief Gulf War, which forced Iraq to withdraw from Kuwait. The imprisoned Shi'ites in Kuwait had been freed. Iraqi troops had withdrawn from Iran and prisoners of war had been exchanged. The

Secretary-General had it within his power to tackle the blame question. He chose a group of European scholars to make a report to the Council.

He also advised Picco to stress during his talks that major donors for a long-languishing UN reconstruction program for Lebanon had been contacted and were ready to contribute. The Secretary-General noted that, though never part of any deal, the United States at a "fortuitous time" during the talks had paid Iran compensation for weapons purchased by the shah's regime that were never delivered.

The UN chief had made it clear that he wanted the situation resolved before his second term ended on December 31, 1991. On August 8, the Islamic jihad released the Irish hostage John McCarthy with a letter for the Secretary-General. The two met at a British Air Force base. The letter chastised the United Nations for failing to support the struggles of oppressed people and asked the Secretary-General personally to see to the liberation of all detainees. McCarthy also told the UN chief that Hezbollah was in serious financial difficulty because it was no longer getting support from Iran or other countries and was convinced that it was time to end the problem. Indeed, an American and a French hostage were freed that same day.[119]

The shuttle diplomacy soon moved into an intense stage of offers and counteroffers. A tentative release schedule was set. Over time, dozens of imprisoned Shi'ites were let go. In all, nine Western hostages were released by three underground groups between August and early December 1991.Terry Anderson, an American reporter, who was taken hostage in Beirut after dropping off his morning tennis partner some seven years before, was the last to be freed on December 3.

Although Iran was unable or unwilling to provide any data on Arad, the missing Israeli, it played a decisive role in ending the hostage episode.[120] Pérez de Cuéllar said that he realized the hostages themselves played no role in their liberation. It was the interplay of incidents and interests and changes in power and the political situation that were major factors.[121]

Still, he was convinced that his good offices and those of Picco also were essential to the outcome. As he told the *New York Times* on December 6, 1991, "I had the advantage that I was personally trusted by all the parties, and they looked on me as totally impartial."[122]

He gave ample credit to Picco for his skill and willingness to put his "life on the line" in going to meetings that even the Israelis advised against.[123]

Though giving primary kudos to the Secretary-General for his timing and judgment in "calling the shots," Bhaskar Menon, the former UN staff member turned journalist, said, "It took absolute raw guts to do what Picco did."[124]

Joe Sills, a former spokesman for Pérez de Cuéllar, agreed, saying, "Picco is probably as good as anybody I ever worked with at the UN. Johnny had a lot of leeway in what he was doing because nobody else wanted to touch it. Nobody knew what to do.... It was a profound embarrassment to the UN that you can have your people taken hostage and held under your nose, and you can't do anything about it.... He did an incredible job."[125]

The United Nations provided a face-saving exit. By then, the hostage takers had probably become convinced that the time for that kind of terrorism had passed.[126] Although various carrots were offered, all sides insisted that no deals were made.

As Thomas Pickering, US ambassador to the United Nations at the time, said, "The United Nations was helpful in putting the Secretary-General in touch with Israel but was not prepared to give even a scintilla of a hint that the US was involved in deal-making with Israel or anyone else."[127]

Picco noted, "We basically made a deal between the freedom of innocent people and telling the truth. I think it was a pretty good deal, very honest and ethical, from every point of view."[128]

Namibia's Long Road to Independence

Although Secretary-General Waldheim viewed progress in Namibia as one of his top accomplishments, the breakthrough to full nationhood did not come until late in Pérez de Cuéllar's second term.

Namibia (formerly South West Africa) had been a German colony. During World War I, South Africa took it over and, after the war, administered it as a League of Nations mandate. South Africa petitioned the United Nations for the right to annex the territory on grounds that the mandate elapsed when the League of Nations ended and was not automatically transferred to UN oversight.

The United Nations did not buy the logic. The Assembly voted in 1966 to terminate the mandate but declared the territory a direct UN responsibility until its independence. The Assembly changed the territory's name to Namibia, established a council to administer it, and asked South Africa to get out. The Assembly also granted Namibia's guerrilla resistance—the South West African People's Organization (SWAPO)—observer status at UN meetings and arranged to give it diplomatic, legal, and military support from the UN budget.[129]

Despite all that, and a 1971 International Court of Justice opinion that upheld the Assembly's legal position, Pretoria firmly refused to give up control. The standoff continued for years.[130]

The plan for an independent Namibia was actually set in 1978 when the Security Council authorized the United Nations Transition Assistance Group (UNTAG) to take on the ambitious task of supervising a cease-fire, monitoring the withdrawal of foreign troops, and observing elections. Though eventually carried out, the plan was mostly on hold for another decade.

Pérez de Cuéllar and his staff were asked to take the lead in several administrative and diplomatic moves. Prodded by the Council, he had finally persuaded South Africa in 1985 to agree to terms for holding Namibian elections. Yet there was one precondition on which South Africa refused to yield: Cuban troops supporting the government in neighboring Angola first had to leave. The concern was that the continued presence of foreign troops there could easily exploit the withdrawal of South African troops from Namibia and fuel instability in the region.

At one point in May 1985, Pérez de Cuéllar flew to Cuba and spent more than 12 hours talking with a "surprisingly likeable" Fidel

Castro, fishing trip included. The Secretary-General hoped to persuade Castro to make at least a symbolic gesture of a troop withdrawal. The UN leader was assured that Cuban troops were in Angola "purely on behalf of internationalism" and would remain there as long as necessary.[131]

Pretoria's refusal to bend on the issue was undoubtedly bolstered by the Assembly's persistent condemnation of South Africa's apartheid policy, the nation's "illegal" occupation of Namibia, and reports of human rights abuses there. South African leaders sometimes accused the Secretary-General himself of bias. In his early days on the job, he received a letter from Prime Minister P. W. Botha accusing him of personal attachment to South Africa's "ideological adversaries."[132]

Pérez de Cuéllar surmised that South Africa wanted a delay on Namibia's transition so it could assess the effect within its own borders and perhaps see a more friendly government installed in Angola.[133]

The situation began to change in the late 1980s, as superpower help for the two sides in the ongoing Angolan armed struggle began to wane. In four-nation meetings over the summer of 1988, US diplomat Chester Crocker managed to negotiate an agreement by which the Cuban troops would begin a gradual pullout from Angola. South Africa then also agreed to withdraw some of its troops from Namibia.

The Secretary-General flew to South Africa that fall to pin down arrangements for its cooperation with UNTAG. A few months later, in January 1989, the Council asked Pérez de Cuéllar to arrange a ceasefire between South Africa and SWAPO. He also helped to develop the UN Angola Verification Mission (UNAVEM) to monitor the withdrawal of the 50,000 Cuban troops in Angola.

UNTAG was deployed in Namibia in April 1989. By summer, the UN team, drawn from 109 nations, numbered close to 8,000 civilian, police, and military personnel.[134]

Voter registration was soon underway for the November elections. Tens of thousands of repatriated Namibian civilians and SWAPO guerrillas were included. The Secretary-General worked out a process by which potentially violent counterinsurgents were removed from the police force by the November 1989 elections. UNTAG monitored the vote and supervised the cease-fire.

Once the election results came through, South Africa withdrew from Namibia. The longtime colony became fully independent on March 21, 1990. Though the civil war continued in neighboring Angola, national elections were eventually also held there in 1992.

Pérez de Cuéllar insisted he had no role in framing the United Nations' policy for Namibia. Yet he was closely involved in many of the administrative and diplomatic efforts to enact it. He also admitted that one of his "proudest" acts was to administer the oath of office to Namibia's first president, Sam Nujoma.[135]

"If you follow Namibia from beginning to end, it is probably the longest standing UN story," noted Thomas Weiss, a codirector of the UN Intellectual History Project at the City University of New York (CUNY) Graduate Center, in an interview. "You have a substantial UN role."[136]

Namibia stands as the only case of UN-supervised decolonization.[137]

A Double Latin American Challenge

As a Peruvian, Pérez de Cuéllar admitted he had a strong special interest in wanting to help bring peace and stability to Latin American nations. He felt the United Nations should do more than "observe with concern."[138]

Intense civil wars were underway in both Nicaragua and El Salvador in the early 1980s. Yet it was not until July 27, 1989, that the Secretary-General was authorized to play an active role in the Nicaragua conflict. As he put it, "After seven years and well into my second term, I finally had a mandate from the Security Council with regard to Central America."[139]

Nicaragua was the first of the two Central American crises to be solved by negotiation. Progress there was viewed as key to forward moves in El Salvador and other regional conflicts. The United

Nations' role in Nicaragua set two important precedents. It marked the first time the United Nations monitored an election in a sovereign state and was the first UN peacekeeping operation in the Western Hemisphere.

Yet from the start, there was a strong reluctance in this case to involve the United Nations. The United States, under President Reagan, had mined some of Nicaragua's active harbors in 1983 and vetoed a Council resolution criticizing Washington for its action. The US administration, wary of Soviet and Cuban involvement in any UN move, was also selling arms to Iran and diverting the profits to the Contra rebels, a practice later known as the Iran–Contra scandal. President Reagan once called the Contras "the moral equivalent of the founding fathers."[140] In 1985, the United States also imposed a trade embargo on Nicaragua, a move the Assembly condemned.

Nicaragua's Sandinista government, supported by Cuba and indirectly by the Soviet Union, wanted no involvement from either the United Nations or the OAS. Both were viewed as dominated by the United States.

Thus the regional peace process first got under way with the Contadora Group, launched in January 1983 by Colombia, Mexico, Panama, and Venezuela. The group proposed a plan that encouraged the five Central American states (Costa Rica, El Salvador, Guatemala, Honduras, and Nicaragua) to eliminate all foreign influence in their domestic conflicts and establish friendly relations with one another through dialogue and negotiation. The Security Council endorsed the Contadora process, asking the Secretary-General to keep the Council informed.

However, violence in the region continued unabated over the next three years. The Contadora effort was on the verge of collapse when Pérez de Cuéllar and the OAS secretary-general, João Baena Soares, made a fact-finding trip to show their support for the plan. During that trip they met the Costa Rican president, Óscar Arias Sánchez, and found that he was proposing a new, more comprehensive plan.

After close consultation with the five Central American presidents, Arias proposed cease-fires among all combatants, amnesties, a halt to all aid to irregular forces, peace talks between the government and guerrilla groups, and the holding of free elections. Known as Esquipulas II, his plan was approved by the five presidents in August 1987. It also won the endorsement of the General Assembly and the US Senate. The Sandinistas and the Contras finally began peace talks in January 1988, and a cease-fire took effect three months later.

The five Central American presidents had agreed to draw up a plan to demobilize and repatriate or relocate the Contras and their families and to ask the United Nations for technical advice. The five also asked their foreign ministers to set up a mechanism to verify the commitments they made. Nicaragua agreed to hold elections in February 1990 and amended its electoral laws to invite international observers, including the UN and OAS secretaries-general, to verify the process.

The Security Council officially approved Esquipulas II and other agreements made by the five presidents on July 27, 1989. The Council also gave its full support to the Secretary-General in his good-offices mission.[141]

The *yes* vote of the United States in the Council marked a major shift in American policy. Some on Pérez de Cuéllar's staff viewed the change as the end of the Monroe Doctrine.[142] The George H. W. Bush administration had replaced the Reagan White House. News of the Iran–Contra scandal now undermined virtually any regional support for the past US policy.

Though it was late in the game, the United Nations did play an important role in Nicaragua's elections and in the demobilization of the Contras.

In response to a request by Pérez de Cuéllar, the Council authorized him in November 1989 to set up a UN Observer Group in Central America, known as ONUCA. Its task was to monitor compliance with Esquipulas II, ensuring the agreed-to halt in international aid to rebel troops and respect for national borders. Pérez de Cuéllar had insisted that the Council, rather than the Assembly (as preferred by Nicaragua), authorize the peacekeeping operation to draw the needed troops from member states.[143]

ONUCA's chief weakness, in the view of the Secretary-General, was its lack of intelligence capacity. Still, he saw it as a worthwhile first step in the peace process. Nicaraguans became accustomed to the group's presence and impartiality. For the United Nations, it marked an important precedent for its control of developments within a sovereign state.[144]

However, ONUCA's deployment was delayed. Rebel conflicts in both Nicaragua and El Salvador intensified. Some 2,000 Contras had moved back into Nicaragua (largely from Honduras), and the government cancelled its 1988 cease-fire.

Pérez de Cuéllar wrote to each of the five Central American foreign ministers, expressing alarm about the increased fighting and urging a revival of the cease-fire.

The five foreign ministers met again in Costa Rica on December 12, 1989, and signed the San Isidro Declaration. It signaled their agreement to international monitoring of their peace efforts, condemned the action of irregular forces, and offered the Contras the chance to take part in Nicaragua's elections. The ministers also wanted ONUCA's role to include cease-fire verification and the demobilization and repatriation of the Contras.

Initially, as one trained in international law, Pérez de Cuéllar was reluctant to see the United Nations take on the job of monitoring a domestic election. The Charter specifically preserved each nation's right to manage its own affairs, and the United Nations had refused similar requests in the past. The Secretary-General was concerned that acceptance might move the United Nations into "treacherous waters." After lengthy discussions with his colleagues, however, he decided a UN role in this case was both desirable and justified.[145]

He set up another UN Observer Mission for the Verification of the Electoral Process in Nicaragua (ONUVEN). Since he wanted the team to oversee more than just the voting, mission members were sent to Nicaragua well in advance of the actual vote.

Pérez de Cuéllar tapped Elliot Richardson, the former US attorney general and secretary of defense, as his special representative to lead ONUVEN. The observers visited more than 2,000 polling stations on the day of the elections—February 25, 1990.

Shortly after the polls closed, Richardson and his team took a quick sample of results and concluded that the Sandinista government had suffered an unexpected defeat.

Though the outcome would not be widely known until the next day, Richardson, along with former US President Jimmy Carter and João Baena Soares of the OAS, who had all helped in the monitoring, called on President Daniel Ortega Saavedra and urged him to accept the defeat peacefully. He was persuaded, but only on condition that the victor, Violeta Chamorro, not publicly brag about her win. Pérez de Cuéllar viewed that early intervention by the three as "crucial" in Nicaragua's return to democracy.[146]

Ortega was the first Latin American head of state that Pérez de Cuéllar had received as UN chief in 1982. The Secretary-General recalled that Ortega seemed to lack both intellectual vigor and a forceful personality. Yet after the election, he praised the Latin American leader for agreeing to the result without protest.[147]

The new government in Nicaragua soon arranged with the Contras to demobilize and repatriate their troops. The Security Council agreed to expand the UN mission to help with that job and authorized its forces to carry light arms, as Pérez de Cuéllar had strongly urged. ONUCA set up five security zones to receive rebel arms and thus became a hybrid diplomatic, military, and psychological effort.[148]

With its postelection job, the United Nations took on a new responsibility for strengthening democratic institutions and monitoring compliance with human rights standards inside a member country. Pérez de Cuéllar saw it as a remarkable and unprecedented UN achievement.[149]

El Salvador: A Deal at Four Minutes to Midnight

As in Nicaragua, a fierce civil war in nearby El Salvador continued during the 1980s. In this case, however, the United States was supporting the government. The Soviet Union was helping the rebels, who joined in a loose alliance as the Farabundo Martí National Liberation Front (FMLN), in 1987. The rebels were also getting arms from Cuba, by way of Nicaragua.

Year after year, various peace efforts floundered. As long as a military solution appeared possible, there was little interest in serious negotiation. In September 1989, however, the Salvadoran government and the FMLN met in Mexico City and agreed to start a political dialogue. After a second meeting in Costa Rica, they agreed further that a political agreement must precede any cease-fire.

It was a decision that proved difficult and complicated. Clearly hoping to improve its bargaining position, the FMLN began a major offensive that November, invading the city of San Salvador for the first time. During the fighting, which left some 75,000 dead, government forces bombed several poor neighborhoods where guerrillas reportedly were hiding. In the process, six Jesuit priests, suspected of sympathizing with the FMLN, were killed. Human rights soon became a major issue in any political settlement.

Both the government and the FMLN now appealed to Pérez de Cuéllar and the United Nations to return them to negotiations. He said the world body thus shifted from helpful bystander to central actor.[150]

The UN mediated almost two years of talks, beginning in February 1990. Álvaro de Soto, the Secretary-General's Special Representative to El Salvador and fellow Peruvian, noted that the mistrust was so deep that only one face-to-face meeting occurred in the following 22 months of negotiations.[151]

"Most of it [the talks] was done by shuttling within the same building—a hotel where we would eat, sleep and work," he explained in an interview. "One party was on one floor, another on another, and I was on a third floor and would shuttle between them. I'd get comments from both sides.... It was all very slow and painstaking."[152]

Salvador's President Alfredo Felix Cristiani was "a man of the right but no ideologue," in the view of Pérez de Cuéllar. As the Secretary-General saw it, the president wanted to end the war but was somewhat distrustful of the United Nations. Cristiani took part in some of the talks but largely sent hard-line representatives who had little flexibility.[153]

The biggest obstacles to reaching a settlement were reform of the armed forces, a halt to human rights abuses, and integration of FMLN forces into the government army. But, by then, both Washington and Moscow were eager for a UN-mediated settlement and encouraged their allies to compromise.[154]

De Soto kept the momentum of the talks going by focusing first on specific issues. The two sides signed a human rights agreement in Costa Rica in late July 1990. It pledged full respect for human rights, spelled out legal procedures for release of political prisoners, and called for a UN mechanism to monitor compliance once a cease-fire had been reached. First, however, the two sides needed to agree on a way to reduce and reform El Salvador's military forces.

Pérez de Cuéllar, convinced that the United Nations should plan ahead as much as possible, told the Council that December that he would send a technical mission to advise him on conditions for establishing a UN Observer Mission in El Salvador (ONUSAL). He felt the human rights portion of its work should begin well before a cease-fire. Though aware of the dangers, he hoped the move would discourage attacks on civilians and give a needed kick to the negotiating process.[155]

Though deployed under civil war conditions, ONUSAL, the United Nations' first attempt to monitor human rights compliance inside a member state, achieved "remarkable results," according to the Secretary-General. The UN observers could travel freely on land controlled by both sides. Rights violations declined sharply.[156]

Parliamentary and local elections were to be held on March 10, 1991. Though President Cristiani asked both the OAS and the United Nations to monitor them, only the OAS agreed. The United Nations had successfully done that job in Nicaragua. However, Pérez de Cuéllar felt that El Salvador, with no cease-fire in place, was a different case.[157]

Though the fighting in El Salvador continued after the elections, the two sides met in Mexico City in early April. Before the end of that month—"almost miraculously," according to the Secretary-General—they agreed on a package of reforms affecting the army, judicial power, and the electoral system. They also agreed to set up a commission to investigate serious acts of violence since 1980.[158]

Yet US criticism of an FMLN tilt by de Soto persisted under the new Bush administration. In May, Pérez de Cuéllar went to Washington to talk with President Bush. The Secretary-General pointed out that de Soto was in the difficult position of serving in a sense as the FMLN spokesman when conveying its position to the Salvadoran government. He argued that any mediator must treat both sides with respect. However, he pointed out that democratizing, especially in military reforms, necessarily makes greater demands on the government than the rebels. Yet the demands, he said, were in both sides' interest for stability and freedom.[159]

"The United States didn't want it [the El Salvador issue] in the UN at all, but Pérez de Cuéllar was someone we had confidence in," recalled Edward Luck.[160]

The Secretary-General, convinced that the talks needed a new high-level impetus, invited Cristiani and five FMLN commanders to the United Nations in New York in mid-September 1991 to solve the central remaining problem: the future size and shape of the army and reintegration of FMLN forces into El Salvador's legal, civilian, and political life. Conditions and guarantees were needed.

Pérez de Cuéllar suggested to Cristiani that rebel forces might be willing to give up their demand to blend into the army for a package of other guarantees. During 10 days of mediated talks—often sustained by pizza deliveries—the two sides finally agreed on measures to reduce and reorganize the armed forces and on criteria to recruit and train a new civilian police force to replace the existing paramilitary one. FMLN members would take up some of those police positions. A National Commission for the Consolidation of Peace (COPAZ) would supervise all agreements.[161]

Still, loose ends remained. The agreements had to be made practical. When he returned to El Salvador, Cristiani faced major public demonstrations for ceding too much to the rebels. His government soon made a new proposal: FMLN members would be barred from participating in the police force. Pérez de Cuéllar promptly phoned Cristiani to express his concern that the new stand could "torpedo" the still-delicate negotiations.[162]

Once again, in a race against time, the Secretary-General asked both sides to come to New York again before Christmas. His term was to end at midnight December 31.

Though his right-wing political party disapproved of his going, Cristiani arrived on December 28. He first went to call on the newly elected secretary-general, Boutros Boutros-Ghali, who would take office in January. Cristiani asked if a better deal might be had if a peace agreement were delayed. The answer was clear. There were other items on Boutros-Ghali's agenda, and it would probably take at least six months to get to the El Salvador question.[163]

With Cristiani able to make the decisions on his own during the ensuing talks, the FMLN moderated its demands. The government agreed to purge its own officer corps, bring rebels into the police force, and adopt agrarian reforms. The FMLN dropped its demand for broader socio-economic changes and accepted the United Nations as the security guarantor.[164]

A final agreement was reached at precisely 11:56 p.m. on December 31.

Pérez de Cuéllar had planned to leave that evening for a vacation in the Bahamas but felt it his duty to stay as long as he could be useful. "It crushed his plans for New Year's Eve," de Soto noted. "He had wanted to put in a normal day's work and go home and board his plane."[165]

The treaty signing date was set for January 26, 1992, in Mexico City. Though invited, Pérez de Cuéllar declined. He felt it was "not in the best taste" to accept since a new secretary-general would be in office.[166] The cease-fire was to take effect February 1, 1992. It had been a long ordeal for all concerned.

Certainly much in the successful outcome was related to the change in attitude of Moscow and Washington. Both decided to hold back support for their "clients" and press for a settlement. Yet UN mediation also played a critical role.

"Only the herculean efforts of Pérez de Cuéllar and Álvaro de Soto saved the peace process in Central America," insisted Benjamin Rivlin, director emeritus of the Ralph Bunche Institute for International Studies at the City University of New York.[167] Indeed, Cristiani himself later admitted that the United Nations played a crucial role that made it very difficult for either side to get up from the table and leave.[168]

Pérez de Cuéllar said of de Soto, "His considerable self-confidence never faltered under the criticism and suspicion [directed at him]. He never failed to seek my guidance or keep me fully informed."[169]

The diplomacy involved required both creative initiatives and sensitivity in timing.

"You have to have a feel for the ripeness of the moment," de Soto insisted. "If you push on blindfolded, without regard for that, you might lose credibility. You have to know when to push on and when to let something ripen by itself.... Fruit doesn't ripen by being thrown against the wall."[170]

Readying Cambodia for a Rebirth

The tough question in the case of Cambodia was how to get Vietnam to agree to a government elected by all factions of the Cambodian opposition. After repeated raids by the Khmer Rouge, Hanoi had invaded

Cambodia in late 1978, ousting Pol Pot's Khmer Rouge government and accusing it of genocide. A Vietnam-dominated substitute was installed.

It would be more than a decade before even the start of a broadly acceptable solution was in place.

The General Assembly was on record, in a series of resolutions dating to 1979, in calling for the immediate withdrawal of all foreign forces [Vietnamese] from Cambodia and for that nation's self-determination. Pérez de Cuéllar was encouraged to use his good offices to make progress in the matter.

Though familiar with the situation, the Secretary-General wanted a fresh start and first appointed Rafeeuddin Ahmed as his special representative for humanitarian assistance in Southeast Asia. That title was a bow to the fact that the United Nations did not recognize the Vietnam-installed government in Phnom Penh. Ahmed, however, also played a political role. He made numerous visits to the region in 1982 to gather leaders' views.[171]

"He traveled almost continuously among the parties and did a lot to bring them together before the actual peace talks," recalled James Sutterlin.[172]

In 1985 Pérez de Cuéllar, hoping to play a mediation role independent of the General Assembly's steady criticism of Vietnam, visited each capital in the region except Phnom Penh in an effort to learn about the varied interests and objectives. Vietnamese leaders assured him they were open to a negotiated solution and willing to withdraw their troops, but not until the Pol Pot "clique" was eliminated. Vietnam's leaders insisted that the Khmer Rouge must not be allowed to take part in any elections.[173]

The Secretary-General also consulted Cambodia's Prince Norodom Sihanouk, then living in exile in Paris. Sihanouk was at peace about including the Khmer Rouge in his loosely organized opposition coalition, despite the fact that the Khmer Rouge had killed two of his sons and nearly destroyed his country. Pérez de Cuéllar professed amazement at such a balanced acceptance in light of those circumstances. Sihanouk said that, in any event, China would also demand Khmer Rouge participation in decisions on Cambodia's future.[174]

Once back at the United Nations, the Secretary-General and his special envoy sat down and worked out the points that had broad agreement. They laid out the basics for what was to become a neutral and nonaligned Cambodia—from a cease-fire and Vietnamese troop withdrawal to elections and guaranteed respect for security concerns in the region. Pérez de Cuéllar was convinced that, despite Vietnam's opposition, the cooperation of both the Khmer Rouge and the Chinese was essential to a settlement.[175]

France and Indonesia then took the initiative to invite Cambodia's four opposition factions and several other countries in the region to a peace conference in Paris in late summer 1989. Pérez de Cuéllar took part but confined his role to suggesting ideas that might be implemented.[176]

Negotiations continued over the next year. Pressure from major UN members increased. The five permanent members of the Council favored an Australian proposal that the United Nations itself administer Cambodia between a cease-fire and elections.[177] Cambodia's opposition coalition accepted the plan. A schedule for national elections was worked out in August 1990, and a cease-fire was agreed to the following June.[178]

An overall agreement was at last signed in Paris on October 23, 1991, and was endorsed a few days later by the Council. The plan provided for broad supervisory and administrative roles for the United Nations. A UN Transitional Authority in Cambodia (UNTAC) would verify withdrawal of the foreign forces, clear mines, disarm factions, organize elections, ensure law and order, repatriate refugees, and begin a reconstruction program.

Under the peace accord, the four factions formed a UN-sponsored interim coalition. The Khmer Rouge later withdrew from the coalition and did not register for the May 1993 elections.

Though UNTAC did not actually begin work until after he left office, Pérez de Cuéllar was quoted in the October 24, 1991, issue of the *New York Times* as saying that UNTAC was probably the most important and complex mission in UN history.[179] The Secretary-General described Cambodia's rebirth as "one of the remarkable triumphs of reason and... negotiations that marked the end of the Cold War."[180]

Increased diplomatic pressure from the United Nations and states in the region played an important role in forcing pragmatic progress on the Cambodian question. So, too, did the increasing expense of Vietnam's occupation and Moscow's readiness to reduce its commitment to Hanoi.[181]

No Compromise in the War in the Persian Gulf

Pérez de Cuéllar tried to play a constructive role in preventing the Gulf War. Despite two trips to the region and many phone consultations, he did not succeed.

The Council took a tough and uncompromising stand that left little room for diplomatic maneuver. Newly unified in what its members saw as a clear-cut case of aggression, the Council returned to the role that its founders had hoped it would play. Yet the victory did not come easily or cheaply.

Kuwait, a former British protectorate and Iraq's oil-rich neighbor, had been independent since 1961. However, on August 1, 1990, Iraq's Saddam Hussein dispatched 100,000 troops to seize the neighboring state. His justification was that Kuwait had once been part of Iraq and, logically, should be again.

The Council, led to action by the United States, saw the move in much starker terms—naked aggression that could not be tolerated. Within hours, the Council formally condemned the action and demanded Iraq's unconditional withdrawal.

More Council resolutions ensued. An embargo was put on all trade except food and medicine. A ban was placed on the purchase of Iraqi oil and on all weapons sales to Iraq. In a show of force meant to deter Hussein from more surprise moves, US President George H. W. Bush sent the first of 230,000 American troops to

Saudi Arabia to protect US allies under the UN Charter right of self-defense.[182]

Iraq showed no signs of heeding the UN demands. Indeed, Hussein formally announced the annexation of Kuwait on August 8. Baghdad at first also refused to let foreigners and UN staff members leave Iraq. The situation was eased only when the Secretary-General sent two staffers to Iraq, including the future secretary-general, Kofi Annan, to try to arrange the hostages' departure.

In late August, Pérez de Cuéllar traveled to Jordan to talk with Iraq's foreign minister, Tariq Aziz, to impress on him the seriousness of the situation. Although under no UN orders to go, the Secretary-General explained later at a press conference, "It was not only important but, I would say, indispensable for the Secretary-General to take his own initiative to try to find the ways and means towards solving this extremely dangerous problem."[183] But he returned to New York with no results.

On November 29, 1990, the Council passed Resolution 698, its 12th on the issue. This authorized the use of force to restore international peace and security (under Chapter 7) unless Iraq withdrew its troops from Kuwait by January 15, 1991. It was the Council's first such authorization of military force since the 1950 Korean War.

The clock was ticking. In October, the Council had suggested that the Secretary-General use his good offices again to pursue diplomacy. It also demanded Iraq's unconditional withdrawal from Kuwait. Several national mediation efforts and one by an Arab group were underway. The American effort involved US Secretary of State James Baker who met for six hours on January 9, 1991, with Tariq Aziz in Geneva. Like the others, it yielded nothing. President Bush, who said he had sent Baker to communicate, not to negotiate, described the response as "a total rebuff."[184]

The so-called "pause for goodwill" was fast approaching the deadline. On January 12, 1991, Pérez de Cuéllar set out for Baghdad in one last attempt to get Iraq's compliance. The Council had not specifically asked him to go. Indeed, many members were nervous about his decision.[185]

As he explained to reporters before he left, "[It] is my moral duty as Secretary-General of the United Nations to do everything in order to avoid war. My only strength is moral strength."[186] He met first with Aziz, who cited a passage from the Quran: "Fighting may be forced on you even if you hate to engage in it. And even if you hate it, it may be good for you."[187]

The Secretary-General was kept waiting for hours for his eventual meeting with Hussein. "This chance was clearly small," he recalled in his memoir. "Yet in my previous dealings with Saddam Hussein, I had found a rational man. If reason was to triumph over pride, then working through the United Nations Secretary-General could make the retreat easier for him."[188]

Pérez de Cuéllar told Hussein that he had the wide support of world leaders and asked him to take at least one step to defuse the crisis. In return, the Secretary-General would urge the Council to review its decisions on sanctions and to consider other forward moves. He said if he returned from the meeting with nothing, those seeking war would see it as reason to go ahead. Hussein insisted that Kuwait was not occupied but reunified with Iraq. He said that all Iraqis knew that Kuwait was Iraq's 19th province and that no Iraqi would "whisper the word 'withdrawal.'" He argued that all the relevant UN decisions were actually US decisions. "What the US wants," he said, "it gets."[189]

The Secretary-General recalled that Hussein "almost jocularly" bid him farewell and told him to come back with a better package next time. The Iraqi leader showed no signs of nervousness or doubt. Yet, for the UN chief, "there was no doubt in my mind that Saddam Hussein knew perfectly well, as I did, that his adamant refusal to withdraw from Kuwait made war inevitable." The Secretary-General gave a full report to the Council on his unsuccessful mission on January 14. He also issued one last appeal to Hussein but received no response.[190]

The first of some 10,000 air attacks on Iraq, led by the United States, began on January 16, 1991. President Bush phoned Pérez de Cuéllar the night before to alert him. The attacks continued for several weeks.

Finally, in late February coalition ground forces moved in. The United Nations had authorized the use of military force. The United States had appointed Norman Schwarzkopf as commander and wanted the coalition troops to wear UN emblems and carry the UN flag. Pérez de Cuéllar refused. He presumably wanted no repeat of the Korean War model in which the United States used the UN name but allowed no interference. Schwarzkopf was never designated a UN commander and never reported to the United Nations on progress made.[191]

On February 27, the "100-hour" war on the ground stopped. Iraq told the Council that it would comply fully with all relevant resolutions. Within days Iraq voided its annexation of Kuwait and promised to pay reparations.

The Council drew up a long list of conditions that Iraq needed to meet before a formal cease-fire could take effect. On April 3, the Council passed Resolution 687, the longest in UN history and promptly dubbed the "mother" of all Council resolutions. It required the United Nations to oversee the destruction of Iraq's weapons of mass destruction. It also called for a continuing arms embargo, reparations for Kuwait, and UN border patrols. A few days later, the UN Iraq–Kuwait Observation Mission (UNIKOM) was established.

In still another resolution two days later, the Council demanded an end to Iraqi repression of its own civilian Kurds and Shi'ites and urged the Secretary-General to pursue humanitarian efforts.

When Pérez de Cuéllar wanted Baghdad's permission, however, to put UN monitors in the northern region where Kurds were being killed, he was refused on grounds of sovereignty. On April 16, President Bush phoned Pérez de Cuéllar to alert the United Nations that he planned to send troops into northern Iraq to provide relief for the Kurds and to limit further government repression there. Bush urged the Secretary-General to make it clear publicly that the military move was in accord with the Council resolution.

The Secretary-General in his memoir said the United States was well motivated and had saved many Iraqi lives by its actions, but that he could not, in good conscience, stretch the meaning of the resolution to say that it authorized Western military incursion. Either Iraq's consent or a new resolution, he felt, was needed.[192]

In time, the United States, France, and Britain, without specific UN authorization, moved ahead to impose no-fly zones in both the north and the south to protect Kurds and Shi'ites from further repression.

Speculation continues to this day as to why Hussein invaded Kuwait despite the many warnings. Some analysts think he probably just thought he could get away with it. After all, the Council took no action against Iraq when it invaded Iran a decade earlier, and Washington supported Iraq during that war. However, the global climate had changed, and so had the pressures on Iraq. On August 15, Baghdad returned land and prisoners to Iran that had been seized during the Iran–Iraq War. Iraq hoped to reduce any incentive Tehran might feel to join the new UN action against Iraq.

Pérez de Cuéllar suggested in his memoir that Iraq's invasion of Kuwait may have been a case in which "an identity with the ancient glory of Babylon was added to a near-maniacal personal ego to produce a man of boundless ambition who could not draw the logical consequence when faced with the certainty of disastrous defeat."[193]

In any case, it was the Council that played the decisive role in the Gulf War. UN secretaries-general have at times managed to divorce themselves from Council resolutions and stake an effective independent path. This was no such case.

Pérez de Cuéllar was "an agent, not an autonomous actor," explained Benjamin Rivlin.[194]

"The Secretary-General felt it was his duty to go [to Iraq], and he did it at considerable risk," Álvaro de Soto recalled. "Not only was there little chance [of success], but he might end up being the one that gave the signal for the firing to begin. That's what the Iraqis accused him of doing. [They say] he wasn't clear enough in telling them, 'Listen, you'll be bombed'.... It should have been obvious but...

it contributed to this image we [the UN] sometimes have of being appeasers."[195]

James Sutterlin agreed. "He knew the trip to Baghdad was hopeless," he said. "He had no wiggle room. Bush had given him nothing to play with in terms of alternative solutions."[196]

"He felt he had to seek a mediated solution," David Malone, a Canadian diplomat and former head of the International Peace Institute, noted, "but he went without much hope and, indeed, achieved nothing with Saddam Hussein."[197]

Looking Back: How Did Pérez de Cuéllar Fare?

The Cold-War thaw of the late 1980s played an important part in UN accomplishments during those years. Yet Pérez de Cuéllar's instincts for timing and his diplomatic skills were also key.

During his first term, as he put it, the Cold War "seemed to congeal international relations into a kind of slow-moving glacier."[198] He said there were times when he felt like the man in the Greek myth, Sisyphus, forever condemned to roll a stone uphill.[199]

By the close of his second term, however, he could look back with considerable satisfaction on the UN role in ending the eight-year Iran–Iraq War, peace agreements and elections in Nicaragua and El Salvador, a Namibia that was gaining its independence, restoration of an independent Cambodia, a Soviet agreement to withdraw troops from Afghanistan, and the freeing of Western hostages from Lebanon.

Many of the United Nations' most important and broad-based peacekeeping operations began during these conflicts. Peacekeepers started to do much more than just patrol cease-fire lines. Their efforts now included overseeing elections, disarming troops, and protecting human rights. Five such new operations were launched during 1988 and 1989 alone.[200] UN efforts in peacekeeping were awarded the Nobel Peace Prize in September 1988 and accepted by Pérez de Cuéllar.

Certainly his lack of ego and soft-spoken manner were major advantages in resolving those later conflicts. He was anything but flamboyant and was often described as quiet, polite, and colorless. In *Calling the Shots*, author Phyllis Bennis, for instance, describes him as "uninspired and lackluster."[201]

Yet he could also be outspoken and very persistent. In researching a book on the Council role, Canada's David Malone recalled in an interview, "It came out again and again that the Secretary-General had put much more pressure [on foreign ministers and ambassadors to the UN] than was ever apparent publicly.... He prodded the Security Council a great deal.... I think he was quite creative in sensing the end of the Cold War by challenging the permanent five to work together...before most of the rest of us realized the Cold War was ending.... I do credit Pérez de Cuéllar for sensing that this provided the UN with an opportunity to play an important role in resolving so-called regional conflicts."[202]

"I think Pérez de Cuéllar did a lot...in a rather unobtrusive way... to restore the office and the UN in a tough time," agreed Inis Claude Jr. "He was not always the shrinking violet, but he was careful and shrewd."[203]

"He had a good capacity to size people up, no matter who they were—from Ortega to Khrushchev," observed James Sutterlin. "It was generally a very accurate perception."[204]

"He is truly a brilliant mind, razor sharp," insisted Bhaskar Menon, former UN staff member. As editor of the staff newspaper, Menon said he was viewed as "a troublemaker" by the Secretary-General. But after leaving the United Nations to become a journalist, he was asked by Pérez de Cuéllar to write some speeches for him. Menon recalled interviewing him after his return from Baghdad in 1991. "I threw every kind of curve ball, and he fielded every one.... He was a master of the nuance."[205]

The Secretary-General briefed the Council when it was locked in vetoes. "He kept the Security Council in the picture—just enough so [members] felt involved...and respected," noted de Soto, "but not so much that they were in a position to second guess him or hijack the effort."[206]

He was adept both at reading the tea leaves and carving out an independent role when one was needed.

"Whenever a [Council] resolution was not formulated or agreed upon, he would sense the consensus and express his position," observed Clovis Maksoud, a former Arab League ambassador to the United Nations. "He was more courageous than he appeared. He steered the UN into a course that laid the foundation for objectivity, planning, peacekeeping, and mediation."[207]

Often, as in his efforts to mediate the Iran–Iraq War, he tried hard to keep his role quite separate from that of the Council. Iran saw the Council as biased against it and refused to deal with it.

The Secretary-General thought the Council did a "very bad job" regarding that war and that the Council's resolution was "absolutely not helpful," noted Sutterlin. "I think [separating his role from the Council] is an absolutely essential distinction...especially because there is frequently considerable resentment and distrust of the Council.... When Iraq invaded Kuwait, the Secretary-General made a special point of making it very clear to Saddam Hussein that he wasn't coming under Council instructions. He was coming as secretary-general in the light of his responsibilities." Sutterlin said the Secretary-General even tried, albeit unsuccessfully, to get the Council resolution reworded and remained somewhat "hamstrung" by it.[208]

The General Assembly's persistent hostility to Israel and to South Africa's apartheid policy also undermined his efforts to settle conflicts involving those two states.[209]

In his memoir, *Man Without a Gun*, recounting the freeing of the Western hostages in Lebanon, Giandomenico Picco wrote that, when asked by one of the ski-masked kidnappers if he had been sent by the Secretary-General or by the Security Council, Picco said Pérez de Cuéllar had sent him. The pleased response was, "That is why we will be dealing with you...[otherwise] we would have had a problem."[210]

Pérez de Cuéllar liked working with a small staff. His top aides were influential in developing mediating positions. He delegated easily to those whom he trusted, such as de Soto in the Central American crises and Picco in the hostage situation.

"His ability to delegate was fantastic," Picco noted. "He was most comfortable just with his inner group...about ten people...like you're more comfortable with your family."[211]

Recalling his work in the El Salvador negotiations, de Soto said, "He said to me, 'You're running this show, but if at some point you need me, let me know.' But I spoke for him. I had the implicit authority to invoke his name."[212]

"Pérez didn't trust many people, but those he did, he had full confidence in," Sutterlin noted, adding that everything was checked with the Secretary-General. "If he felt something was being done wrong, he told them."[213]

Despite seeming remote to many staffers outside his inner circle, he was very protective of the Secretariat as a whole. He conceded, however, that in the past some staffers were too close to their governments and sometimes were pressured to follow national interests.[214] Though the permanent five Council members expected to hold the five most senior UN posts and traditionally provided the candidates, Pérez dc Cuéllar insisted on choosing from a list.[215]

When he first took office, the Secretary-General promised to revitalize the international civil service and set the United Nations on a new course. Yet the roadblocks were many, and reforms were few.

He did trim the Secretariat staff by 17 percent during his tenure.[216] He also started the Office for Research and the Collection of Information (ORCI) in 1987 to equip him with better data with which to alert the Council to potential global crises, but it was abolished in the 1990s.

Pérez de Cuéllar also launched an important new approach with the Council. He tried to attend every Council meeting, something his predecessors had not done. He also hosted a series of luncheon meetings for the five permanent members. Those meetings in the late 1980s, made possible by the winding down of the Cold War, helped form the basis for the US ability to get unanimous support to expel Iraqi troops from Kuwait and for the effort to bring the two sides in El Salvador to Mexico City for joint talks.

"The Council for the first time reached a consensus on any number of things," recalled Fred Eckhard, a former spokesman for the Secretary-General. "The Russians voted right along with the Americans, and the Chinese seemed to not want to be left out.... They either abstained or voted for..."[217]

By contrast, in the early 1980s the Secretary-General had to host separate lunches for Council members from the West, China, and the Soviet Union. "We couldn't put them together around a table," Pérez de Cuéllar recalled.[218]

Of his own style in his good-offices capacity, he noted in his memoir that he always tried to distance himself from "obsession." He wanted to be able to "stand back and see a problem in perspective."[219]

Yet what could he really offer in mediation beyond his own powers of persuasion?

In the Iran–Iraq War he offered Iran a UN report on the question of which nation—Iraq—actually started the war. His success was also due mostly, however, to the slowly dawning realization in Iran that it was pointless to continue a costly war and that the UN provided a way out without losing face.

"The fundamental thesis of our operation was that, by definition, we do not have the tools of a state—weapons and money," Picco said. "We had to invent our negotiating cards. [They need to be something] that your opponent wishes to have. [Neither side] ever asked, as a quid pro quo, for anything that was tangible. Too many people in the West believe that money and death are the ultimate rewards and threat. They never were."[220]

This Secretary-General wrestled, like others before and after him, with the question of the United Nations' right to interfere in questions of national sovereignty, action specifically barred in the Charter. The UN role in national elections was a new problem that arose with the end of the Cold War, especially as domestic conflicts intensified. Nicaragua wanted UN help. Pérez de Cuéllar initially resisted but eventually agreed. The General Assembly also authorized a UN Observer Group for the Verification of Elections in Haiti (ONUVEH) to monitor the December 1990 election process.

"Once it was done, [an election role] was seen to be a legitimate UN operation," said Thomas Weiss, chairman of the Academic Council on the UN System (ACUNS) and co-director of the UN Intellectual History Project. "It became politically less onerous to call on the UN as a way out of a crisis."[221]

Humanitarian issues began to firm up the United Nations' resolve to act in internal conflicts. Preventing human rights abuses and other adverse developments that could affect global peace were increasingly seen as a UN responsibility. Pérez de Cuéllar favored incorporating the Declaration of Human Rights directly into the Charter. Nongovernmental organizations (NGOs), working inside nations began to be seen as attractive UN partners. As the Secretary-General once told a *Christian Science Monitor* journalist, "I think we are rather close to a reconsideration of noninterference."[222]

Pérez de Cuéllar told a University of Bordeaux audience in April 1991, "We are clearly witnessing an irresistible shift in public attitudes towards the belief that defense of the oppressed in the name of morality should prevail over frontiers and legal documents."[223]

Before any of his trips, the Secretary-General said he met with Amnesty International leaders on individual cases of human rights abuse that he might usefully broach with national leaders. He kept no records but estimated a 90-percent favorable outcome. "I call this 'my discretion diplomacy,'" he said in his memoir.[224]

Though critical of what she saw as some early missteps in his diplomatic career, Felice Gaer, director of the American Jewish Committee's Jacob Blaustein Institute for the Advancement of Human Rights, said that the Secretary-General appeared to undergo an evolution in his thinking on human rights issues. She noted he used some "rousing language" on the importance of NGOs to the United Nations during his second term and "some rhetorical positives about human rights which were good."[225]

The Secretary-General also viewed UN-defined norms as playing an important role in shaping a more just world. He saw the United Nations as a power broker and mobilizer in areas such as the control of nuclear and chemical weapons, environmental protection, and population planning.[226]

Yet he claimed disappointment that the United Nations did not function more effectively as a system for economic and social development during his tenure. He urged his successor to try to arrange a North–South dialogue, something he had been unable to achieve.[227]

In his memoir, written six years after leaving the United Nations, Pérez de Cuéllar described it as a "world unto itself...of numbing meetings, interspersed with far-off crises...where the truly significant is sometimes lost in the flood of words and paper."[228]

Still, he managed to remain patient and take a broad view of his own role. Good offices for him went well beyond the role of messenger: "The secretary-general must be mediator and standard bearer, moderator and guide, conciliator and arbiter, impartial in all... I was called on to fill all these roles."[229]

Sutterlin said he regarded the Secretary-General's two major achievements as his mediating role in the Iran–Iraq War and in the Central American peace process: "I actually think he should have gotten the Nobel Prize [for those], but he didn't."[230]

Pérez de Cuéllar, like most others before him, did not get high marks for his administrative skills.

"He resented and resisted suggestions for change, taking them as personal criticisms," wrote Bonnie Angelo in a lengthy *Time* article that termed his stewardship "flawed." His most serious shortcoming, she wrote, was his unwillingness to bring the UN bureaucracy under control.[231]

His varied diplomatic efforts also occasionally drew criticism. Some analysts say he did as much as he could to stave off the Gulf War. Others argue that he could have done more.

"He took the position that this was a Chapter 7 affair [allowing the Security Council to authorize force in cases of aggressive threats to global peace] and not within the sphere of the secretary-general," noted Princeton's Leon Gordenker. [232]

As Edward Luck put it, "He didn't try to block [the war] or say the UN wouldn't cooperate, but he was in many ways uncomfortable with the whole Desert Storm exercise."[233]

Still, as his second term ended, Pérez de Cuéllar was satisfied that the United Nations was no longer on the sidelines but at the center of world affairs. He credited the change in the global climate, the revived Council role, and the eventual readiness of those fighting each other to accept the UN role as providing a way out.

"It would have been self-defeating hubris," he insisted, "to assume that the United Nations or the Secretary-General could independently bring peace in any of these cases.... But the United Nations' contribution in each...was central and indispensable."[234]

"The Security Council did what the secretary-general never could have done in the Gulf War," Picco contended. "And in Beirut with the hostages, the secretary-general did what the Security Council never could have done. This is not a zero-sum game between two organs. It's an 'everybody wins' situation."[235]

"The Secretary-General can't claim credit for having saved the world," said Edward Luck. "The world changed in the middle of his tenure. He looked good because he was honest and had his ego under control. He took advantage of changes in the international political climate. By the time he left, North–South relations were much better, and the organization seemed to revive."[236]

"I think Pérez de Cuéllar teaches us that leadership has to be exercised in a very discreet way," de Soto observed. "If the leader is too obvious about wanting to take the lead, he will be knocked down. The Security Council likes an envelope-pushing secretary-general so long as he doesn't tear the envelope."[237]

Pérez de Cuéllar was asked by several Council members to stay on at least two more years. President George H. W. Bush, who awarded him the US Medal of Freedom for his service, urged him to stay for a third term. But, noting that to everything there is a season, the Secretary-General was convinced that the time was right for a new voice and a fresh perspective.[238]

He returned to Peru and, in time, ran for his nation's presidency. Unlike Waldheim, he was not elected.

CHAPTER EIGHT

Boutros Boutros-Ghali: An Egyptian Steps In after the Cold War

There was nothing either swift or automatic in the Security Council's 1991 election of Boutros Boutros-Ghali as the United Nations' sixth secretary-general.

True, African nations were demanding "their turn" and had persuaded the other nonaligned nations in the Group of 77 to back their claim.

However, Boutros-Ghali, Egypt's deputy prime minister of foreign affairs and a former law professor, still had to campaign hard for that "African" post. Admitting that he saw the "political animal" in himself, he viewed campaigning for the position as a "wonderful adventure."[1]

Once he actually got the job, he reported, almost incredulously, "I began a new career at age 69."[2]

He considered working for the United Nations while he was a visiting Fulbright professor at Columbia University in New York in 1954 but said he would never have wanted the top job while the Cold War was on. As he told the *London Observer* in 1991, "If I were offered the job five years ago, I would have turned it down. The UN was a dead horse, but...[now] the UN has a special position."[3]

As he tells it, the idea of his candidacy first came up in June 1991. As a government official representing Egypt, he attended a summit of the Organization of African Unity (OAU) in Nigeria. In a closed-door session, talk focused on an African successor to Pérez de Cuéllar. Five possible candidates were suggested. Gabon's president, Omar

Bengo, noted that none, however, spoke French, the United Nations' all-important second language. He turned to the Egyptian, who spoke Arabic, English, and French, and asked, "Boutros, why don't you present yourself?"[4]

In all, the OAU eventually suggested six candidates, including Boutros-Ghali. The Security Council held anonymous straw polls to narrow the field. Finally on the fifth and last round, Boutros-Ghali got an 11-vote majority and no negative votes.

The United States, caught somewhat by surprise, had originally backed Canada's prime minister, Brian Mulroney. He eventually withdrew amid third-world protests. Boutros-Ghali later learned that US President George H. W. Bush and Secretary of State James Baker had failed to agree on a candidate and gave no definite instructions to the US ambassador to the United Nations, Thomas Pickering, who abstained in the final vote.[5] Word was that the United States at the time was still searching for an acceptable candidate and viewed Boutros-Ghali as too old-fashioned, too senior, and too passive for the job.[6]

Boutros-Ghali had headed the Egypt–USSR Friendship Association, and Moscow favored his candidacy. France, where Boutros-Ghali learned to speak flawless French and earned his doctorate in international law at the Sorbonne in 1949, strongly promoted him right from the start.

"The US was outfoxed by the French—it didn't think he was ever going to be elected," noted Benjamin Rivlin, a former director of the Ralph Bunche Institute at the City University of New York.[7]

After the Assembly confirmed the Council's choice on December 3, 1991, Boutros-Ghali took his oath of office in Arabic and gave his first speech in Arabic, French, and English. He insisted from the start—though he later changed his mind—that he would serve one term only.

The new Secretary-General came from a wealthy and prominent Coptic Christian family. His grandfather, Boutros Ghali, was Egypt's prime minister until his assassination in 1910 by a radical Muslim nationalist.

The grandson felt a strong calling to a political career from his early years. However, he started as an academic. He chaired the political science department and taught international law at Cairo University for close to 30 years. Finally, in the last half of the 1970s, he took on a variety of government jobs. As a minority Christian married to a Jewish woman from Alexandria, he never rose to the top ranks.

He was probably best known globally for his role in helping negotiate the Camp David accords. He accompanied Egypt's president, Anwar Sadat, on the trip to Jerusalem that led to establishment of Egyptian–Israeli relations. Two of Boutros-Ghali's superiors resigned rather than endorse that trip.

"People tend to forget that he had a key role in backing up Sadat," noted George Sherry, a former UN assistant secretary-general for special political affairs. "That's a move very much to his credit."[8] Not everyone, of course, read it that way. Some considered him a traitor.

His extensive government experience in Egypt doubtless helped him weather the storm of criticism that he would later attract from the United States and others for the UN role he played. As journalist and author Stanley Meisler put it, Boutros-Ghali knew how to "shrug off insults."[9]

Optimism in the Air

When he first took on the UN post, the climate for more effective UN action looked particularly promising. With Russia and the United States no longer automatically on opposing sides, the Council began to pass resolutions much more easily. The number of peacekeeping missions swiftly multiplied.

The United Nations was basically a new organization in 1992. "Until then, superpower rivalry had pervaded almost every aspect [of UN work]," recalled Richard Thornburgh, a former Pennsylvania governor, in an interview. Thornburgh had been chosen by President George H. W. Bush and appointed by Boutros-Ghali for a one-year assignment as undersecretary-general for administration and management. "Often it had been the silly things—like, if you hire one

Soviet nominee in this place, you have to hire one for the US in another.... It had just been surreal."[10]

While the official residence of UN secretaries-general on Sutton Place was undergoing minor repairs, Boutros-Ghali lived briefly at the Waldorf-Astoria. He termed the rent—$40,000 a month—an "unthinkable sum." When he was finally able to move into the four-story Georgian townhouse, he took along his prized collections of bronze birds and Ottoman pen cases. His mother started the latter collection during his student days with a pen case of his grandfather's.[11]

Soon, the Secretary-General began to map out broad themes that he hoped would characterize his tenure: peace and preventive diplomacy, development, reform, and democratization among and within states.[12]

As the African candidate, he also felt a special obligation to his home continent. "I have loved Africa and tried so hard throughout my life to help her," he wrote in his memoir. "Africa is the mother of us all, and Egypt is the oldest daughter of Africa."[13]

However, in looking back on his record, he conceded that, as much as he wanted to advance the cause of Africa's nations, UN members soon became preoccupied with the increasing number of post–Cold War conflicts. UN obligations to the poorest nations were neglected in the process.[14]

Still, hoping to take advantage of the generally more positive global atmosphere as he started his term, Boutros-Ghali quickly convened the first-ever Council meeting at the head-of-state level. He hoped the meeting, held on January 31, 1992, would help him to play a more effective role as secretary-general.

"Boutros-Ghali was no shrinking violet," noted David Malone, a former Canadian ambassador to the United Nations and former president of the International Peace Academy (now called the International Peace Institute). "He had very few doubts about his own capacity and was eager to seize the moment shortly after his election when he felt the UN could play a much more active role in international security affairs."[15]

Yet as the special Council meeting drew near, "I felt like the new boy in school who would have to sit for an examination before 15 world leaders," the new Secretary-General recalled.[16]

Ultimately, the leaders asked him to come up with recommendations by that July on how to strengthen and streamline the United Nations' capacity for preventive diplomacy, peacekeeping, and peacemaking. He was also asked to find ways to make greater use of his good-offices role under the Charter.

"It [the summit] was kind of a first-class funeral to the Cold War," said Álvaro de Soto, a former senior political adviser to Boutros-Ghali and a former UN assistant secretary-general. "Both [Boris] Yeltsin and [George H. W.] Bush were there. They served the secretary-general with a unique opportunity on a silver platter."[17]

Boutros-Ghali was well aware that he was breaking new ground. "I was at the center of a political effort at consensus building with a mandate that had no precedent in UN history," he recalled. "I had won my post through politics and now I was being asked to become a political leader." He was also mindful of the irony involved: "I would have to assert the independence of my office, and that could destroy me politically."[18]

The summit discussion ranged from democratization to collective security but without full recognition of the problems or costs involved. It was an "over-optimistic climate," in the view of Edward Newman, author of *The UN Secretary-General from the Cold War to the New Era*.[19]

A few UN-watchers had their doubts that the Council summit was really that serious in its request for recommendations from the Secretary-General. "I think it was a ceremonial meeting," insisted Leon Gordenker, Princeton professor emeritus of international relations. "I suppose you could say that Boutros-Ghali made a serious mistake in taking at face value the Council instructions to work out a time frame for the future."[20]

Internal Reform

In those early days on the job, Boutros-Ghali also managed to focus—if only briefly—on UN internal reform. At the time, the organization was strongly criticized as inefficient, wasteful, and even corrupt.

"He inherited a very difficult situation—the hangover from premature jubilation about the end of the Cold War," remarked Sir Brian Urquhart, former UN undersecretary-general for special political affairs, in a session with UN reporters. "Boutros-Ghali was obliged to do massive reorganization on a machine which had been grossly overstretched and going at full speed."[21]

The new Secretary-General wrote in his UN memoir that the organization had many dedicated and intelligent workers, but that the staff as a whole lacked "intensity and independence" and was "bloated, slack, and out of touch." He said many people owed their jobs and often part of their salaries to their home countries.[22]

He also told Paul Lewis of the *New York Times* that he had learned from his experience in Egypt's bureaucracy that "stealth is essential," a comment that did not endear him to the Secretariat.[23]

He energetically began to make changes, giving himself a 60-day deadline. He consolidated many of the 35 departments and abolished 18 high-level posts, saving some $4 million. High-level political appointees were put on one-year contracts, instead of the more usual three- or five-year contracts. Boutros-Ghali stipulated that no undersecretary-general was to travel without his approval.[24]

The response, not surprisingly, was less than appreciated by those affected. Many of the remaining staff complained that the changes left them overworked and underpaid. As for those who lost their jobs or were transferred or demoted, ambassadors from their home countries besieged the Secretary-General. They wanted to know why he had taken such "punitive" action.[25]

Overall, Boutros-Ghali managed to cut some 1,000 staff positions and consolidate several UN field operations. Yet several of his proposed changes were defeated in the Assembly. He attributed that to the North–South split between developed and developing nations.[26]

In addition to the need for staff reform and savings, Boutros-Ghali also faced an alarming budget crisis. A *Time* magazine article likened the situation to that of a new chief executive taking over a corporation in danger of going into a Chapter 11 bankruptcy.[27]

Members owed almost $1 billion in unpaid assessments. Only 67 of the 159 members had paid their regular dues in full. Peacekeeping costs had tripled, and the United Nations was forced to borrow from the few solvent operations to keep the others going. The Secretary-General wrote personal letters to leaders of nations in arrears and slashed several UN services such as conference translations and weekend meetings.[28]

He drew up a list of suggestions, including some already made by Pérez de Cuéllar. Boutros-Ghali proposed an emergency peacekeeping fund of $50 million, an endowment fund of $1 billion, a small tax on air tickets and arms transfers, and interest charges on past-due assessments. He urged that peacekeeping costs be considered part of each nation's national defense budget.

At his request, an independent advisory group headed by the former US Federal Reserve chairman Paul Volcker and former deputy governor of the Bank of Japan, Shijuro Ogata, studied the problem and incorporated several of the Secretary-General's suggestions in their report issued a year later.

In time, the uphill nature of the reform battle and pressing global challenges that first year combined to divert Boutros-Ghali's attention to other matters.

"Almost on a daily basis, Boutros-Ghali's ability to handle administration and management matters—and, frankly, his interest—flagged substantially," said Thornburgh, whose job was to help with the reform effort. "In the final analysis, whatever desire the Secretary-General brought to the office to handle these things was eroded, overtaken by events."[29]

Boutros-Ghali began to guard his own time more carefully. Unlike Pérez de Cuéllar, he rarely attended sessions of the Council, which was meeting almost daily. Boutros-Ghali appointed a deputy, Chinmaya Gharekhan, to attend Council meetings on his behalf.

"If the Secretary-General...attended every Security Council meeting or consultation, he would have done nothing else but sit in the Security Council all day—so that's a dramatic change [from Pérez de Cuéllar's routine]," explained Fred Eckhard, former UN spokesman.[30]

Admittedly, there were some drawbacks to the new pattern.

"You'd ask a question, and his [designated Council] spokesman would say, 'I'm not informed,'" Diego Arria, a former Council member who was Venezuela's ambassador to the United Nations, said. "The Secretary-General didn't want anybody from the Secretariat giving opinions or information.... He tended to go more to the public meetings of the Council where everything is already decided and there are no surprises."[31]

"The relations between him and the Council were not fantastic," confirmed Álvaro de Soto, who sometimes substituted for Ambassador Gharekhan. "The Council felt he was being very aloof."[32]

Boutros-Ghali still had one major internal job ahead of him. He had been asked at the January 1992 Council summit to suggest ways to improve UN security, particularly peacekeeping, by July.

In response, he produced *An Agenda for Peace*—one month ahead of deadline. It was essentially his first published policy statement, intended as a blueprint for a more ambitious brand of peacekeeping. Boutros-Ghali spent more than 40 hours reading and revising the suggestions of his staff and academic experts to produce a 52-page document.[33]

He proposed deploying UN troops as a preventive measure, when at least one government agreed, to discourage potential conflict. In the past, the United Nations was often unable to act unless both sides agreed and often only after a signed cease-fire.

That suggestion was put into practice later that year in Macedonia, without the specific consent of Serbia. UN peacekeepers were posted inside Macedonia's borders with Albania and Serbia to block expansion of the Yugoslav conflict.

Boutros-Ghali's report also suggested that as many member governments as possible make available up to 1,000 troops each on a standby basis for possible speedy deployment. He stressed that it was not a call for a standing army but for troops to be more readily available to Council requests. There had often been long delays.

He further suggested that some troops should be more heavily armed than traditional peacekeepers to enforce the peace in dangerous situations such as acts of aggression, tentative cease-fires and the delivery of humanitarian goods. Action would be taken in clearly defined cases only and under the authorization of the Council and command of the secretary-general.

His report also urged a review of peacekeeper and police training, a larger role for regional organizations in preventive diplomacy and peacekeeping, and increased coordination efforts in UN fact finding.

UN peacekeeping duties had been slowly but steadily expanding over the years. They sometimes now included supervising elections, shoring up democratic institutions, disarming militias, and even helping refugees return to their homeland. In some ways, *An Agenda for Peace* simply aimed to solidify trends already started. Indeed, many proposals had been made before by think tanks and were not considered all that radical.

Yet some governments thought the *Agenda* was much too ambitious and unrealistic. The concepts of preventive deployment and peace enforcement gave them pause. Some nations were also concerned that the report did not address the increasing dilemma of conflict within, rather than just between, states. Developing nations were happy with the prospect of more UN involvement in postconflict nation building but concerned that any charge of human rights abuse or lack of democracy on their part might trigger a UN violation of their sovereign rights.

In autumn 1992, the Council encouraged members to advise the Secretary-General of their willingness to provide troops and equipment. The Council also urged a larger role for the Secretary-General in alerting the Council to potential security dangers and in mediating disputes.

The General Assembly established a working group to study each chapter of the report. The Council did its own review. Peacekeeping and political affairs departments were established.

However, by spring 1993, the Council insisted anew that peace-keeping operations still required a precise mandate and consent of all involved governments or parties, except in rare cases.

Though the initial reaction had been positive, support soon seemed to taper off. As Boutros-Ghali put it in his memoir, "My idea at first sparked great interest, but soon it was ignored or declared to be politically impossible."[34]

Leon Gordenker, a prolific author on UN matters, said, "It's a trait of every bureaucratic organization to try to do its work better. A lot of what Boutros Boutros-Ghali attempted [in *Agenda*] was what bureaucrats thought they could do. I thought it was all old stuff.... The one thing that was quite unusual was asking for a military force which would be at the secretary-general's disposal without an earlier policy decision. And that disappeared without a trace."[35]

During his time in the United Nations' top job, Boutros-Ghali's devotion to work and his energy were never questioned. He expected the same focus on hard work from his staff.

"If you came to a meeting unprepared, you took your life in your hands," recalled one close aide. "He knew the stuff, and he expected you to know it. He would drive everybody nuts because of his attention to detail."[36]

Sophisticated and intellectual in his dark-frame glasses, he was professorial, outspoken, and often critical if he felt others were mistaken or ill informed. He was not a great communicator. His manner was often aloof and appeared arrogant. Some even dubbed him "the little pharaoh."[37]

Yet, according to one staffer, he never began a meeting by saying what he thought. He generally drew high marks for his ability to analyze an issue from mixed vantage points before reaching a decision.

"He was honest and honorable but was considered to have an abrasive personality," noted George Sherry. "He was very demanding and not very appreciative of what was done."[38]

Some UN ambassadors said he tended to appoint people he could control to high posts, those who would follow his mandate to the letter. Some also resented the fact that, rather than deal with them in person, the Secretary-General would often consult their foreign ministers or heads of state.

A former Indonesian ambassador to the United Nations once told a reporter that he had been given a total of 120 seconds in presenting his credentials to Boutros-Ghali in his office and was not even asked to sit down.[39]

"As Arabs go, he was remarkably un-Arab," Thomas Franck, a former director of the Center for International Studies at the New York University School of Law, observed. "He was terrifically aristocratic and very much the intellectual. He was basically a French mandarin, a very high civil servant. He would go to a meeting with some of his political masters but otherwise do his work in his office. [He felt] there was no point of sitting around all day while people sounded off."[40]

In Boutros-Ghali's defense at this busy stage in UN history, it should be noted that the Council was constantly handing him problems and asking him to report back with suggestions for action.

He felt that the press and politicians tended to blame him for years of UN mismanagement. He also complained that the Assembly defeated even some of his "modest" reform proposals.[41]

He viewed the Council's job as one of setting policy and his role as guide and catalyst.

"You cannot be neutral," he insisted in a 1995 TV interview with David Frost. "You cannot be passive, waiting [to see] what will be the direction of member states. You have to push everybody."[42]

The British journalist William Shawcross suggested in his book *Deliver Us from Evil* that the Secretary-General would, by giving his own opinions, try to limit the Council's freedom to make choices that might be politically expedient but that he saw as inadequate or inappropriate. Such self-confident behavior often showed the tension between his role as chief administrative officer and his duty to warn the Council of security threats.[43]

The United Nations had been successfully involved in settling the Iran–Iraq War, resolving many of the problems in Cambodia and Namibia, and getting Soviet troops to withdraw from Afghanistan. That rapid level of progress, however, was not to continue. Many more stiff challenges lay ahead.

Inherited Tasks

Part of any new secretary-general's job is to keep up UN projects already under way. Halfway through his first month on the job in 1992, Boutros-Ghali flew to Mexico City to oversee and celebrate the signing of the El Salvador peace agreement reached by Pérez de Cuéllar just two weeks before.

Another major UN project was going on in Cambodia. After the Khmer Rouge rule and genocide of the mid-1970s, the Vietnamese army had invaded and, by 1979, installed a new government led by Hun Sen. In the years since, the regime was the target of increasing criticism and attacks from the Khmer Rouge and two other internal factions. Moscow's once-firm support for Vietnam and its chosen government in Phnom Penh also was slipping.

In October 1991, while Pérez de Cuéllar was still in office, a Cambodian peace agreement was signed in Paris by 19 nations, including the five permanent members of the Security Council. The ambitious plan called for an interim UN administration (UNTAC) to organize, rather than just monitor, elections. The United Nations was also charged with supervising the withdrawal of foreign forces, disarming internal factions, repatriating refugees, and helping with reconstruction. The job would not be easy. An advance UN observer team was to pave the way. It arrived in Phnom Penh in November 1991.

It fell to Boutros-Ghali to name a special representative to head UNTAC. The night before he took office, he met with Yasushi Akashi of Japan, UN undersecretary-general for disarmament, and easily persuaded him to take the job. The Secretary-General then phoned Cambodia's Prince Norodom Sihanouk to be sure he approved the choice. Boutros-Ghali and the prince were French speakers who knew each other well from the days when Egypt and Cambodia first established diplomatic relations. To the Secretary-General's dismay, however, Sihanouk soon publicly announced the Akashi appointment. The Council had not been told. Fortunately for the Secretary-General, it confirmed the choice several days later.[44]

The Council, which formally created UNTAC in February 1992, authorized a force of almost 20,000 troops, police, and civilians. It was to be the largest UN peacekeeping operation to date.

Akashi faced a major challenge. UN troops were slow in coming. A Supreme National Council, representing the four Cambodian factions and headed by Prince Sihanouk, was operating as an interim government of sorts. Akashi had the right under the Paris accords to make a final decision in any impasse. However, he chose to continue negotiating with the four factions instead of overruling them.[45]

The Khmer Rouge and Hun Sen deeply distrusted each other. Violence and intimidation continued nonstop. The Khmer Rouge had been granted the right to take part in the election, but suspected that the U N favored Hun Sen's Vietnam-installed regime.[46]

Some UN forces were poorly trained. Communication and control of the troops were weak.[47] The United Nations was unable to disarm the fighting factions and did not take over the civil administration. As Boutros-Ghali acknowledged in his memoir, the United Nations never could exercise the authority envisioned in the Paris accords.[48]

The Secretary-General was convinced that Sihanouk, intelligent and cultured but also volatile and easily discouraged, was the "pillar of all hopes" for a unified Cambodia.[49]

Boutros-Ghali flew to Phnom Penh, where Sihanouk met him at the airport on April 18, 1992. They drove to the royal palace where servants were everywhere, bowing reverently, in awe of the prince. "To them, he was not only a king but a god," Boutros-Ghali noted.

During their conversations, Sihanouk noted that Cambodia was under the constant threat of domination by Thailand and Vietnam. He urged the Secretary-General to let the United Nations remain for at least three months after the elections, which were scheduled for May 23, 1993, to deter any possible coup. But Boutros-Ghali faced strong pressure from the United States and other nations to get UN forces out promptly after the vote.[50]

Fierce fighting went on. The Khmer Rouge even attacked some UN troops and helicopters, and Boutros-Ghali faced pressure from some advisers to postpone the elections but decided to press ahead. He visited Phnom Penh again a month before the 1993 elections, finding Sihanouk discouraged and depressed. The prince had publicly criticized the United Nations before his guest's arrival and had threatened to resign as leader of the Supreme National Council. Boutros-Ghali begged him to stay on for the good of his people.[51]

At a gathering in the throne room of the palace, the Secretary-General urged the leaders of all four Cambodian factions to respect the voters' decision. He recalled later that the young and unsophisticated Hun Sen, a former Khmer Rouge leader who had defected, looked, in the palatial setting, like "a militant peasant in a field of golden grain." Hun Sen had always wanted maximum foreign aid for Cambodia but a minimal international presence.[52]

To keep the elections on track and successful, the Secretary-General also appeared on TV to remind voters to cast their secret ballots with a clear conscience for the good of their families and Cambodia's future.[53] UNTAC helped end much of the fighting and resettled close to 400,000 refugees from camps along the Thai–Cambodian border so they could vote.

After his return to New York in April, Boutros-Ghali learned from Akashi that Sihanouk had gone to North Korea for medical treatment, where he had been pushed to support the Khmer Rouge. The prince was currently in China, and his doctors there ordered him not to travel. The Secretary-General promptly sent him a message, noting that the next meeting of the Supreme National Council certainly could be held in Beijing and that Akashi could attend. Boutros-Ghali's aim was to be sure that Sihanouk returned to Cambodia by election day as reassurance for voters.[54]

Sihanouk returned the day before the elections. The turnout, despite rain, was 90 percent of the five million registered voters. The process was conducted under the watchful eyes of 900 supervisors from 44 countries and 50,000 Cambodian officers.[55] The two winning parties met with Sihanouk in September and agreed to form a unified government. Boutros-Ghali later said, "There would be repeated setbacks, but the UN operation had been a success."[56]

The Balkans Erupt

The post–Cold War breakup of Yugoslavia planted the crucial seed for the fierce Balkan War. It began in the summer of 1991—before Boutros-Ghali took on the UN job—and lasted for four long years. He would assume significant decision-making authority over time but not without controversy.

Serbia, eager to be the dominant power in a united Yugoslavia, had opposed the disintegration from the start. Yet, one by one, the ethnically diverse regions began to secede. Croatia and Slovenia, following citizen referendums, were first to declare independence in June 1991.

In an effort at preventive diplomacy that did not work, former UN Secretary-General Pérez de Cuéllar and others had strongly warned against swift international recognition of the two regions before protection of ethnic minorities could be firmly guaranteed. He twice wrote the foreign minister of Germany, which had strong ties to Croatia, warning against recognition.[57] Before the end of 1991, however, both Germany and the European Community formally recognized both Croatia and Slovenia. A few days later, Bosnia and Herzegovina announced its intention to become independent and internationally recognized.

Boutros-Ghali later described this rush to recognition in the former Yugoslavia as "foolish" and a definite trigger for the Muslim–Serb battles that followed.[58]

On his second day as Secretary-General, though, he was called on by UN special envoy and former US Secretary of State Cyrus Vance. Vance urged Boutros-Ghali to send UN peacekeepers in to back up the cease-fire Vance had negotiated between Croat leaders and their Serb counterparts who had close ties to the Yugoslav National Army (JNA). The Secretary-General was wary. He shared the concern of the UN peacekeeping chief at the time, Marrack Goulding, that UN troops were likely to come back "in body bags."[59]

A Creeping Mission for UNPROFOR

Despite the Secretary-General's reservations, the Council, which had imposed an arms embargo on all of Yugoslavia the previous fall, soon authorized a group of 50 lightly armed military liaison officers to help keep the new cease-fire. They were assigned to three tense, and substantially Serb, areas of Croatia to protect Croats living there and to ensure the withdrawal of the Yugoslav army from the new nation.

Their efforts, initially intended to be temporary, marked the start of a gradually expanding mandate for the new UN Protection Force (UNPROFOR). War soon broke out in Bosnia as the JNA helped Bosnian Serbs there to secede. Their newly independent republic put its capital at Pale, near Sarajevo.

The humanitarian situation was fast deteriorating for Bosnia's Muslim majority. Sarajevo was the target of heavy shelling. On May 12, 1992, Boutros-Ghali told the Council that "all international observers" now agreed that the Serbs were trying to create ethnically pure regions.[60] Three days later, the Council authorized UN peacekeepers to provide armed escorts for relief convoys in Bosnia and ordered the disarming and disbanding of all irregular forces.

The Secretary-General had argued that the UNPROFOR mandate was not workable since the Bosnian Serbs strongly opposed any increase in the UN presence. The needed respect for the United Nations did not exist. Nor, in his opinion, had the troops been given the tools to do what the Council asked. The UN troops could not respond with force if challenged and were increasingly threatened and humiliated.[61]

As Boutros-Ghali recalled it, the Council's demands were "the beginning of the unrealistic 'mission-creep' that was to lead the UN into its disaster in Bosnia."[62] He said he knew that it was hopeless to ask peacekeepers to be impartial observers while challenging Serb aggression.[63]

The Serb attacks on Sarajevo, where the United Nations had set up its regional headquarters, continued without letup. By the end of 1992, the Serbs had taken control of 70 percent of Bosnia's land area.[64]

On New Year's Eve 1992, Boutros-Ghali and Vance landed in Sarajevo to visit UN troops. Later, when leaving the building that housed the Bosnian presidency, the Secretary-General was met by an angry crowd, calling him a "Fascist" and "murderer" and denouncing the United Nations as not doing nearly enough to help. He tried to explain the limitations of UN actions without much success.

It was here that the Secretary-General told citizens during a press conference that their situation was better than that in at least 10 other places on earth that he could easily list. He later explained that he was referring mainly to the "orphan conflicts" in Africa which, in his view, few people knew or cared about. He said he intended his message as one of hope, to assure the civilians that they had the support of the international community. But his remarks were widely interpreted as brutal and unfeeling.[65]

He had previously voiced a similarly strong opinion in accusing the Council of a double standard in its preoccupation with the "rich man's war" in Yugoslavia while virtually ignoring crises in Somalia and elsewhere.[66]

Bosnia's Muslims had long complained that the UN arms embargo was unfair and that they were uniquely vulnerable. Serbs had access to more weapons through the Yugoslav National Army. The United States accordingly favored a lift of the UN embargo for Bosnia's Muslims, but the Council did not buy it.

An Early Try at Peace Falls Flat

A peace plan proposed by Vance and Lord David Owen, the European Community envoy, in the fall of 1992 would have divided

Bosnia into 10 Swiss-style cantons. Each ethnic group would have three, and Sarajevo, the 10th, would be jointly governed. The plan viewed Bosnia as an independent nation with three aggressors who deserved equal blame. The Bosnian Serbs rejected the proposal because it gave them only 49 percent of the territory.[67]

Additionally, to the disappointment of Vance and Boutros-Ghali, the Clinton administration opposed the plan, on grounds that it appeased the Serbs. The plan also would have required some 30,000 troops to police it, half of whom would have been American.[68]

Encouraged by Washington's opposition, Bosnia's Muslims and Croats were unenthusiastic as well. When Radovan Karadžić, the Bosnian Serb leader, came to New York in early March 1993, Boutros-Ghali strongly suggested that he endorse the plan and quickly. "The entire world is against you," insisted the Secretary-General. Karadžić, whom Boutros-Ghali described as a "burly, posturing, pompadoured" figure and "accomplished diplomatic actor," countered that the plan would make the Serbs the most deprived community in Bosnia. "Karadžić was clearly playing for time," noted the Secretary-General.[69]

A disappointed Vance resigned in April. The Serbs stepped up their attacks and seized even more Bosnian territory. Relief efforts were blocked and sabotaged. The lightly armed UNPROFOR troops found themselves trying to do a dicey combination of peacekeeping, limited enforcement, and delivery of humanitarian aid.

Meanwhile, a lively debate was underway at UN headquarters as to how best to protect predominantly Muslim areas from further Serb bombardment and conquest. Gradually the talk was shifting from the need to defend such areas to the presumably more doable task of deterring attacks against them. In yet another important shift, it was decided that the United Nations' job would be to promote, rather than enforce, withdrawal of hostile forces from Muslim areas.[70]

The "Safe Areas" Myth

In April 1993, Srebrenica, where thousands of Muslims had sought refuge, was on the verge of being seized by Serb forces. To help prevent the invasion, the Council demanded that all parties treat the town as a "safe area." Boutros-Ghali was asked to increase the UN presence there, to arrange for the safety of the sick and wounded, and to ensure delivery of humanitarian aid to civilians. A few weeks later, the Council added Sarajevo and four more Bosnian cities to the "safe areas" list.

Diego Arria, Venezuela's former ambassador to the United Nations and onetime head of the United Nations' nonaligned group, led the push for the Council's first "safe area" resolution.[71] Later, he recalled his shock at what he saw when he led a Council visit to Srebrenica soon after. When he got back, he told Council members, "We have created a monstrosity. These people are hostage to the Serbs. It's like a concentration camp.... We're going to be accomplices to murder."[72]

Boutros-Ghali and Kofi Annan, then undersecretary-general for peacekeeping, were convinced that many more troops would be needed to deter attacks against the six "safe areas." In a closed door session with the Council in May 1993, the Secretary-General proposed that at least 34,000 troops would be required for the expanded task. The numbers were based on a preliminary UN military study. The troops would be under the operational and tactical control of the North Atlantic Treaty Organization (NATO), while the Council would keep the strategic and military authority. Boutros-Ghali warned the Council that if the recommended troop increase were not approved, UN troops might have to withdraw if they came under heavy military pressure.[73]

The United States thought the Secretary-General's proposed troop numbers were too high. In the end, the Council authorized a mere 7,600 troops. It was the so-called light option. The approach was to be gradual, beginning with the redeployment of troops already based in Bosnia. Boutros-Ghali noted that Sir David Hannay, the British ambassador to the United Nations at the time, warned him that he could never get Council approval for the larger troop figure: the Secretary-General reluctantly agreed.[74]

It was a major retreat that would have dire consequences.

"The numbers were whittled and we got them [the troops] very late," said Álvaro de Soto, a senior political adviser to Boutros-Ghali from 1992 to 1994. "It [the idea] was really very ill conceived."[75]

Boutros-Ghali had essentially been told to "shut up" about his troop number request, noted David Malone. He said he thought the Secretary-General and Annan were correct in their original assessment. "At that point, there should have been some consideration by both men to resign," Malone said. "They were being ordered to do an impossible task."[76]

"Boutros-Ghali certainly said what he needed," noted Thomas Weiss, presidential professor of political science at the City University of New York. "The question in retrospect is whether the secretary-general can say, 'If you're not going to give me what I've asked for, then I'm doing nothing' or whether he is a servant of the UN...and can make it clear that, 'if there are major massacres, the blame should be not on the organization but squarely on you folks.' It seems to me that more could have been done than blithely proceeding."[77]

Although over time the United Nations drew pledges of more than three times the number that the Council had authorized, the troops were slow in coming and often poorly equipped. Bangladesh, for instance, withdrew its offer of 1,200 troops when it realized the supply of armored personnel carriers, on which its pledge depended, was not forthcoming.[78]

The Two Sides of Airstrikes

The other major Balkan debate underway at the United Nations concerned the use of NATO air power—both in strikes against attackers and in providing close air support for ground troops.

On June 6, 1993, the Council (in Resolution 836) authorized UNPROFOR to take "all necessary measures," including the use of force, in "safe areas" if troops there were acting in self-defense against attacks or incursions. Airstrikes thus could be included.

However, key governments in both NATO and the United Nations were sharply divided on the advisability of a bombing program. The Clinton administration, which had no troops on the ground, was strongly in favor. France and Britain, nations that did have troops on the ground, were strongly opposed.[79] The Russians, traditional Serb allies, wanted to be sure that the United States took no airstrike action on its own.[80]

Boutros-Ghali, who had been asked by the Council to report back on its latest resolution, wanted a strong UN voice in any bombing decision. His top concern, he said, was whether troops on the ground would be subject to retaliatory attacks or kidnapping.

He made a distinction between airstrikes, which he saw as an offensive move, and the more defensive option of close air support to protect troops under attack. He told NATO that leaders of ground troops needing protection should be able to request air support. He would then make the decision in consultation with the Council.[81]

The United Nations was still championing an impartial approach, hoping to keep the trust of every party in the fight. The Secretary-General again chose Yasushi Akashi as his special envoy to act as the civilian chief of UNPROFOR. Often later, when NATO leaders wanted permission to bomb, Akashi would meet with Bosnian Serb leaders, trying to negotiate a peaceful way out instead. In his view, any NATO humiliation in that process was not a factor.[82]

President Clinton wrote Boutros-Ghali on July 30, 1993, saying that if Serb efforts to strangle Sarajevo continued, NATO air power should be used. US Secretary of State Warren Christopher later told the Secretary-General that such strikes would be fully coordinated with the United Nations but that no specific request or authorization from UNPROFOR would be needed.

For Boutros-Ghali, such a green light could not be tolerated.

He told Christopher that NATO nations with troops on the ground felt that the UN ground commander must first approve airstrikes in the interests of troop and civilian security and progress in peace talks. Thus, as he had told the Council earlier, he as Secretary-General would initiate the call for air power upon advice from the UN ground commander and Akashi.[83]

Boutros-Ghali found it ironic that "safe areas" could not really be safe because the United Nations did not have the means to prevent attacks from the inside or deter them from the outside. Yet the world body was expected to agree to use NATO airstrikes against Serb targets that could then lead to retaliation or hostage taking.[84]

Still, his demand for a first call in enforcement decisions was widely criticized.

"Boutros-Ghali has always said the reason for his insistence on holding one of the keys was that the two members of the Council who had troops on the ground wanted an additional circuit breaker," de Soto recalled. Yet "there was considerable internal debate as to whether he should really hold the key in airstrikes. We—his staff—advocated his distancing himself from it entirely."[85]

"The [UN] founders had it right: keep enforcement in the Security Council, whether it's economic sanctions or military decisions," said Edward Luck, a former director of the Center on International Organization at Columbia University. "If the secretary-general is involved in a Chapter 7 [enforcement] operation, then he's involved in carrying it out. It makes him more than half-pregnant. It's the dual key problem of command and control. Also, it damages his ability to be an impartial mediator."[86]

In the end, it was the United States, the chief proponent of airstrikes, who criticized the Secretary-General most sharply for his stand. In what Boutros-Ghali called an "outlandish assertion," Jeane Kirkpatrick, US ambassador to the United Nations, insisted that he was "guilty of the most sweeping power grab in the history of international organizations." Four days later in a press conference at The Hague, Boutros-Ghali insisted that he was ready to approve requests for air power but had not yet been asked.[87]

On February 5, 1994, the Serbs launched a devastating mortar attack on a market in Sarajevo, killing 68 and wounding some 200 civilians. NATO promptly demanded that the Serbs withdraw their heavy weapons from areas around the city. But Akashi, the UN civilian chief on the scene and a man prone to negotiate when possible, allowed some tanks and artillery to stay on, subject to UN monitoring. In effect, he said, the Serbs were in compliance. His diplomacy and the continuing threat of airstrikes combined to halt the shelling of Sarajevo for most of the remaining year.[88]

When Serb gunners then began to shell UN observers in Goražde that April, however, Akashi allowed two small bombing attacks on the perpetrators. Bosnian Serb leader Karadžić countered that UN troops would be treated from then on as a hostile force.

When the Serbs at first defied a NATO demand to get troops and heavy weapons out of the area around Goražde, Akashi again vetoed a NATO bombing proposal. He said he was negotiating the withdrawal directly with Karadžić instead. When the Serbs finally left, they looted and burned hundreds of homes in the process.[89] They also attacked peacekeepers. In response, NATO bombed the Serbs a few more times in 1994. The Serbs promptly took more than 400 UN peacekeepers hostage.[90]

On January 1, 1995, the Serbs joined the Bosnian government in signing on to a four-month cease-fire negotiated by former US President Jimmy Carter.

Yet when the agreement expired that May, the Serbs began again to shell Sarajevo and other "safe areas" and to retrieve the heavy weapons they had stored nearby.[91] More NATO airstrikes followed, and the Serbs took another 370 peacekeepers hostage, using several as human shields.

Noting that each airstrike seemed to incite a new round of hostage taking, Boutros-Ghali asked the Council in late May for its advice "at this moment of crisis," adding that he, of course, would still make any final decision on airstrikes. He recalled only silence in response. Despite earlier Council micromanaging, he said, no member made "the slightest effort to be constructive or helpful." He called the absence of American leadership at that moment "appalling."[92]

Boutros-Ghali was convinced that changes in the mandate and/or size of the UN troop contingent were necessary.

He asked the Council to approve a British, French, and Dutch proposal to deploy well-armed mobile units to respond to threats to UN personnel. This rapid reaction force would be part of UNPROFOR and operate under the UN flag and command but wear national uniforms. Accordingly, on June 16, 1995, the Council authorized the deployment of 12,500 more heavily armed troops, while noting that they remained part of the impartial UN peacekeeping operation.[93]

Tragedy in Srebrenica

Despite the new order for added help, the worst war crime since World War II was about to take place.

The Netherlands had been the only Western nation to respond positively to Boutros-Ghali's request for more troops to deter attacks on "safe areas" in Bosnia. So it was that 450 lightly armed Dutch troops were assigned to Srebrenica.

On July 6, 1995, Serb forces began to fire rockets into the town. At first the United Nations suspected a limited operation. Dutch soldiers were ordered to withdraw rather than fire back. As the shelling continued, however, the Dutch ground commander requested close air support for his troops. According to an in-depth report ordered later by peacekeeping chief Kofi Annan, the request was either unheeded or denied. UN civilian and UNPROFOR officials apparently thought such action could bring the United Nations directly into the war, endanger troops, and perhaps kill the peacekeeping operation.[94]

After another major attack on July 10, the Dutch commander was expecting massive airstrikes against the Serbs, but a mistake in the UN chain of command translated into many hours of waiting in vain for help. Finally, two bombs in support of the besieged Dutch troops were dropped. However, by that time, Serb threats of retaliation led the Dutch minister of defense to call for a bombing halt because it was endangering his troops.[95]

Akashi felt he had no choice but to comply with that request.[96]

As the world now knows, the UN troops were outnumbered and overwhelmed. Thousands of Muslim women and children were forced to leave Srebrenica, and an estimated 7,500 men and boys were eventually murdered. Srebrenica was gone. The town of Žepa fell soon after. The worry was that Goražde would be next.

To prevent that, the United Nations and the European Community held a hurriedly arranged meeting on July 20 in London. As Boutros-Ghali arrived, he saw demonstrators with a huge sign showing his picture beside that of Karadžić, labeling them "Brothers in Crime." Those attending the conference managed to agree before disbanding that any further attack on Goražde or other "safe areas" would be met with major NATO air attacks. They also approved a proposal to reduce UN personnel to make possible greater use of such air power.[97]

Then, in response to a request made at his Sutton Place residence by the British, French, and US ambassadors to the United Nations, Boutros-Ghali formally delegated his decision-making authority on airstrikes to the UN commander on the ground.[98]

The debate continues over what else might have been done to keep the Serbs from doing what they did. Though Boutros-Ghali accepted no blame in his account, some people argue that he could have acted more decisively.

"Srebrenica was the beginning of the end for the UN in Bosnia," noted David Malone. "There was this sense that neutrality had to be maintained between the Serbs and other combatants. Faced with the horrors of Srebrenica, preceded by plenty of other horrors, the absurdity of [UN] neutrality was highlighted.... I think Boutros-Ghali was wrong in not calling for NATO air support to defend Srebrenica. There were of course good operational reasons why it might have been risky, but it's hard to imagine a worse outcome."[99]

The Serbs launched another major mortar attack on Sarajevo on August 28, 1995. More than 30 people were killed and 100 wounded. At 8 p.m. the next evening, as dinner guests were arriving at his home in Sutton Place, Boutros-Ghali was handed a note by his steward. It said that waves of NATO aircraft were striking targets all over Bosnia. This time, the Secretary-General, though stressing that the United Nations was "not at war with the Serbs," asked his spokesman to tell the media that the raids had his full support.[100]

Washington Takes Over

The United States, which pushed for and got Council approval for a Yugoslav war crimes tribunal in 1993, was slowly taking over the lead role for a solution in Bosnia. Washington had been secretly arming Croat forces there to persuade them to join a federation with Bosnia's Muslims to balance the Serbs' Republika Srpska in Pale. The Croats managed to roll back several Serb land seizures.[101]

In early September 1995, Richard Holbrooke, President Clinton's envoy to the region, chaired a meeting in Geneva to discuss ending the conflict. A UN representative was allowed to attend as an observer but only in a closed session and at the last minute. As Boutros-Ghali recalled, "The United States was finally ready to get involved and wanted no more UN role whatsoever." Still, he told the Council that he welcomed the US initiative. As it was, the Bosnian operation was absorbing almost all of the United Nations' $3 billion peacekeeping budget.[102]

In *To End a War,* Holbrooke wrote that the Secretary-General was indeed originally reluctant to involve the United Nations in Bosnia and visited Sarajevo only once in 1992. After a few meetings with him, Holbrook said he concluded that "this elegant and subtle Egyptian... had disdain for the fractious and dirty peoples of the Balkans. Put bluntly, he never liked the place."[103]

In any case, the war in Bosnia was at last winding down. After weeks of discussion, the leaders of the three ethnic groups agreed on November 21, 1995, to establish a multiethnic country with a unitary government under the so-called Dayton accords. The single job left to the United Nations was to organize a civilian police force and arrange for the return of refugees. NATO and some 60,000 international Implementation Force (IFOR) troops under its command were to enforce the agreement.[104]

The Balkans Scorecard

In an overall sense, the UN role in Bosnia has been widely regarded as a failure. Many of the more than 150 Council resolutions and statements that were passed had little, if any, effect.

Yet peacekeepers protected UN relief operations. Close to three million Bosnians received food and other aid. Many lives were saved. The Serb attacks might have been even more intense and successful if the United Nations had not occasionally badgered the Serbs into accepting (though not often keeping) cease-fires. Though the United Nations did not stop the aggression or recover conquered territory, the war did not spread. Former UN correspondent Stanley Meisler said the UN mission was "hapless and star crossed" but not a total failure. He argued that the UN accomplished as much as it could with a "confused and limited mandate."[105]

Boutros-Ghali certainly let the Council know on several occasions that its demands were not equal to its supply of authority or resources for UN troops. UN peacekeepers never had the political or military support to effectively counter "safe area" violations.

The Secretary-General had also made it clear to Council members that he wanted to be consulted rather than bypassed on certain issues. A May 23, 1992, article in the *Economist* noted that Boutros-Ghali was not "a table thumper, a politician or even a good speaker." Yet, he was beginning to show a "sure touch" and might be "less worried than his predecessors about making enemies."[106]

Still, placing the Secretary-General's office so close to the use of force and giving him new powers challenged his reputation for impartiality. In the process, however, the change also allowed the Council to cover its own divisions on use of force.[107]

"A number of decisions taken by the Security Council were essentially copouts," said Álvaro de Soto. "Members wanted to do something to counter the impression that they were just standing there.... But this was a peacekeeping operation where there was no peace to keep.... Peacekeeping is ultimately a narrow concept. It's not a cure-all."[108]

Sir Brian Urquhart agreed:

> "I don't think the Security Council gets half enough blame for what happened. Its decision to declare six safe areas in Bosnia was ridiculous."[109]

Yet the criticism persists that military decisions, particularly those involving enforcement, were outside any secretary-general's realm of competence and, in that respect, potentially dangerous.

"You [need to] save the secretary-general to be a valuable interlocutor for both sides," said Thomas Weiss, chair of the Academic Council on the United Nations System. "I don't think you can be neutral and simultaneously participate in a Chapter 7 operation. Using military force is anything but neutral.... I'm one who argues that everything is political, and that it's impossible to be neutral. But in certain situations you can pretend to be more neutral than in others."[110]

Fouad Ajami, a senior fellow at Stanford University's Hoover Institution, argued that Boutros-Ghali never found his "compass" in Bosnia and forfeited the United Nations' "moral standing" along the way. As Ajami put it in a *Foreign Affairs* article, "All along, the Bosnians and their cause were a great irritation to this secretary-general—the Bosnians refused to do him the favor of a quiet surrender."[111]

In the view of Indar Rikhye, the late Indian general and a longtime friend of Boutros-Ghali, the Secretary-General became too involved in detail and his own attempts to keep control of the situation. Rikhye advised him to choose people he trusted, decentralize, and never recommend the use of force in Bosnia or anywhere. "He was a typical professor—everything was on his desk," Rikhye recalled.[112]

Certainly relations with the United States were tense. Boutros-Ghali said his insistence that he needed a vote on the use of airstrikes allowed Washington to blame him for blocking decisive action. When Akashi once mentioned in April 1994 that the United States should contribute ground troops if it wanted its views taken seriously, Madeleine Albright, US ambassador to the United Nations, lashed back, "International civil servants should remember where their salaries come from." [113]

All in all, the Bosnian experience proved an extremely difficult one for the United Nations. As the 1999 Annan report concluded, "Through error, mismanagement, and an inability to recognize the scope of evil confronting us [the UN], we failed to do our part to help save the people of Srebrenica from the Serb campaign of mass murder.... The tragedy of Srebrenica will haunt our history forever."[114]

Trouble in Somalia

From almost the first day on the job, Boutros-Ghali was determined that the United Nations must help the broken nation of Somalia. As in the Balkans, the United Nations' first step was to be based on the humanitarian need. The challenge was to keep an image of neutrality amid an intense civil war. That goal was not met.

The Siad Barre dictatorship had collapsed in late 1990, and the internal fight for power among rival warlords was fierce and unrelenting. Schools were closed. Basic services, such as electricity, had become nonexistent. Armed clan members roamed the streets in light trucks. Relief aid from varied sources was not getting through.

In January 1992, Boutros-Ghali dispatched James Jonah, under-secretary-general for political affairs, to try to arrange a cease-fire between the two top leaders—Mohammed Aideed and Ali Mahdi—and secure the delivery of food and other needed aid. Both leaders had said they favored a UN role, but Aideed was strongly opposed to any deployment of UN troops.[115]

Varied efforts to reach an effective cease-fire finally succeeded that March. The Secretary-General asked the Council for a small force to monitor it and protect aid deliveries. In April 1992, the Council authorized a lightly armed advance force of 500, to be known as the UN Operation in Somalia, or UNOSOM I, for the task. They had no mandate to use force. As it happened, the troops, all from Pakistan, did not get to Somalia until September.[116] When they arrived at the harbor in Mogadishu, their efforts to protect relief supplies were largely blocked. They were abused and humiliated by the Somali clans.[117]

Boutros-Ghali, who had been working with the OAU and the Arab League to reach a political solution, was convinced that the United Nations must do more and that its troops needed enforcement power.

At an OAU summit in Darfur, Sudan, various leaders complained to the Secretary-General that the United Nations seemed all too ready to involve itself in the "rich man's war" in the former Yugoslavia while doing far too little to help in Somalia.

"Boutros-Ghali very ably parlayed what they said to him in Darfur into leveraging the Security Council to do something [more] about Somalia," de Soto recalled.[118]

The Secretary-General accused the Council of setting a double standard. It was, he said, a practice, that must stop.[119]

In August 1992, the Council authorized an additional deployment of more than 3,000 troops for the UNOSOM I relief effort.

Boutros-Ghali also had been working hard to get the United States more involved. He visited the White House in May to talk with President George H. W. Bush. Although Washington had been providing millions of dollars in food aid to Somalia for more than a year, the help was not getting to those most in need. The Secretary-General suggested that the lack of a more vigorous effort by the West was costing the United States a loss of prestige in the Middle East.[120]

Under added pressure from Congress and the media, President Bush announced his decision in late November to send up to 30,000 troops to Somalia if the United Nations were to endorse the use of force to ensure relief deliveries. On December 3, 1992, the Council accordingly authorized the Unified Task Force on Somalia (UNITAF) with the power to use "all necessary means" under Chapter 7 of the Charter in their mission. The US-led effort, also known as Operation Restore Hope, planned to transfer its authority back to United Nations command and leave Somalia once secure conditions were established. By early 1993 some 44,000 troops were on the scene, including 20,000 from 20 other nations.

Disagreeing to Disarm

From the start, Boutros-Ghali had a far more ambitious view than Washington did of what the United Nations should accomplish in

Somalia. In his September 1992 *Report on the Work of the Organization to the General Assembly,* he said he saw the UN operation there as contributing to a broad "reconstruction of an entire society and nation."[121] He was also convinced that the US-led UN operation must include disarmament—by force if necessary. In separate letters to the Council before its December vote to authorize UNITAF and to US President Bush, he stressed that effective enforcement must at least include neutralizing the clans' heavy weapons by putting them under international control.[122]

UNITAF succeeded in stopping much of the violence and thievery. However, the United States was not on board with the stronger push for disarmament. The subject had not been mentioned in the actual Council resolution. The United States saw itself on a temporary mission and had no wish to risk more casualties by challenging the warlords.

John Bolton, then US assistant secretary of state, told a reporter at the *New York Times* that the United Nations was trying to change the goalposts in the middle of the game. If Somalis kept their weapons out of sight, he said, no one would take them away.[123] Robert Oakley, the US special envoy to Somalia and a former US ambassador to the country, had extracted a pledge from the warlords that they would not target US troops if Somalis were not disarmed.[124] Boutros-Ghali said in his memoir that US forces simply refused to disarm militants and were under orders not to seize heavy weapons even when a major cache was found.[125]

The Secretary-General periodically tried to arrange reconciliation talks in Ethiopia with Somalia's warlords. However, he was not high on the popularity list with Aideed and his supporters. Many clan leaders had been suspicious of Boutros-Ghali since his days as an Egyptian diplomat when he was responsible for maintaining good relations with Somalia's former dictator, Siad Barre.[126]

So when Boutros-Ghali tried to visit the UN compound in Mogadishu in January 1993, he was blocked by Aideed supporters, who pelted the building with rocks and garbage and yelled curses at him. He tried to make it clear (without notable success) in a press conference at the time that no nation wanted control of Somalia. He insisted that the United Nations and the United States were simply offering Somalia a last chance for peace.[127]

Washington Wants to Leave

The real challenge for the Secretary-General and the United Nations came when the Clinton administration wanted to transfer the US-run Somali operation back to the United Nations in spring 1993. On March 26, the Council, responding to Boutros-Ghali's request, voted to give a new UNOSOM II contingent enforcement power that UNOSOM I never had. The Council also expanded the new peace-keeping group's mission to include establishing a police force and judicial system, repatriation of refugees, and promotion of national reconciliation. It was close to an impossible mission.[128]

At the suggestion of Washington, the Secretary-General named retired US Navy Admiral Jonathan Howe, a former deputy national security adviser under Bush, as his special representative and the civilian overseer of UNOSOM II.

In an April 30, 1993, TV interview with David Frost, Boutros-Ghali, explaining the new Council rules, said, "We are doing a political operation." He predicted that it would take Somalia another two years to form a government.[129]

Unlike the Bush White House, the Clinton administration, which came to power in January 1993, was increasingly interested in the political rather than the humanitarian aspect of the UN operation. It wanted to help Somalia become a democracy.[130]

The official US-to-UN transfer date was set for May 4, 1993. The United States was to leave some combat forces behind. These would remain under US command. The remaining few thousand US logistics personnel would operate under UN command. Yet the Secretary-General was clearly concerned that US troops were leaving faster than the United Nations could replace them. He was worried not only that other governments might follow the US lead, but also that the US failure to disarm the Somali factions would leave the UN troops in a more vulnerable and dangerous position.[131]

A Hate Campaign against the United States and the United Nations

Meanwhile, Aideed thought UN policies were aimed directly at weakening him. The United Nations had dropped support for a peace conference he had convened in central Somalia, though Howe, the UN special envoy, had said it was only because the Somali leader backed down on promises made. Aideed-controlled Radio Mogadishu began a hate campaign against both the United Nations and the United States, suggesting they wanted to make Somalia a trusteeship.[132]

On June 5, 1993, UN Pakistani soldiers were helping to distribute food and inspecting several sites where Aideed's troops had agreed to store weapons. One site was in the same building as Radio Mogadishu, and rumors spread quickly that a shutdown might be imminent. An angry crowd gathered. In its midst, Aideed's militia shot and killed 26 Pakistani soldiers.

The next day, the Council reaffirmed its stance that the Secretary-General had authority to take all necessary measures, including arrest and detention for trial and punishment, against those responsible for armed attacks.

The humanitarian mission of the United Nations now took second place to the organization's determination to capture Aideed. Howe announced a $25,000 bounty for his capture. UN forces launched several days of air and ground attacks on weapons sites and broadcast facilities of Radio Mogadishu to try to restore law and order in Aideed's stronghold south of the city.

Boutros-Ghali was convinced that Aideed should be punished and that, in light of the newest Council resolution, no political deal with him now could be made.[133]

The war with Aideed and his supporters went on for four months.

On July 12, a US rapid reaction force, acting on US authority, staged a raid on a suspected Aideed command center. Weapons were seized and prisoners taken. Somalis said more than 70 people died in the attack. Four journalists who came to cover the story were killed by the angry crowd that had gathered.[134]

US public support for the Somalia operation was fast eroding. The Clinton administration was rethinking its strategy. In his first speech to the General Assembly in September 1993, Clinton insisted that the United Nations must learn when to say "no" to peacekeeping ventures. That same month, US Secretary of State Warren Christopher suggested in a letter to Boutros-Ghali a possible new approach in Somalia: try to refocus media attention on the UN operation as a humanitarian effort, stop the hunt for Aideed, and explore ways to put him under house arrest in another country.[135]

The Secretary-General replied in writing that the Council mandate obliged the United Nations to stay on course. It directed that those who committed or ordered attacks on UN personnel must be held responsible. Boutros-Ghali said that he made every effort over the past months to bring Aideed and his Habar-Gidir clan into the political process, but that it was Aideed's refusal to share power after Barre's overthrow that led to Somalia's civil war in the first place. The Secretary-General said he was still open to other ways of neutralizing Aideed (such as house arrest elsewhere), but that the Council mandate must be followed.[136]

The Fateful October Raid

At Howe's request, the United States in the late summer of 1993 had sent a joint unit of Army Rangers and Delta Force commandos from Fort Bragg, North Carolina, to help the UN mission. In a move that went disastrously wrong, a decision was made at the Florida headquarters of the US Special Operations Command to begin an attack on October 3, 1993, on a suspected Aideed stronghold in southern Mogadishu.

The US force of 160 troops arrested 24 of Aideed's colleagues. A major firefight of many hours followed, later immortalized in the US movie *Black Hawk Down*. In the end, one American helicopter pilot was captured and 18 US soldiers and 1 Malaysian peacekeeper were killed. Scores of others were wounded. The dead body of an American was dragged through the streets and flaunted in TV videos. Aideed boasted about the October killings.

At first many, including the United States, were quick to blame the United Nations for the raid that the United States had launched. Yet all American combat forces had functioned under the command and operational controls of the United States during the entire episode.[137] Still, the Council had called for the capture of Aideed. Agreement was widespread that some kind of forceful action was needed to stave off more attacks on US and UN personnel.

"American leadership really was not prepared to conduct a mission of that kind," General Rikhye former UN military commander, said. "The chain of command...conveniently bypassed the whole UN system."[138]

In a speech to the American people four days after the October raid, President Clinton said he would send the US ambassador, Robert Oakley, to try to get the captured pilot released and reach a political settlement with all factions. The hunt for Aideed would stop during that effort, he said. Clinton then pledged to take all US forces out of Somalia by March 31, 1994.[139] He backed away from earlier pledges, telling the *Washington Post* on October 10, 1993, "It is not our job to rebuild Somalia's society."[140]

In mid-November 1993, the Council authorized Boutros-Ghali to appoint members to a commission of inquiry. At Washington's request, however, the scope was limited to the June 5 killing of the UN Pakistani soldiers. Boutros-Ghali suspected that the restriction was placed so that the United States might find a way to exonerate Aideed, who had proudly claimed responsibility for the October killing of US Rangers. That way, the Secretary-General reasoned, Aideed might play a role in political reconciliation, which would help to justify the US withdrawal.[141]

The commission, headed by a Zambian chief justice, found Aideed and his faction responsible but accused Howe and his advisers of naïveté in their dealings with the warlord.

Aideed was again holding news conferences and issuing threats but the Council made no attempt to punish him.[142] Over time, other factions refused to deal with him. He was eventually ousted by his own clan before his death.

In February 1994, as US troops were leaving Somalia, the Council once again changed the UN peacekeepers' mandate. They were now to protect roads and ports and guard relief convoys, using their weapons in self-defense only. Yet little seemed to change, and the United Nations was spending $2.5 million a day. The Council finally voted unanimously to pull UN forces out of Somalia by March 31, 1995.[143]

All US troops had left the year before. At that point Clinton issued Presidential Decision Directive 25, setting tight limits for any future US involvement in UN peacekeeping efforts. US support, he said, would depend on the conflict's threat to international peace and security or on a decision that the operation would serve the US national interest.[144]

The Secretary-General viewed those conditions as stifling and almost insurmountable. He said he thought any future US involvement would thus be limited to small-scale, benign, UN–directed classical peacekeeping operations.[145]

Even after all US and UN troops were gone, Boutros-Ghali continued UN efforts to bring political peace to Somalia. He set up a small UN office in Nairobi to help the reconciliation process.[146]

The Report Card

The US–UN Somalia action in the 1990s has been widely viewed as a disaster. Yet the experience, besides saving some lives, offered valuable lessons.

The United Nations' traditional peacekeeping role clearly was inadequate to deal with a failed state. Remaining neutral proved impossible.

The US failure to disarm the fighting factions, though most clan leaders were willing, suggested that Washington was not that serious about stability and restoring order. The factions realized they could wait until the US forces left. The United Nations would then take over, with fewer arms and a more fragile command structure. By not disarming the Somalis, the United States, and the United Nations in effect, sided with those who had the most weapons.[147]

"The term 'peace enforcement' is no longer used—it became tainted," said James Sutterlin, former Yale University fellow in international security studies. "It is one thing to use weapons against anyone interfering with the delivery of humanitarian aid but quite another to use military force against one particular party as opposed to another."[148]

Intervention in civil violence inevitably affects the political situation and nation building. Oakley, the former US ambassador, defined the key problem as one of mixed objectives. In looking back, he said that the political and military sides of intervention must be united. If not, there can be trouble. As he saw it, the United Nations was trying to build a new political structure while the United States was withdrawing its troops and handing the security job back to the United Nations.[149]

In the view of Howe, the United States basically was unwilling to provide the resources and the military power necessary to stabilize the country.[150]

Yet many analysts insist that the earlier Bush–Oakley approach— limited humanitarian security and some cooperation and dialogue with the warlords—was actually the more realistic one.[151]

Boutros-Ghali came close to having a policy-making role in the deepening UN involvement in peace enforcement in Somalia. He supported ongoing talks with all Somali factions. However, his use of force and abandonment of a neutral stance affected his usefulness as a mediator and may well have tainted the reputation of his office, according to British political scientist Edward Newman.[152]

During the experience, the Secretary-General often remarked that others made him a scapegoat. He was quick to fire back accusations of his own. He insisted, for instance, that the United States had not completed its promised task and wanted to get in and out of Somalia too quickly. Still, he said he was willing to accept blame since the United Nations' job was precisely to help nations solve their problems. "If it helps the Americans solve theirs by blaming me, I'll be a scapegoat," he once told a reporter.[153]

"I think he was quite right in saying he was made a scapegoat because that [October] fiasco was American," argued Lawrence S. Finkelstein, a former political science professor at Northern Illinois University.[154]

Unlike most other secretaries-general, Boutros-Ghali tended to compare his own powers with those of national governments. In that sense, he saw himself as politically weak. After the US troop pullout from Somalia, he noted, "I can do nothing. I have no money. I have no experts. I am borrowing everything."[155]

Rwanda: "An Overpopulated Little Country" That "Destroyed Its Own People"[156]

Rwanda won its independence from Belgium in 1962. Ethnic tensions between minority Tutsis and majority Hutus ran high there for many decades. However, it was not until the spring of 1994, after the Hutu president's plane was shot down, that the friction led to mass slaughter. The genocide continued for more than three months and left more than 800,000, largely Tutsi and moderate Hutus, dead.

Though it was not for lack of trying on Boutros-Ghali's part, the United Nations did not act decisively to prevent or stop the killing.

Brutal and bitter recent experience in Somalia and Bosnia played a major role in that failure. The experience had prompted US President Bill Clinton to issue those strict guidelines on future US support of and involvement in UN peacekeeping, a position that Boutros-Ghali described as a "deadly blow" to multilateral cooperation.[157]

The United Nations authorized deployment in June 1993 of a military observer mission on the Ugandan side of Rwanda's border where the Tutsi-dominated Rwandan Patriotic Force (RPF) was stationed in exile. The Council voted that October to establish a small UN Assistance Mission in Rwanda (UNAMIR) as well. Its job was to monitor a new peace agreement signed two months earlier by the government and RPF leaders in Arusha, Tanzania. Both parties had asked for UN help. The Council's limited mandate also asked UNAMIR to help maintain security in Kigali, Rwanda's capital, and to assist with aid and refugee repatriation. Boutros-Ghali promptly appointed Canada's Lieutenant General Roméo Dallaire as commander of the new UN mission.

Later that year, the Secretary-General reported to the Council that the Arusha agreement had failed to hold and that the situation was increasingly fragile. Though the Council earlier had urged him to find a way to reduce UN troop strength in Rwanda, he instead asked the Council to authorize an additional battalion. It did so on January 6, 1994.[158]

A few days later, while Boutros-Ghali was away on official travel, General Dallaire cabled the UN peacekeeping head, Kofi Annan, to report a highly placed informant's insistence that Hutu extremists had been ordered to register all Tutsis in Kigali and were stockpiling weapons. The suspicion was that the Hutus were readying for a mass killing of Tutsis.

Dallaire wanted authorization to seize the weapons. He was told that the UN mandate was too limited. He was urged, however, to share his information with Western ambassadors in Kigali (including those from the United States, Belgium, and Britain), and he did. In his memoir, Boutros-Ghali thus insisted that the powers that could have acted to prevent the massacre that followed were "indisputably and immediately informed" of the seriousness of the threat.[159]

The incident that sparked the start of the mass killing that lasted for three long months was the April 6, 1994, crash of the plane carrying the Hutu presidents of Rwanda and Burundi. Both had made recent concessions to their Tutsi populations. Suspicions were strong that Hutu extremists had shot down the plane. Soon after, gunmen killed Rwanda's interim president and 10 Belgian UN peacekeepers. Belgium promptly withdrew its troops and equipment, despite Boutros-Ghali's pleas to leave at least its heavy weapons behind.

Belgium's foreign minister pushed for the full withdrawal of UNAMIR. Over the next several weeks, Boutros-Ghali discussed with the Council the options—from full withdrawal to reinforcement. He favored the latter and a stronger mandate, as did Dallaire. But the Council voted on April 21, 1994, to reduce UNAMIR to a force of 250 from 2,500 and to limit its mandate to mediation and humanitarian aid.[160] The slim UN contingent could do little or nothing about the continued killing. Dallaire was extremely frustrated not to get more troops and enforcement power.[161]

Boutros-Ghali warned the Council that civilian evacuation might be needed if more troops were not provided. "We were facing a kind of 'tropical Nazi genocide,'" he recalled, adding that his view was not well received.[162]

He strongly urged the Council to reconsider its troop decision. Finally, on May 17, 1994, after more than two weeks of heated debate, the Council agreed in principle to the Secretary-General's push for an expanded UNAMIR II force of 5,500 peacekeepers. However, the approval hinged on conditions—that a cease-fire must be in place and that the parties welcomed a UN presence.[163] Madeleine Albright, US Ambassador to the UN, held to Clinton's directive and pressed the Council to delay the send-off until those conditions were met.[164] The United States and France would not agree to fund or equip the troops or to grant UNAMIR II Chapter 7 enforcement power.[165]

By late May, more than 200,000 Rwandans had been killed. In June, France, which had been deeply involved with the Hutus, offered to protect civilians and stay until the UN force was strong enough to take over. In what was known as "Operation Turquoise," France sent 2,500 troops to set up a humanitarian protection zone in southwest Rwanda.

Most of the new UNAMIR II troops did not arrive until late summer. By then, several governments had cut back on previous pledges or had withdrawn troops on the scene.[166]

By August 1994, the Tutsi-dominated RPF had taken military control of most of the country, declared a unilateral cease-fire, and was on the verge of taking over Rwanda's government. Close to two million Hutus soon fled to Burundi, Tanzania, and Zaire.

In a visit to the region in July 1995, after the fall of Srebrenica, Boutros-Ghali emphasized the UN mission's shift from a military focus to one geared more toward peace-building and rehabilitation. The Rwandan government wanted the UN forces out by December 1995, when their mandate was to expire. However, the Secretary-General and the Council convinced the government to accept a smaller force with a changed mission.[167]

During his African trip, Boutros-Ghali visited Burundi where tension between Tutsis and Hutus had also been high. After listening to leaders from both sides blame one another, the Secretary-General, never one to mince words, said it made him ashamed to call himself an African. As originally reported by the *New Yorker* writer Michael Ignatieff, who traveled with him, Boutros-Ghali told the gathering, "Your enemy is not each other but fear and cowardice. You must have the courage to accept compromises.... If you don't, nobody will save you."[168]

During the 100-day civil war in Rwanda, Boutros-Ghali had clearly helped draw media attention to the civilians' plight. Yet the Council was not ready to act in any forceful way to stop the killing. The United States, still smarting from its experiences in Somalia and Bosnia, took great care not to describe the situation as "genocide," which would have legally obligated signers to fulfill their treaty obligations under the 1948 Genocide Convention. The Council followed the US lead, behavior that Boutros-Ghali described as "shocking."[169]

The Secretary-General insisted later that if the swift intervention he urged in April 1994 had occurred, thousands of lives might have been saved. He also maintained that if a UN standby force for rapid deployment had been created, as he had suggested in 1992, the genocide might never have begun.[170]

General Dallaire agreed with Boutros-Ghali that earlier UN action could have prevented the slaughter. In his memoir, Dallaire insisted that the key Western members of the Council—the United States, France and Britain—who might have prodded the Council to act, just "sat back and watched it all happen."[171]

Venting his exasperation with the whole situation as it unfolded, he argued that "we are in desperate need of a transfusion of humanity."

Still, Dallaire conceded that the genocide was ultimately the responsibility of the Rwandans who planned, ordered, supervised, and conducted it.[172]

Eventually the United Nations established a war crimes tribunal to try those accused of atrocities in Rwanda, just as it had done with Yugoslavia. In 1999, Kofi Annan, the Secretary-General at the time, commissioned an independent report on the UN role in the tragedy. It concluded that the United Nations had failed the people of Rwanda at every level.[173] Did Boutros-Ghali do all that he might have done?

"The secretary-general has a real duty to speak up," Herbert Okun, a former US deputy ambassador to the United Nations, said.

> Boutros-Ghali tried very hard to get the Security Council interested in the Rwandan genocide and got nowhere.... It's a terrible blot...against the Security Council, which turned its back on him. Was there something more that could have been done? Should he have asked the networks for air time? Called a huge press conference with the International Committee of the Red Cross head there and announced his resignation? I think it would have worked![174]

Taking Aim at Common Goals

In one sense, the early 1990s offered the United Nations a golden opportunity. With the Cold War over, the United Nations had decided to begin an ambitious new series of world conferences. Though the United Nations hosted an earlier wave of these in the 1970s, little had been achieved. The hope this time was to reach broad areas of agreement in tackling the common challenges of poverty, environment, human rights, population, and women's issues.

The General Assembly actually adopted the 1990s conference plan before Boutros-Ghali came aboard, but he quickly embraced it as his own.[175] As the one UN leader responsible to all members, the secretary-general is in a unique position to champion the moral principles underlying the Charter. His responsibilities were slowly expanding to include promotion of common values.[176]

Boutros-Ghali looked on the conferences as a totally new way to reach global agreement on shared problems. Nothing binding would emerge. Yet it was hoped that areas of consensus would gain moral, and perhaps some legal, force over time. In theory at least, governments violating adopted norms could no longer easily duck responsibilities by claiming the overriding right of sovereignty.[177]

Still, sensitive aspects required special care and skill. When Boutros-Ghali arrived in Vienna in June 1993, for instance, to open the UN human rights summit, he found that Austria had invited the Dalai Lama without telling the United Nations. China had insisted that it would withdraw if he came. That would leave, as Boutros-Ghali put it, one-fourth of humanity unrepresented. The standoff was resolved by the Dalai Lama's "gracious" acceptance of an offer to participate instead in an earlier nongovernmental human rights session in Vienna. When Boutros-Ghali finally convened the UN conference, China was present and the Dalai Lama was not.[178]

Four months later, the Assembly established the post of UN high commissioner for human rights. When a representative of the Carter Center in the United States first suggested the idea to Boutros-Ghali, the Secretary-General said he was not in favor and thought such a move would create a largely unnecessary layer of bureaucracy. He said he preferred dealing with such problems on a case by case basis. The Carter delegation "stiffened in their chairs and looked stricken," he recalled. After the Assembly took action, however, he quickly concurred and nominated José Ayala Lasso, Ecuador's foreign minister, for the job. Lasso had lobbied hard for creation of the post and was backed by Washington.[179]

Boutros-Ghali viewed the UN global conferences as democratic in the largest sense of the word. He described them as beginning a new form of people's control of their own destiny on issues that domestic politics often could not resolve. He saw democracy as a crucial link between development and peace—far more than just an issue of free elections. The Charter itself makes no specific mention of democracy. Yet the Secretary-General insisted in *Unvanquished: A US–UN Saga,* "The key theme of my term...was democratization."[180]

James Sutterlin agreed: "The strong talk on democracy really began pretty much with Boutros-Ghali and was carried further by Kofi Annan."[181]

In his last year on the job, Boutros-Ghali on his own initiative produced *An Agenda for Democratization*, calling it his "swan song." He wrote the General Assembly president, asking that the report be distributed as an Assembly document. Some nations were critical, labeling the report socially disruptive and an impediment to development. In the end, the report attracted relatively little attention or comment.[182]

At the time, Boutros-Ghali had issued two other major reports— one, an update of his original *An Agenda for Peace*, and another called *An Agenda for Development*. These were much more widely discussed.

His peace agenda update, issued in January 1995, drew on the United Nations' bitter experiences in Bosnia and Somalia. He still felt there was a need for UN peace enforcement but admitted that, except on a very limited scale, it was beyond the United Nations' current capacity. He said three principles must guide future UN peacekeeping efforts: consent of the warring parties, impartiality of UN troops, and use of force only in self-defense. As he explained at a news conference, the United Nations could continue to authorize others to undertake enforcement in its name, as it had done when the United States organized the coalition that chased Iraqi soldiers out of Kuwait in 1991.[183]

Though Boutros-Ghali renewed his call for a rapid reaction force, the Netherlands was the only nation to endorse the idea. Others, particularly the United States, were wary of giving the United Nations any more military power.[184]

The peace update had not been solicited by either the Council or the Assembly. Boutros-Ghali called it a position paper for the United Nations' 50th anniversary. The report criticized the Council and the United States for micromanaging conflicts and advocated a greater focus on patient diplomacy. Boutros-Ghali also urged a larger role for the secretary-general's office in mediation and peacekeeping.

Madeleine Albright, the US ambassador to the United Nations, promptly accused him of trying to take more power for himself rather than leaving those tasks more appropriately to member states.[185]

Still, analysts agree that the Secretary-General's updated peace report was far more nuanced and realistic than the one he gave at the beginning of his term.

"I think peacekeeping is always being reexamined, but one element is clear, even in Boutros-Ghali's time," said Canada's David Malone. "As he [the Secretary-General] said in his addenda to *An Agenda for Peace*, 'The UN simply isn't good at enforcement. It's good at peacekeeping.' He argued at the time, and I think it's still true, that where enforcement is necessary, it is better carried out by a highly motivated and well-funded coalition of the willing rather than by an often indifferently equipped and poorly funded UN peacekeeping force."[186]

Boutros-Ghali tried to increase support for his update by pairing it in one volume with his 1995 *Agenda for Development*. He had been asked specifically by the Assembly to prepare the development report but quickly realized how politically explosive the topic had become. He saw that rich nations were worried that the focus would create a demand for redistribution of wealth. They preferred to tackle the problem with bilateral aid. Poorer nations, by contrast, were worried that the United Nations, under such pressure, would fail to be a major advocate for their cause.[187]

Boutros-Ghali's report argued that economic growth was the engine of development and that national policies aimed at creating a healthy private sector were crucial. In a related effort that he admitted was controversial, he also wrote letters to leaders of the Group of 7 (G-7) nations every year before their June summits. Though his aides told him his efforts were presumptuous, he urged the leaders to consider Africa's special development challenges. His plea was mentioned at the summits each time, but no action was taken. The Secretary-General took some satisfaction, however, in that US President Bill Clinton introduced what he called his own "Africa Initiative" at the G-7 Summit in Denver in 1998.[188]

Boutros-Ghali resented criticism that his desire to help developing countries necessarily made him anti-West. In his view, any secretary-general from any background, "in a world of big and wealthy powers," must be an advocate for those marginalized by ethnicity, gender, religion, age, or poverty. Globalism, he insisted, is "an irreversible force."[189]

The Assembly held hearings on the *Agenda for Development* report but it never received as much attention as his original *Agenda for Peace*.[190] Stanley Meisler said in his UN history, published on the organization's 50th anniversary, that Boutros-Ghali's tentative skills as a communicator and diplomat created ill will, resentment, and misunderstanding. Meisler suggested that this shortcoming prevented the Secretary-General from making many of the changes he had hoped to accomplish.[191]

Still, Clovis Maksoud, the former director of American University's Center for the Global South, insisted that Boutros-Ghali did far more than any predecessor in addressing the needs of developing nations. "This was sort of a victory for the global South," he said. Boutros-Ghali's efforts actually spurred the UN specialized agencies to do much more research in the field and develop new statistical techniques to measure and emphasize development, Maksoud added.[192]

Second Thoughts on a Second Term

Boutros-Ghali had assured everyone at the start that he would serve just one term. But when asked during a May 1994 press conference if he still held to that stance, he said he would reassess the issue in 1996. It would depend in part on his physical condition. He added, pointedly, "I believe that only stupid people don't change their minds."

That hint of a turn was to prove a major challenge for the Clinton administration. US elections were to be held in early November 1996, shortly before the end of the Secretary-General's first term.

The Republican presidential nominee, Bob Dole, spoke mockingly of "Boo-trus Boo-trus Ghali" and pledged that no American boys would ever serve under the "command" of the UN chief once Dole was in the White House. A few politicians on the right even spoke of a UN conspiracy to deprive nations of their sovereignty. There also was talk of black UN helicopters hovering over the Rocky Mountains in preparation for a US takeover.

Though Republicans were the most outspoken, members of both parties in Congress had been sharply critical of Boutros-Ghali's handling of the crises in Bosnia and Somalia. Hopes had been high. Disappointment with the reality was widespread.

Some on Capitol Hill accused the United Nations and its Secretary-General of appeasing the Bosnian Serbs. Many criticized Boutros-Ghali's insistence on controlling airstrikes over Bosnia and his hesitance to authorize them. "More than any other issue, it was his performance in Bosnia that made us feel he did not deserve a second term," Richard Holbrooke, chief architect of the Dayton Peace Accords, noted in his book, *To End a War*.[193]

Congress had been holding back US dues to the United Nations as leverage for what it saw as essential reforms. The public focus of US opposition was heavily on finance and administrative issues. There was also talk of his age—then 74—and whether or not he would have the energy for another term.

Boutros-Ghali's prickly relationship with Madeleine Albright also became a factor. Actually, the relationship had started rather well. The Secretary-General recalled that at their first meeting, when she presented her credentials, she seemed "shy and very nice." They even discussed their parallel shift from academia to diplomacy. "She asked me to help her learn," he recalled.[194]

But the growing tension between them soon became abundantly clear to all. She felt he overstepped in trying to become a policy-maker. He saw her as putting up every possible obstacle to his building effective personal relationships in Washington. It was, as the international law expert Thomas Franck put it, "a poisonous chemistry."[195] Boutros-Ghali himself spoke of "her campaign against me" and described theirs as a "love–hate" relationship.[196]

Certainly the Secretary-General was widely respected for his intellect. However, he had a reputation as a man difficult to work with and prone to lecturing. At UN headquarters, he was seen by some as condescending and reluctant to share his authority.

"I did get the sense that his management style was such that he didn't like saplings growing up in his shade—that as soon as they got to be of a diameter a little too large...[he would] cut them down," noted Ruth Wedgwood, a lawyer and professor at Johns Hopkins University's School of Advanced International Studies.[197]

Boutros-Ghali was sharply critical of the US Congress' failure to pay its assessed UN contribution. In reaching for temporary answers in a speech in Oxford on January 15, 1996, he repeated Pérez de Cuéllar's suggestion that a modest international tax on airlines might help the United Nations pay its bills. That drew another storm of criticism on Capitol Hill. Senator Dole called it an "outrageous attempt to create an international IRS."[198] A bill was soon introduced in Congress to bar the United Nations from directly collecting taxes from US citizens, calling it a violation of the US Constitution.[199]

"Though some of the US objections [to Boutros-Ghali's reelection] were legitimate, probably three-quarters of the people talking about reforming the UN really wanted to kill the organization," said Hurst Hannum, professor of international law at the Fletcher School of Law and Diplomacy at Tufts. "Boutros-Ghali was the one whose head was on the chopping block."[200]

As it was, the Secretary-General felt that he had tried hard to bow to US wishes in everything from personnel appointments to reforms and policy.

"His position on most things was actually that which the US should have welcomed," James Sutterlin observed. "Boutros-Ghali was relatively conservative on policy issues. It comes back to a question of communication. He just wasn't terribly skillful in handling relations in Washington.... I don't think he came across as very likeable."[201]

Veteran US diplomat Herbert Okun agreed, saying, "It wasn't that he was opposing the United States on policies—he just wasn't very articulate."[202]

Boutros-Ghali first got word of US opposition to his reelection at 8 p.m. on Sunday, April 14, 1996, at his Sutton Place residence. He recalled that a "deeply embarrassed" Cyrus Vance was at his front door. The former US secretary of state read aloud a note from the current secretary of state, Warren Christopher. It said that the Clinton administration had decided not to vote for him. Boutros-Ghali admits to surprise but said he was undeterred. Though the United States eventually tried to negotiate a face-saving one-year extension, he turned it down. "I don't take *baksheesh*," he told Vance, who telephoned in June with the offer.[203]

The Secretary-General was in Germany later when he got another phone call, this time from his New York office, telling him that news of the US stance against his reelection had been leaked to the *New York Times* and would appear in an article on June 20, the next day. The article would say that the Clinton administration was prepared to veto his candidacy, if necessary. By 6 p.m. on the day he got word, Boutros-Ghali put out a statement through UN headquarters that he was definitely a candidate for reelection and hoped the United States would change its mind.[204]

He knew very well that risk was involved and that his decision could get mired in American politics. Yet many diplomats at the United Nations had encouraged him to stay. He felt that leaving would be a slight to both Egypt and Africa. "And to be honest," he recalled in his memoir, "my own pride and sense of achievement drove me to seek a second term."[205]

Rumors soon began to circulate in the United States that UN staff and resources were being used to help him win. On July 23, 1996, Sylvana Foa, his spokeswoman and an American, shot down the talk as intimidation and "a disgraceful disinformation campaign" with roots in the "McCarthy era."

In this case, Washington was the decider. The United States was Boutros-Ghali's only public opponent and cast its veto to his reelection bid on November 19, 1996. In his book, *Mixed Messages: American Politics and International Organization 1919–1999*, Edward Luck argued that the United States, because of its raw power and the strength of its political convictions, felt less need to rely on diplomatic skills than most other nations.[206] In his memoir, Boutros-Ghali accused Albright, similarly, of a tendency to lecture and assert rather than practice the difficult diplomatic work of persuasion.[207]

The Secretary-General was well aware that a veto was coming, and he managed to get in the last word.

Both the Council and the Assembly passed unanimous resolutions of praise for his past efforts. In his farewell remarks before the Assembly, where he received a standing ovation, he argued that the United Nations was at a financial crossroads—not because of mismanagement—but because of member failure to fulfill treaty obligations.

With a new secretary-general, he said, all excuses for foot dragging would be gone. "All arrears should be paid at once," he insisted. In one last head-held-high moment, he said no secretary-general should ever be seen as acting either from fear or to curry favor with members: "If one word is to characterize the role of the secretary-general, it is independence."[208]

Unvanquished

That word is the title of Boutros-Ghali's candid and absorbing UN memoir. It is also clearly the proud way he looks back on his first and only term. He quotes both critics and admirers and clearly enjoyed spelling out the many challenges he faced. He had taken office at a euphoric moment when many thought the United Nations could do almost anything it set out to do.

Midway through his term, however, a sobering sense of caution and realism began to set in. Civil conflicts—no longer the traditional wars between states—in Bosnia, Somalia, and Rwanda brought the United Nations into the fray but took a decided toll. In the end, all three were largely seen as UN failures. Conventional peacekeeping operations were unable to enforce cease-fire agreements or give adequate protection when guns were firing.

"We fell flat on our face...partly because of the hubris of applying [traditional] peacekeeping recipes to situations where they didn't apply," observed Álvaro de Soto. "We overextended ourselves...getting involved in a lot of areas where we probably shouldn't have."[209]

In Boutros-Ghali's view, the United Nations—despite some successes—emerged "seriously damaged" in the mid-1990s. He described his memoir as mostly about the loss of an opportunity to build an "an agreed-upon post–Cold War structure for international peace and security."[210]

Certainly the issues arriving at the Security Council for action had been streaming in at a rate almost faster than they could be voted on. The number of Council resolutions, usually no more than 15 a year, suddenly jumped in 1993 to more than 90. The 22 UN peacekeeping missions launched between 1988 and 1996 were almost double the number of those authorized during all of the United Nations' first four decades.[211]

The concept of peacekeeping was fast expanding to include humanitarian aid and even some efforts at nation building. This new climate sharply increased the demands on the secretary-general as mediator, adviser, planner, and the one in charge of implementing Security Council decisions.

Though cautious in some instances, Boutros-Ghali often felt he pushed the Council far harder than it was willing to go. The Council, for instance, authorized only a fraction of the number of peacekeepers he recommended to protect the "safe areas" in Bosnia and refused to get more deeply involved in the Rwanda conflict.

The United States, of course, held the vital vote on the Council. In all three major conflicts, Boutros-Ghali argued, it was Washington that "abused, scapegoated and obstructed UN peacekeepers, placing the future of UN peacekeeping in doubt."[212]

As he saw it, the United Nations' chances for success improved in such cases as Cambodia, El Salvador, and Mozambique, where the United States supported operations but did not intervene. However, the United Nations "failed tragically and horribly" in Bosnia, Somalia and Rwanda. In those cases the United States wanted to appear actively involved, he insisted, while actually avoiding the hard decisions and blaming the United Nations. The challenge, in his view, was to find a balance between too much and too little US involvement.[213]

Boutros-Ghali's relations with Washington became especially difficult after President Clinton took office. The Secretary-General's reluctance to use force in Bosnia and his insistence on a virtual veto over NATO bombing operations while UN troops were on the ground clearly nettled the United States.

"He very foolishly took on the responsibility of calling for bombing strikes," recalled Sir Brian Urquhart. "The British and French conned him into that, putting him and the peacekeeping force in an impossible situation.... If you have troops dedicated not to use force, you can't put on a different hat and order NATO to bomb. If they were going to bomb, they should have changed the mandate to one of fighting the Serbs. Of course they were not prepared to do that."[214]

Summing Up

Most analysts suggest that the Boutros-Ghali's strongest legacy may well lie in his ambitious and thoughtful documents—particularly his *Agenda for Peace* and its update and the *Agenda for Development*.

According to his former spokesman, Joe Sills, the Secretary-General had hoped to play a positive mediating role both in North Korea, which he visited despite strong US opposition, and in Kashmir. He said the UN leader did not receive the support he needed to create change.[215]

Boutros-Ghali faced a major hurdle in trying to recruit enough troops and equipment for the spate of peacekeeping operations that the Council did authorize. The situation had changed radically from the time when the United Nations could rely on 12 to 15 members as traditional suppliers.

"In the early 1990s, those nations could no longer meet the demand," said Canada's David Malone. "New countries willing to provide troops and equipment had to be found, and it was a serious challenge for the Secretary-General." Malone said that many of those newer suppliers who helped in Somalia and Bosnia were not well prepared for the job and not used to working with other countries. The result was often long delays and reversed promises.[216]

In addition, most mandates assigned to UN peacekeepers were not strong. General Rikhye argued that most troops needed to be better prepared to exercise effective self-defense if challenged. He said that, in both Somalia and the former Yugoslavia, many UN troops had their weapons taken away and were sometimes jailed. UN forces there had been "disgraced, dishonored and robbed," he said.[217]

Concern over troops and money were almost always at the top of Boutros-Ghali's agenda. He personally beat the bushes with phone calls to recruit troops. As a reporter interviewing him from time to time, I vividly recall his sense of frustration. In desperation for the money side of the equation, he occasionally suggested other funding options. Usually, they were promptly shot down.

"I think he was deeply disappointed by the amount of time he had to spend on finance and budget issues," said Joe Sills. "He felt strongly that it's the right of member states to control the budget process and make him justify everything, but that once the budget is approved, he should have that money to work with."[218]

"He tried in every way to make the job workable," confirmed Benjamin Rivlin. "It wasn't his fault that the Security Council decides certain things and then gives him peanuts with which to do it. He was under a lot of pressure."[219]

As Boutros-Ghali told it, he implemented Council mandates in Bosnia that he was sure would fail. In Rwanda, he said he tried to "cobble together" a mission "out of scraps thrown...by member states."[220]

The secretary-general's role, and that of the UN, did expand significantly in the course of hosting the series of UN megaconferences in the mid-1990s. Stephen Burgess, a Boutros-Ghali biographer, contended that these defined the United Nations as much as its major peace operations at the time.[221]

"Boutros-Ghali sort of nursed the conferences along and provided a sense of direction," noted Clovis Maksoud. "His intellectual input gave them a heightened level of purpose. He was able to articulate the consensus in favor of progress."[222]

Stabs at Reform

Like most secretaries-general, Boutros-Ghali did not shine as an effective administrator. "Early on, he saw himself as a political secretary-general and not one that was going to repair the plumbing and... the bricks," observed Johns Hopkins' Ruth Wedgwood. "As a matter of time, you can't combine mediation and good offices with tough-nut CEO duties, even if you have both capacities."[223]

The Secretary-General said in his memoir, however, that he carried out more reforms than any previous secretary-general. But needed structural reforms would have to come, in his view, from the most influential member states.[224]

Most analysts agree that he did make a promising start at trimming the UN bureaucracy when he first took office. But within a few years, he virtually reversed the process. By 1994, nearly 50 under-secretaries-general were again reporting directly to him, according to Rosemary Righter in her book, *Utopia Lost: The United Nations and World Order*.[225]

"I think Boutros-Ghali deserves credit for beginning steps in trying to reform the UN," said Sir Brian, who worked in a senior capacity at the United Nations for most of its first half-century. "I think the trouble was that he did it along the wrong lines." Urquhart, who often issued reports on recommended reforms during his career, recalled one in 1993, suggesting that, for greater efficiency, the United Nations should be divided into four main departments, each headed by a deputy who could act as a cabinet officer.

"Boutros-Ghali told me that it was ridiculous, that it would weaken the secretary-general," Sir Brian recalled. "I said, 'Since when have four strong pillars weakened the structure of a house?' It's nonsense unless you run the whole operation as a secret society—in which case, God help you!"[226]

Leon Gordenker confirmed, "Boutros-Ghali couldn't delegate anything. He didn't want to. Everything went to the top."[227]

Still, this secretary-general is credited with enlarging the role and number of special representatives. Each was to act as a roving ambassador on the scene, reporting directly to him in the context of the assigned mandate. Such emissaries are important to act as negotiators for the secretary-general and earn the confidence of governments and parties to disputes, noted former UN assistant secretary-general George Sherry.[228]

"I think this was a major development," said Joe Sills. "No one had done this before to the extent that Boutros-Ghali did. When these special representatives are back in New York, they brief the Council but don't 'report' to it. That's [a] very important [distinction]."[229]

As an example of how important the position can be, Sills noted that Lakhdar Brahimi, the Algerian diplomat who was Boutros-Ghali's special representative in Haiti, very skillfully directed the transition there in 1995 from a US-led force to a UN peacekeeping contingent when the Aristide government was reinstated. "Brahimi was the critical person in getting Haiti to come together," said Sills.[230]

During the Secretary-General's brief tenure, there were other important forward moves. For example, the Council established international criminal tribunals for both the former Yugoslavia and Rwanda.

"This was a magnificent step forward, the most important development in international civil society of the previous 25 years," Giandomenico Picco, a former Pérez de Cuéllar senior aide, said. "For the first time in human history, we have tribunals which dare to look at the action not only of the victims but of the victors."[231]

Goals Too Limited?

Still, there were gaps. Hurst Hannum of the Fletcher School said he would rate Boutros-Ghali a 7 on a scale of 10 for his reform efforts:

> I don't think people had the sense that he was committed to building the organization in a long-term way as opposed to making himself look good and maybe accomplishing something in the short term. That, combined with the payments problem, contributed to a great drop in morale...and I think Boutros-Ghali deserves at least some of the blame for that.[232]

Hannum also argued that Boutros-Ghali could have done far more to champion the cause of human rights than he did. He pointed to the Secretary-General's initial reluctance to support Washington's long-time goal of creating a UN high commissioner of human rights.

"Once it was established, he wasn't particularly supportive," Hannum said. "Evenhandedness has not been a hallmark of any secretary-general—or any government, for that matter. But I think with Boutros in the human rights area, it's almost a Kissingerian sense that human rights simply isn't appropriate for the UN in some respects—that it really is an organization that should be run by diplomacy."[233]

Widespread agreement exists among analysts that when things went well, Boutros-Ghali tended to take the credit. When they did not, he would usually stress that he lacked power and was just the "humble servant" of the Council, a convenient scapegoat. Sir Brian recalled that he strongly urged the Secretary-General not to describe himself that way.

"I told him that we've all spent 50 years trying to build up the office of the secretary-general," Sir Brian explained. "His answer was some long and totally ridiculous academic reason."[234]

"Few people have suggested that humility is one of Boutros-Ghali's strong points," noted Edward Luck. "He was very bright and capable—more capable than I thought he would be—but he also had a way of alienating, not listening enough, not drawing on his advisers' judgment. He was the leader of a large political machine which had a lot of analytic capability."[235]

"It's true that member states often let down the UN, but secretaries-general also have ways of prodding member states to behave better," said Canada's David Malone. "I think he was not notably successful in his efforts to mobilize member states."[236]

Isolation from the Council

Many feel that Boutros-Ghali might have fared better if he had worked to build a closer relationship with the Council and had made a greater effort to make outsiders aware of the limits on UN action in crisis situations.

"One of his problems was that he believed he was two cuts above an ambassador—basically at the same level as a head of state," Sir Brian insisted. "I think he was distanced from the Security Council very dangerously. If you're running peacekeeping operations or very complicated negotiations, you really need to take part in a very informal way in the Council and explain to people what you're doing and what's needed. You can't just appoint a bureaucrat to sit there like a dummy.... I think it cost Boutros a great deal. When he needed the Council, they weren't really there for him, and it was a pity."[237]

The secretary-general's presence at informal sessions of the Council is "absolutely essential," Diego Arria, former president of the Council, agreed. "It's the place of give and take. The secretary-general not only gets the views of the P5. It's also the only chance of the other members to debate the issues with him."[238]

Though at first he was considered by some as too old for the job, Boutros-Ghali approached his task with an intelligence and energy that largely impressed most skeptics. He rarely took time for a concert or movie. He told me during an interview that he managed once, in his first four years, to get to a museum to view Matisse. As he once remarked, "I am a monk."[239] He often took files home at night to prepare for meetings the next day and admitted he was hard on the people who worked with him.

"In a way, he treated the UN as sort of a postgraduate seminar," observed his friend Maksoud. "This led to positive as well as negative vibes. It sort of gave the impression that the rest of the international representatives are the graduate students, and they resented that."[240]

Arria noted, "Sometimes when you sat next to him, you could almost hear his brain churning. In one-on-one, he was an extremely gifted and very engaging man."

Arria added that the Secretary-General, probably as a protective effort to keep his reactions from showing, sometimes would sit with arms folded across his chest—"like a sphinx."[241]

On occasion, the Secretary-General could be obstinate and confrontational. Accordingly, some think his efforts at leadership were a little too public and assertive.

"I think Boutros-Ghali sought to exercise very strong leadership on a personal basis in crisis areas by putting forward his positions publicly—only to see them not followed," James Sutterlin said. "I think he is, in a sense, an illustration of how dangerous it can be to try to exercise too much leadership in an aggressive sense. You have to bring Security Council members along. The kind of leadership that I think is most effective is leadership of persuasion and trust."[242]

"He wanted to be a leader like Hammarskjöld but he really didn't have the temperament," agreed Sir Brian.[243]

The Secretary-General's speaking style was highly quotable. "I think in many ways he's been a breath of fresh air," Luck noted.[244] Of course, Boutros-Ghali's outspokenness occasionally got him in trouble. The West, for example, in no way welcomed his description of the war in Bosnia as a "rich man's war." He also urged fellow Africans to get their own house "in order" because no one was going to rescue them.

"His speaking [to the Africans] that way was not accidental," Sills said. "It was a very conscious decision, because he felt it needed to be done, and he saw the rest of the world completely losing patience with these people."[245]

Fortunately, along with his sharp tongue, Boutros-Ghali had a sense of humor and sometimes poked fun at himself. Near the end of his term, at a UN Correspondents luncheon in September 1996, he said he had been bored on vacation and was happy to be back in New York: "It's much more fun to be back here blocking reform, flying my black helicopters, imposing global taxes, and demoralizing my staff."[246]

Tough Balancing Act

Ultimately, it was really his often-tense relationship with the United States that curtailed his UN service. To a degree, it is the catch-22 problem of every secretary-general. Each wants to further UN efforts to solve global problems. Yet, in the process, none can afford to lose the support and confidence of key members, especially the five with veto power.

"It's a difficult line to walk," conceded Hurst Hannum. "You can be so independent that you make the institution irrelevant. In some ways, I think Boutros-Ghali did as good a job of balancing these issues as anyone."[247]

"People in Congress had it in for the UN long before Boutros-Ghali became Secretary-General," insisted Benjamin Rivlin. "It's unfortunate that some people decided to use him as a whipping boy.... He really tried very hard to get along with the US."[248]

As David Malone said, "Boutros-Ghali's personality contained the seeds of his ultimate Waterloo at the UN. He was an intelligent but extremely arrogant figure who was a difficult boss. And he was tone-deaf to the American political world.... He never seemed to understand that the US was serious about getting rid of him."[249]

Hannum observed, "I think Boutros-Ghali was both lucky and unlucky at the same time. He came into office when hopes were the highest they'd been since 1945. But expectations were so extraordinarily high that I think he suffered when you compare the reality. Circumstances required him to respond in a fairly active way to developments. I'm not sure anybody else would have been much different."[250]

"Countries in some ways set him up," Hannum added. "NATO and the US knew that nothing could be done in Bosnia so they didn't want to get involved. 'Let's let the UN do it.' It's like the old commercial for cereal: 'Let Mikey try it—nobody else likes it.'"

William Luers, a veteran US diplomat and former president of the UNA-USA, noted, "It was a terribly difficult five years. After Somalia, things seemed to go from bad to worse as the US resisted constructive participation. It's a classic case of the US shaping, really limiting, what the UN could do." Recalling that he was with the Secretary-General on his last night in New York, Luers added, "I think his wife was more upset than he about how he'd been treated. He was trying to be a good soldier."[251]

When this author once asked if he felt obligated to respond to virtually every crisis, the Secretary-General's answer was essentially yes. He said, "It is my duty to try to bring the spotlight on those conflicts which nobody wants to pay attention to. We are talking about equality."[252]

For all his setbacks, Boutros-Ghali remained an independent and energetic UN leader who clearly expanded the role of the secretary-general as an international player.

CHAPTER NINE

Kofi Annan: A UN Insider from Ghana Pushes Hard for Human Rights

Boutros-Ghali's decision to run his race for reelection right to the bitter end essentially blocked chances of open campaigning or sharing of resumes by others interested in the job.

The situation was delicate. Kofi Annan, an undersecretary-general from Ghana, who spent most of his 30-year career working for the United Nations, was one of five Africans whose names were being whispered about as possible successors. It was assumed that with "Africa's turn" in the top job only half completed, another African would follow Boutros-Ghali for at least one term.

Annan was well aware of the rumors. As Boutros-Ghali noted in his memoir, Annan came to his office one day to say that he would never present himself as a candidate for the United Nations' top post.[1] Privately, Annan wasn't all that sure he wanted the job or that it was really doable. He once remarked, "If it's to come to me, it will; if not, it won't."[2]

Washington had decisively vetoed Boutros-Ghali's nomination on November 19, 1996. The US preference for Annan, though he had sometimes criticized US policies, was a well-known secret. The United States quietly encouraged Ghana to promote his candidacy.[3]

However, it was several straw polls later, on the evening of December 13, when the Council finally settled on him in a unanimous vote. The breakthrough came when three other African candidates withdrew earlier that day. One was from the Ivory Coast, a fluent French speaker long favored by France but vetoed by the United States and Britain. France had favored Boutros-Ghali's reelection and was unhappy with the US veto of his bid. France had cast its own veto of Annan's candidacy as recently as December 12 but, by the next day, agreed to support him.

The Assembly confirmed the Council's choice a few days later. In his inaugural speech to the Assembly on December 17, Annan, the first UN insider elected to the top job, pledged to create a more open United Nations—one closer both to the people and to nongovernmental organizations.[4] He stressed that the United Nations' success or failure depended on its members.

"The United Nations is an instrument for peace and justice," he said. "Use it; respect it; defend it.... Applaud us when we prevail. Correct us when we fail, but, above all, do not let this indispensable, irreplaceable institution wither, languish, or perish as a result of indifference, inattention, or financial starvation."[5]

At long last, the United Nations was to have as its seventh secretary-general a CEO with management experience and one who knew both the United Nations and the United States well. He would be the first black African and the first UN staff member ever to hold the United Nations' top job. As the former League of Arab States ambassador Clovis Maksoud, put it, "He's a secretary-general who was not so much elected as...promoted."[6]

Annan's Family and Career

Annan came from a prominent Ghanaian family of tribal chiefs. His father Henry, a noble of the Fante coastal tribe, managed the United African Company, a Lever Brothers subsidiary that dealt in cocoa exports and varied imports. After retiring, he was elected governor of the Ashanti Province. Kofi Annan has described his father as a man with an "almost innate" sense of dignity and very "centered." Kofi's older sister Essie said that often, after family dinners, their father would hold mock court sessions to "try" his children for their misdeeds. He was less interested in their excuses than in their behavior and holes in their logic. Essie recalled that Kofi often inserted a well-timed joke.[7]

Once his basic education in his hometown of Kumasi was behind him, Kofi received a Ford Foundation scholarship to attend Macalester

College in Minnesota. He graduated in 1961 with a BA in economics and went on to further studies in Geneva at the Graduate Institute of International Studies. He began his UN career there as an administrative and budget officer with the World Health Organization. He worked in two of its field offices and eventually joined the UN Economic Commission for Africa in Ethiopia, where he worked for five years.

He returned to the United States in 1971 as a Sloan Fellow at the Massachusetts Institute of Technology, earning an MS in management. He went back to Ghana to work briefly in national tourism development but soon decided to return to the United Nations, taking a job with the UN High Commissioner for Refugees in Geneva. At a party in Geneva, Annan met Nane Lagergren, a Swedish lawyer and artist. They married in 1984. Both had been divorced and had children. Kofi's son, Kojo, would later figure prominently in the United Nations' oil-for-food scandal involving Iraq.

The couple moved to New York where Annan held numerous UN jobs, including assistant secretary-general for program planning, budget, and finance. In 1992, he was tapped as assistant secretary-general for peacekeeping operations and was later promoted to undersecretary-general.

Annan had already proven his skills along the way as a mediator and manager. Pérez de Cuéllar in 1990 asked him to go to Iraq to help work out the repatriation of more than 900 international staff and thousands of other citizens from Western and Asian countries. Saddam Hussein was essentially holding them hostage, using some as human shields against bombing by US coalition forces. After Annan's visit, all UN staff members, women and children, and many citizens of other nations were allowed to leave.

His "gutsy performance" as peacekeeping head in August 1995—in effect, authorizing the retaliatory NATO bombing of Bosnian Serb positions around Sarajevo by asking UN civilian officials to temporarily give up their authority to veto airstrikes—helped pave the way to the Dayton Peace Accords. In the view of US ambassador Richard Holbrooke, that step also helped to persuade many Americans that Annan was the best man to lead the UN.[8] His candidacy got a further boost that November when Boutros-Ghali asked Annan to oversee the transition of UN forces to the NATO-led multinational coalition in Bosnia.

Annan took on the United Nations' top post at a time of much less euphoria about the organization's possibilities than when Boutros-Ghali took the helm. The United Nations' peacekeeping experience in the first half of the 1990s had been sobering. UN troops still serving in 1997 numbered about 22,000, down three-fourths from their peak number a few years before. Regional organizations had taken over many of the jobs usually given to UN troops. The financial situation was precarious. Many nations, rich and poor, had not paid regular dues. Money was borrowed from the peacekeeping budget to finance regular operations.

Critics had been concerned that Annan, consistently calm, patient, and soft spoken, might be just too nice and conflict averse to make hard decisions. Though aides say he could get angry on occasion, Annan once explained, "Screaming and getting bitter and being angry is negative energy that takes a lot out of you and doesn't help me."[9]

Over time he was to prove he had considerable mettle in his own quiet way for the challenges he faced. As Sir Brian Urquhart observed, "People mistook Kofi's great civility for weakness. He comes from a family of African chiefs. That's the low-key way they function. I think he's very courageous."[10]

Sporting a well-trimmed beard and always impeccably dressed, Annan's outgoing manner was a distinct change from Boutros-Ghali's image as a workaholic. Annan and his wife, Nane, had a burst of real celebrity soon after his election when the couple was invited to many New York parties. Annan saw it as a welcome chance to meet people and learn. As the journalist and Annan biographer James Traub noted, he "understood that the only way to get your story out is to personalize it."[11]

Despite some rumblings of criticism that the socializing amounted to too much partying, Sashi Tharoor, then UN communications director and the person who arranged most of the outings, made no apology for using the Annans to enhance the United Nations' image. As he told the *New York Times*, "Putting a warm and honest face" on the United Nations is "almost basic PR."[12] The Annans usually reserved their weekends for long walks, listening to music, and seeing an occasional movie.

Annan came to be viewed as a respected and accessible leader by both his staff and UN diplomats. Many applauded his tact and considerable political skills. David Malone, Canada's former ambassador to the United Nations, said that the new Secretary-General expressed himself on UN problems in a much more balanced way than his predecessor.[13] Thomas Weiss, director of the City University of New York's Ralph Bunche Institute for International Studies, said Annan was very conscious of his own limitations and had a talent, in his gentle but firm way, for extracting good ideas from others. He would push the ideas into the public domain and get others to take them seriously.[14]

In traveling with Annan, British journalist William Shawcross noted that the Secretary-General had an unusual "presence" and a way of dealing with people in a familiar but persuasive way. Annan almost always managed to keep his dignity and authority intact. Shawcross also insisted that Annan had a "lively and sometimes mischievous sense of fun."[15]

First Things First

Like most secretaries-general, Annan began his first term with a fresh spurt of in-house reforms. The pressure was intense. Washington was particularly demanding, holding back its share of UN dues until more progress was made. US conservatives were lashing out at the United Nations as corrupt and wasteful.

Having worked for the organization for close to 30 years, Annan knew the system well. He wanted to make it more inclusive and decentralized. He hoped to open UN doors more widely and was eager for good input on how a leaner United Nations might perform its tasks more efficiently. He described his approach as "a new diplomacy" that could give the United Nations renewed energy and inspiration.[16]

In spring 1997, for instance, he held a dinner party that included leading journalists and statesmen. He asked the Holocaust survivor and writer Elie Wiesel to talk about the principle of humanitarian intervention. Each table was then urged to discuss the issue and tap a speaker to recap the highlights during dessert. As James Traub recounts the story in *The Best Intentions: Kofi Annan and the UN in the Era of American World Power*, Annan said little, and no conclusion was reached at the time: "He marinated himself in the thoughts of people more verbal and philosophical than he."[17]

When Annan traveled, he did not confine his visits to top government leaders. He also spoke with legislators who appropriate UN funds. He courted some of the United Nations' most vocal critics such as North Carolina Senator Jesse Helms, then chairman of the US Senate Foreign Relations Committee. Helms had been known to describe the United Nations as "the nemesis of millions of Americans"[18] and a threat to US sovereignty. However, he soon began to call Annan by his first name and agreed later to pay up the US debt over a three-year period.[19]

Annan developed a set of proposals in a March 1997 report called *Renewing the United Nations: A Program for Reform*. He said he wanted more time and feedback to refine his suggestions and eventually scaled back some of his more dramatic proposals.[20]

For the most part, members accepted his ideas. The Assembly also usually gave its stamp of approval where its action was necessary.

Annan began by reorganizing UN departments into a few key areas such as development and peace and security. In contrast to Boutros-Ghali, who had senior officials reporting directly to him individually, Annan enlarged his circle by holding weekly cabinet sessions. Senior UN officials, department managers, and heads of the UN programs and specialized agencies, including the World Bank and International Monetary Fund, attended. Some of the more than 30 people taking part were stationed abroad and tuned in by teleconference. Elisabeth Lindenmayer, a senior official attending, recalled that Annan would ask for opinions on pressing UN issues, listen, and usually announce a clear decision.[21]

Noting that the practice was a first in UN history, Bhaskar Menon, a former UN staff member and journalist, insisted, "Real work got done."[22]

"Annan recognized, maybe more clearly than his predecessors, the necessity of bringing together all the resources of the UN system to consider problems," noted James Sutterlin, a former distinguished fellow in UN Studies at Yale. "There was more mutual consultation, especially with financial issues."[23]

"There's no question that he's a gifted manager who is very good with people and knows how to delegate," said former UN senior staff member Álvaro de Soto. Stressing that most of the Secretary-General's predecessors lacked that ability, de Soto added, "Sometimes you strike gold."[24]

For the first time in UN history, Annan also appointed, with the Assembly's approval, a deputy secretary-general—Louise Fréchette. She was Canada's former deputy minister of defense and finance and was to take on the daily management and reform chores. "It was completely his initiative," said Canada's David Malone.[25]

Besides his appointments and internal reforms, Annan scuttled Boutros-Ghali's practice of sending a deputy representative to Council sessions to act as a briefer where information was needed. Annan chose a different tack. As his former spokesman Fred Eckhard explained, "Realizing there was a limit to the detail that one person could give the Council on any one of a wide variety of subjects, he instead delegated [the job] to department heads, or to whoever could give the Council the most detailed response to its questions. The quality of information given...improved dramatically under Annan."[26]

As part of his first wave of reforms, the Secretary-General also held down the next year's budget by a one-third cut in administrative costs and elimination of 1,000 Secretariat positions, about ten percent of the total staff. In addition, he strengthened the United Nations' independent auditing department.[27]

Annan believed that ultimately reform was a matter of political will and said that government attitudes were often at fault. He pointed to the practice of some members' refusal to pay UN bills promptly to try to get the changes they want and to a tendency to use the United Nations as a scapegoat by crafting unrealistic mandates.[28]

From the start, Annan had a deep concern for human rights and consistently paired it with the need for more widespread economic development. In his *Renewing the United Nations* report, he insisted the global body's highest priority must be to lessen poverty and improve the prospects of developing countries. He pledged to earmark some of the funds saved from cost cutting to use as a "development dividend."[29]

Africa: An Early Concern

As the "African candidate," like Boutros-Ghali before him, Annan had a strong commitment to his home continent. As he once stressed to a reporter, "My roots are deeply, deeply African."[30]

In fact, while head of UN peacekeeping operations during the first half of the 1990s, he supervised the dispatch of UN forces to a broad mix of African postings, including Angola, Western Sahara, Somalia, Mozambique, and Rwanda.[31]

When Annan took on the United Nations' top job, 15 of Africa's 54 nations were involved in civil wars or fighting across borders.[32] During his first term, he made several visits to the continent. What he thought and said about Africa may have been more significant than what he actually accomplished.

In April 1997, he issued a report titled *The Causes of Conflict and the Promotion of Peace and Sustainable Development in Africa*. He sent it to the Assembly and the Council. In essence, it urged Africans to stop blaming colonialism for their troubles. "Africa must look to itself," he insisted. He criticized an attitude he saw in many African leaders that, as victors, they had the right to keep wealth, jobs, and power within their own small circle. In such situations, he argued, conflict is almost inevitable.[33]

The report noted that the United Nations was often asked to intervene in intrastate conflicts where the aim seemed more intent on destroying ethnic groups and civilians than militias. Annan insisted that preventing such wars was really a question of "defending humanity itself." The report urged African leaders to hold their defense budgets to zero-growth for the next decade and strengthen democratic rule.[34]

During the summer, Annan spoke to leaders of the Organization of African Unity (OAU) in Ethiopia at its annual summit. He encouraged them to stop tolerating governments that come to power in military coups. Respect for human rights, he said, was neither a luxury of the rich nor a plot of the West, but a needed response to the "yearning for human dignity that resides in every African heart." His remarks were greeted at first in silence but soon prompted a standing ovation. OAU Secretary-General Salim Salim told Annan that he was probably the only one who could have made such a statement and get out of the room "without being lynched."[35]

During his first year in the new job, Annan visited South Africa and Angola as well. He planned to attend the inauguration of a new government of national unity in Angola that was to cap more than two decades of civil war, but the event was postponed. Instead, he visited the Angolan rebel leader Jonas Savimbi, urging him to move forward with the peace process.

By the following year, however, Angola was embroiled once again in a bitter civil war.[36] The government accused the United Nations of failing to persuade Savimbi to stay in the peace talks that had been underway and said that UN peacekeepers stationed there must leave at the end of their mandate. The Secretary-General told the Security Council that the United Nations' 1,000-person force in Angola thus had no further basis for staying and must comply.[37]

Meanwhile, another crisis had erupted in Rwanda and Zaire.

More than one million Hutu refugees who fled to Zaire in the aftermath of the 1994 genocide had come under attack by Rwanda's Tutsi-led army. The Council had voted in late 1996 to send a Canadian-led force to protect the refugees. But before the UN troops arrived, the Tutsis killed thousands and forced hundreds of thousands of other Hutus to return to Rwanda. Annan was eager to conduct a UN investigation at that point. However, Laurent Kabila, who had taken control of Zaire and renamed it the Democratic Republic of the Congo, managed to delay and block the UN investigators at almost every turn. Annan had to withdraw the team, which had little to show for its efforts.[38]

In May 1998, Annan again visited several African nations to focus more UN attention on the continent's special challenges. During the trip he had advance word of an article by Philip Gourevitch in the *New Yorker* that took Annan to task, in his former peacekeeping role, for not having urged stronger UN action in Rwanda after receiving a January 1994 cable from Lieutenant General Romeo Dallaire, the man in charge of the small UN force there. He had warned of a possible genocide and wanted to seize a cache of Hutu arms in Kigali.[39]

It was an issue that would haunt much of Annan's first term and eventually push the Secretary-General to order a thorough investigation. At various stops in Africa he was questioned repeatedly in press conferences—and sometimes by government leaders—about his role in the 1994 tragedy.

During a stop in Kenya, Annan, now obviously on the defensive, argued that too much was being made of one cable and that not all of the information flowing into the peacekeeping department was necessarily accurate. He said few understood the limiting conditions facing Dallaire. At one point, Annan said, the general had one Ghanaian battalion only. Those soldiers risked their lives, Annan added, to protect people in the local stadium and at the Hôtel des Mille Collines.[40]

Annan biographer Stanley Meisler argued that it was "wrongheaded" to task Annan with major responsibility for the tragedy. Annan insisted in a news conference in Nairobi that the failure was not a lack of information but a lack of political will to act by UN members.[41]

In Kigali, Annan faced a blistering attack by Rwanda's foreign minister, Anastase Gasana, who charged that the United Nations knew well ahead about the planned 1994 genocide and did nothing. The Secretary-General replied that he had not come "to get into polemics." He turned the focus back on Rwanda by asking rhetorically what it was that caused people to turn against one another so violently. "It was a horror that came from within," he suggested.[42]

"He was criticized for not being contrite enough," recalled his spokesman Fred Eckhard. "He said, 'You share in the guilt.' They didn't like to hear that, so he was a very unpopular visitor."[43]

The Rwandan presidential spokesman called the UN leader's comments "arrogant, insensitive, and insulting." In contrast, William Shawcross, who was traveling with Annan at the time, termed Annan's remarks "subtle and rather brave."[44]

In July 1998, Annan played a brief good-offices role in Nigeria. After the death of the military dictator General Sani Abacha, Annan was invited by the general's temporary successor to visit Nigeria to help bring the country out of its long global isolation. Annan believed that the nation was moving toward democracy, and he wanted to encourage it.

During the visit, he worked to do that and urged the temporary leaders to free all political prisoners. Voters chose members of an assembly later that year and elected Olusegun Obasanjo as Nigeria's new president the next May. Obasanjo began to attack corruption and became the first Nigerian leader in more than a decade to come to the United Nations and speak to the annual Assembly meeting.[45]

Annan later said, "If only as a bridge, my presence may have served to support a democratic transition at a perilous moment."[46]

Still, intense and widespread fighting continued in many African nations. As Annan told Barbara Crossette, a *New York Times* reporter, in December 1998, Africa at that stage in his first term was a "deep disappointment." The resulting state of affairs, he said, was "a tragedy, a real tragedy."[47]

Standoff in Baghdad

As part of the 1991 Gulf War ceasefire, Saddam Hussein had agreed to unrestricted UN weapons inspections. However, the road ahead for those United Nations inspections would prove very difficult.

As the first step, the UN launched the UN Special Commission (UNSCOM) and charged it with finding and disarming all weapons of mass destruction (WMDs) in Iraq. However, Rolf Ekeus, the Swede tapped as first chairman of the group and who approached the job with persistence, found the challenge extremely frustrating. As he explained to a gathering of nonproliferation experts, "We are nothing in Baghdad.... We are at their complete mercy. They can just stop our work at any time."[48]

Ekeus finally opted to resign, and Annan chose Australian diplomat Richard Butler in July 1997 as UNSCOM's new chairman. However, Butler's confrontational style soon triggered Iraqi complaints. By November, Iraq, having already drawn up a list of sensitive areas barred from inspection, demanded that all inspectors from the United States exit the country immediately. Butler decided to leave with his whole team.[49]

The Security Council was deadlocked as to what should be done next. The United States, already practicing bombing missions from a carrier in the Persian Gulf, was threatening to bomb Iraq.

Though only just beginning his second year as Secretary-General, Kofi Annan felt he had a moral right and duty to step into the fray. Pressure from religious groups was particularly strong. "There was overwhelming public sentiment that there must be a peaceful way to get out of this mess," Fred Eckhard, Annan's spokesman, recalled.[50]

Annan decided to fly to Baghdad to try to break the impasse. Washington and London had strong reservations.

"I decided to go myself because the stakes were extremely high," Annan recalled in an oral history interview with Yale University. "The Council had given us a mandate. We had inspectors on the ground.... I was worried that if the [US-threatened] bombing went ahead...it could mean the end of the inspections and could have a negative impact on the humanitarian efforts we were doing for the Iraqi people."[51]

Annan met first with the five permanent members of the Council, then the 10 elected members, and then all 15 together in his 38th-floor conference room. "He said, 'I'm not going to go until you give me marching orders,'" Eckhard recalled. "He eventually squeezed out of them parameters within which he could operate."[52]

Unlike Pérez de Cuéllar, who had made a similar trip just before the Gulf War, Annan wanted to make sure that he still had some room for maneuvering. He wanted to be seen as an independent actor with enough flexibility to solve the impasse while allowing Iraq to save face.

"He [Annan] had gone to great pains to really work it out with the Council before he went," Sir Brian noted. "He knew what he was going to negotiate, and he had the latitude to do it.... Of course, he was also very lucky in a way with the [US] military buildup [as backup]."[53]

The Secretary-General arrived in Baghdad on February 20, 1998. He was met at the airport by the Iraqi foreign minister, Tariq Aziz. Eventually, he managed to meet alone for three hours with Hussein.

"I had always seen him in a military uniform so it was interesting to walk into the palace and see him in a coat and tie," Annan said. "He seemed to have been well briefed...and was asking very pertinent questions." The Secretary-General noted it was the first time he had met with someone, however, who left him briefly to "go and pray."[54]

The Iraqi leaders knew their nation faced not only the threat of US bombing missions but also continued strict economic and trade sanctions if it stayed on course. The Council resolution was clear: disarm and the sanctions would be lifted.

"In the end, they [the Iraqis] were cooperative, but they began [the talks] in a rather hostile attitude toward the resolution and the organization that, in their mind, tried to humiliate them, trample on their sovereignty and dignity, and prevent them from developing their country," Annan noted. He recalled that, at the end of the talks, Hussein offered him a cigar—"like a peace pipe."[55]

On February 22, the Secretary-General signed a memo of understanding with Aziz. Iraq agreed to reopen sites previously closed to UN inspectors—such as the presidential palaces—and set no deadlines for completion of the work or conditions on the identity or nationality of the inspectors.

After the signing, Aziz told the gathered crowd of reporters that it was diplomacy and not "sabre rattling" that led to the agreement.

Yet Annan readily conceded that the bombing threat from Washington helped to seal the deal: "You can do a lot with diplomacy, but of course you can do a lot more with diplomacy backed up by firmness and force," he said.[56]

Skeptics were dubious from the start that the agreement would last. Yet there was also widespread relief that Annan had managed to do what he did. The United States called off the bombing. On his return to the UN headquarters in New York, Annan was greeted in the foyer by a crowd of cheering UN staffers.

In trying to reassure those who were still doubtful, he said of Hussein during a press conference, "I think I can do business with him, and I think he was serious."[57]

US conservatives promptly branded the statement a naïve mistake. Some thought Annan sounded like Britain's Neville Chamberlain, too trustingly taking Hitler at his word. The *New York Times* columnist A. M. Rosenthal termed Annan's policy one of "diligent appeasement" and said Annan was clearly "Saddam's single greatest asset at the UN."[58]

"Annan took a lot of heat," Eckhard said. "The whole thing became very partisan and political, and it hurt him."[59]

"Annan's was a neutral statement, not a value judgment," said Álvaro de Soto. "Annan did do business with Hussein. He struck an agreement. It doesn't mean that the man [Hussein] is a stalwart citizen or that you'd trust him with the family jewels...but you've got to be able to deal with the dangerous ones."[60]

However, by fall 1998, the Annan–Aziz agreement clearly collapsed, just as the skeptics had predicted. This time Iraq said no more UN weapons inspectors would be allowed inside its borders.

In response, on December 16 American and British planes embarked on a four-night barrage of airstrikes and missile bombardments on Iraqi military installations. Hussein held to his refusal to readmit UN inspectors or make any more weapons concessions. UN economic sanctions and the ban on Iraqi trade, both of which Hussein wanted lifted, remained in place.

Annan now was viewed as having merely delayed war. In January 1999, in a major speech at the Council on Foreign Relations, he described Iraq's turnabout in the fall of 1998 as "a flagrant and deeply troubling violation" of both his agreement with Baghdad and its obligation to heed Council resolutions. He admitted that his good-offices mission had been risky, both for the United Nations and for his own position. Yet he argued that impartiality requires strict and unbiased adherence to the principles of the UN Charter. It is not, he said, "neutrality in the face of evil."[61]

Stepping Up the Pressure on Libya after Lockerbie

By the time Annan dealt with the Libyan issue, it had been almost 10 years since Pan American Flight 103 blew up over Lockerbie, Scotland, in December 1988.

Most of the more than 270 people killed were British or American. Early on, Syria and Iran were thought to be involved. Over time, Western intelligence agents became convinced that the culprits were two citizens of Libya. That nation had been on Washington's state-sponsored terrorism list since 1979. In 1986, the United States also imposed economic sanctions and launched an air attack on Libya when that nation was thought to be behind an attack on a Berlin disco that killed two Americans.

In the fall of 1991, the United States and Britain issued warrants for the arrest of the two Libyans in the Lockerbie case. The Security Council passed three resolutions in 1992–93 imposing tough sanctions on Libya that covered everything from a ban on flights in and out of that nation to a ban on the sale of arms, aviation spare parts, and oil-producing equipment. The Council authorized Boutros-Ghali, Secretary-General at the time, to try to get Libya's cooperation in turning over the suspects.

But Colonel Muammar Qaddafi, highly suspicious, showed no signs of willingness to yield. Boutros-Ghali, whose relations with the Libyan leader had been strained since he accompanied Anwar Sadat on the 1977 trip to Israel, had held many talks with Qaddafi in person and through emissaries. The UN chief assured Qaddafi that the Western powers had no secret agenda and that the Council would make no more demands once the suspects were turned over. Yet Boutros-Ghali's impression was that the Libyan leader was stalling, fearing Libya's destabilization and hoping that his lawyers would find a way out.[62]

As the years went by, the Council's stiff sanctions faced new challenges. In response to an intense Libyan protest campaign, the Arab League, the OAU, the nonaligned group, and the General Assembly all denounced the Council restrictions in 1996 and demanded their removal.

Qaddafi wrote a sharp letter to Boutros-Ghali, complaining of bitter injustice against Libya. In a twist on words, he cited the 1986 US air attack on his country—calling it the "Locker-A Massacre"—as the real cause of the current crisis. Boutros-Ghali said that, by the time he left office, Qaddafi was "furious" with him and criticized him publicly—proof, in Boutros-Ghali's view, that he had performed his role effectively.[63]

By summer 1998, when Annan was Secretary-General, the 53 nations of the OAU decided to resume commercial flights in and out of Libya in direct defiance of the UN sanctions.[64]

Like Boutros-Ghali, Annan also tried hard, both personally and via emissaries, to resolve the Lockerbie affair. Both Washington and London had been holding out for a trial on their own turf. Libya, adamantly opposed, finally agreed to hold the trial in a neutral third nation. Annan urged the Western nations to agree to the plan, and they did. In August 1998, a Dutch proposal to hold the trial in the Netherlands was accepted. At the same time, the Council agreed to lift the sanctions as soon as the two accused Libyans were safely transported to the trial site.

Most legal and logistical problems had been resolved. Still, there was no sign of any forward movement by Libya.

Annan was convinced that the Council could do little more to end the standoff and that the sanctions were fast losing broad support. He applied to the Council's sanctions committee for permission to fly to Libya himself on December 5, 1998, to try to break the impasse.

He met first with Libya's foreign minister, Omar al-Muntasser, and stressed the importance of the shift in Washington and London in now accepting a third nation trial site. Annan also assured the foreign minister that the two nations would make no attempt to involve more senior Libyans or the government itself. "No one wants to drag this out," he said.[65]

Finally, Annan traveled to a tent in a remote part of the Libyan desert to talk with Qaddafi, who still had strong doubts about turning over the suspects. At one point, the Libyan leader launched into a lengthy discussion of what it means to be a terrorist versus a freedom fighter. Annan told him that he was convinced that the Americans and the British were acting in good faith. The Secretary-General added, "In life sometimes we have to have the courage and wisdom to do what is good for our people and nation.... You have taken some tough decisions, and I think you are capable of one more. I would encourage and urge you to do it."[66]

The two agreed that when Annan was questioned by the press he would say only that he found Qaddafi to be in good health, so it would not look as if the Libyan leader had been overly influenced by his UN visitor. Annan saw his trip largely as a confidence-building measure.[67]

Yet Libya made no immediate pronouncement. The British and Americans decided to turn up the heat again. On February 26, 1999, they warned of more sanctions within 30 days if the two suspects were not surrendered. Finally, in mid-March, Qaddafi agreed to the transfer. The two men were sent to the Netherlands on April 5. The Council lifted the sanctions the same day.

The trial took place in May 2000. The three presiding judges, who were Scottish, reached a unanimous decision on January 31, 2001, to convict one man and free the other.

Certainly the ultimate outcome was a joint effort. The months-long process included mediation by Nelson Mandela of South Africa and diplomats from Egypt and Saudi Arabia. Speaking only for himself, after his return from Libya and well before the trial began, Annan told the Council on Foreign Relations, "If my visit speeded up, even by one day, the closing of this tragic chapter, I believe it will have been worth it—to me and to the UN."[68]

Human Rights Dilemma in Kosovo

Annan, surely one of the strongest promoters of human rights ever to sit in the secretary-general's chair, faced a tough challenge in finding the right role for the United Nations in the post-Bosnia crisis in Kosovo.

Kosovo, the southernmost province of Serbia in the former Yugoslavia, once had self-governing powers like Serbia itself and the five other Yugoslav republics. In 1989, Serb President Slobodan Milošević abruptly reversed the situation, placing Kosovo under Serb jurisdiction in the Federal Republic of Yugoslavia.

Yet a full 90 percent of Kosovo's two million residents were ethnic Albanians. Milošević brought in Serb police, dismissed Albanian teachers from schools and universities, and ushered in a more Serb-centered curriculum. Ethnic Albanians now had to get permission even to buy or sell property.[69]

One group that took full advantage of the growing resentment among Albanians was the well-armed Kosovo Liberation Army (KLA), which was formed in 1996 as a peaceful resistance movement. Over time, supplied with weapons from nearby Albania, it started attacking Serb police and militias. The Serbs responded by killing many of the province's ethnic Albanians and burning many of their villages. Thousands fled to nearby Albania, Macedonia, and Montenegro.

The pace of such ethnic cleansing was particularly intense by spring 1998. Kosovo was becoming a major problem for the international community. What, if anything, should be done?

Annan made his strong feelings on human rights in this case very clear. In a major speech that June to the prestigious Ditchley Foundation in Britain, he said that, because he was African, people might mistakenly assume that he would preach against intervention in any nation's domestic affairs. Yet the UN Charter protects the sovereignty of the world's "peoples" rather than its governments, he said, and was never meant as a license for governments to "trample on human rights and dignity."

Mindful of the UN failure to act promptly and effectively in Rwanda and Bosnia, he insisted that state boundaries must no longer be seen as "watertight protection" for war criminals or mass murderers. "Sovereignty implies responsibility, not just power," he said. The Security Council, he added pointedly, has the authority to decide when intervention is needed.[70]

Still, the burning of Kosovo villages and the civilian killings continued. That summer a leader of the Albanian opposition met with Annan, asking him to do what he could to stop the bloodshed. The Secretary-General sent a report to the Council in August 1998, warning that the global community's commitment to humanitarian work results in dealing with only the symptoms of the Kosovo problem.[71] In a closed briefing to the Council, the UN High Commissioner for Refugees (UNHCR) similarly warned of an impending humanitarian disaster if the Serb offensive continued.[72]

In a statement that month, the Council president condemned the attacks by the Serb forces. On September 23, 1998, the Council passed a resolution demanding that the Serbs withdraw from Kosovo and that the leaders of the Albanian opposition, for its part, condemn all terrorist acts. Both sides were urged to work toward a negotiated solution. The Council also authorized the dispatch of international monitors to keep watch on the situation.[73]

In a similar move, NATO officials warned Milošević to stop the Serb violence or face possible airstrikes.

Richard Holbrooke, who had been President Clinton's successful envoy in the Dayton accords and now awaited his appointment as US ambassador to the United Nations, spent much of October negotiating with Milošević. The Serb leader finally agreed to a cease-fire with the KLA, to reduce his security forces in Kosovo, and to allow Albanian refugees to return. He also agreed to allow up to 2,000 unarmed observers from the

Organization for Security and Cooperation in Europe (OSCE) to verify the process.[74]

However, recruitment of the observers took an extraordinarily long time. Meanwhile, mass killings and more forced departures continued. In January 1999, the KLA murdered four Serb police. The Serbs retaliated with a vicious attack on the village of Račak, where some of the KLA leaders were thought to be hiding, and murdered at least 45 Albanian residents.[75] Annan called for a full investigation.

Monitors from the OSCE blamed Yugoslav security forces. Serb leaders accused the OSCE of lying, insisting that the KLA itself staged the massacre, using its own dead. In a huff, the Serbs expelled American diplomat William Walker, head of the OSCE group, and refused to allow Louise Arbour, the UN prosecutor for war crimes in the former Yugoslavia, to enter Kosovo.[76]

Diplomats from the United States, Europe, and Russia met with leaders from both sides of the dispute at the French castle of Rambouillet near Paris that February. The diplomats presented their solution. Though still designated as a Serb province, Kosovo would have increased powers of self-government, and a NATO force would be sent to police any violence. The Kosovo Albanians agreed. However, Milošević did not attend the meeting, and the Serb delegation simply walked out.

Holbrooke again met with Milošević in Belgrade to argue that the deal must be accepted or NATO bombing would begin. On March 23, with no concessions in hand, Holbrooke flew from Belgrade to Brussels. There he told NATO officials that the Serb leader would accept no international force in Kosovo.[77] Annan withdrew UN aid workers from Kosovo the same day.

The long-threatened NATO bombing began March 24, 1999. In response, Milošević immediately began a massive ethnic cleansing operation in Kosovo by Serb forces. In a few days, as many as 4,000 ethnic Albanians were fleeing the province every hour.[78] In a statement on March 30, Annan described himself as "profoundly outraged by reports of a vicious and systematic campaign of ethnic cleansing" by Serb forces.[79]

The situation posed a huge challenge for both Annan and the United Nations. Technically, the United Nations had not authorized the NATO bombing as it had done for its strikes in Bosnia in the mid-1990s.

On the day the bombing began, the Secretary-General issued a statement that blamed Belgrade for rejecting a political settlement. While it was "tragic" that diplomacy had failed, he said, "there are times when the use of force may be legitimate in the pursuit of peace." Yet he also expressed regret that NATO acted without specific UN authorization. He stressed that, under the Charter, the United Nations has primary responsibility to maintain international peace and security.[80]

The United States and other NATO nations argued that the Council, in effect, had endorsed the action by its September 1998 resolution demanding a Serb troop withdrawal. Yet any specific military go-ahead from the Council would almost surely have drawn a veto from Russia, still a firm Serb ally, and China, which viewed itself as the often lone champion of inviolable sovereign rights. Washington, accordingly, had been working hard to avoid almost any UN involvement in the crisis.

Annan, of course, did not want to see the UN sidelined. Yet he also did not want to be seen as supporting Milošević by insisting on specific Council authorization. The Secretary-General's critics said he tried to have it both ways.

In a speech at The Hague that spring, he said he knew it was sometimes difficult for the Council to reach a united position. Yet what worried him, he said, was that states seemed unable to reconcile national interests when "skillful and visionary diplomacy would make unity possible." To underscore the point, he warned, "Unless the Security Council is restored to its preeminent position as the sole source of legitimacy on the use of force, we are on a dangerous path to anarchy."[81]

Meanwhile, Annan worked to stay involved in the continuing diplomatic efforts. He praised—and criticized—all parties, trying to keep solutions moving forward while providing political cover.[82] On

April 7, 1999, in an address to the Commission on Human Rights in Geneva, he said, "We will not and we cannot accept a situation where people are brutalized behind national boundaries. A United Nations that will not stand up for human rights is a United Nations that cannot stand up for itself."[83]

He later issued a statement, spelling out the exact steps Yugoslav authorities must take for the bombing to stop. He then flew to Brussels and conferred at the airport with Javier Solana, NATO Secretary-General. In late April, he flew to Moscow to talk with Russia's President, Boris Yeltsin. By then, Russia had become very interested in being part of the solution. Although Annan did not view the conversation as particularly helpful, Yeltsin spontaneously bid the Secretary-General farewell with, "Together, you and I are invincible. Together we can end this war."[84]

By mid-May, NATO was running out of targets for its airstrikes. Though President Clinton at first resisted, the United States finally agreed to a NATO plan to send in as many as 50,000 ground troops. Another blow for Milošević came with news on May 27 that he and four senior colleagues had been indicted by the Yugoslav war crimes tribunal.[85] Milošević was facing intense pressure to seal a deal.

Finally on June 1, Viktor Chernomyrdin, the former Russian prime minister, Martti Ahtisaari, the president of Finland, and US Deputy Secretary of State Strobe Talbott met in Bonn, Germany, and worked out a common position. All Serb forces must be withdrawn from Kosovo and a NATO-led ground force allowed in—or the bombing would continue. Milošević agreed to their demands on June 3, 1999.[86]

The NATO airstrikes had gone on for more than two months. During that span, another 10,000 Kosovars died, largely in Serb attacks.[87] The UNHCR estimated that one million more ethnic Albanians also had been forced to flee.[88]

Both NATO and the United Nations would now take on major roles in Kosovo's future. As Annan later told TV interviewer David Frost, "I don't see NATO as a rival. I think NATO should be seen as an ally."[89]

On June 10, the Council ratified the peace agreement. While reaffirming respect for the sovereignty and territorial integrity of the Federal Republic of Yugoslavia, the Council granted Kosovo more powers of self-administration. A NATO-led peacekeeping force was authorized to oversee the departure of Serb troops and the return of Albanian refugees.[90]

The United Nations was to be the interim administrator, and Annan was asked to appoint a special representative to oversee the civilian and humanitarian side of the job. He chose Sérgio Vieira de Mello of Brazil as the temporary head of the UN Mission in Kosovo (UNMIK).

Vieira de Mello was then UN undersecretary-general for humanitarian affairs and emergency relief coordinator. In May, he led the first international team into Kosovo to assess the humanitarian situation since the bombing started. Belgrade insisted that he travel with Serb escorts. He gave a full report to the Council on June 2. It covered both the NATO bombing damage to Serb cities and the extent of ethnic cleansing in Kosovo. His biographer, Samantha Power, termed it a "daredevil mission" that brought important new data to light.[91]

By June 20, 1999, less than a month after the bombing stopped, all 40,000 of the Serb troops once in Kosovo had left.

It had been a difficult time for the United Nations. Although the Secretary-General had worked hard to stay involved at every step of the crisis, the United Nations had not been directly involved either in NATO's bombing decision or in the negotiations that followed.

The United States had been eager to keep UN involvement minimal. Stanley Meisler wrote that Madeleine Albright, who was named US Secretary of State in 1997, had phoned Annan frequently during the crisis and was unhappy with what she saw as his "meddling" in the situation. She treated him with disdain, Meisler said, judging him "too soft to negotiate with the big boys."[92]

Yet through his outspoken concern for human rights during the Kosovo crisis, Annan left a lasting moral legacy.

In his annual speech to the Assembly in September 1999, Annan said that the doctrine of humanitarian intervention is consistent with the language and spirit of the UN Charter, which allows the use of armed force in the common interest. He criticized the United Nations' uneven record in that regard and said Council members must accept a much broader definition of national interest.[93] At the same session, President Bill Clinton argued that if NATO had not acted, the result might have risked discrediting everything the United Nations stood for.[94]

A year later, at the September 2000 Assembly opening session, Jean Chretien, Canada's prime minister, announced that he would form a panel to study the human rights issues that Annan had raised. This group, called the International Commission on Intervention and State Sovereignty, released a report in December 2001 known as the *Responsibility to Protect*.

The 12-member commission, chaired by Gareth Evans, former Australian foreign minister, and Mohamed Sahnoun, a senior Algerian diplomat, concluded that the international community had a duty to intervene on humanitarian grounds if a state were unable or unwilling to protect its own citizens or had committed atrocities against them. The report said that the world community's responsibility extended to prevention, reaction, and rebuilding.[95]

Annan praised the report later at a seminar organized by what was then known as the International Peace Academy. He said the commission was "taking away the last excuse of the international community for doing nothing when doing something can change lives."[96]

An earlier study, issued in 2000 as the *Kosovo Report*, had been started by the Swedish prime minister Göran Persson and conducted by the Independent International Commission for Kosovo. Focused specifically on the crisis there, it concluded that NATO's military action was technically illegal in skirting a Security Council vote but was politically and morally legitimate.[97]

"Annan was always torn about Kosovo," said Thomas Weiss, who has written extensively on the UN and its challenges. The Secretary-General was "ambivalent" about it and actually used the NATO precedent to ask if anyone would have complained if any country had been willing to act on Rwanda without a Council mandate, Weiss wrote in a February 10, 2011, e-mail to this author.

Both of the reports effectively endorsed the Secretary-General's position. As journalist and Annan speechwriter Edward Mortimer concluded, "I firmly believe that if Kofi Annan had achieved nothing beyond gaining broad acceptance for the responsibility to protect, that by itself would constitute a major achievement."[98]

East Timor: Human Rights on the Line Again

Speaking in Dili, the capital of East Timor, a few minutes before midnight on May 19, 2002, Annan insisted that he was just as excited as he was 45 years earlier when Ghana gained its independence. As the UN flag was replaced by that of the new East Timor nation, he complimented the Timorese on their courage and persistence. "Your independence day is a day of pride for all of us," he insisted.[99]

The journey for the former Portuguese colony had been long and costly. Shortly after the colony declared its independence in 1975, Indonesia, which had long regarded East Timor as one of its provinces, invaded the island nation. The Security Council quickly condemned the act and demanded that Indonesia withdraw its troops. The Council made clear its support for the right of the East Timorese to determine their own future. Yet the impact of the UN action was minimal. Indonesia formally annexed East Timor as its 27th province in July 1976.

Thus began a violent and brutal occupation that lasted for more than 25 years. Tens of thousands of East Timorese were killed or forced to flee to the mountains or to the western half of the island. The CIA estimated that 100,000 to 250,000, possibly one-third of the entire population, died under Indonesian rule.[100]

At the urging of the Assembly and two UN secretaries-general, Portuguese and Indonesian diplomats held talks over the years on East Timor's future, but the discussions made little progress.

The crucial change occurred when Indonesia's president, Mohamed Suharto, was overthrown in 1998 and replaced by his vice president, Bacharuddin Jusuf (B. J.) Habibie.

Annan had long been concerned about reports of increasing violence on the island. After his considerable prodding, Habibie suddenly announced on January 28, 1999, that he would consider allowing a referendum. The choice for the East Timorese would be full independence or stepped-up autonomy within Indonesian rule. Habibie reportedly assumed that voters would opt for the latter.[101]

The United Nations was to help prepare for the referendum. A small UN Assistance Mission in East Timor (UNAMET) would be allowed in but with no armed troops. Though the United Nations wanted to have the semiofficial Indonesian military on the island disarmed and confined to their barracks during the voting, Indonesia nixed the idea. It also opposed attempts to bring in foreign troops. Habibie assured Annan in a memo that the army-controlled Indonesian police would keep order.[102]

Yet the continued violence and threats to voters during the days of preparation were such that Annan twice postponed the date of the referendum.[103] The vote was finally held on August 30, 1999. An impressive 98 percent of those eligible to vote cast their ballots. Almost 80 percent supported full independence for East Timor.

The reaction was immediate. Ragtag militias supported by the Indonesian military destroyed buildings and phone lines, killing hundreds of East Timorese, and forcing thousands of others to flee.[104]

Under an earlier UN–Indonesia agreement, Jakarta's military was to stay in charge of East Timor security until the Indonesian parliament formally cancelled the 1976 annexation.[105]

It was an agreement that clearly was not working. The university in Dili was set on fire, and the city center looted. UN and foreign aid workers were among those targeted. Annan, in his good-offices role, spoke frequently with both Habibie and José "Xanana" Gusmão, East Timor's chief proindependence leader, then under house arrest. Gusmão had been eager for the referendum and now urged the United

Nations to intervene to stop what he called "the new genocide." Yet the Council was not about to approve any UN intervention without Indonesia's consent.[106]

Annan warned Habibie that the situation was out of control. Habibie continued to assure Annan—even as late as September 8, 1999, in a lengthy 3 a.m. phone call—that the army was quite able to maintain order on its own. All this occurred while as many as 3,000 refugees an hour were being trucked to West Timor, and the street violence continued unabated. Annan told the Council the next day that, under the circumstances, he did not want to pull the UNAMET troops out completely. Instead, he authorized a partial withdrawal, asking for volunteers to stay behind as added protection.[107]

Meanwhile the Council had sent a mission of five ambassadors to Indonesia to visit Dili and to talk with Habibie. Their report of the devastation they saw and their conclusion that Habibie was not in control of the situation, prompted Annan to issue a strong public statement on September 10. He said that Indonesia had failed in its security responsibilities and that it was time for international help. Noting that those responsible for crimes against humanity must be held accountable, he said, "No one in their wildest dreams thought what we are witnessing could have happened."[108]

Habibie telephoned Annan two days later. Insisting that he was speaking to Annan as "a personal friend," he asked the United Nations to send in a multinational force as soon as possible. He set no conditions. Habibie then announced his request on Indonesian television, saying that too many Timorese had already lost their lives and that the United Nations would now help Indonesia restore security.[109]

With permission granted, the Council unanimously authorized, on September 15, a Chapter 7 peace enforcement operation that could use "all necessary means" to restore order. It was to be a force of 8,000 soldiers led by Australia, which had long been ready to help out. Troops began to arrive within five days.[110]

Still, the situation remained grim. In early October, Annan told the Council that the water and electrical systems were barely operating and that there was no longer any judicial system.[111] He proposed a broad plan by which the United Nations would take over full control of East Timor until its actual day of independence. He would appoint a civilian administrator with wide authority to pass new laws and amend existing ones.[112]

The Council unanimously approved his plan for a UN Transitional Authority in East Timor (UNTAET) on October 25, 1999. Those deployed would include close to 10,000 peacekeepers and observers (replacing the earlier Australian-led force), more than 1,600 police, and hundreds of civilian administrators and aid workers. They would establish an interim government under the UN flag. As in Kosovo, Annan again appointed Vieira de Mello as his special representative. It was a nation-building job not unlike those in Kosovo and Cambodia, though the United Nations in this case had some ability to work with local advisers.[113]

The UN job involved reconstruction, refugee resettlement, and establishment of a legal and judicial system. "Never before has there been such a broad and ambitious [UN] mandate," Vieira de Mello later told Dan Murphy of the *Christian Science Monitor*.[114]

At the time, Annan ignored a recommendation from the UN Human Rights Commissioner Mary Robinson to set up a war crimes tribunal. He said it was preferable for Indonesia to first make its own effort to carry out trials.[115]

The first democratic elections in East Timor were held on August 30, 2001, exactly two years after the referendum. Voters chose 88 members of an assembly to draft and adopt a constitution. Full independence—for the first time in 500 years—arrived May 20, 2002. The guerrilla leader, José "Xanana" Gusmão, was elected president.

The challenge was daunting. More than half of East Timor's population was illiterate. The new nation was ranked as one of the world's 20 poorest. However, in the two and a half years of its UN administration, it showed an "admirable diplomatic tendency," as a *New York Times* editorial put it, and clear signs that it would be relatively well governed.[116]

The new nation of Timor-Leste soon joined the United Nations, which remained actively involved there for several more years. As

Annan told the East Timorese at the independence ceremony, "The United Nations will stay.... Your friends around the world will continue to help."[117]

Annan had patiently and persistently exercised his good-offices role, offering a face-saving way out for Habibie.

Yet the United Nations, coming in late, had been unable to prevent the violence. As an International Peace Academy report noted later, the United Nations had agreed early on to Indonesia's insistence that it could handle East Timor's security alone because of concern that Habibie might otherwise cancel the referendum.[118]

However, the very fact that Habibie ultimately decided to hold the referendum and later welcomed UN peacekeepers was widely seen as a diplomatic victory for Annan. He proved that, even when the Council is unable to act, the secretary-general can keep an item on the UN agenda and the options open.[119]

Lessons from the Massacres in Srebrenica and Rwanda

The United Nations obviously could have done more to prevent or contain such massive slaughter as was seen in Srebrenica and Rwanda. It is the political will to act that is crucial. It is not clear if today's United Nations is any better equipped to deal with similar future challenges than it was then.

Two UN reports published in late 1999 look back at the role the organization played in both cases. No one escapes blame. Each report is sharply critical of the Secretary-General at the time, the Secretariat, and the member states. Annan was then head of peace-keeping operations.

The General Assembly, prodded by the UN ambassadors from Bosnia, Croatia, and Jordan, requested the Srebrenica report.[120] When the Security Council established a handful of "safe areas" in Bosnia, Secretary-General Boutros-Ghali asked for 32,000 extra troops to handle the job. The Council was unwilling to authorize so many. In the end, the Dutch troops, far outnumbered and short on weapons and support, were stationed in the "safe area" of Srebrenica. They faced an onslaught of some 2,000 Serb forces, backed by tanks and heavy artillery. It was no match. Thousands of Bosnians were raped, tortured, and murdered there in 1995.

The only possible help for the heavily outnumbered UN troops in Srebrenica lay in NATO airstrikes. Boutros-Ghali had been reluctant to approve them out of concern for Serb reprisals against UN ground troops. Also, the Security Council had given the UN Protection Force (UNPROFOR) a strictly humanitarian mandate—not one focused on war with the Serbs. The 100,000-word Srebrenica report accuses the UN Secretariat of failing at times to give an honest account of Serb atrocities in its efforts to appear neutral. The report claims that for far too long the international community was trying to reach a negotiated settlement with a "murderous regime" when force was obviously required to stop the killing and expulsions.[121]

Annan has admitted that, in his former peacekeeping role, he relied too much on the judgment of ground commanders. Yet he noted that they, too, had conditions placed on them by troop contributors, curbs that "played into the hands of the Serbs."[122] Annan conceded that the United Nations, in sticking to its traditional peacekeeping rules, was trying to "keep the peace when there was no peace to keep."[123]

Unlike the Srebrenica report, it was Annan himself who requested the report on Rwanda. He created the commission to do it and chose Sweden's former prime minister Ingvar Carlsson as chairman.

As the United Nations' top peacekeeping official at the time, Annan was criticized in that report for his low-key response to General Romeo Dallaire's January 1994 warnings, three months before the massacre, that extremist Hutus were stockpiling weapons for a possible Tutsi massacre. Dallaire wanted permission to seize the weapons. He was told, in a cable actually written by an Annan aide, Iqbal Riza, that such action did not fall under the United Nations' mandate. Instead, Dallaire was told to share the information he had with Western ambassadors in Kigali.[124]

No action was taken. In the tragic aftermath, some 800,000 Tutsi and moderate Hutus were killed between April and June of 1994.

During a stop in Brussels on 1999 European trip, the Secretary-General was approached by Belgian and Rwandan families who lost relatives in the Rwandan tragedy. They wanted a full investigation of the UN role—particularly of what they saw as the peacekeeping department's failure to prevent the killings.[125] In March, Annan ordered the Rwanda report and asked the Council to support it by granting full access to its diplomatic cables at the time.[126]

The report, completed nine months later, concluded that even the modest force of 2,500 UN peacekeepers who were posted in Rwanda when the violence began should have been able to limit or stop the killing. They did not do so, according to the panel, because the peacekeeping mandate was impossibly weak and the United Nations did not take sufficient account of the warning signs.[127]

This same report claimed that the UN Assistance Mission in Rwanda (UNAMIR) was not deployed or instructed in a way that would have allowed it to stop the genocide. Senior UN officials and member states alike made errors in judgment. The report concluded that there was a "lack of will to identify the massacre...as a genocide." It was a failing that the report called "deplorable." The Rwanda panel, also critical of the United Nations' failure to apologize to the Rwandan people earlier and with more candor, urged the United Nations to develop specific plans to prevent another such tragedy and to improve troop capacity for faster responses in the future.[128]

On receiving the Rwanda report, Annan declared that, as secretary-general, there was no aim that he was more committed to than that of "enabling the UN never again to fail in protecting a civilian population from genocide or mass slaughter."[129]

Annan generally rated high marks from all sides for his courage in making these two self-critical reports public.

"Annan decided that the only way to put this thing to rest was to welcome the results," Fred Eckhard, his former spokesman, said. "He felt, like others before him, that the UN was blamed for more than was justified...but the report was also pretty rough on the US, and until then, the US had pretty much escaped blame. It was the US that refused to allow the UN to keep peacekeepers in Rwanda (after the tragedy in Somalia).... No modern, effective armies were ready to go into Rwanda except the Belgians and the French who went in to extract their nationals...and then let the killing begin."[130]

"I do think that Annan deserves a lot of credit," said Thomas Weiss. "In fact, I think a new standard was set.... Both reports reflect the fact that he was pushing out the limits of what is acceptable for a UN report. It's still not as hard hitting as an academic report, but no academic would have had the same kind of access. The kind of information that has to come out—a spade being called a spade on occasion—is exactly the kind of credibility the UN needs.... The organization does not have a comparative advantage in serious military operations, but it does [have it] in peacekeeping and observation."[131]

John Bolton, a former US ambassador to the United Nations and one of its strongest critics, faulted Annan for making such reports public. He has written that such open criticism of the Security Council "is a matter above his pay grade" and raises "questions of insubordination."[132]

Sir Brian Urquhart has called the two reports "brutally honest." He dismissed the whole concept of "safe areas" in the former Yugoslavia—established without consent of the parties and with no credible military deterrent—as a "sham" from the start. As a man who has issued many major reports on needed UN reforms, he admitted to skepticism that the reports' recommended reforms would ever be implemented. In his view, they may only add to "the already towering pile of admirable but unacceptable plans for UN reform." In his view, nothing short of radical change is needed, both in the United Nations' institutional nature and in member attitudes.[133]

That position is seconded by Canada's David Malone who predicted in an interview that the United Nations "may continue to flounder on peace and security issues." He added, "Even the lessons of the two reports in which Annan was so involved do not seem to have any practical application at the United Nations today. Root and branch changes as to how peacekeeping is planned and executed are still very much required. It's not enough to be well intentioned. One needs to be effective as well." Yet Malone also praised Annan's decision to admit collective UN and personal responsibility for past mistakes. "It doesn't negate the mistakes, but it's the first time in UN history I've known it to happen."[134]

An Update for Peacekeeping?

It was becoming abundantly clear that the United Nations needed to rethink its peacekeeping strategy.

The Council, though often paralyzed by inaction, sometimes sent peacekeepers on missions impossible. The United Nations had come in too late in Rwanda to prevent genocide. In the Kosovo crisis, the United States, foreseeing a Council veto, headed straight for NATO, which took action without UN authority.

In the civil wars and complex humanitarian emergencies of the 1990s, paramilitary forces and other factions often attacked civilians, UN personnel, and aid workers during their battles with the enemy. UN efforts to remain politically neutral often led to military caution and the failure to protect civilians. Also, UN secretaries-general were increasingly hard pressed to recruit enough troops quickly enough for the assigned job. Political tolerance for casualties was receding, particularly among those most able to supply soldiers. Developing nations that did respond to the calls for volunteers often sent troops with little training or equipment.

By this time, Annan had strong views as to what was most needed. In his opening speech to the Assembly on September 20, 1999, he stressed the importance of developing a global consensus to allow intervention to protect civilians from "wholesale slaughter." He said, "Nothing in the Charter precludes a recognition of rights beyond borders." The Council, required by the Charter to protect the "common interest," must find a way, he argued, to act more quickly and effectively.[135]

The changes he urged, however, were not universally applauded. Smaller, developing nations saw any "right" to humanitarian intervention as a direct threat that smacked of neocolonialism. Algeria's president Abdelaziz Bouteflika, who chaired the OAU at the time, insisted, for instance, that consent of the concerned states still must be required. Sovereignty, he said, is "our last defense against the rules of an unequal world."[136]

Yet Annan persevered. After a half-century of well over 50 UN peacekeeping missions, it was time, in his view, to look ahead at the new realities of a changing world. In March 2000, he tapped a panel of experts to take a fresh look. As chairman, he chose Lakhdar Brahimi, the former Algerian foreign minister who had headed up UN operations in Haiti and South Africa and served as a former special envoy to Afghanistan.

The goal was to craft a more workable peacekeeping doctrine to guide future operations. Not surprisingly, the Brahimi report, as it came to be known, included many of the points Annan previously raised. The *Report of the Panel on United Nations Peace Operations*, published in August 2000, said the Council must issue "clear, credible, achievable" mandates with the resources to back them up. If unable to meet those conditions or get the needed troop commitments, the Council should take no action. Peacekeepers must try to move unfinished conflicts to the political stage.[137]

The report also called for greater rapid deployment ability so that well-trained and well-equipped forces would be available on call. That suggestion had often been made in vain in the past. Though all peacekeeping troops would still be under orders to fire only in "self-defense," the report urged nations to define the term more broadly.[138]

The report said the United Nations should stop treating both sides equally if one side clearly violated the terms of a peace agreement. "No failure did more to damage the standing and credibility of UN peacekeeping in the 1990s than its reluctance to distinguish victim from aggressor," the report said. If violence against civilians is observed, the report said, it must be assumed that UN troops may move to stop it, regardless of whether the Council specifically authorized it.[139]

The report noted that only 32 officials in the Department of Peacekeeping Operations were expected to supervise more than 27,000 peacekeepers. In addition to recommending a larger staff, the report called for stronger support from UN headquarters in planning and intelligence gathering and improved coordination among

UN bodies and troop contributors.[140] The panel said that in the past there had been too much reliance on personal networks and ad hoc support.[141]

The Brahimi report had been carefully timed to gain the endorsement of top government leaders gathering in New York for the September 2000 Millennium Summit. Accordingly, both the Council and the Assembly approved the report. Afterward, the United Nations tried to improve coordination. The world body increased its peacekeeping staff in a few years to about 600.[142] The United Nations also began to work more closely with international financial institutions to improve strategic planning and to assess needs more accurately before sending out peacekeeping missions.[143]

Certainly the report had its critics. For instance, John Bolton, who became the American ambassador to the United Nations in 2005, saw it as an attempt at a "quiet coup d'état" by Annan. Bolton said the report aimed to expand the power of the UN Secretariat at the expense of the authority of the five permanent members of the Security Council.[144]

In fact, many of the suggested institutional changes did not happen. No nation volunteered forces, civil administrators, or police that could be readily on call. The Assembly was also reluctant to urge greater intelligence-gathering capacity. As one South Asian ambassador put it, "What we need in this building is political will, not intelligence."[145]

Most of the core principles developed from peacekeeping's early days remained intact. Both consent of local parties to UN missions and the use of force only in self-defense were still viewed as vital conditions. As Annan biographer James Traub noted, the report gave the Secretary-General the "courage and the cover" to be more candid with the Council in assessing mission needs and in prodding the Council to be more realistic about mandates. Yet Traub added that "the members did not, at bottom, want peacekeeping to be much more forceful, or perhaps much more effective, than it already was."[146]

The report, which adopts the broader term of *peace operations* rather than *peacekeeping*, was well received by Annan and the major donor nations, according to Yale's James Sutterlin. Some developing nations, however, had reservations because the new term implied nation building. "I don't know how many praised the report without qualification," Sutterlin said, "but the one thing the report did not provide was guidance as to how to get the money for the [extra] police, judiciary, and other resources that would be needed."[147]

The Global Compact

From the start, Annan made it clear that he couldn't do anything alone—that he would need to reach out in partnership with other leaders and organizations.

With the new century in mind, he convened a high-level meeting on July 26, 2000, of global business, labor, and civil society leaders at UN headquarters. Chief officers of close to 50 multinational companies in every field from mining and footwear to cars and computers attended. Annan's hope was to launch a campaign in support of common values and responsible business practices.

He had first broached the idea of a Global Compact at the January 1999 Davos meeting of the World Economic Forum. He told business leaders there that he wanted to build a cooperative relationship between the United Nations and the private sector. He urged the leaders to encourage their governments to give the United Nations the needed resources and authority to do the job.

Annan and his staff—led by John Ruggie, assistant secretary-general and his chief strategic planning adviser—then carefully drafted a list of nine principles on which there had been fairly widespread agreement in UN conferences and resolutions. These focused largely on human rights, fair labor standards, and good environmental practices. They ranged from a right to collective bargaining and a commitment not to hire children as workers to a ban on bribery and extortion.

At the high-level July meeting, Annan encouraged business and other leaders to include their aims and practices in mission statements and annual reports. He said he also hoped that the new partners would work with the United Nations on projects such as helping villagers link to the Internet and strengthening small- or mid-size firms. Annan asked everyone present to pledge support to this collective effort by the end of the year. They were to report their progress and lessons learned on a new Global Compact Website.

Annan basically wanted to humanize globalization, a word that had long triggered suspicion in some developing countries that it would widen the gap between rich and poor. Some skeptics assumed that colonial powers, deserving no trust, were behind the push. Annan hoped to encourage powerful corporations and other labor and civil society leaders to make it clear to all that there is a better way: workers can be treated more fairly, streams can be made cleaner, and human rights can be honored.[148]

In short, everyone could benefit if the global marketplace, in tandem with labor and civilian groups, acted more like a global society. In Annan's view, globalization must become "an engine that lifts people out of hardship and misery, not a force that holds them down."[149]

Critics of the Compact, including some nongovernmental organizations (NGOs), argued that its voluntary nature allowed companies to wrap themselves in the UN flag and get undeserved bragging rights when no one was actually monitoring or enforcing the standards. They also argued that no provision was made for filing complaints or weighing the relative merits of one action versus another. Children removed from "sweatshop" jobs, for instance, might then take up prostitution instead. Even within the United Nations there was concern that payments to lower ranking UN officials for special favors and other possible forms of corruption might be hard to detect.[150]

Ruggie, by then a professor of international relations at Harvard's Kennedy School of Government, defended the Compact as a "learning model" rather than a code of conduct. Its aim is to identify and promote good corporate practices rather than praise individual companies, he argued. The logistical and financial requirements for monitoring company conduct were far beyond the United Nations' capacity, in his view. Also, businesses naturally would object to any imposed code of conduct. The message is simply that "it pays for companies to do 'good' things and to be seen to do them," he said.[151]

Thomas Weiss agreed. "There is this notion that the UN can regulate everything—it can't," he said. "This is a new and different model for the UN.... I think it's a worthwhile experiment."[152]

Indeed, the Compact did attract a good deal of support, particularly among those convinced that the emphasis of the future must be on foreign investment rather than on foreign aid. As Mark Malloch-Brown, a former administrator of the UN Development Program (UNDP) said, "At the end of the day, everybody has to acknowledge that the primary source of finance for development is going to come out of the private portion of the global and national economy."[153]

Within a few years, some 2,500 companies formally accepted the Compact's principles. Noting that this was one of the Secretary-General's favorite initiatives, author James Traub claimed that the Compact clearly repaired the United Nations' relationship with the corporate world and changed...[the global organization's] "reputation as a nest of socialism."[154]

William Luers, a former American diplomat, concurred:

> Traditionally, I think the UN has been sort of distrustful of the private sector—very distant. But Kofi has approached the private sector in practical ways. He's gone to Davos. And he quietly and persistently changed attitudes within the UN regarding the role of the private sector.[155]

"Given Annan's rather compelling personality, which corporations know that publics are sensitive to, corporations have inclined, very gingerly at the outset, toward engaging with him," David Malone observed. "Many NGOs are deeply suspicious of corporate motives—though they rarely question their own—and have not reacted well to this, having almost entirely occupied the nongovernmental field by themselves for years."[156]

Call for a Summit

In one more forward-looking move in spring 2000, Annan spelled out his vision of UN goals over the next 10 to 15 years in a report titled *We the Peoples: The Role of the United Nations in the 21st Century.*

He quietly sent out invitations to leaders of the world's governments to come to a Millennium Summit in September to discuss the document at UN headquarters. He had first broached the idea of a summit shortly after his 1997 election.

The goals that he hoped the public leaders would embrace, just as he had put them before business and civil society leaders that July, included values already broadly agreed on at UN conferences. Annan, Ruggie, and others added a sense of urgency in this case by setting specific dates for reaching precise goals. Extreme poverty—experienced by one-fifth of the world population earning less than $1 a day—was to be halved, for instance, by 2015.

The Secretary-General wanted, not just stated support, but a real plan of action. He freely admitted that the targets were very ambitious. Yet he felt strongly that the United Nations, as the only body with such broad membership and scope, must play a major role in ending global poverty and speeding up economic and social development. He wanted the focus on people, rather than governments.

"The Millennium Summit was a vehicle for him to get a mandate," recalled Fred Eckhard. "Because he knew it would take those governments 10 years to agree on any kind of agenda, he did all the work for them. He took ideas that nations had already committed themselves to, but he quantified them and gave the governments something to shoot for. It was a way of getting everyone at the highest level to say, 'Yes, here's what we want to do.'"[157]

At a press conference on April 3, 2000, Annan distributed copies of the report. He stressed that those coming to the summit would have to decide on priorities and strategies. "What we need, above all, is brains...the one common commodity...equally distributed among the world's peoples."[158]

In early September, some 152 government heads of the United Nations' 189 members at the time arrived for the discussion. They ranged from the United States' Bill Clinton to Cuba's Fidel Castro. Each of the leaders was allowed a five-minute speech. However, the summit was not all "hot air and diplomatic license plates," noted Annan biographer Traub.[159] Meeting over a three-day stretch, just before the annual opening session of the General Assembly, the leaders carefully reviewed what soon became known as the Millennium Development Goals (MDGs).

In addition to attacking poverty, the MDGs aimed at improving education and women's rights, fighting HIV/AIDS and reducing malaria, and protecting both the environment and humanity from violence. The goals covered eight pages of pledges with 48 time-based targets. Among those for 2015, for instance, were pledges to cut by half the number of people without access to safe drinking water, to reduce child mortality by two-thirds and maternal mortality by three-fourths, and to provide at least a primary education for every child.[160]

It was to be a blueprint for a new and more effective United Nations. One underlying premise was that the only long-term solution to deep poverty was income growth. In signing on, developed countries would be expected to help with more aid and investment, as well as to reduce trade barriers to exports from poorer nations. It was also hoped that developing nations, in turn, would do more to curb corruption and authoritarian rule. A UN Development Program report had recently labeled those two factors as major barriers to eliminating poverty.[161]

Annan wanted to keep the process open and transparent. He gave himself the job of returning to the General Assembly at least once a year to make a progress report on the goals. In late 2001, he asked the economist Jeffrey Sachs to head the Millennium project. Sachs told a US audience at the annual Chicago Humanities Festival in 2008 that food and water are the primary needs, but that all targets, not just one or two, must be met. Pointing to what he called "powder kegs" if progress is not made, he noted that Africa's population doubles every generation and added that the United States stands first in the world in prison population.[162]

The 2000 summit marked the United Nations' most extensive goal-setting reform effort. Many progress reports would follow.

"Kofi is always straight," said William Luers. "No nation is being asked to give up sovereignty. It's about changing the way nations think about their laws and internal behavior.... I think the *Millennium Report* is really quite a document. It was a mammoth task that set out a practical agenda, saying, 'We have 15 years to make changes—let's do it.'"[163]

Second Term, Ready or Not

Reaction to Annan's several reports was largely favorable. He was applauded for his candor—a willingness to criticize the United Nations—and for his look-ahead efforts to make the organization more efficient and effective.

Although it had been a challenging first term, Annan had gained a reputation for being pragmatic and idealistic without becoming an ideologue. Relations with the United States, which had hit a new low during Boutros-Ghali's term, and with the other Council members were on the mend. David Malone observed, "The P5 seemed quite comfortable working with Annan, despite his very sharp criticism of the US on its Iraq policy and...of the Russian Federation over...the targeting of civilians and the many casualties in its military campaign in Chechnya."[164]

Annan also won praise both for his diplomatic skills and his varied stabs at UN improvement. He had introduced a cabinet-style administrative team and was trying to reform the politicized management system. He had also opened the UN door more widely to the private sector. As an African, he steadily urged more international help for his home continent. As Nigeria's ambassador to the UN Arthur C. I. Mbanefo remarked, "We in the African group are all proud of this great son of Africa."[165]

So it was that the soft-voiced, calm, and courteous Secretary-General was voted in for a second term at a date far earlier in the calendar game than any of his predecessors. Though some Asian nations suggested it was their turn at the helm, none came forward. Annan was considered virtually unbeatable.

The Council unanimously renominated him on June 27, 2001. The Assembly followed with a vote of acclamation two days later though his new five-year term would not begin until January.

Early on, Annan had promised his wife, Nane, that he would serve only one term. She was concerned about the invasion of their privacy and the steep demands on her husband's time. He admitted having wrestled with his decision to accept a second term, ultimately deciding to take it on. In the end, Nane, being "a good soldier," he said, went along with his change of heart.[166]

In his acceptance speech before the Assembly, he said he had tried to turn "an unflinching eye" on past UN failures and carefully assess what it would take for the United Nations to succeed in the future. He renewed his pledge to keep a sharp focus on human rights, calling it "the touchstone of my work."[167]

He still felt he had an important job to do. As he had told author Shawcross in Davos in 1999, "Everything, I think, is a race against time—to save lives, to stop killing. One of the areas where we have really tried to make a difference is...to get governments and the public engaged in good governance, to respect [the] rule of law and human rights—to let people know they do have rights and not everything is at the beck and call of governments."[168]

The sometimes-delicate balance between such rights and the job of government was about to be tested again right there in New York City, even before Annan's new term began.

The Secretary-General was at his Sutton Place residence in the early morning of September 11, 2001, when two planes hit the World Trade Center. He issued a strong public statement later that day, labeling the attacks "deliberate acts of terrorism, carefully planned and coordinated," adding, "I condemn them utterly.... A terrorist attack on one country is an attack on humanity as a whole." In support of the American position, Annan agreed that, under the UN Charter, the United States could invoke the right of self-defense without Council approval in its hunt for Osama bin Laden and his al-Qaeda terrorists and in the effort to bring down Afghanistan's Taliban government.[169]

When the Assembly opened on September 24, Annan reiterated the importance of the United Nations in the fight. He said the United Nations alone "can give global legitimacy to the long-term struggle against terrorism."[170]

A welcome, if brief, respite was soon to come for the Secretary-General.

His spokesman Fred Eckhard phoned Annan at 5 a.m. on October 12 to tell him that both the Secretary-General and the United Nations had been named joint winners of the Nobel Peace Prize. Annan was the second UN chief—after Hammarskjöld, who won the prize posthumously—singled out personally for the honor. When Annan arrived at UN headquarters that morning, he was greeted by several hundred applauding staff members. He called the announcement a "shot in the arm" for the United Nations, both needed and deserved.[171]

The Nobel citation noted that the United Nations, after the Cold War, was at last able to "perform more fully the part it was originally intended to play" and that Annan himself had been "preeminent" in bringing "new life" to the United Nations. Though keeping the United Nations' traditional responsibility for peace and security in place, Annan, according to the citation, also stressed the United Nations' obligations in human rights and took on new challenges such as HIV/AIDS and global terrorism.[172]

Two months later in Oslo City Hall, amid tight security including a NATO surveillance plane enforcing a no-fly zone over the city, Annan stood to receive the Nobel Prize. In his acceptance speech, he said that international terrorism had made everyone aware of "a new insecurity" but also of the "bonds that bind us all." He said his goals for the new century were threefold: eliminating poverty, preventing conflict, and promoting democracy. "Peace must be made real and tangible in the daily existence of every individual in need," he said.[173]

Annan donated all of his prize money—close to $500,000—to the United Nations. It was set aside to start a fund for the education of children of those UN civilian staff members killed in the line of duty.

Washington Takes On Iraq—Without the United Nations

For a short time after the World Trade Center bombing, the United States and the Council were in sync in their reaction to terrorism. The Council confirmed the United States' right to attack al-Qaeda in self-defense and called on UN members to deny safe haven to terrorists and to share pertinent intelligence. The Council also established a Counter-Terrorism Committee to monitor compliance.

However, the United States soon parted company with most other UN members with respect to the terrorist threat posed by Iraq. The George W. Bush administration developed a fixation with that issue.

The Council-imposed economic sanctions on Iraq of 1991 were still in place. Iraq had allowed no UN weapons inspectors back into the nation since December 1998. During the following year, the Council laid down conditions for return of the UN inspectors, but little progress had been made. The White House strongly suspected that Baghdad had a link to al-Qaeda and was harboring WMDs that it wanted no one to see.

Annan had long been concerned that the United States might decide to go it alone in attacking Iraq. In his acceptance speech at the Nobel ceremony in December 2001, he warned the United States against enlarging its war on terrorism to include Iraq. He said any decision to attack Baghdad would be unwise and could lead to a major escalation in the region.[174]

At the opening of the Assembly session on September 12, 2002, Annan once again urged Iraq to meet its UN disarmament obligations. "If Iraq's defiance continues," he said, "the Security Council must face its responsibilities." He added that, while any nation has a right to self-defense if attacked, the UN has a "unique legitimacy" in handling broad threats to international peace and security.[175]

Speaking shortly afterwards to the Assembly, US President Bush described Saddam Hussein's regime as a "grave and gathering danger." He said that Baghdad had answered "a decade of UN demands with a decade of defiance." If Council resolutions were not enforced, he said, "action will be unavoidable.... A regime that has lost its legitimacy will lose its power."[176]

Indeed, Bush began to argue that needed UN authorization for a military attack was already in place. A few months earlier, in June 2002, US National Security Adviser Condoleezza Rice told State Department Director of Policy Planning Richard Haass, who felt specific UN authorization was both necessary and desirable, that President Bush had already decided to go to war with Iraq.[177]

The Secretary-General and top UN disarmament officials met three times in 2002 with Iraqi officials to try to find a way to return UN inspectors to Iraq. Baghdad continually set conditions—such as preliminary technical talks—that UN officials saw largely as stalling tactics. However, Annan did manage to persuade Iraq's foreign minister in mid-September to accept the inspectors' return without conditions in a clearly stated letter. The Secretary-General announced the development on September 16. The White House was dismissive. A US spokesman, Scott McClellan, called it a tactical step, aimed at avoiding Council action. Rice phoned Annan, saying that the letter did not strike her as very important.[178]

Finally on November 8, 2002, the Council unanimously adopted Resolution 1441. Basically an ultimatum, it authorized the inspectors' return, including visits to so-called "sensitive sites" that Iraq had barred, and vowed to consider further steps if Iraq were found in "material breach" of its duty to disarm. Iraq was ordered to submit a complete declaration of its WMD program. The inspections began again later that month. In early December, Iraq submitted its report, totaling a full 12,000 pages.[179]

By the time the leaders of the two UN inspection teams submitted their report in January 2003, the United States had 100,000 troops stationed in the Persian Gulf. The UN teams reported no evidence of a revived nuclear program since UN inspectors had declared the program finished back in 1997. However, the UN reports indicated that they had only half-hearted Iraqi cooperation in the search for other kinds of weapons.[180]

Annan stressed that the inspectors needed a more reasonable amount of time to do their job. "I'm not saying forever," he added.[181]

In his annual State of the Union speech that month, President Bush again charged that Hussein was defying the will of the international community and had tried to buy "yellow cake" uranium from Niger. A UN International Atomic Energy Agency official later insisted that the Niger charge was based on a transparent forgery.[182]

Annan spent much of January and February of 2003 on the phone with US, British, and French officials in search of a solution. At one point, during a private dinner, Bush told Annan, "Kofi, you've got to do what you've got to do, and I've got to do what I've got to do."[183]

It was obvious to almost everyone by February that the United States was preparing for a major move. The number of US troops stationed in the Gulf had doubled. Europeans opposed to any attack on Iraq were staging mass protests. On February 5, US Secretary of State Colin Powell, an administration official who enjoyed unusually broad global respect, was dispatched to the Security Council to argue the US case—backed by myriad photos and detailed assertions—for Iraq's blatant failure to disarm as ordered. "I can't say that he was convincing, but he made a powerful presentation," Annan recalled.[184]

In a speech on February 8 at William and Mary College, Annan warned once again, as antiwar protestors marched outside in the hall, of the dangers in unilateral attacks. He said the United Nations is most useful to all its members, including the United States, when it works as a source of collective action. War is "always a human catastrophe," he said, and the international community has a duty to prevent it.[185]

Britain's Prime Minister Tony Blair and the US State Department wanted a return to the Council for clear UN authorization for a military strike. The Pentagon and US Vice President Dick Cheney were opposed. The United States thought it could get 9 of the 15 votes on the Council, but France had threatened a veto. On March 5, the foreign ministers of France, Germany, and Russia met in Paris and jointly agreed not to allow UN authorization of force. The United States and Britain pulled back their resolution.[186]

The United States now insisted that it really needed no further authorization to disarm Iraq by force than the November 8, 2002, Security Council resolution that promised consideration of further steps if Iraq failed to disarm.[187]

Bush announced his decision on March 17, 2003, in a TV address. He said Hussein and his sons must leave Iraq within 48 hours or military conflict would begin. They did not leave. The bombing began in earnest two days later.[188]

Speaking to the Council, Annan called it "a sad day" for the United Nations and the international community. However, as he told a reporter 10 days later, he was still hopeful that a peaceful resolution would be possible. He cited a peacekeeping doctrine that argues, "You sometimes have to show force in order not to use force."[189]

Annan had made a consistent pitch for collective UN action at every turn. Some critics say he therefore should have immediately branded the US action as illegal. That was not his style. As he put it, "I had said enough for everyone to know where I stood on this issue."[190]

Still, for him, the US move was a serious psychological blow. James Traub reported that the Secretary-General felt a "profound sense of failure" and noted that people around him said that he was losing his voice and his face its usual luster.[191]

Yet the United Nations was not through with the situation in Iraq. It was to be a long, long war.

Reeling the United Nations Back into Iraq

Soon after the US invasion, the Secretary-General began to receive a number of phone calls from top American officials. The steady message was that the United Nations was needed to play a major role in Iraq's recovery and reconstruction.

Annan, who was trying to deal with low staff morale, certainly would have been more pleased if the United Nations had taken part in the decision-making in the first place. As he told biographer Stanley Meisler, Washington's mood was "victorious" and there was "a certain hubris" in its attitude and approach to the United Nations.[192]

US Secretary of State Colin Powell had been urging Annan to appoint Sérgio Vieira de Mello, the charismatic Brazilian who was then UN High Commissioner for Human Rights, to head the UN mission in Iraq. However, Vieira de Mello had been in his current job only a year and was reluctant to leave for another post—especially one with a somewhat vague mandate. He finally agreed to go on a temporary basis for four months.[193]

In late May 2003, under US pressure, the Council passed Resolution 1483. Noting that the United States and its allies were now the occupying powers in Iraq, the Council spelled out a specific role for the United Nations in reconstruction, humanitarian relief, and institution building and authorized Vieira de Mello to help build an interim administration.

Paul Bremer, an American counterterrorism expert and the top US civilian official in Baghdad, had already dissolved the Iraqi army and disqualified the upper echelons of the Bath Party from holding government jobs.[194] He was trying to put together an Iraqi advisory council to help write a new constitution and prepare for elections. Bremer gave the United Nations a role in recruiting the council.

As a UN official, Vieira de Mello was much freer than US officials to travel and interview a broad mix of Iraqis, including the minority Sunnis. In the course of that work, he met with Grand Ayatollah Ali al-Sistani, the most powerful Shi'ite cleric in the country and a man who refused to meet with the Americans. In his talks with Vieira de Mello, the cleric insisted that the new constitution must be written by elected Iraqis, not foreigners with Iraqi advisers, and that elections must be held soon.[195]

Vieira de Mello agreed but said the needed groundwork for elections would make them impossible to hold before 2004. He also told Bremer that the group they were jointly putting together should have real powers and responsibilities rather than just serve as advisers. "Iraqis feel humiliated," he told Bremer. "There is a huge power vacuum there." The name of the group was accordingly changed to the Governing Council. About half of its 25 members were chosen by Vieira de Mello. In July 2003, it became the first indigenous authority in Iraq since the fall of Hussein's regime.[196]

After its selection, however, Bremer appeared to have little further use for Vieira de Mello or his advice, according to Mark Malloch-Brown, who would become Annan's deputy secretary-general. He reported that Annan was appalled that the United Nations had lent its good name to an American effort that was doing things in a "deeply damaging way," thus tainting the United Nations' role as an honest broker.[197]

Meanwhile, the Iraqi insurgency was rapidly gaining strength. As a protective move, the Americans placed armored vehicles in front of the UN Mission in Baghdad at its Canal Hotel headquarters. The United States also blocked the access road with a truck and put an observation post on the hotel roof. But UN officials, viewing their mission as separate from that of the United States, were uneasy with such a large American military presence and asked for its removal.[198]

Annan, who was vacationing with his wife in Scandinavia, phoned Vieira de Mello on August 18 to arrange a meeting in Europe on Annan's return to New York. Annan later recalled that Vieira de Mello was laughing at the other end of the line, reminding Annan that he would be taking the month of October off. Annan replied that the respite was well deserved and that he would call again the next day to suggest a meeting place.[199]

The second phone call was never placed. At 4:30 p.m. on August 19, 2003, an orange flatbed truck raced down an access road toward the United Nations' Baghdad headquarters. Driven by a suicide bomber, the truck pulled up beside the security wall near Vieira de Mello's corner office and exploded. His office fell two floors to the ground. Buried beneath rubble, he was briefly alive, responding to UN officials who called to him. He was heard by one American soldier to say, "Don't let them pull the UN out."[200] By the time his body was retrieved four hours later, he was dead.[201] More than half of the 22 killed in the blast were UN employees. Annan was devastated.

Back in New York the next day, he stood somberly with Council members in a silent vigil. Later, he assured them, "The blue flag has never been so viciously assaulted as it was yesterday." He noted that wherever the United Nations had gone in the past, it was always sustained by the local view that the world organization was there to help. In a taped televised statement to UN staff around the world, Annan termed the bombing "an act so savage and senseless that we can hardly believe it really happened. It feels like a nightmare from which we are still hoping to wake.... If only it were."[202]

The United Nations had become a target. "The hope of meeting terrorism with a balanced response was gone," Malloch-Brown, said.[203]

A UN staff committee immediately asked Annan to suspend all operations in Baghdad and withdraw all employees, at least until security could be improved. However, Annan insisted that the United Nations would not be deterred from its job. A key aim of the bombers, he said, was to scare away the international community.[204]

Over time though, he reduced the size of the UN field staff and changed its locale. After a second suicide bombing outside the Canal Hotel on September 22, killing a UN security guard and two Iraqi police, Annan ordered UN officials in Iraq to go to Jordan but said humanitarian work would continue with the Iraqi staff on the scene.

Annan had also ordered an investigation into UN security in Baghdad by an independent panel to be led by Martti Ahtisaari, the former president of Finland. That group's report, issued October 20, 2003, noted that UN security practices had been lax, leaving the Baghdad mission vulnerable. Safety procedures were "sloppy" and greatly needed reform, according to the report.[205]

Annan then pulled all UN workers out and ordered a report from a new panel to determine responsibilities for any security lapses and mismanagement at the UN mission. That report, not released until March 2004, accused top UN officials in Baghdad and humanitarian agencies of having been overconfident in their conviction that the United Nations would not be attacked.[206]

The Secretary-General normally kept a tight lid on his emotions but later admitted that the August bombing was the most painful episode of his career. "You live through a war that you neither defended nor supported, and then you have a mandate to do something about it in the aftermath," he told author James Traub. "And I sent in some of my best people and friends, and they got killed.... Why did it have to be them?... These are civilians who are there to help, who didn't have to be there."[207]

Iraq in Search of a Government as US–UN Tensions Increase

Iraq's Grand Ayatollah Ali al-Sistani still needed to be persuaded that elections could not be held as soon as he had hoped. Thousands of street protesters were backing up his demand for an early vote.

Bremer and some members of the Iraqi Governing Council sent letters to the Secretary-General, pleading with him to intervene. Annan invited Bremer and the others to confer with him in New York on January 19, 2004. Ironically, the United Nations was being asked for help again after it had been shunted aside both in the decision to invade Iraq and after having played an advisory role on self-government steps just before the bombing of its Baghdad headquarters. Yet Annan, who steadily insisted that the stability of Iraq was "everyone's business," eventually agreed to send a technical team and Lakhdar Brahimi, to help out.[208]

Brahimi, like most other UN staff members, had opposed the 2003 US invasion. Yet he had valuable past experience in helping to organize elections in Afghanistan. Though resistant at first, after two meetings with President Bush, he agreed to take on the assignment.[209]

As Annan's special adviser for Iraq, Brahimi visited al-Sistani in February 2004. The cleric, though demanding that Americans must not control the makeup of Iraq's government, soon agreed to the idea of postponed elections. Brahimi then worked with Bremer's Coalition Provisional Authority (CPA), run by the United States and Britain, to create a sovereign interim caretaker government by the end of June 2004. Its job was to administer and conduct elections. After consulting with several Iraqis, Brahimi drew up a list of possible leaders from which a prime minister—Dr. Ayad Allawi, a Shi'ite politician whose exiled political party had received CIA funding and who was the US choice for the job—and 31 other cabinet members were selected.[210]

The first set of Iraqi elections was scheduled for January 2005. The United States would be holding its own presidential elections the previous fall, and the Bush administration's handling of the war in Iraq was becoming a major election issue in the United States.

It was a time when US–UN relations were clearly cool. The United States was not pleased, for instance, that Annan had sent to Iraq only 35 UN election officials. The Secretary-General insisted that, given the security conditions at the time, that number was all he could recruit. Annan later insisted that the United Nations had played a key role in selecting an interim government, opened hundreds of registration stations, and trained some 6,000 election registrars.[211]

Another major irritant for Washington, however, was the fact that in a September 4, 2004, interview with the BBC's Owen Bennett-Jones, Annan, under persistent questioning, finally conceded that the US invasion of Iraq was "illegal" from the "[UN] Charter point of view." He said there should have been a second Council resolution since it is the Council's job to decide the consequences for noncompliance with its own resolutions.[212]

"The [US] political failure was to seek UN support without being able to secure it, then to act without sufficient international support to provide any cloak of UN legitimacy," Malloch-Brown said.[213]

Later, in his September address to the General Assembly, Annan repeated his concerns about legitimacy. Though pointing no direct finger, he said, "Every nation that proclaims the rule of law at home must respect it abroad, and every nation that insists on it abroad must enforce it at home."[214]

The Bush White House was also clearly unhappy with what it viewed as UN interference in its military strategy. US Marines had begun an assault on the insurgent Sunni stronghold of Fallujah in spring 2004. Brahimi, greatly concerned about potential civilian casualties, warned that he would abandon his mission if the attacks continued. The United States stopped them—but just temporarily.

When the attacks on Fallujah began again that fall, Annan sent letters requesting a halt to President Bush, Britain's Tony Blair, and Iraq's prime minister, Ayad Allawi. The Secretary-General's concerns were the potential negative impact on the upcoming Iraqi elections (the Sunnis largely did boycott them), more civilian casualties, and the likely spread of alienation and terrorism.

As Annan explained to a journalist, "It [the continued attacks on Fallujah] is a bit like kicking the hornet's nest." He argued that the problem of insecurity "can only be addressed through dialogue and an inclusive political process." Though he assumed that the letters he sent to the three leaders would remain private, his message was leaked to the press. The Bush administration, concerned about the possible effect on US elections, was described as "livid." Annan insisted that, since the United Nations was so closely involved in the Iraqi elections, he had every right to speak out.[215]

"Annan has steel under his placid exterior," Malloch-Brown observed, "and I suspect he simply wanted his complaint on the record." Malloch-Brown said he tried to arrange a Bush–Annan meeting to ease the tension, but the United States cited schedule difficulties.[216]

Iraqis elected a Transitional National Assembly on January 30, 2005. Its job was to draft a constitution in March that would be subject to a fall referendum and a further set of elections.

Meanwhile, the United Nations was getting a large dose of unwelcome publicity over a series of small scandals that culminated in a damaging report on its handling of the Oil-for-Food Program (OFF) with Iraq.

Scandals That the United Nations Did Not Need

Charges that UN civilian and military personnel had hired child prostitutes in exchange for money and food in the Democratic Republic of the Congo (DRC) were both rumored and denied in early 2004. However, after an investigation by the UN mission there and the UN's Office of Internal Oversight Services (OIOS), the Secretary-General was given a specific briefing that November. He promptly announced that there was clear evidence of "gross misconduct" by a small number of UN personnel and that he was "absolutely outraged" by it. He said it must be stopped and the perpetrators held accountable.[217]

Annan then sent two teams to further investigate the charges and recommend ways to rectify the situation. Their report, issued in March 2005, advised strengthening troop contributor legislation to ensure that the UN peacekeepers responsible would be punished by their home countries. The United Nations has little legal authority to discipline offenders other than to send them home. The report urged that the pay of offenders be put into a fund for victims and that the United Nations make counseling and medical care available to victims and "peacekeeper babies."[218] One UN staff member was fired over the scandal and six others suspended.

On May 31, 2005, the Council weighed in on the issue for the first time. It strongly condemned all acts of sexual abuse and exploitation by UN personnel, noting that such behavior tarnished the United Nations' otherwise honorable record of accomplishments.[219]

Another case, this one of sexual harassment against UN employees, involved Ruud Lubbers, the UN High Commissioner for Refugees and a former prime minister of the Netherlands. He was officially accused by one UN staffer, backed up by five others, of making unwanted advances at his Geneva office in December 2003. He strongly denied the charges, calling his accusers "liars" who mistook courtesy and gentlemanly behavior for harassment. Again, the OIOS investigated. Its confidential report, confirming the charges, somehow leaked to the press. Lubbers promptly labeled it "no proof at all."[220]

Despite the report's findings, Annan's lawyers warned him that he did not have strong enough legal grounds to fire Lubbers.[221] Though the refugee chief at first refused to resign, the adverse publicity persisted. And Annan eventually persuaded him to step down.[222]

By far the biggest and most publicized UN scandal during Annan's tenure, however, concerned the UN humanitarian venture in Iraq known as the Oil-for-Food (OFF) Program.

Started by the Council in December 1996 while Boutros-Ghali was still in office, the plan was considered a way to modify the sanctions imposed on Iraq after the Gulf War. The intent was to allow Baghdad to sell oil in exchange for food and medicine to benefit Iraq's hard-pressed civilian population.

From the beginning, Boutros-Ghali expected Saddam Hussein to undermine the effort because it might interfere with his ultimate goal of getting sanctions lifted.[223]

In the program's seven-year run, some $64 billion of Iraqi oil was sold. The United Nations' job was to monitor the imports and exports to prevent any abuse. Benon Sevan, a senior UN staffer, was tapped by Annan to head the project. His job was to help select the contractors and supervise the program.

Within three years—by January 1999—news reports of possible corruption began to surface. One of the most damaging charges concerned Annan's son, Kojo, who had worked for Cotecna, a Swiss firm that had an OFF contract to inspect goods entering Iraq. The suspicion was that Kojo might have used his father's name to influence the company's selection. Kojo insisted that he left the company before any contracts were awarded. The Secretary-General asked his chief of staff Iqbal Riza to investigate any possible conflict of interest. Riza soon reported that UN officials were unable to confirm any link of Kojo to the awarding of the contract.[224]

However, rumors of payoffs and kickbacks (involving Cotecna and various other contractors) persisted. Finally, in April 2004, Annan asked the highly respected former US Federal Reserve Chairman Paul Volcker to investigate all charges. Assisted by a South African judge, Richard Goldstone, and a team of 50 investigators, the new Independent Inquiry Committee produced a series of reports over a year-long period.

The first reports exposed some small-scale corruption and other shortcomings in the OFF Program, which Annan promptly pledged to correct. With respect to the Cotecna contract, the committee charged that Kojo actually had a continuing relationship with the company that both he and company officials had tried to conceal from the Secretary-General and others.

Two UN staff members were suspended in February 2005. One was the United Nations' top OFF man, Benon Sevan. He was accused of "a grave and continuing conflict of interest" and unethical conduct in repeatedly asking for and receiving oil allocations for an Egyptian friend's company.[225] He was charged with taking more than $140,000 in kickbacks.[226] Sevan insisted he was innocent but opted for retirement in Cyprus, his home country, before being indicted by a US federal court in January 2007.

Also suspended, and later fired in June 2005, was Joseph Stephanides, supervisor of contract selection for the UN Security Council. He was charged with violating UN procurement rules by taking actions that hampered competitive bidding for contracts.[227]

Annan's chief of staff Riza had announced his resignation in connection with OFF in December 2004. He had been accused by the Volcker group of having ordered the shredding of records and documents from 1997 to 1999. He claimed his assistant was simply clearing out cluttered files and that it was a question of needing more space. The Volcker probe said he had acted imprudently but found no violation of staff rules.[228]

The final Volcker report was issued September 7, 2005. Though noting that no secretary-general had ever been chosen for his managerial skills, the report accused Annan of failing to curb corruption and mismanagement in monitoring the program. Though the committee again found no evidence of any role by the Secretary-General in the awarding of the Cotecna contract, it did find that Kojo had tried to use the link with his father to get the contract. Kojo also apparently bought a Mercedes-Benz, taking advantage of a diplomatic discount and avoiding the usual import fees in taking the car into Ghana.[229]

Many thousands of contracts were negotiated under the OFF Program. The Volcker panel concluded that Saddam Hussein himself had managed to skim some $1.8 billion of illegal income from the program.[230]

The Volcker investigation also noted a general lack of efficiency by an "overpoliticized" United Nations that was in urgent need of reform and a "strong organizational ethic." Observing that thousands of new UN employees had been hired, for instance, without much vetting, the report said several instances of corruption and unethical behavior had been found among low-ranking staff members in the field. Also, several private companies, "manipulated" by Hussein, were pronounced guilty of "wholesale corruption."[231]

Annan viewed the final Volcker report as a "great relief" in holding him personally blameless for the many "distressing and untrue allegations." He confessed that he was "deeply saddened" by his son's failure to cooperate fully with the Volcker committee. He said the most painful moments for him personally were those that suggested that Kojo might have "acted inappropriately or might not have told me the full truth about his actions."[232]

"He has learned a lot and has grown, [but] he withheld information from me...[and] caused me lots of grief," the Secretary-General told biographer Stanley Meisler a few months later.[233]

Throughout the scandal, Annan survived numerous calls for his resignation from US newspapers and politicians. One of the loudest and most persistent voices was that of Senator Norm Coleman, a Republican from Minnesota, who was chairman of the Senate Permanent Subcommittee on Investigations. In a December 1, 2004, *Wall Street Journal* op-ed titled "Kofi Annan Must Go," Coleman said Annan must be held accountable for the United Nations' "utter failure to detect or stop Saddam's abuses." Coleman said that the world organization could not root out its own corruption while Annan remained in charge.

Representative Dana Rohrabacher, a California Republican and chairman of the House Subcommittee on Oversight and Investigation agreed: "Something stinks about this situation, and the smell is emanating from the executive office of the UN."[234]

In all, five US Congressional committees held their own investigations into the scandal. The minority staff of Coleman's subcommittee released its report in April 2005, claiming that more than half of the illegal deals carried out in the OFF Program involved American imports of Iraqi oil. Senator Carl Levin, a Democrat of Michigan and minority chairman of the subcommittee, remarked, "We need to look into the mirror at ourselves, as well as point fingers at others."[235]

Mark Malloch-Brown, named Annan's chief of staff in January 2005, argued that the Volcker reports showed that the major source of corruption in OFF was not at the United Nations but between the Iraqi government, which devised an elaborate kickback scheme, and the companies dealing with it. Describing himself as the "lead gladiator for the defense" during the long investigation, Malloch-Brown concluded that the United Nations was more incompetent than corrupt.

"The Volcker Report basically cleared Annan of any wrongdoing," Jean Krasno, a lecturer in political science at Yale University, noted in an October 11, 2011, interview with this author. "Really, the scandal of OFF was the oil companies and the food companies that were paying kickbacks and bribes. That's where the money was—not the UN."

The United Nations' failures were largely supervisory and operational, Malloch-Brown argued. The Volcker committee had charged that UN auditing of the program had been inadequate and that faults discovered often went uncorrected. Annan's chief of staff added that when the investigative panel interviewed Annan and Louise Fréchette, his deputy secretary-general at the time, each thought the other one was in charge of the program. In fact, Annan had sent her a note shortly after she took office assigning her the OFF job, but she did not recall it.[236]

Certainly there were other OFF Program links to the UN, besides those involving Secretariat personnel. Indeed, Annan saw it as the offspring and responsibility of the Council. He had assumed that its sanctions committee would carefully monitor compliance, just as it had been doing since the end of the Gulf War.[237]

In one unguarded moment while talking with UN communication officials, Annan remarked that by far the largest portion of Hussein's illegal profiting from the long sanctions regime occurred on "the American and British watch" rather than during the more recent OFF Program.[238]

In the end, only a few of the UN officials involved in the OFF Program were accused by the Volcker panel of taking bribes or other unethical behavior. Malloch-Brown's conclusion was that "the UN took the fall for a scandal that was much bigger than its own part of it."[239]

One Last Push for Reform: A Limited Success Story

The need was clear. The Volcker reports and other recent UN studies left no doubt that major reform was crucial to UN credibility. Indeed, in a private meeting with veteran foreign policy experts at the Manhattan apartment of Richard Holbrooke in December 2004, Annan listened for more than three hours to suggestions on the urgent need to repair his relationship with both Washington and his staff and to make major changes in the United Nations itself.[240]

There was no shortage of suggestions. Everything from management reform to emergency aid was on the table. Annan had set up a 16-member high-level panel a year before on threats, challenges, and change to tackle the full spectrum of needs. That group's

101 recommendations in late 2004 ranged from expanding the Security Council to specifics on reaching the ambitious Millennium Development Goals (MDG). Early in 2005, the Secretary-General also asked three top officials to suggest reforms in UN procedures.

Annan distilled most of these ideas in his own sweeping reform agenda—*In Larger Freedom*—which he distributed to General Assembly members for their review in March 2005. He urged a review of all mandates more than five years old, establishment of a $1 billion fund to provide relief after sudden disasters, the crafting of a broad antiterrorism agreement, and a draft of new steps to stem nuclear proliferation. He also suggested a one-time staff buyout to help younger, more energetic workers to rise in the organization.

He clearly wanted a bold reshaping of the United Nations.

However, as he well knew, great ideas are one thing. Acting on them is often quite another. Annan hoped to capitalize on the opportunity afforded by the scheduled world summit of September 2005 to push through a major reform package. The gathering of world leaders was the scheduled follow-up to the 2000 summit that adopted the MDGs. He saw the 2005 meeting as the ideal moment to get things moving.

Various committees studied the reform document for several months before the summit. Yet on the day before the big meeting, members still could not agree on language in at least 100 cases. So Annan and his colleagues hastily assembled a compromise document. Terrorism, for instance, was condemned but not specifically defined.[241]

On the morning of the summit, UN ambassadors were called in for an advance look at the text. When the world leaders convened later that day, Annan encouraged them to sign the declaration even if they strongly disliked parts of it. Though they did endorse the text, it was clearly just the beginning. The reforms still had to go through many other internal hoops. Once the leaders went home, the driving energy behind the reforms quickly tapered off, and nit-picking began in earnest.

Despite all that, two new institutions endorsed by the summit leaders survived the added scrutiny and debate and won the needed Assembly approval.

One was a slimmed-down new Human Rights Council (HRC). It was to replace the Human Rights Commission which, by this time, lacked almost any credibility. On April 7, 2005, Annan told a commission gathering at its Geneva headquarters that its performance had "cast a shadow on the reputation of the UN system as a whole." Insisting that human rights are at the very "core of the United Nations' identity," he said a new council committed to and accountable for the job was necessary.[242]

The Human Rights Commission had been meeting for only six weeks each spring, and its 53 rotating members, including such poor performers as China, Cuba, and Sudan, often were more interested in protecting themselves against criticism by joining the body than in judging others. Members were chosen by regional blocs from a closed slate of volunteers and approved by majority vote in the UN Economic and Social Council.

The new Human Rights Council, in contrast, would have 43 members, and, in a late compromise, be chosen by a secret ballot majority vote of the Assembly. They would exist year-round and meet whenever necessary. Periodic reviews would be conducted of each nation's human rights performance. The Assembly approved the new HRC in mid-March 2006.

The other new institution to survive the debate and win Assembly approval was the Peacebuilding Commission. Its aim was to help countries recover from the damaging effects of war. It would have no decision-making power but act as a forum for planning and coordinating postconflict strategy.

Also surviving the summit and winning unanimous Assembly approval in late 2005 was the concept of a UN Responsibility to Protect (R2P), the doctrine aimed at protecting civilians in cases where their governments either could not or would not do so. Annan had pushed hard for this concept after the Rwanda and Srebrenica reports.

Mark Malloch-Brown considered the approved text short on details but still one able to provide more political traction for the concept of humanitarian intervention. Yet he noted the idea also carried a potential second message, in the eyes of some, of a United Nations that chooses sides: "The blue flag...was no longer above the conflict but rather became a soft target."[243]

Malloch-Brown said that all three reforms that passed the Assembly were weaker than those originally proposed. Half-finished reforms remained unfinished. "The UN went back to dysfunctional business as usual," he said.[244]

The West's chief concern was to improve administration and security. The Group of 77 (actually by that time, 132 nations) wanted a much stronger emphasis on development and tended to see the Secretariat as a tool of the West.[245]

The United Nations at this point was a highly diverse organization of 192 members and six official languages. Sweden's Jan Eliasson, the Assembly president, argued that if the proposed reform package had been less ambitious, it might have won consensus approval. Yet he called it a "serious effort to ask for more."[246]

US Ambassador to the United Nations John Bolton wanted a fresh start for the whole reform process. Both before and after the summit, he made what were widely considered impossible reform demands. When he threatened to tell Congress that the Secretary-General did not want any debate on procurement issues, Annan reportedly replied, "John, this is intimidation. You really have to stop doing this."[247] Malloch-Brown wrote that Bolton's "tantrums" left the summit declaration in "tatters" by seeking massive cuts in almost every area.[248]

At one point, Bolton threatened that, without management reform, the United States would block passage of the United Nations' usual biennial budget at the end of the year. Annan, aiming to avert what he saw as an impending disaster, made it known that the United Nations could survive on an interim budget. Accordingly, the Assembly accepted a six-month budget in late 2005 as negotiations continued.[249]

Mark Malloch-Brown had little patience with Bolton and his mode of operation: "Bolton used the oil-for-food crisis to shame and tar the organization, and he used the reform proposals as a stick with which to beat the UN, rather than strengthen it."[250]

Even though Annan was disappointed by the United Nations' failure to adopt more major reforms, he actually proposed and made smaller changes virtually every year since taking office.[251]

When reforms could be made by executive power, without lengthy committee review and debate, they were. In a more open attempt to attract top-quality staff, for instance, the United Nations began publishing job descriptions and criteria, reaching out not just to governments but also to NGOs. Once appointed, senior staffers were briefed for the first time on the broader system of UN rules and regulations and codes of conduct.[252] They now were told that they served at the pleasure of the Secretary-General and could be dismissed with a three-month notice. UN rules for procuring supplies also were tightened and made more transparent.

Certainly the toughest challenge at the United Nations is to make large reforms, though everyone knows they are needed. Further expansion of the Council or any change in the veto power and makeup of the five permanent members remain—so far—forever debatable topics. The more focused and subtle changes are the ones that tend to get through, noted Edward Luck.[253]

Annan had given sweeping reform his best try. In his last speech before leaving the UN, at the Harry S. Truman Library in Independence, Missouri, on December 11, 2006, he once again urged all members, especially the major powers, to adopt a larger world-view in casting votes. The Council, he said, is not "just another stage on which to act out national interests."[254]

Looking Back: A Strong Legacy in Human Rights

Annan was not a particularly tall or physically imposing man, yet he carried himself with a quiet dignity and strength that seldom failed to impress those who dealt with him.

He effectively broadened the United Nations' embrace during his two terms as secretary-general. In crafting the Millennium Development Goals, he reached out to include nongovernmental organizations, the private sector, and academic institutions. He also was the first secretary-general to address world economic leaders in Davos at their annual gathering in 1997.

He surely will be most remembered, however, for his steady emphasis on human rights and his conviction, in the aftermath of Srebrenica and Rwanda, that the United Nations has both a right and a duty to protect civilians when their governments fail to do so or, worse, when they abuse their own citizens. He challenged the long-held UN view that sovereignty is inviolable.

"Kofi was like a sea change," noted the human rights expert Felice Gaer, former chair of the US Commission on Religious Freedom. "There is no question but that he was the best secretary-general for human rights issues that the UN has ever had.... It was a matter both of his conviction and his personality. I think it had a lot to do with his quest for a UN that people would look up to and that Americans would want to support."[255]

"He took what I think is a very courageous position," said Yale's James Sutterlin. "If there is a threat of genocide someplace, and if the Security Council is unable or unwilling to act, it is better for one country or a group of countries to use force [rather than take no action at all]."[256]

"He consistently championed human rights as the unifying theme of his mandate," insisted former International Peace Academy president David Malone. "It is not what the US or any other country expected of him.... He constantly preached the supremacy of the individual's security as opposed to the rights of the state.... It was not a particularly neutral stance. He implied strong personal support of NATO's action in Kosovo, for instance, even though it was opposed by several of the permanent five members and probably a number of others."[257]

William Luers, former president of the USA-UNA, admitted, "That conceptual [human rights] shift is what a lot of nations are resisting, but it's a response to globalization. No nation is being asked to give up sovereignty. It's about the way nations think about reshaping their laws and internal behavior."[258]

Annan also worked hard at making the United Nations and its business far more transparent. He drew high praise from all sides for making public those reports on crises that were poorly handled by the United Nations.

"He showed great courage in [asking for] the report on Rwanda... and in accepting the one on Srebrenica, knowing full well that they would be very critical of him," Sutterlin said.[259]

Certainly the sharpest US criticism aimed his way focused on his behavior during the Iraq crisis. Though Washington championed his selection as secretary-general at the start, much of the enthusiasm on Capitol Hill soon waned. His trip to Baghdad in 1998 to try to strike a deal with Saddam Hussein was criticized when it eventually fell apart. Some never forgave him for describing Hussein as "a man I can do business with."

"I suspect that he [Annan] meant that he understood the insecurities, fears, and vanities that drove the dictator, rather than that Hussein was a man to be trusted," observed Malloch-Brown, Annan's former deputy.[260]

As Annan explained to Barbara Crossette, the UN correspondent for the *New York Times*, "We are operating in a world which is quite brutal, and there are some very wicked people around.... In the business I'm in, we sometimes have to shake the hand of the aggressor, to lend an ear in order to save lives.... I go where I have to go and talk to those I have to talk to.... Self is not involved."[261]

Far more troubling to many in Washington was Annan's criticism of the unilateral decision by the Bush administration in 2003 to intervene in Iraq without specific UN authorization. Some in Congress were demanding his resignation. Sir Brian Urquhart suggested that Annan just happened to have the "bad luck" to be in office when Washington was run by a "band of ideologues.... If the United States had been on his side, he would have been regarded as in the class of Dag Hammarskjöld."[262]

"The campaign against him was a shameful maneuver by neoconservatives who had not forgiven Annan for having criticized the Iraqi invasion as illegal," added Sir Brian. He said that the call for the Secretary-General's resignation was "ultimately nothing more than a campaign of revenge.... The [OFF] program was not subject to the Secretary-General's review. The fact is that the Security Council gave a fraud like Saddam Hussein the power of attorney to control oil exports and food imports and to select the receivers. The UN was simply incapable of handling such an extensive undertaking."[263]

Annan hoped to leave behind a revitalized and more efficient United Nations. With his extensive in-house experience—working in the personnel, budget, and peacekeeping areas—he knew better than most secretaries-general what needed fixing. However, he also knew that major efforts at change often ended in intergovernmental gridlock. He did manage to get a results-based budget reform through the Assembly, but it took about three years. He also created the Office for the Coordination of Humanitarian Affairs, establishing it as the chief focus for global relief efforts.[264]

In the end, he focused largely on reforms that he could make on his own. "Rather than come in and shake everything up, I think he was after change in places where he thought it was possible," Luers said. "He knew that everything takes a long time."[265]

Although Annan did not succeed in getting Assembly approval to strengthen the UN peacekeeping department as much as he would have liked, some 17 new peacekeeping missions were launched during his tenure.

He also made some impressive appointments, often bringing in outside experts. These included UN scholar John Ruggie as assistant secretary-general for strategic planning and journalist Edward Mortimer as UN director of communications. He created the position of deputy secretary-general and tapped Louise Fréchette for the job. When she stepped down during his second term, he appointed UN Development Program chief Mark Malloch-Brown to the post. He also selected Mary Robinson, Ireland's former president, as UN High Commissioner for Human Rights.

The Secretary-General was a comfortable delegator. "He wanted to shift more responsibility to department heads and unit managers and rely less on committees formed by the departments," explained Fred Eckhard, his former spokesman." He knew the rules inside out, and he was very good at preparing the ground and not springing dramatic new ideas on people."[266]

Many of Annan's mediation efforts ended successfully in ceasefires. He made a strong pitch for careful listening before responding and suggesting.

"A lot of the mediation that he did personally was over the telephone, far from the public eye," noted David Malone. "It was often hard to know what was going on unless he signaled it directly or through his spokesman."[267]

"I've been amazed at his willingness to become engaged in controversial issues—to do it quietly and not pound his chest over it," Luers said. "I think he played a very subtle role, for instance, in moving Indonesia out of East Timor."[268]

Malloch-Brown said Annan invested "great emotional intelligence" in trying to understand the people he dealt with. In his view, if the Secretary-General had a fault, it was that he was probably too cautious. Annan's UN career had convinced him that risk taking was not always possible. Malloch-Brown reasoned that successful secretaries-general may always be "better balancers than drivers of policy."[269]

"Kofi Annan was a very, very good diplomat and conciliator," Thomas M. Franck, New York University law professor, said. "He had a sense of humor, a sense of proportion, and a sense of history."[270]

Shortly before Annan left office, President Bush held a dinner in Annan's honor. John Bolton, a steady critic of the world body and Annan, was asked afterwards by a reporter if he had at last "made peace" with the Secretary-General. Bolton replied that "nobody sang 'Kumbaya' [the African song of fellowship]." When told of the comment, Annan said, "But does he know how to sing it?"[271]

Annan took great pains to stay in close touch with governments and their legislatures. He often went to Washington, for instance, and spoke with members of Congress.

"That was something none of his predecessors had done," noted Princeton's Leon Gordenker. "I think it [the lack of a precedent] was strictly a hang-up in diplomatic protocol.... This notion of getting into forums where governments make decisions is perfectly acceptable."[272]

Yet a few people, such as Richard Thornburgh, former Pennsylvania governor and a former UN undersecretary-general, saw a downside to the practice. "It's a slippery slope," he remarked in an interview. "You spend a little time with those folks and they get used to it. Pretty soon you're spending a lot of time with them. Also, it creates an impression that the United Nations is too much in the thrall of the United States if the secretary-general is hobnobbing constantly with members of Congress."[273]

Though Annan did appear at a number of New York social functions, friends and colleagues insist he has always been a private person who did it mostly to focus needed attention on the importance and role of the United Nations.

"Kofi felt that one way to get things done was to make friends," noted Jean Krasno, a Distinguished Fellow at Yale's Center for International Security Studies. "He went to a lot of parties and dinners and created friendships."[274]

"I've seen a lot of him, and he's a very serious presence," Luers said. "He dances, but he's not a party guy. When he's around, people talk about the issues. He wanted to provide access and knowledge for New York's power structure to know what the United Nations is all about. Traditionally there's been the New York world and this little '*demi-monde*' on the East Side, and they don't meet."[275]

Though initially viewed as a candidate of reform and sound management, Annan probably will be most remembered for his moral leadership and focus on shared values. "He helped the global community find its conscience," noted former American diplomat Stephen Bosworth.[276]

Annan became a strong advocate for helping HIV/AIDS victims and refugees and continued the push begun by his predecessor for more democratic rule. Annan reasoned that democracies tend to avoid not only wars with one another but also civil wars.

He became known as a polite but strong leader who was sometimes surprisingly decisive and direct. Helmet Kohl, the former German chancellor, once said that it was impossible to "keep up barriers" when approached by Annan.[277]

"He's got a point of view, and he says it in a very courteous way," Gordenker said. "He has great personal charm. I've been in situations with him where he had to decide something and he did. You know? Boom! I'm impressed with that."[278]

"He's not weak—he's very clear headed and doesn't give an inch," noted former UN staffer and journalist Bhaskar Menon. "He's always been exactly the same, no matter what job he's had. Everyone in 'the house' felt they had a special relationship with him, even the guards."[279]

Annan also worked hard at trying to keep an optimistic approach. While flying with the Secretary-General to Iraq in 1990 to negotiate the release of foreigners held hostage, Elisabeth Lindenmayer, then one of his top aides, recalled asking him about contingency plans in case the effort failed. He told her never to speak to him negatively when he was about to negotiate. He said, "We'll make it." In retrospect, she called it a highly useful motivational strategy.[280]

While in office, Annan focused strongly on the need for development as a key to a more peaceful world. He was sometimes critical of his own African roots in that regard. He often remarked that Africa was the only continent unable to feed itself. He urged its leaders to help heal their nations' crises and divisions to attract desperately needed investment. He told author William Shawcross that he "hammered" the point home to African leaders as often as he could. They would agree, Annan reported, but then go home and do nothing about it. "They carry on their wars," he remarked.[281]

Before leaving the United Nations, he made it clear that he intended to focus on two African problems: the poor state of agriculture and the low level of women's education.[282] In 2007 he was chosen to head the Alliance for a Green Revolution in Africa (AGRA). He later created the Kofi Annan Foundation with the twin aims of fostering peace and sustainable development.

CHAPTER TEN

Ban Ki-moon:
A South Korean Works
around the Clock

Ban Ki-moon definitely wanted the United Nations' top job. He announced his candidacy in February 2006 and campaigned energetically most of that year. As his nation's foreign minister, he visited all 15 nations with seats on the Security Council. Backed fully by the South Korean government in his quest, he signed numerous trade deals with European countries and promised aid to developing nations. It was a practice that sparked some criticism. However, his steady, professional campaign—combined with an earlier diplomatic gaffe that he later counted a blessing in disguise—eventually led to his election.

He had been summarily dismissed in 2001 as South Korea's ambassador to Austria by President Kim Dae-jung after supporting renewal of the Anti-Ballistic Missile (ABM) Treaty in a joint communiqué with Russia. The United States had already signaled that it would pull out of the agreement. The implication, in the eyes of some onlookers, was that South Korea was moving closer to Russia. South Korea's president publicly apologized, saying he hoped that the incident would not mar good relations with Washington. As Ban recalled, "I was out of work for the first time in my life."[1]

Though he expected to be sent to some remote diplomatic post as punishment, he was soon tapped as chief of staff by the UN General Assembly president, who happened to be a South Korean. While in that position, Ban gained valuable mediating experience and helped with Assembly passage of the resolution condemning the 2001 terrorist attacks on the United States. In his view, his work with the GA gave him the all-important entrée to become UN Secretary-General.[2]

Four straw polls were conducted among Council members from July to October 2006. By that time, six others had entered the race for what was widely considered Asia's turn at the post. Vying with him were candidates from Afghanistan, Jordan, Sri Lanka, Thailand, Latvia, and India.

Ban had strong ties to the United States, having studied at Harvard and served twice in South Korea's embassy in the United States. Washington was pleased that Ban had pushed for the participation of South Korean troops in the US war on Iraq. His heavily accented English and modest manner were also reassuring to US conservatives. "They knew he would not be a counterweight to America's power if the US was charging off in its own direction," noted Jeffrey Laurenti, senior fellow at New York's Century Foundation.[3]

During the informal polling period, Ban gave important speeches to such groups as the Council on Foreign Relations and the Asia Society. He said he viewed the United Nations' top post as a catalyst in rallying member states' political will and vowed to be a "bridge builder." He made it clear in interviews that he intended to improve the United Nations' image and make the organization more relevant.[4]

In the early stages of the polling, voting nations were asked to choose among three options regarding the candidates: encourage, discourage, or no opinion. At first, no distinction was made between ballots of the five permanent members (P5) with veto power and the ten others. Though the results were supposed to be secret, word soon leaked out that Ban and Sashi Tharoor, the Indian candidate then serving as UN undersecretary-general for communications, were leading the race. In the end, Ban emerged the victor with the support of the P5 and no "discourage" votes from the others.[5]

The General Assembly formally voted him in as Secretary-General on October 13, 2006, four days after the Council vote. Chungju, South Korea, the town where he grew up, was so proud of his win that tens of thousands of residents gathered in the local soccer stadium to celebrate.[6]

Despite warnings from the global community, North Korea chose to test a nuclear weapon a few days before Ban's election. Partly because of that and to emphasize its support of Ban, the South Korean government voted for the first time in three years to abstain rather than vote as usual with Russia and China against an annual General Assembly resolution criticizing North Korea for human rights abuse.[7]

In his first press conference, the Secretary-General said that while his selection should have been a moment of joy, he stood before the media "with a very heavy heart" because of North Korea's action.[8]

In an interview some days later with *Newsweek*, he said that North Korea was following a "dangerous and negative path," while the United Nations was trying to help with diplomacy and humanitarian aid. He said the tests were a "total display of disrespect to our goodwill."[9]

Still, he had the new job, and he promised to be a good listener, work hard to reform the United Nations' management system, and try to narrow the gap between developing and developed nations. "Without eradication of poverty, you will always see conflicts," he said.[10]

"Ban in '07, not Bond 007"

Ban brought to his new UN post well over 30 years of experience as a diplomat. His overseas posts included India and Austria as well as the United States. He has said that, at first, he deliberately picked embassies where he could live economically enough to send money home to family members.[11]

Over the years, he had served as chairman both of the Preparatory Commission for the Comprehensive Nuclear-Test-Ban Treaty (CTBT) and the Six-Party Talks on North Korea's nuclear program. He was South Korea's foreign minister from 2004 through 2006. In that capacity, he worked with Kofi Annan in urging North Korea to give up its nuclear aims. Yet neither he nor Annan approved of Washington's added emphasis on North Korea's human rights violations.[12]

Ban was born in 1944 in a small village, Eumseong, in a still-united Korea but one under Japanese occupation. He was the oldest of six children. His father had a warehouse business that eventually went bankrupt. The family fled during the Korean War to a remote mountain village, where they lived for three years. They managed to escape much of the fighting and bombing but were, in Ban's description, both poor and hungry.[13] When he returned to one of the many bombed-out schools, he recalled sitting in the schoolyard dirt, studying, until classrooms could be rebuilt.[14]

Ban taught himself English, partly by listening to American soldiers during the war and by talking with Americans who were helping to build a fertilizer factory nearby. In 1956, when he was 12, he was selected by his classmates to send a message to UN Secretary-General Dag Hammarskjöld about the Hungarian uprising against the Soviet Union.

While still in high school, in the early 1960s, he won an English essay contest sponsored by the American Red Cross and Volunteers in Service to America (VISTA). At the time, he says he was still a "country boy" who had never been out of Korea.[15] The prize was a trip to the United States that included a home stay with a family in San Francisco. He adapted quickly. Libba Patterson, his hostess, later recalled that she had bought some rice and offered to cook it up for him but that Ban said he would actually prefer a hamburger.[16]

The key celebrity moment of the trip was a meeting for the winners with President John F. Kennedy. Ban recalled being inspired by both the President's decisiveness and his strong contributions to world peace and security. He credits the visit with strengthening his resolve to become a diplomat. A framed photo reminder of that visit, given Ban by the late Ted Kennedy, sits in the Secretary-General's study at his UN residence on Sutton Place.[17]

Ban went on to graduate from Seoul National University in 1970 with a bachelor's degree in international relations. He soon married his high school sweetheart—Yoo Soon-taek. She had been student council president when he won the Red Cross contest, presenting him then with the traditional good-luck symbol of bamboo strainers. She later studied library science and took a university library job but was advised to resign after her marriage since Korean jobs were then in short supply.[18]

Years later, Ban assured a *New York Sun* reporter, "I've had 35 years of honeymoon."[19] He and his wife have three grown children and three grandchildren. His wife has been active in the United Nations Children's Fund (UNICEF), and one daughter has worked for that agency in Kenya.

The Secretary-General insisted that he has always put public service first in his life and that the UN job definitely required a "sense of mission.... I'm deeply grateful to my wife, who has never complained."[20]

In the mid 1980s, he and his family returned to the United States where he earned a MA from Harvard University's Kennedy School of Public Administration. Ban recalled that, unlike Korea where memorizing what teachers taught was key, there was much more "mutual two-way traffic" in Harvard's approach.[21] Joseph Nye, one of his professors there, later described him as having a rare combination of analytic clarity, humility, and perseverance.[22]

Dr. Sung-Yoon Lee, a fellow South Korean and assistant professor at the Fletcher School of Law and Diplomacy at Tufts, was a 16-year old high school student in the Boston area when he first met Ban, then studying at Harvard. Lee's father was a South Korean diplomat, and the two families got together often. "Ban came across as a genuinely warm person with no shred of arrogance," Lee recalled in an interview. "He's very good with people-to-people social skills—but not in a flashy way."[23]

Indeed, Ban is widely seen as quiet and low key. Journalist Tom Plate, a scholar at Loyola Marymount University in Los Angeles, interviewed Ban several times for a biography in his "Giants of Asia" series. "Ban's way can be...perhaps so spice-less," he wrote, "as to give a whole new haze to the term *unflashy*."[24]

Ban readily concedes he is not one for "fiery rhetoric." In his acceptance speech before the General Assembly, he urged members to view his approach as a cultural attribute rather than as lacking needed passion or decisiveness.[25]

Ban admitted that he once wrote letters of apology to 120 colleagues in South Korea's foreign ministry for having been promoted ahead of them. "I was able to lessen the sorry feelings of my senior colleagues," he explained.[26]

"In the Korean context, that would be somewhat expected from one surging ahead in a promotion," noted Professor Lee. Ban took the trouble after the election to phone and meet with Lee's father, who was then retired and happened to be a vocal critic of South Korea's "sunshine" policy toward North Korea. "Ban doesn't forget people to whom he owes even a small intellectual debt," said Lee.[27]

By his own description, the Secretary-General is a workaholic, usually sleeping no more than five hours a night. According to an assistant, he told his wife she should count on his office hours being even longer than those of Kofi Annan.[28]

These days, Ban's spokesman often starts at 4 a.m. to gather needed news items and send pertinent e-mails to Ban at home. The two then meet at 8:45 or 9 a.m. Ban, technologically adept in manipulating his Blackberry, has said that he usually accepts phone calls whenever they happen to come in, since time zones vary so widely. "I'm open all 24 hours," he insists.[29]

"He really doesn't do anything lightly," said Edward Luck, one of Ban's former special advisers who worked closely with him. "One of his strengths is the energy he brings to the job. He likes to focus with a laser-like determination and get things done."[30]

While foreign minister, Ban was nicknamed "Ban-jusa" by some people in his office, meaning "the bureaucrat" or "administrative clerk."[31] He was known for attention to detail and skillful diplomacy. South Korean reporters sometimes referred to him as "the slippery eel" for his ability to dodge tricky and sometimes nasty questions. "They could never grab me," he recalled.[32]

In his spare time, Ban has said he enjoys classical music. Vacations are rare, but he did take a short one for a daughter's wedding. Sports are not on his agenda except for a rare game of golf or soccer.

The Secretary-General tends to wear tailored suits with monogrammed French-cuffed shirts. A man with a ready smile and sense of humor, he once introduced himself at Harvard as J. F. K.—"just from Korea."[33]

Early on, he also made fun of his name, insisting that it was pronounced "bahn" and not "ban"—"I don't want to ban anything," he said.[34] He told audiences then that he was "Ban in '07," and not "Bond 007."[35] At a UN Correspondents Association dinner in December 2006, before taking on the United Nations' top post, he managed to sing a bar or two of "Santa Claus is coming to town," substituting his own name for the popular symbol of Christmas.[36]

Repairs Needed: At Home and at Work

The five-story, UN-owned Georgian townhouse on Sutton Place—traditional home of UN secretaries-general—was 85 years old when Ban took office. It was in dire need of repairs to everything from plumbing and elevators to the kitchen exhaust system. He and his family thus spent most of that first year at the Waldorf Astoria, the traditional living quarters of US ambassadors to the United Nations.

Like each of his predecessors, Ban inherited a raft of challenges. The wars in both Iraq and Afghanistan were still going strong. Fierce fighting in the Darfur region of Sudan had been underway for three years, leaving more than 200,000 dead. Ban quickly termed the Darfur situation a top priority. General problems in Africa, the Middle East, and the environment—especially climate change—were also on his "to do" list. So were reducing the threat of terrorism and the spread of HIV/AIDS.

One other early goal was to do what he could to curb the spread of nuclear weapons. Progress in persuading Iran and North Korea of the issue's importance had been exceedingly slow. Just a few days before Ban took office, the Council imposed sanctions on Iran and ordered all nations to ban the sale of any technology and materials to Iran that might be used for nuclear programs.

At the start of his job, Ban asked his top staff to name two or three issues on which his office could focus most effectively. They discussed what was needed and the timing. It took about two years to craft a global strategy, according to Robert C. Orr, a US diplomat who was on Ban's executive team.[37]

In an apparent bow to developing nations and his pledge to promote gender equality, he soon appointed an Indian diplomat as his chief of staff and two women to top posts—a Haitian broadcaster as his spokesperson and a former Tanzanian foreign minister as deputy secretary-general.

In a brief advance piece in the *Interdependent,* a publication of the United Nations Association of the United States of America, a former deputy secretary-general, Louise Fréchette, had urged more appointments of women to top posts—"not just out of fairness, but because, in my experience, women are less inclined to indulge in turf wars and power games." She argued that the United Nations needs more team players and fewer prima donnas.[38]

"The Secretary-General puts a great deal of weight on the character and style of the people who work for him," noted Edward Luck, a member of Ban's team from 2007 to 2012. "He tries to pick people who will work well together. He will not stand for turf differences. He hates that."[39]

Shortly after taking office, Ban learned a few important lessons from some early mistakes.

On his first day on the job—January 2, 2007—reporters asked for his views on capital punishment. Saddam Hussein had been executed a few days before. Ban's comment that Hussein was responsible for "unspeakable atrocities" but that the death penalty was for each nation to decide drew some flak from human rights activists. The United Nations had long been formally on record as strongly opposed to capital punishment. Within a few weeks, implying his apparent approval of the UN stance, Ban told a Washington audience that he recognized a growing move globally to end the death penalty altogether.[40]

He had hoped to capitalize on his first days in office by proposing two structural reforms that he wanted enacted by the time he returned from a late January trip to Africa and the Middle East. Yet at the United Nations, even the mildest-sounding changes are never easy.

Ban proposed dividing the UN peacekeeping department in two. One part would focus on operations. The other would concentrate on administration. He also urged that the then-separate disarmament department be brought under the umbrella of the Department of Political Affairs. Neither proposal had appeared before on any outsider reform list.[41]

Developing nations often see proposed reforms as aimed at reducing their power. They strongly prefer consultations with a General Assembly committee as a first step.

In one closed-door discussion on Ban's proposals while the Secretary-General was away in Africa, Ambassador Nirupam Sen of India said that Ban should have consulted with Assembly committees first, since the nonaligned Group of 77 (actually 130 members by then) accounted for two-thirds of the Assembly votes. As he put it, "The Secretary-General is not a king, and the Secretariat is not a king's court."[42]

When Ban returned from his trip, he faced a heated debate on both reform proposals. Nobuaki Tanaka, head of the disarmament department, saw Ban's change as a demotion. He said he did not understand the rationale and that the idea was rather like asking a turkey to present itself for Christmas dinner. Ban, red in the face, said that the disarmament chief should become a team player or get out. Tanaka resigned.[43] Ban soon abandoned the proposal himself, asking the disarmament department instead to report directly to him and restoring its top post to the undersecretary-general level.

The head of the peacekeeping department, consulted only briefly before Ban's trip, did not support the proposed division and said he also would resign. Ban rejected his offer. Eventually, the peacekeeping proposal was streamlined and accepted in mid-March by the Assembly. Ban has since touted that the split was a major reform that few expected would work, but it has.[44]

He resolved from then on, however, to engage in consultations before, rather than after, proposing reforms.

In addition to Ban's other challenges, the Secretariat faced continuing charges of inefficiency, corruption, and mismanagement. Ban said from the start that he wanted to make the Secretariat more accountable and transparent and to raise its standard of ethics.[45]

To his credit, he became the first secretary-general to make his own financial situation public—placing his net worth at somewhere around $2.5 million—and urged other senior UN officials to follow suit. He also opened staff positions to wider competition, inviting others in the broad UN family of funds and programs to apply for Secretariat jobs.[46]

He said that all positions would be considered five-year appointments with annual reviews. He also continued Annan's practice of allowing the UN staff to speak to the press on matters within their areas of expertise.[47]

Ban also worked to stay on top of any charges of UN fraud. When questions arose about the use of funds given North Korea by the UN Development Program (UNDP), for instance, he quickly tried to limit the damage. North Korea was charged with making millions of dollars in cash payments to the government and local staff rather than investing in programs that would benefit the wider population. A series of internal audits by the accounting firm KPMG found that controls on use of the funds had been lax and that UN staff had failed to visit and monitor UNDP projects.[48] After a January meeting with Ad Melkert, UNDP associate administrator, Ban requested an outside examination.[49] He also called for a system-wide external inquiry into the financial activities of all UN programs.[50]

Meanwhile, the Six-Party Talks on North Korea continued during Ban's first year and made some progress. In February 2007, North Korea agreed to close its nuclear reactor and stop the production of plutonium in Yongbyon. In exchange for allowing an international inspection team to verify the action, North Korea was to get some 50,000 metric tons of fuel oil. The reactor was shut down in July. Another agreement was reached later that year regarding the shutdown of other nuclear facilities in exchange for more economic aid.[51]

Middle East peace and stability was another of the Secretary-General's top concerns. At his first formal news conference on January 11, 2007, he said he wanted to see a meeting as soon as possible of the Diplomatic Quartet—the United Nations, European Union, United States, and Russia—to develop a more effective mechanism to move toward a two-state solution between Israel and Palestine. He also pledged support for Lebanon's reconstruction in the aftermath of the 2006 war there.[52]

The Secretary-General set off again in March for a 10-day tour of the Middle East—visiting Egypt, Israel, the West Bank, Jordan, and Saudi Arabia. His first stop, a surprise, was Baghdad's Green Zone where, during a press conference at Prime Minister Nouri al-Maliki's home, a mortar exploded in a nearby field. Ban ducked. Shaken, he later conceded that the turmoil and the wind and dust then swirling around him seemed "very dangerous."[53] The United Nations, after all, had already lost 22 of its staff in Iraq in the 2003 attack on its Baghdad headquarters. This time, no one was hurt.

Though the UN role in Iraq was limited after the 2003 incident, Ban said he wanted to do more to help Iraq's social and political development.[54] The George W. Bush administration had been pushing the United Nations to increase its staff and play a larger political role there.[55] In August 2007, the Security Council unanimously passed a resolution extending the four-year-old UN Assistance Mission in Iraq (UNAMI) for another year. Its job was to promote economic reform and political reconciliation. That September, at a New York meeting with al-Maliki and others, Ban said the United Nations would add to its staff in Erbil in the north and establish a new southern office in Basra.[56]

Ban's Push for Peacekeepers in Darfur and the Need to Deal with Climate Change

During that first year in his new job, Ban worked energetically to persuade Sudan's President Omar Hassan al-Bashir to accept a UN peacekeeping operation. The bloodshed had been horrific. In addition to the hundreds of thousands killed in the western province of Darfur, some 2.5 million Sudanese simply fled. Adding to the pressure was the January arrest of some 20 aid workers from the United Nations and other agencies. Five UN staff members were beaten.[57]

The Sudanese leader, who firmly denied all charges of human rights abuse, had actually agreed in November 2006 to allow UN peacekeepers to join the 7,000 African Union (AU) troops already in Darfur. Largely underpaid and poorly equipped, the AU forces were overwhelmed by the task. However, Bashir was insisting on a voice both in the size of the UN force and the chain of command. He wanted to keep a strong African representation in the UN operation. Otherwise, the United Nations personnel could be seen as invaders and occupiers, he argued. With those caveats, he wrote Secretary-General Kofi Annan that December that he would agree to let in UN troops.[58]

Yet Bashir had a long history of backtracking on his promises and of setting up new roadblocks.[59]

When Ban set off in late January 2007 for an AU summit in Ethiopia, discussions with Bashir were at the top of his agenda. At their first meeting, Ban recalled looking the Sudanese president in the eye and telling him that the continuing violence in Darfur was "unacceptable," a word he was to use time and again during his tenure. He said that Sudan must live up to its agreement with the United Nations. "I made this case as hard as I could," Ban recalled. Bashir again agreed during the talks to accept a joint UN–AU force but wrote Ban a few weeks later to back out.[60]

A 35-page report released in March by the UN Human Rights Council added to the sense of urgency in New York that more needed to be done and soon. The report argued that the Sudanese government and its militia allies had failed to protect their own citizens, had "orchestrated and participated" in international crimes, and should be tried for war crimes.[61]

Ban persisted in quiet diplomacy. Later that month, at a meeting in Saudi Arabia, Bashir finally told Ban he would accept as many as 20,000 UN troops but only under full AU command.[62]

The George W. Bush administration was threatening to up the ante by imposing sanctions. Ban urged Washington to hold off, arguing that such action would interfere with the diplomatic approach.

Finally in June, Sudan agreed to let in the UN troops as a hybrid UN–AU force as long as there was an African majority. On July 31, the Council authorized up to 26,000 troops for Darfur. Tagged the African Union–UN Mission in Darfur (UNAMID), it was the largest such force the United Nations had yet called for. It marked the close of a nine-month struggle with Khartoum.[63] The UN mandate insisted on a UN command and allowed the use of force, if necessary, to protect civilians and aid workers under Chapter 7 of the UN Charter.[64]

Yet the roadblocks continued. Despite having agreed to the UN deployment, the Sudanese government was unwilling to turn over the land needed to house and supply the soldiers and to ease visa and travel restrictions to allow night flights. UN members also had not come up with helicopters needed to ensure troop mobility. Ban insisted that failure put the entire mission at risk.[65]

He took his first trip to Sudan in the early fall, saying he wanted to see the situation on the ground. He spoke with government officials and visited the al-Salam camp where 45,000 civilians had fled. He said he could feel the refugees sense of hopelessness and frustration.[66] Ban reported a strong need for new roads and education help but advised postponing these until a peaceful solution to the conflict could be found.[67] Later that month, he announced creation of a trust fund to support more talks on Darfur.

From the beginning of his involvement with the Darfur situation, Ban saw a definite link with another topic on which he held strong views: climate change.

On June 16, 2007, in a *Washington Post* essay, he wrote that a primary cause of the violence in Darfur was a severe drought. Though the conflict was often described as one between government-supported Arab militias in the north and black African rebels and farmers in the west and south, Ban insisted its real roots lay in water and food insecurity. Rains in Darfur began to dry up in the late 1980s just as temperatures were rising in the Indian Ocean. Arab nomadic herders and black African farmers worked harmoniously together, he reasoned, until food and water grew scarce in the early years of the new century. UN peacekeepers could help, he said, but only as a first step.[68]

Ban gave the climate change issue a strong, fresh impetus. Global warming, in his view, was "as great a threat to the world as modern warfare." He said it would be a "major driver of war and conflict" in the decades ahead.[69]

The new secretary-general said that reduction of greenhouse gases was one of his top priorities. He urged the Bush administration to take the lead in getting global support for a new treaty to replace the 1997 Kyoto Protocol, due to expire at the end of 2012. That agreement limited the amount of carbon dioxide emitted by the factories and power plants of industrialized nations.[70] In a speech to the General Assembly two months after taking office, Ban had said that, for his generation, fear of a "nuclear winter" was the leading threat, but that the danger to the planet and humanity from climate change was now at least as great.[71]

The United States had been the largest emitter of carbon dioxide until China moved into the lead. Neither nation was a party to the Kyoto agreement. President Bush had argued that nations should be allowed to set their own carbon limits and that too much environmental regulation could curb economic growth.[72] In his attempt to get the United States more fully on board in the effort to reduce climate change, Ban went to San Francisco in July 2007 to meet with California officials and tour several businesses using green technology. That state had set its own limits on greenhouse gases. Ban told reporters there that strong global action was crucial and should have been taken "yesterday."[73]

At a high-level, one-day meeting in New York of more than 150 nations that September, Ban tried to lay the ground work for an upcoming climate meeting in Indonesia in December. He again urged decisive action to replace the Kyoto Protocol with a new agreement. As an in-house move, he announced a new initiative to reduce the organization's own carbon footprint. In what some observers saw as an unusually impassioned message from the mild-mannered Secretary-General, Ban stressed that the time for doubt had passed and that action was crucial. He later termed the climate session "highly successful."[74]

That November, Ban became the first secretary-general to visit Antarctica. He met with scientists there and witnessed the melting and breaking off of ice shelves. At a meeting later that month of a UN-assembled Intergovernmental Panel in Valencia, Spain, Ban said that what saw in Antarctica was "more terrifying" than any science-fiction movie. Noting that China and the United States were the largest emitters of greenhouse gases, he again challenged them to come up with solutions.[75]

The nearly 200 nations that attended the December 2007 climate conference in Indonesia did not agree on an action agenda but did pledge to begin two years of formal talks on global warming.

Timothy Wirth, former president of the United Nations Foundation, an independent charity founded by media mogul Ted Turner, has called Ban a revolutionary and an "evangelist" on the subject of climate change. Noting that the UN leader's home base of South Korea had no special history on the issue, Wirth said that Ban has made the United Nations "the world's most important political player" in the field.[76]

Unfortunately, while Ban was at the Indonesian conference, in an increasingly common development, one more major attack was launched on UN workers in the field—this time in Africa. On December 11 in Algiers, the UNDP offices and an Algerian government building were attacked, killing 17 UN staff members and injuring another 40. In a statement issued from Bali around midnight, Ban called the attack an "ugly reminder" that terrorism remains "the scourge of our times." Soon after, he asked the veteran Algerian diplomat, Lakhdar Brahimi, to head a new independent panel to probe the vulnerabilities of all UN missions and recommend improved security measures.[77]

It was a sad close to the Secretary-General's first year in his new job.

Inching toward Those Millennium Development Goals

Ban has steadily prodded UN members to work harder to achieve the eight ambitious Millennium Development Goals (MDGs) adopted in 2000 under Kofi Annan. Both the midpoint assessment and the 2015 end date were to occur under Ban's watch. He has frequently raised the issue of their close relationship to world peace and security.

At his first press conference in 2008, for example, Ban told reporters that the year should be known as that of the "bottom billion"—the time to help the poorest of the poor. Those living in Africa and on the small island nations of Asia, he said, were among the neediest. He established a special MDG African Steering Group, urging all members to give fresh thought to ways the UN goals could be met.[78]

A 2007 UN midterm MDG report showed significant gains in most goal sectors. For instance, some 46 nations in four regions had universal primary education for boys and girls. Yet more than one-third of the world's developing nations were considered unlikely to reach the 100 percent goal by 2015.Though the number of those living in extreme poverty was down one-fifth from 1990 levels, an estimated 850 million people were still going hungry. Also, some 500,000 women were still dying each year of preventable complications during pregnancy and childbirth.[79]

Both the 2008 economic downturn and the rising cost of food spurred riots in close to 30 nations. Some MDG advocates urged that the shrinking portion of development aid aimed at improving agricultural production—a 10-percent drop since the early 1980s—must be reversed for continued progress.[80]

In March 2009, Ban wrote leaders of the Group of 20, gathering in London, to prod them to establish a $1 trillion global stimulus package to help the economies of the poorest nations over the next two years.[81] A few months later he distributed a report titled *Voices of the Vulnerable*. It cited an International Labor Organization prediction that as many as 222 million workers around the globe were in danger of joining the ranks of the working poor, earning less than $1.25 a day.[82]

At a development summit of world leaders before the 2010 GA fall session, the Secretary-General announced a major new $40 billion pledge from governments and private aid organizations aimed at improving the health of women and young children. Progress in that area had not been keeping pace with other gains.[83]

"I think, over time, Ban has developed a real passion on development issues," noted Edward Luck. "He's very determined."[84]

By the summer of 2011, an annual UN report on MDG progress yielded some guarded good news. Poverty was continuing to decline.

Universal primary education was still increasing. Strategies to fight malaria and HIV/AIDS were progressing. More people, particularly in urban areas, had access to clean drinking water. However, the report also noted that the decline in extreme poverty was not matched by a corresponding drop in the number of those going hungry. The world was still far from meeting sanitation targets, particularly in South Asia, and some 215 million women still had no access to contraceptives.[85]

A 2011 World Bank report on the MDGs cited economic progress in China and India as responsible for many of the gains against poverty.[86] The 2012 annual UN report on MDG progress noted that goals in three of the eight areas had been met well ahead of the target 2015 date. The major gains were in reduced poverty, access to safe drinking water, and improvement in the lives of urban slum dwellers.

"There has not been as much progress as we'd like to see in Africa, but there's been huge progress in some other countries," said Michael Meyer, a former UN undersecretary for communications. "The SG [Secretary-General] has spent a lot of time in Africa and has put a big push behind women's and children's health.... We've been a pioneer in the new brand of partnership that brings together governments, UN agencies and programs, nongovernmental organizations, and civil society groups.... We're starting a similar set of partnerships in the energy area.... We have to find inexpensive and efficient ways to bring light and electricity off grid."[87]

Eleven nations—ranging from Afghanistan to Vietnam—joined forces to protest that the goals have been cast too narrowly. Arguing that wars and environmental disasters can easily slow progress, they urged adoption of a ninth goal that takes risks and vulnerabilities into account.[88]

Indeed, a high-level panel of experts set up by Ban Ki-moon to look at the post-2015 development agenda agreed that the goals had been set in too narrow a context. Their report, issued May 31, 2013, argued that the MDGs had failed to focus sufficiently on reaching the very poorest of the poor, said little or nothing about the significant effects of conflict and violence on development, and neglected to take into account the important role of open and accountable government.

Ban has since called for a broader set of targets that take into account new economic realities and technological advances.

A Wedge in Myanmar

So often, it is a mix of pressures that stimulates change on the world scene. Yet the United Nations and Ban Ki-moon clearly played a key role in prying open the door to a more democratic Myanmar.

The military junta that seized power in a September 1998 coup in the former Burma showed little respect for human rights and, for many years, stubbornly resisted any outside pressure to change.

In late August 2007, fast-rising fuel prices suddenly sparked unusual and very angry public protests. The ruling junta promptly imposed a curfew and arrested many protestors. The George W. Bush administration further tightened the 10-year-old US sanctions on Myanmar. The UN Security Council had tried earlier that year to pass a resolution demanding a halt to further violence against civilians and urging a broad political dialogue. However, both Russia and China vetoed the measure.

In his annual address to the General Assembly in September 2007, Ban said the situation in Myanmar was being closely monitored. He urged that nation's military leaders to show "utmost restraint" in dealing with protestors and to begin a dialogue with opposition parties. He then dispatched Special Adviser Ibrahim Gambari to Myanmar on a four-day emergency trip.[89]

At a Security Council briefing on Gambari's return, Ban termed the continuing use of force against peaceful protesters "abhorrent and unacceptable" and called on the Myanmar government to release all political prisoners. China's Ambassador to the United Nations, Wang Guangya, argued that such pressure could lead Myanmar to a confrontation or loss of dialogue with the United Nations. US Ambassador to the United Nations Zalmay Khalilzad countered that such pressure was absolutely essential to give the government the incentive to cooperate. Gambari told Council members that he had conveyed strong messages from the Secretary-General to Myanmar's leaders to stop night raids and release all protesters. Gambari added that the response so far was unclear.[90]

"Ban was basically trying to sell a military junta not yet convinced...that it was going to have to go," observed Jeffrey Laurenti. "Often these things require time."[91]

In some ways, it was a natural disaster that paved the way to more persuasive UN pressure. In early May 2008, a devastating cyclone hit Myanmar. At first, outside help was definitely not welcome. Ban tried several times to phone that nation's military leader, Than Shwe. He would not accept the calls.[92]

Yet, over the next several weeks, the Secretary-General did manage to convince the ruling generals to reverse their stance. He flew to Myanmar where he met with General Shwe and toured the hard-hit Irawaddy Delta. Myanmar rulers finally agreed to accept foreign aid and allow use of the Yangon International Airport as a distribution center.[93] Ban then also chaired an international donors' conference in Yangon that drew contributions and pledges of close to $100 million.[94]

Ban again visited Myanmar in July 2009. Before he left New York, he said he realized that, by going, and by asking for a meeting with Aung San Suu Kyi, the major opposition figure then still in prison, he was taking a risk. Western diplomats had cautioned him that the government could use his presence to claim its own legitimacy. They urged him to wait until after reforms were made. Ban countered that quiet, one-on-one diplomacy was important and could succeed. Leaders, he insisted, "don't want to be lectured in front of many of their senior advisers." Sensitive issues raised in public, he said, often tend to bring on an emotional and hard-line reaction.[95]

Though Ban did not manage to meet the chief opposition leader, he spent almost two hours with General Shwe in a frank exchange of views. Ban said he was assured that elections, then scheduled for 2010, would be fair and transparent. Once again, he urged that all political prisoners, including Aung San Suu Kyi, be released so that the elections would be inclusive.[96]

Later Ban gave an unusual public speech in Myanmar to an audience of diplomats and humanitarian workers. He warned that the nation's prosperity depended on its opening up to the outside world.

He called again on the government to respect human rights, meet humanitarian needs, and commit to civilian leadership.[97]

The 2010 elections were held on schedule but were not widely considered free and fair. Though Than Shwe did retire, the new leadership included several former generals from the junta. Still, the new president, U Thein Sein, one of those former generals, soon surprised everyone by speaking out on the importance of fighting poverty and corruption, reducing taxes, and working toward political reconciliation. Banking and investment rules were redrafted. He called for new peace talks with the rebels and invited Myanmar exiles to return home. Later, Ms. Suu Kyi, by then under house arrest, was freed.[98]

In October 2011, the new Myanmar government also ordered an abrupt halt to a long-planned, but highly controversial, Chinese-funded hydroelectric dam project that was to span the Irrawaddy River. Citizens who used the river for everything from washing clothes to brushing their teeth had been strongly opposed to the project.[99] President Thein explained that, in cancelling the plan, the elected government was simply responding to "the aspirations and wishes of the people."[100]

Though many have been skeptical of the government's sincerity, further signs of a loosening up in Myanmar gradually surfaced. Some political prisoners were freed, and President Thein later said all others would be freed by 2014. Workers gained the right to join unions and strike. Press censorship eased somewhat.[101]

The Secretary-General welcomed the ongoing political and economic reform effort in a personal meeting with President Thein in New York in November 2011. Ban encouraged everyone in Myanmar to seize the opportunity to strengthen national unity and to keep pushing for reform.[102]

In January 2012, the government took another step forward in signing a cease-fire agreement with ethnic Karen rebels. The rebels later denied they had agreed, however, and fierce fighting resumed later that year. Still, the January move did prompt the United States to announce a full restoration of diplomatic relations with Myanmar.[103] Also, at President Thein's invitation, Ban paid a third visit to Myanmar that spring. He spoke to the Parliament and urged Western nations to lift any remaining sanctions.[104] Later that year, the Myanmar government allowed the United Nations to establish a human rights office there.

Despite strong initial resistance from the nation's military regime, Ban had used his bully pulpit to gain admission of humanitarian aid that surely helped to save lives. "He tried to make a symbolic gesture," noted Stephen Schlesinger, author of *Act of Creation: The Founding of the United Nations* and a senior fellow at the Century Foundation. "That, [the] sanctions, US criticism, and global isolation all contributed to pushing Burma in a new direction."[105]

Helping Haiti

Haiti, the poorest nation in the Western hemisphere, had long been considered a "basket case" by much of the world. And that was well before the string of natural disasters in the 21st century that pushed it even further behind.

When charges of government corruption and inefficiency led to violence and the overthrow of President Jean-Bertrand Aristide in 2004, a group of Caribbean nations urged the Security Council to send in UN peacekeepers to restore order. The mission known as the UN Stabilization Mission in Haiti (MINUSTAH) soon took over the operation of essential services from security and health to education and job creation.[106]

Though crime lessened and security improved, rising food prices set off a new round of civilian protests in April 2008. Haiti also was hit by four hurricanes in less than four weeks that year.

Shortly after urging the Group of 20 to come up with $1 trillion over two years to aid the world's poorest nations, Ban paid a symbolic visit to Haiti in March 2009. Despite the global economic downturn, he wanted to emphasize the scope of the remaining need there and urge nations to do what they could to help.[107]

Less than a year later—at 4:53 p.m. on January 12, 2010—a devastating earthquake leveled half of Port-au-Prince in a mere 47 seconds. The toll was extremely heavy. More than 200,000 people were killed. The UN headquarters collapsed, killing 102 UN personnel, more than the total lost by the United Nations in any other single event. An estimated 300,000 Haitians were injured and two million left homeless. Despite the heavy UN losses, UN search-and-rescue teams helped seek out survivors. Some UN workers, armed with knives and guns, slept on the streets to protect civilians from gangs.[108]

The Secretary-General paid a second visit to Haiti several days after the earthquake. "We are here to help you—you are not alone," Ban stressed. He asked the Security Council for authorization to send 3,500 more peacekeepers and police to help with the emergency. The Council agreed.

Elections, originally scheduled for February 2010 were postponed until May 2011. Later, the Security Council did reduce the number of peacekeepers, essentially removing the surge ordered after the quake. Some Haitians wanted a full UN exit. They were concerned about rumors, later confirmed, that UN troops from Nepal were responsible for a cholera outbreak that killed thousands and that other UN troops from Uruguay and Pakistan had sexually abused Haitian civilians.

However, Haiti's new president, Michel Martelly, a former musician known as "Sweet Micky," wanted UN forces to stay, and they did.[109] Indeed, in fall 2012, Ban urged the Security Council to extend the peacekeeper mandate to October 2013. He has since recommended a reduced UN force to focus on police and judicial reform and appointed Sandra Honoré of Trinidad as his Special Representative in Haiti.

"There was some criticism when the earthquake happened that Ban didn't step up to the plate fast enough, but he did organize donor meetings, and he was effective in making sure that UN forces were not withdrawn—and the UN did help with the 2011 elections," noted Stephen Schlesinger. "Given the limitations of Ban's office, I think he responded in the right way."[110]

Human Rights Questions in Sri Lanka

The fierce civil war between Sri Lanka's government and the separatist Tamil Tigers had been underway for close to 30 years before the government's decisive victory in May 2009.

Representing the Sinhalese ethnic majority, the government had insisted all along that it was fighting an intolerable terrorist-fueled rebellion that recruited child soldiers and used women suicide bombers. In the government's view, theirs was a humanitarian effort to liberate civilians. Human rights groups, watching from the outside, argued that both sides had pushed violence to the extreme. In addition to the estimated 70,000 killed over the years, the United Nations recorded more citizen "disappearances" during 2007 in Sri Lanka than in any other country. Yet the government in Colombo refused to allow any human rights monitors or foreign journalists to go to the front lines to view the situation for themselves.[111]

Nations convinced that the fight was an internal matter kept the UN Security Council from acting on the issue. China, a strong ally of Sri Lanka, was supplying it with arms and financial support and played a key role in keeping the United Nations from acting.[112] A narrow majority led by the nonaligned nations in the new UN Human Rights Council similarly decided that violation charges existed against both sides and were a domestic issue.[113]

Yet the atrocities committed were widely considered horrific—particularly in the final phase of the war. Hundreds of civilians were trapped in the northeast corner of the island by the forces of the Liberation Tigers of Tamil Eelam (LTTE), who refused to let them leave. In an effort to get at the rebels, the government targeted several schools and hospitals, killing many of those civilians in the process.[114]

Finally, just after the war ended, Ban Ki-moon flew to Sri Lanka to confer with its president, Mahinda Rajapaksa, and to inspect the refugee camps, then home to some 300,000 internally displaced Sri Lankans. Ban urged the president to open up the camps to international aid groups. The two men issued a joint statement on May 23, 2009, expressing their commitment to reconciliation for Sri Lanka and to accountability for human rights violations.

Ban created a three-member advisory panel to report on the human rights violations—particularly those occurring near the end of the civil war. The group was to advise Ban only on accountability issues and the law, not to investigate individual charges of misconduct. Still, it was not a popular move in the eyes of the Sri Lankan government or its supporters. Protests erupted outside UN offices in Colombo. One cabinet member began a hunger strike, vowing to fast to the death if the panel were not disbanded.

The Secretary-General sharply criticized the government's failure to prevent disruption of normal operations at the UN offices. He closed the UNDP regional center in Colombo and called the UN resident coordinator back to New York for consultations.[115]

The UN panel issued its findings in April 2011. These included credible reports that both sides had committed war crimes during the final months of the war. The panel urged the government in Colombo to begin "genuine investigations."[116] The United Nations estimated that as many as 40,000 civilians were killed in government attacks on "no-fire zones" in rebel areas during the closing months of the war.[117]

Not surprisingly, Sri Lanka called the report "fundamentally flawed," based on biased accounts with no verification.[118] An *Asian Tribune* article charged Ban with bowing to US and Western pressure and thereby ending his own chance for a second term. By failing to support "a sovereign democratic member fighting terrorism," the writer said, the United Nations actually set back the process of reconciliation.[119]

A commission set up by the Sri Lankan government released its own report in December 2011. Close to 6,000 civilians testified orally or in writing. Though the government clearly was blamed for some of the violence, the report was described by one Sri Lankan journalist as "largely an apologia for the army" during the final brutal weeks of the war.[120]

In November 2012, Ban ordered a second UN investigative report. It directly criticized the United Nations itself—from the Security and Human Rights councils to the Secretariat and local staff—for failing to respond to early warnings and to protect civilians during the last days of the 2009 war. The self-critical report also accused the United Nations of keeping silent on the fact that the majority of deaths in those final months were caused by government troops. In releasing the report, Ban said he was determined to see the United Nations draw the "appropriate lessons" from the findings. The independent Human Rights Watch applauded the United Nations for conducting the report and urged it to follow up with specific steps.[121]

Ban had long been the target of heavy criticism from human rights groups about his general handling of the Sri Lanka situation.

Stephen Schlesinger suggests that the Secretary-General may have felt that quiet diplomacy in this case was his proper role: "Ban sort of ducked the issue of whether there was going to be any punishment for the final days of that uprising and of whether the UN was ever going to take a position on International Criminal Court prosecution of the government."[122]

"Ban got moral commitments from the government, which have not been followed through in the way that he would like," noted Edward Luck, "but he didn't hide and say it [the question of the government's role] was going to be too controversial."[123]

In late 2013 the Tamil National Alliance won a strong victory in northern Sri Lanka in the first provincial elections held in 25 years. President Mahinda Rajapaksa faces strong pressure to follow through on his promised reconciliation efforts.

Sovereignty No Longer Implies the License to Kill

The idea that the sensitive subject of sovereignty—a bedrock concept in the UN Charter—carries not only rights but responsibilities has been steadily gaining ground at the United Nations. The organization's failure to act quickly and effectively to prevent mass atrocities of civilians in Rwanda, Srebrenica, and Sri Lanka has helped to fuel that push.

Known informally as R2P (the responsibility to protect), the idea was vigorously championed by former Secretary-General Kofi Annan and endorsed by leaders of UN member nations at the 2005 World Summit. Annan had been asking key questions on the subject for some time. In his annual address to the General Assembly in 1999, for instance, he asked, "If humanitarian intervention is indeed an unacceptable assault on sovereignty, how then should we respond...to gross and systematic violations of human rights that offend every precept of our own common humanity?"[124]

If a government will not or cannot protect its own people, what must the United Nations do? Annan decided early on to tap the wisdom of outside experts. He thought an insider analysis could prove too divisive. The resulting 2001 report of the International Commission on Intervention and State Sovereignty (ICISS) was intended to "sow the seed" regarding the problem and its possible solution in hopes that members over time would "digest" it, Annan explained in an oral history interview on file at Yale University.[125]

However, a number of nations that signed onto R2P as a worthy goal in 2005 have since had "buyer's remorse." Indeed, the concept—particularly if it goes beyond humanitarian aid to the point of UN military intervention—remains hotly controversial. Just as one man's terrorist is another man's freedom fighter, everything about R2P hinges on one's vantage point. Some worry, for instance, that it could encourage deliberate provocation by protesters to push governments into human rights violations that might then require UN action.

When Gareth Evans—a committed early supporter of R2P, coiner of the phrase, and cochair of the ICISS report—gave a lecture on the subject in Sri Lanka in 2007, the response was distinctly hostile. Some of those present, in fact, viewed the concept as a license for whites to intervene whenever they saw fit in sovereign black nations.[126]

For his part, Ban Ki-moon has warmly embraced R2P.

He raised it often during his 2006 campaign for the United Nations' top post, insisting he would put the concept into action. Once in office, he created the position of Special Adviser on R2P and chose Edward Luck for the pro bono job. Ban gave a major speech in Berlin on the subject in the summer of 2008 and published a report on progress made on R2P in 2009.

Luck insisted that one of Ban's innovations, a concept never referred to or agreed to before, was that armed groups inside a nation, like their governments, also have R2P responsibilities.[127]

Ban chose civilian protection as the theme of his remarks at the February 3, 2011, Cyril Foster Lecture at Oxford University, a long-awaited talk that secretaries-general traditionally give at the close of their first term. Though his remarks might have jeopardized his standing for a second term, he took on R2P in a major way. He insisted that "our words are ahead of our deeds" and that human protection would remain a "hallmark" of his administration. "I condemn any act against peaceful protest," he said.[128]

"Ban has been extremely outspoken [on R2P]...more than any other leader, hands down," said his former communications director Michael Meyer.[129]

The Secretary-General had published annual reports on R2P progress, and, in the summer of 2013, appointed Dr. Jennifer M. Welsh to succeed retiring Edward Luck as Special Adviser on R2P.

"Ban was determined to be the implementer—to turn R2P into action," noted Luck, who explained that not much had been done since 2005 to institutionalize the idea or create a strategy to move it forward. "People sometimes wonder why he has so much passion about the United Nations' responsibility for human protection. One reason is the personal connection in his growing up years. But also, he was determined that it wouldn't just be one of those high-sounding phrases that often come out of the UN."[130]

Traditional UN peacekeeping calls for lightly armed, neutral soldiers. They are to act as a third-party physical buffer between enemies who have already agreed to a cease-fire. Military intervention under R2P still requires neutrality but with a proviso. Brahimi's peacekeeping report argued that impartiality should not translate into complicity with evil. The report noted that political neutrality has too often degenerated into military timidity.[131]

Of course, UN members were already clearly on record for years in support of the Declaration of Human Rights and the Genocide Convention. Translating that theoretical commitment into politically acceptable action has always been the challenge.

One early diplomatic example of the growing UN focus on human rights occurred in Kenya. As the top two presidential candidates each claimed victory in a fall 2007 election that was peppered with charges of fraud, violence broke out in January 2008. Though more than 1,100 died and several hundred thousand civilians were internally displaced, most analysts say that if the African Union and the United Nations had not stepped in to mediate when they did, the results might have been far worse.

Ban flew to Kenya that February, after attending the AU summit. He raised the issue of civilian protection with both the president and the leader of the opposition. "He stressed that they had a responsibility and that he was worried that 'your people are inciting violence,'" recalled Luck.[132]

Both Ban and the AU asked Kofi Annan to mediate the ongoing dispute. Some 41 days of stormy sessions followed. The Kenyan leaders finally agreed on a deal to prevent genocide and share power.

"What was in my head," Annan later told journalist Roger Cohen, "was that we can't let this [genocide] happen in Kenya." That nation had become a safe haven for many refugees fleeing other African conflicts. Annan was convinced that without mediation, the situation might become hopeless. "That's why I stayed five weeks," he said.[133]

The fact that the negotiations had the backing of the broad international community—the United States, the European Union, the African Union, and the United Nations—and that Ban himself had visited Kenya during the talks were all important in the positive outcome, according to Elisabeth Lindenmayer, then a senior UN staff member who was there at the time. She wrote a lengthy report on the negotiations for the International Peace Institute. She noted, "It became clear that everyone was walking in the same direction and speaking with one voice."[134]

Kenya had a more recent election in March 2013 when Uhuru Kenyatta, who had withdrawn from the 2007 election at a late stage, was elected president and William Ruto, deputy president. However, both men have been charged by the International Criminal Court with having a role in planning and funding ethnic violence following the 2007 election.

R2P to the Rescue after Ivory Coast Elections

Though clearly defeated at the polls, Ivory Coast president Laurent Gbagbo just would not go.

He had been in his job in the West African nation since first elected in 2002. Further elections had been repeatedly postponed as continuing instability involving the military, the Muslim north, and the Christian south edged into civil war. Finally, in late 2010, an election was held. The winning presidential candidate was Alassane Ouattara, a former prime minister and International Monetary Fund (IMF) official. Gbagbo immediately rejected the results and refused to step down.

Ban Ki-moon staunchly defended the election results and urged Gbagbo to accept his defeat. "Ban was...very outspoken," recalled R2P adviser Luck. The Security Council echoed Ban's demand that Gbagbo respect the voters' choice. The General Assembly also offered its unanimous support. Yet a state body that Gbagbo controlled promptly invalidated the results. Gbagbo and his family remained entrenched in the presidential palace, surrounded by loyal troops and supporters.[135] The defeated president managed to hang onto power for four more months.

After his 2002 election, Gbagbo had asked the Economic Community of West African States (ECOWAS) and France to send peacekeepers to help settle the violent civil war then underway in the former French colony. In 2004, the Security Council authorized the UN Operation in Côte d'Ivoire (UNOCI) of about 10,000 to replace ECOWAS troops and provide further help with reconciliation and the peace process.[136]

UN troops thus were still in place when the 2010 elections were finally held. Once the results were in, Gbagbo asked the United Nations and remaining French forces to leave the country immediately, accusing them of favoring his opponent. The United Nations did not back down. Ban insisted that UN peacekeepers there would fulfill their mandate and continue to monitor and document "any human rights violations, incitement to hatred and violence, or attacks on UN peacekeepers."[137]

On March 30, 2011, the Security Council stepped up the pressure by calling on the UN forces in the Ivory Coast to "use all necessary means" under Chapter 7 of the Charter to protect civilians in the continuing violence after the 2010 elections. Ban had argued that intervention was vital to save lives. UN peacekeeping operations chief Alain Le Roy stressed that the UN move was a moral choice and a military and legal necessity.[138]

"Suddenly, a rather theoretical human rights framework (R2P) became a real live, on-the-ground test case," recalled former UN communications director Michael Meyer. "The Arab Spring, Libya, the Ivory Coast—they're all part of that continuum."[139]

UN troops were attacked by Gbagbo's forces. Many UN employees were evacuated. Gbagbo's state-operated TV station accused French troops of preparing a genocide similar to that in Rwanda.[140]

In an effort to stop Gbagbo's troops from using mortars and machine guns against civilians, UN peacekeepers began a series of strikes against the president's military bases.[141]

Just 12 days after the Council vote, forces loyal to Ouattara, supported by UN and French troops, captured and arrested Gbagbo. The move paved the way for political change. Ouattara was inaugurated as president on May 20, 2011. The Security Council opted to keep the UN mission at its crisis-level strength to help restore law and order. By late fall, Gbagbo was flown to The Hague to be tried for crimes against humanity.

Both internal and external investigations into responsibility for the many atrocities were launched. In September the new Ivory Coast government, like South Africa before it, established a truth and reconciliation commission. The government later said that suspects charged with crimes by the International Criminal Court, including first lady Simone Gbagbo, should be tried in the nation's own courts rather than in The Hague.

At his year-end press conference in 2011, Ban Ki-moon said that Gbagbo had tried to subvert the will of his people but that the United Nations "stood firm for democracy."

Though the UN intervention in the Ivory Coast did not receive much media attention, Richard Gowan, associate director of New

York University's Center for International Cooperation, argued that the UN move narrowly averted what might well have been a disaster.[142]

"The result wasn't perfect," confirmed Edward Luck, "but it's certainly a more hopeful situation now than it was."[143]

Ban and the Arab Spring

As citizen protests against authoritarian rule began to sweep across the Middle East and North Africa in early 2011, Ban Ki-moon steadily cited the United Nations' R2P obligation. At his December 14, 2011, press conference, he said the desire for democracy was "spreading like wildfire." He offered the United Nations' help in holding elections to establish inclusive interim governments.

A month later, at a high-level conference on democracy in Beirut, he told the leaders: "The flame ignited in Tunisia will not be dimmed.... The old way is crumbling." Ban argued that the desire for dignity and an end to corruption rather than regime change were the initial sparks. In an unusually blunt remark directed specifically to Syria's president, Bashar al-Assad, he urged, "Stop killing your own people. The path of repression is a dead end."[144]

"Ban has kept on top of Arab Spring issues as they have bubbled up—he has certainly been rhetorically in the right place," noted the Century Foundation's Jeffrey Laurenti.[145]

"The Secretary-General really led the global reaction to the Arab Spring," insisted the United Nations' former communications head Michael Meyer. "And he called for rapid and decisive action in Libya, helping to get Security Council resolutions through."[146]

Robust Protective Action in Libya

Though most UN efforts to protect civilians in danger had been limited to public statements and diplomacy, a new precedent was set in Libya in early 2011.

In light of the fast-deteriorating situation there between rebel forces and the government, Ban Ki-moon telephoned Colonel Qaddafi, warning him of the urgent need to respect the human rights of the Libyan people. They spoke for a full 40 minutes.[147]

Yet the situation did not improve. The violence intensified. On February 25, 2011, the UN Human Rights Council (HRC) demanded that the Libyan government end all violations of human rights. The HRC dispatched an independent investigative team to the scene and asked the General Assembly to suspend Libya's HRC membership.[148]

The very next day the Security Council voted to impose an arms embargo on Libya, freeze its foreign assets, and refer the situation to the International Criminal Court.

By March 1, the General Assembly had voted to suspend Libya's HRC membership.

Several days later, the Security Council moved its pressure a giant step forward. The Council imposed a no-fly zone over Libya for that nation's military planes. The Council also authorized the use of "all necessary measures" to protect civilians and enforce the arms embargo, giving a green light to military intervention. The vote was ten to zero with five abstentions, including China and Russia. Under other circumstances, the two might well have vetoed any such intrusion of sovereignty.

What made the difference? Certainly the United Nations' past failures to act swiftly and effectively in both Rwanda and Srebrenica were a factor. So, too, was Qaddafi's aggressive pledge to show no mercy or compassion to the protesters. Another crucial element figuring in the abstentions was the prod from regional organizations.

The Arab League, the African Union, and the Secretary-General of the Organization of the Islamic Conference had all strongly condemned Libya's violations of human rights and humanitarian law.[149] In an early March open letter to the Security Council, the Arab League had urged the United Nations to move decisively to protect civilians in Libya by establishing a no-fly zone. The letter concluded,

"The Arab League will not stand with its hands tied while the blood of the brotherly Libyan people is spilt."[150]

Eventually, Qaddafi fled and was killed. The UN-authorized campaign, largely carried out by NATO, was deemed a success. As Britain's Prime Minister David Cameron put it in his September 22, 2011, address to the General Assembly, "The UN has to show that we can be not just united in condemnation but united in action" in accord with the United Nations' founding principles.[151]

Libya's National Transitional Council announced the nation's full liberation on October 23, 2011. The UN Support Mission in Libya (UNSMIL) began working with the interim government to help in Libya's transition to modernization and democracy. During a visit to Tripoli in early November, Ban declared that "Libyans inspired the world in throwing off tyranny" and confirmed that the United Nations would continue to be their "partner."[152]

Whether or not the same degree of UN political cooperation can be reached in any other case is still an open question. Several government leaders and analysts have argued that NATO's lengthy bombing operation went well beyond UN-authorized limits of protecting civilians, amounting to taking sides in the civil war. Comments from Western leaders that Qaddafi must go clearly contributed to that impression.

"In the view of some of the [SC] abstainers, the resolution was hijacked for more than it was supposed to be," said Jeffrey Laurenti. "In effect, NATO became the air force of the rebels and angered Russia and China. It contributed to their refusal [at a later date] to... lecture Syria."[153]

The HRC issued a follow-up report in March 2012, charging that NATO did not adequately investigate the impact on civilians of its air raids on Libya. The report added that Libya's interim government had committed war crimes by failing to do enough to stop revenge violence on loyalists.[154]

Former UN High Commissioner for Human Rights Louise Arbour has cautioned that the world is not necessarily in for a new era in civilian protection. "The best form...[of that]," she has stressed, "is to prevent deadly conflict in the first place."[155]

Yes to a Second Term

In the midst of the Arab Spring protests, on June 6, 2011, Ban made an unusually early announcement that he would run for a second term. US President Obama quickly welcomed the news. Terming the United Nations "an imperfect but indispensable institution," he said that Ban had played a "critical role" in responding to its many challenges and had made important reforms. France's foreign minister echoed his support, saying Ban had shown "courage and determination in a period of crisis."[156]

There was little opposition to Ban's candidacy. Within two weeks, the Security Council offered its unanimous support. The General Assembly officially elected him on June 21.

Declaring that he was both "proud and humbled" to accept a second term, Ban placed his hand on the original UN Charter and promised to act in the interests of the whole UN membership: "We must do more to connect the dots among the world's challenges, so that solutions to one global problem become solutions for all....Together, anything is possible."[157]

Syria Resists Global Pressure

Steadily increased sanctions have had little effect on the Syrian government's behavior during its lengthy Arab Spring challenge. The continuing civilian protests and the government crackdown on them began in mid-March 2011. Syrian President Bashar al-Assad has long insisted that his fight is against terrorists armed by foreign powers intent on overthrow of the government.

Yet Ban Ki-moon has used his bully pulpit and private persuasive efforts more vigorously in the case of Syria than in any other Arab nation. The day after his election to a second term, he renewed his earlier demand that Syria must allow fact-finding and humanitarian missions into the country to investigate human rights violations and provide needed humanitarian aid.

The Secretary-General spoke frequently by phone with President Assad. The Syrian leader made several promises—from a national dialogue to amnesty for political prisoners—but failed to follow through. In late June 2011, Ban told Al Arabiya, the Saudi-owned Arab-language news channel, "I don't see much credibility in what he has been saying.... He really has to take firm measures."[158]

The Security Council, which had been debating its stand on the issue for months, finally issued a statement several weeks later condemning the Syrian government for human rights violations. The spur for the Council then was a devastating new attack on the city of Hama. Three days after the Council vote, the Secretary-General again phoned Assad, who had refused to accept Ban's calls for much of the summer. This time the call got through. Ban, citing the rising death toll, pressed again for an immediate halt to the use of force against the demonstrators.

In mid-September at UN headquarters, Ban told a news conference that Syria had consistently broken its promises. Insisting that "enough is enough," he said it was time for the international community to take measures and "speak in one voice."[159]

Yet such unity is more easily called for than achieved at the United Nations. On October 5, a Security Council resolution condemning Syria's oppression of antigovernment forces was vetoed by China and Russia. Brazil, South Africa, and India abstained. The suspicion again was that the West was encouraging the protesters to further its own interests.

Several days later Ban renewed his call for a team to investigate the deaths in Syria. Speaking in Bern, Switzerland, he told reporters that Syria must make political reforms "before it is too late." He said, "This killing must stop immediately."[160]

Assad signed a pledge with the Arab League on November 2, 2011, promising to pull back his forces from urban areas, release political prisoners, and begin a dialogue with the opposition on political reforms. On the same day, Ban, then on an unannounced visit to Tripoli, told reporters that the Syrian people had been suffering "too much, too long" and that he hoped the Arab League peace plan would be carried out soon.[161]

The Arab stance gradually toughened. King Abdullah of Jordan became the first Arab leader to demand that Assad step down. The Arab League imposed broad new trade sanctions on Syria and suspended Syria's Arab League membership. Officials in Damascus, furious at both League moves, called for an emergency summit of the group.[162]

The UN Human Rights Council issued a report in late November charging the Syrian government with major human rights violations. The list included torture, rape, and the shooting of unarmed demonstrators. A few days later, UN High Commissioner for Human Rights Navi Pillay accused Syrian authorities of "continued ruthless repression" and urged international intervention.[163]

In one more attempt at a united stand, the Security Council called on Assad in February 2012 to cede power, but the resolution was vetoed again by both China and Russia. Though he rarely comments on Council decisions, Ban called it a "great disappointment" that undermined the United Nations at a moment when a unified voice was most needed.[164] Noting that Assad is surrounded by "all those hardliners who believe that if Assad falls, they will fall," Ban later said the Syrian leader "has gone too far, too deep" and it is "too late for him to return to normalcy."[165]

By mid-2013, the United Nations estimated that 1.6 million Syrians out of the nation's population of 20 million had fled to neighboring nations. The world body issued its largest appeal to date for humanitarian aid for Syrian refugees. Another 100,000 Syrians are thought to have been killed. The best efforts of an Arab League observer team and UN envoys—first Kofi Annan and later Lakhdar Brahimi—to find a workable compromise yielded little progress.

After a massive sarin gas attack killed more than 1,000 people in a Damascus suburb on August 21, 2013, Ban commissioned a United Nations investigation, which eventually confirmed the use of chemical weapons but did not attribute blame to one side or the other. Ban announced on September 21 that he had received a letter from

President Assad who, while still denying that his government used such weapons, said he had decided to sign and abide by the 1992 treaty banning the development and use of such weapons.

The Secretary-General had been sharply critical of America's unilateral military threat to punish Syria for its alleged use of chemical weapons, insisting that use of force is only legal in self-defense or when authorized by the Security Council. After more than a two-year deadlock on the Syrian issue, the Council finally did pass a binding resolution on September 26 that required Syria to give up its chemical weapons and allow verification. However, the text added no automatic penalty for noncompliance. Ban welcomed the resolution as "historic," noting that "the international community has delivered." [166] He earlier had praised Russia's offer to disarm Syria of its chemical weapons.

Looking to Nuclear Disarmament—With Slim Results

Ban Ki-moon has often stated that a world free of nuclear weapons is a top priority. As a South Korean who grew up in a divided country after the Korean War, his experience and hopes for peace were deeply personal. Eight years before he became secretary-general, he was elected chairman of the CTBT Preparatory Commission. In the early 1990s, he had served on a Joint Nuclear Control Commission of the two Koreas.

The United Nations has long served as a multilateral forum for disarmament talks but has never really been a central player.[167] More than one secretary-general has voiced frustration with the glacial speed of progress. After a 2005 world summit came to no further agreement on nonproliferation and disarmament, Secretary-General Kofi Annan called the result "inexcusable" and "a disgrace."[168]

Ban Ki-moon often has been similarly frustrated. He has consistently prodded UN member nations to do more. In October 2008, he laid out a five-point plan aimed at moving closer to a nuclear-free world. Noting that well over 25,000 nuclear weapons already exist, he urged the permanent five Security Council members to hold disarmament talks and assure nonnuclear nations that they would not be subject to the threat or use of nuclear weapons.[169]

It was the Conference on Disarmament (CD) in Geneva, an autonomous body but one with links to the United Nations, which finally agreed to the CTBT in 1996. Though the treaty, which bans all nuclear tests, has been signed and ratified by a majority of nations, it is not yet in force. All 44 members of the Conference on Disarmament with nuclear reactors, mostly of the research variety, must first sign and ratify it. The United States (which signed the treaty but has yet to ratify it), China, India, Pakistan, Egypt, North Korea, Israel, and Iran are among the holdouts.

By contrast, the CD's 1968 Nuclear Nonproliferation Treaty (NPT) became operational in 1970. It is generally considered a success in discouraging nonnuclear states from acquiring nuclear capability. It has had much less success in implementing the major goal of nuclear disarmament. As such, the treaty essentially has not moved forward since 1996. India, Pakistan, and Israel have not signed on. North Korea, once a signer, withdrew in 2003.[170] Ban has often reminded UN members that they all have an "obligation" to join the NPT, as well as to sign and ratify the CTBT.

The Secretary-General has been sharply critical of the Conference on Disarmament. After its May 2011 seven-week session in Geneva, he accused it of giving in to "a paralysis" that puts the conference's "very legitimacy at risk." He blamed its rule that "consensus" must underline any agreement. One or two nations thus can easily block any forward move. He urged the group to find ways to revitalize its work: "The tide of disarmament is rising, yet the Conference on Disarmament is in danger of sinking."[171]

In this case, Ban has singled out Pakistan for most of the blame. That nation, reluctant to accept a possible treaty on the agenda that would ban the production of fissile material for nuclear weapons, has for years essentially blocked the resumption of CD nuclear talks. In a conversation with author Tom Plate, Ban noted that the international community normally works on a consensus basis. In a rare concession to direct national criticism, he said, "But now just one country can block everything.... Is that reasonable? Do we have to just accept it as a fact?"[172]

Iran has been an especially troubling case for the United Nations. With initial assistance from the United States, the shah started the nation's nuclear program in the 1960s as part of his modernization plan. After Iranian dissidents accused Tehran in 2002 of secretly building a uranium enrichment facility for a military program, Iran did suspend its enrichment program and allow inspections. When President Mahmoud Ahmadinejad came to power in 2005, however, Iran's position toughened. Tehran began building centrifuges for uranium enrichment. In 2006, the Security Council required Iran, under Chapter 7 of the Charter to suspend all uranium enrichment activity.[173]

Though Tehran continues to insist that its nuclear program is strictly for peaceful use (thus still technically legal under the NPT), reports by the International Atomic Energy Agency (IAEA), the United Nations' nuclear proliferation watchdog, suggest otherwise. Its November 2011 report found "credible" evidence that Iran may be secretly working to develop a nuclear explosive device and ways to deliver it.[174]

An article in the *Bulletin of Atomic Scientists* promptly insisted, however, that the IAEA findings were not that different from previous reports. The article said that although Iran pursues activities "highly relevant" to a nuclear weapons program, there is no evidence yet that the nation has decided to build such weapons.[175] American nuclear engineer and former IAEA inspector Robert Kelley also labeled the IAEA report "very thin" with "little new information." [176]

For his part, Ban Ki-moon has urged restraint and continued diplomacy. He said a military strike on Iran might not seriously disrupt any Iranian nuclear program and could trigger unintended consequences. However, he also had made it clear at a May 2010 conference on the NPT that he fully supports Council sanctions against Iran. "The onus is on Iran," he said, "to clarify the doubts and concerns about its program."[177]

The Security Council has imposed several rounds of sanctions on Iran. After one early round, President Ahmadinejad blithely dismissed their effect. He said such sanctions "are like used tissues which should be thrown in the trash."[178] Yet several outside analysts insist that more recent sanctions have been taking a noticeable toll in currency devaluation and reduced oil exports.

In the late summer of 2012, Ban was sharply criticized, by Israel and its American supporters among others, for his decision to attend the 120-nation Nonaligned Movement annual meeting in Tehran. Many thought the visit would send the wrong message. However, while there, Ban seized the opportunity, in frank discussions with Iranian leaders and in public statements, to urge Iran to take "concrete steps" to prove that its nuclear program has no military element. He also voiced "serious concern" about the status of human rights in Tehran.[179] "Overall, I think Ban has been quite active on the [disarmament] issue and has tried to bring it back to public awareness," noted *Act of Creation* author Steven Schlesinger.[180]

Ban has largely steered clear of direct involvement on North Korean issues, including the nuclear program and the Six-Party Talks. However, when a North Korean submarine torpedoed a South Korean naval vessel in March 2010, killing more than 100 sailors aboard, he admitted that, as a South Korean, he had a difficult time knowing what role to play. North Korea denied responsibility but the evidence, according to the United Nations, was clear. In the end, he urged the Security Council to meet and take necessary action. When a senior North Korean official came in person to protest, the Secretary-General insisted he was acting in his UN capacity, not as a South Korean: "Period."[181]

"I think he has tried hard NOT to come across as too engaged on Korean issues," said Fletcher's Sung-Yoon Lee. "But he has also come across as [often] trying too hard not to say anything that may be taken as a critical position on North Korea's multifaceted problems, including human rights."[182]

South Sudan Gains Independence—With UN Help

After a lengthy civil war, the Republic of South Sudan at last gained both its independence and UN membership in 2011.

The Secretary-General flew to Juba for the July 9 celebration, delivering the usual congratulatory messages. Yet in interviews afterward, he stressed that there were still immense challenges ahead for the new nation and its northern neighbor. He cited the enormous lack of infrastructure in the south and the pressing need to establish both the rule of law and institutions, such as schools and hospitals.[183]

A 2005 peace agreement between the Khartoum government in the Muslim, Arab-dominated north and the rebel Sudan People's Liberation Movement in the largely Christian south had called for a new government of national unity and a semiautonomous government in the south until a January 2011 referendum could be held. The South would then decide its own future. To no one's surprise, it opted for independence.

"Everyone was afraid it [the referendum] was going to be an absolute disaster, but it wasn't," recalled Ban's Special Adviser Edward Luck. "It's remarkable that a new state was created in Africa. I think the whole UN system deserves a lot of credit."[184]

"It was a big accomplishment for change along the border," agreed Ban's former communications director Michael Meyer. "We've worked hard to keep the situation in Sudan from exploding out of control."[185]

To help keep the peace and nurture development after South Sudan's independence, the Security Council authorized a new peacekeeping operation—the UN Mission in South Sudan.

Yet the new troops were slow to form and arrive. Ban noted that it took only days to get UN forces on the ground in the Korean War but that more recent deployments, partly because Africa has so many ongoing crises, often take as long as two years. He said it is increasingly hard to find enough troops.[186]

The situation between Khartoum in the north and Juba in the south is still far from settled. Fierce fighting and bombings have continued. The status of the border in the Abyei region, an area both sides claim, remains tense and unresolved. Ban has expressed deep concern over incursions on both sides and cross-border support of rebel groups.[187]

Also, the oil-rich south relies on refineries and pipelines in the north to process and export the oil, but agreeing on a fair transport fee has been difficult. Juba suddenly shut down its pumps in early 2012, hurting both nations economically. Though the north and the south finally agreed to a profit-sharing arrangement later that year, implementing it was a slow process.[188] Each nation has accused the other of supporting rebel groups in the other's country. Adding to the instability of the situation, Sudan's President Omar al-Bashir, in power for more than two decades and now indicted by the International Criminal Court on charges of crimes against humanity and genocide, has faced increasing criticism—even from Islamists and hard-liners in the north. Human rights groups have called for his immediate detention if he travels out of the country.

For its part, the United Nations also has faced its own challenges in the region. In December 2012, a UN helicopter carrying Russian peacekeepers was shot down by the South Sudan army. The explanation offered later was that the plane was mistakenly assumed to be from Khartoum, carrying supplies to rebel forces. Ban quickly countered that the plane had been clearly marked and urged an immediate investigation. He was further angered by a South Sudan attack on a UN convoy in April 2013 that killed five UN peacekeepers and seven civilians. He called it a war crime that falls under ICC jurisdiction.

Ban Keeps the Pressure On for a Greener Planet

Nations often talk of the need to curb global warming but argue vehemently over the specifics. The toughest decisions are usually postponed. It has been a long, slow slog.

Ban Ki-moon, a cheerleader for bold action from the start, has tried hard to focus public attention on the need to tamp down the heating of the planet. In the words of his former communication director Michael Meyer, "Ban went around beating the drums on climate change like some tinpot evangelist."[189]

The Secretary-General has tried to get the message across through his frequent travels—visiting melting glaciers in the Antarctic and stopping in Switzerland and Norway for a personal look at the impact of climate change. He has also tried hard to keep a spotlight on the problem. At a world climate conference in Geneva in September 2009, he told delegates, "Our foot is stuck on the accelerator, and we are heading towards an abyss."[190]

Similarly, at a forum in Los Angeles in February 2011, he prodded the 400 Hollywood directors, producers, and writers there to make movies that treat global warming as a pressing topic. Making the earth environmentally sustainable, he said, is "a political and moral imperative.... Animate those stories," he urged. "Set them to music. Give them life. Together we can have a blockbuster impact on the world."[191]

Each major UN gathering on climate change has taken at least some forward steps. Often these are formalized or added to at the next meeting. Major conferences in Copenhagen in 2009 and in Cancun in 2010, for instance, were precursors for decisions made at the Durban, South Africa, climate conference in December 2011 and later gatherings.

In South Africa, delegates from close to 200 nations picked up on a promise made in Cancun to establish a UN-managed Green Climate Fund to raise and spend some $100 billion a year in public and private money by 2020 to help developing nations shift to clean energy sources. There were no specifics, however, on how the money would be raised or distributed. "It may be a challenge, but it is doable," Ban insisted.[192]

Negotiators at the Durban conference also agreed to extend by five to seven years the 2012 expiration date of the Kyoto Protocol, the last strong emissions-cutting agreement reached at a UN climate conference.

The protocol set specific pollution reduction targets for advanced nations but not for developing countries, a distinct point of controversy. Although the United States helped craft the Kyoto treaty, Congress did not ratify it. American lawmakers did not accept the unequal obligation to comply. China, exempt from major cuts under Kyoto and now the world's largest emitter of carbon dioxide, did sign.[193]

The extension agreed to in South Africa was meant to give nations time to come up with a new global treaty by 2015 that would feature strict targets to be applied equally to all nations. The plan was to have that new, binding agreement ratified and enacted by 2020. "That, I think, is the most important achievement in the history of climate change," Ban said.[194]

Yet some reviews on the progress made at Durban were not nearly as glowing. One environmentalist said it was as if one spent all day negotiating contract terms with a plumber while watching a burst pipe flood the kitchen.[195]

Others felt that, with the distraction of the economic downturn, it was remarkable that Durban achieved any deal at all. Ban Ki-moon, a man inclined to view progress from a glass-half-full standpoint, insisted at his 2011 year-end press conference that the results at Durban "defied the skeptics." He said the conference achieved a consensus on a clear target and a timeline for reaching a legally binding agreement. "For the first time, the international community is going to work in one framework," he said. "We will build on this Durban spirit of cooperation."[196]

Much of the debate over the warming of the planet has centered on the need to find the right balance for both developed and developing countries—steps that will help the planet but not limit or reverse economic growth.

In that spirit, a UN Conference on Sustainable Development was held in Brazil in June 2012. It was billed as a follow-up to the 1992 Earth Summit held in Rio de Janeiro. Ban termed it a fresh opportunity to set a new, more balanced course. He called for a goal of universal access to sustainable energy and a doubling both of energy efficiency and use of renewable energy sources by 2030.[197]

Yet the lack of specific dramatic results following the second Rio conference also drew sharp criticism from some environmentalists. Many termed the summit a waste of time and money. Still, the gathering drew close to 50,000 people, including many business leaders and heads of state. It clearly moved the global discussion forward. In a social media chat in China, Ban hailed the conference as "a great success that put all of us towards a greater sustainability path."[198]

Hundreds of initiatives and side agreements, though little noticed, did emerge. Microsoft, for instance, pledged to impose a carbon fee on operations in more than 100 nations by 2030. Also, a group of development banks pledged $175 billion to promote public transportation and bike lanes in the world's largest cities by 2030.[199]

The Povertymatters blog of the *Guardian* called the results "modest" but insisted that the very fact that the three-day conference did not "fall apart" was in itself a "fantastic achievement." The blog noted that the United States and developed nations had appeared "hell bent" until the last day on returning negotiations to where they were more than two decades before.[200]

The second Rio conference also drew praise for the breadth of its social media participation. A Natural Resources Defense Council staff blog noted that the Twitter hashtag *#RioPlus20* was viewed more than one billion times. The United Nations used Facebook, Google+, Tumblr, Pinterest, and Weibo, with postings in six different languages to encourage participation. The world body estimates that more than 50 million people took part electronically in the conference.[201]

"I think Ban has played an important role in getting the issue of climate change back on track," said American diplomat Robert Orr. "Everyone was paying lip service to it, but the issue had come to a screeching halt.... We have a new dynamic in negotiations. We implement more things. They [participants] agree to more things."[202]

The Israeli–Palestinian Deadlock

Many feel that Ban could have done more than he has to help ease the longstanding Israeli–Palestinian dispute. He left the negotiating largely to the Diplomatic Quartet. Yet early in his first term, he did urge Israel to stop building new homes in the Occupied Territories. On a March 2010 visit to the West Bank, he repeated that call, saying that his very presence there should send a clear message of international support for a Palestinian state.[203]

The 2011 admission of Palestine as a full member of the UN Educational, Scientific, and Cultural Organization (UNESCO) triggered an automatic cutoff (by law) of US funds to that agency. Asked about that at a year-end press conference, Ban said he was indeed concerned about the 20 percent loss of funds but said that full UN membership for Palestinians was a separate issue: "I support their aspirations to be admitted into the UN and to work in other organizations...within the context of the two-state vision."[204]

Though a bid for its full UN membership was defeated in the Security Council in 2011, the Palestinian Authority was recognized as a nonmember observer state in an overwhelming vote on November 30, 2012. That status allows it to take part in debates and possibly join such bodies as the International Criminal Court. Ban said the UN vote underscored the need for Israel and Palestine to resume meaningful peace talks.[205]

While ceasefires in the volatile region tend to come and go, often quickly, Ban has spent a good deal of time in that effort. Sometimes, he has argued, aiming for a unilateral rather than a simultaneous ceasefire is the best choice. In a series of personal meetings and phone calls in 2008, for instance, Ban recalled persuading Israeli Prime Minister Olmert to adopt a ceasefire "because the Israelis started this [latest] war." Later he flew to Damascus and urged President Assad to talk with Hamas officials based there so that Hamas leaders in Gaza might then be persuaded to follow suit. Accordingly, Hamas agreed to a ceasefire within 12 hours of the Israeli announcement.[206] Needless to say, however, it did not hold.

An investigative report commissioned by the UN Human Rights Council and headed by widely respected South African judge Richard Goldstone concluded that both the Israeli Army and the Hamas fighters were guilty of war crimes during a later—2009—three-week Israeli invasion of Gaza. However, Goldstone soon retracted a specific assertion that Israel had intentionally targeted Gaza civilians as a matter of policy. He explained that Israeli evidence had since emerged that "skewed" that finding. The original charge had so angered Israel that Prime Minister Benjamin Netanyahu insisted that the whole report be shelved.[207]

Ban Ki-moon did manage to get Israel to reimburse the United Nations for most of the $12 million he had demanded for damage to schools and other UN facilities in Gaza. Yet a small group of Palestinian protesters threw shoes and sticks at him when he arrived from Israel in February 2012 on his third visit to Gaza. Their complaint: though he had heard Israel's side of the story, he had made no plans to meet with the residents of Gaza to hear their side or to demand the release of political prisoners in Israel.[208]

The Secretary-General did commission an independent report on the May 2010 Israeli raid on the Turkish ship that was trying to bring aid to Gaza. Israel wanted to do its own inquiry, but Ban convinced Israeli leaders that the results would not be seen as credible.[209] The report Ban commissioned confirmed that the Israeli blockade of Gaza was a legitimate security measure intended to block any flow of weapons into the Strip. However, neither nation was considered free from blame. Israel's use of force was deemed "excessive and unreasonable," while the Turkish ship acted "recklessly" in trying to breach the blockade.[210]

"Ban was actually quite critical of the attacks on Gaza," recalled Steven Schlesinger. "However, in my view, he could have taken a more proactive role in the Israeli–Palestinian situation. He's been rather silent most of the time." [211]

"He pushed the envelope more than Washington would have wanted on some of these issues, but he has not created problems for the US administration," agreed Jeffrey Laurenti.[212]

Looking Back

Ban Ki-moon may well be the most traveled secretary-general to date.

If it was not Somalia or the Gaza Strip, it was Antarctica or Pakistan. He even made it to Chicago during a blizzard in February 2008 to talk with business leaders and kick off a student-run model UN program focused on climate change. In his first year alone, he traveled more than 125,000 miles, more than any predecessor in a similar period.

A few saw it as travel in excess. Ban Ki-moon has been "trotting the globe collecting honorary degrees, issuing utterly forgettable statements and generally frittering away any influence he might command," insisted Jacob Heilbrunn, senior editor at the *National Interest*, in 2009. "He has become a kind of accidental tourist."[213]

Yet right from the start, the Secretary-General viewed travel as a vital part of his job—touching base with the people of UN member nations. Visiting after natural disasters to show the flag of UN solidarity and attending regional conferences were high on the agenda.

The Secretary-General has been trying to "revive the UN Charter" by this focus on its "we the peoples" constituency, insisted former UN communications head Meyer. "Ban sees his role as the voice of the voiceless," explained Meyer. "He travels to see the poverty and the problems people face, to give them hope and faith in the future."[214]

"Maybe he travels more than he should," conceded Edward Luck, "but he's determined because he believes very much in one-on-one personal diplomacy…. Even with Assad in Syria, he tried to keep up his phone calls and press the message."[215]

Ban's tenure also will be remembered—though the Secretary-General did not personally initiate it—for the massive $1.9 billion renovation of the United Nations' physical plant. Staff and diplomats alike were forced to relocate, often to smaller and more Spartan spaces.

"There was much grousing," recalled the Century Foundation's Jeffrey Laurenti, who said the boxy, three-story building erected as a temporary substitute had no carpets, few windows, and no escalators. "It was widely derided by UN staff and diplomats as Guantanamo," he said.[216]

What did Ban Ki-moon really achieve during his time in office? The best answers may well lie in the realm of quiet diplomacy.

Certainly his persistence in pressing Sudan's President Bashir finally to accept UNAMID, the joint UN–African peacekeeping force, played an important role. An earlier UN peacekeeping mission in Sudan, established in 2005 to implement the peace agreement reached after two decades of fighting between the north and south, helped provide security and supplies for the south's important January 2011 vote for independence. The panel appointed by Ban to oversee the referendum agreed that the process had been fair and credible. Since then, South Sudan has become the United Nations' newest member—the 173rd.

As a mediator, Ban also was very clear in telling Ivory Coast president Laurent Gbagbo that the leader must accept his 2010 election defeat. Ban stood firm against the Gbagbo demand that UN peacekeepers must leave. Eventually, the defeated leader was arrested. The peacekeepers stayed on.

Likewise, Ban's efforts to persuade Myanmar military officials to accept international aid after the devastating cyclone there may well have helped convince the government to open the door politically another inch or two.

The Secretary-General also firmly resisted efforts by the Sri Lankan government to block any investigation into war crimes committed by the government's army against the rebel Tamil Tigers. He created an advisory panel to report on human rights violations.

Ban was similarly strong in his public support for the democratic protests during the Arab Spring. He insisted early on that both Libya's Qaddafi and Egypt's president Hosni Mubarak must go.

"He related, recalling his days as a student when Korean students were protesting the repressive, military-dominated regime and the sacrifices people made to make Korea a more democratic society," said Edward Luck. "He's said this on several occasions."[217]

Despite his energetic efforts to spotlight the need for more steps to protect the environment, progress on climate change has been slow. Ban has said that he intends to hold a high-level meeting in 2014 to build political strength for a binding climate agreement by 2015. As he stressed in a June 2013 speech to scientists at the National Center for Atmospheric Research in Colorado, "The facts don't lie."

Though progress on disarmament also has been slow, Ban applauded the General Assembly's overwhelming 2013 vote aimed at deterring what he called the current "free for all" in global weapons transfers. The new arms trade treaty, debated for more than a decade, will take effect 90 days after 50 nations have ratified it. Calling it "substantial and robust," Ban said the treaty should make it much harder for illegal weapons to be diverted to warlords, terrorists, and criminals.

Some have argued that Ban could afford to be much stronger on human rights issues. "We're not Human Rights Watch or Amnesty International," countered Michael Meyer, noting that quiet diplomacy is often a more effective tool in that realm. "There are times when we sing from the same score sheet but not always."[218]

"Some people have been uncertain about just how visionary Ban is on human rights," said Jeffrey Laurenti, "but I don't think the human rights community sees anything about his performance that is dismaying."[219]

Though criticized by some for surrounding himself at first with a small cadre of South Korean staffers—often accused of blocking access to their boss—Ban is not alone among UN leaders who have relied heavily on trusted nationals. His rebuttal is that all South Koreans on his staff are highly qualified.

He is proud of helping to establish UN Women, the superagency aimed at women's empowerment, first headed by former Chilean president Michelle Bachelet. Only a few women were in important positions in the Secretariat when he took office. He says he has increased their numbers at the assistant secretary-general level by 40 percent. He also changed the gender composition of the staff selection committee to make it more balanced and insists that at least one woman's name must appear on any suggested hiring list. After the gang rape and death of a 23-year-old Indian woman in December 2012, Ban urged the government to reform its laws and punish the attackers. "Every girl and woman has the right to be respected, valued, and protected," he said.[220]

Ban has tried to make a number of other reforms in UN staffing and programs. Some succeeded. Some did not. Once in a long while, his frustration would surface.

"When you are trying to change the status quo, people will resist," he once reminded a UN audience. "Here at the UN, unfortunately, I see people too often putting their own interests first.... I see too many turf fights. Department heads squabble among themselves over posts and budgets...as though they somehow owned them. People forget. We are here to act... When you work for the UN, please leave your ego at the door." [221]

Ban certainly has done a great deal of talking over the years, making as many as 10 speeches a day. Yet he rarely makes headlines. His low-key delivery has been known to lull a few listeners to sleep. As one UN official put it, "No matter what he says, he just can't make a splash." A June 2009 *Wall Street Journal*/NBC News poll found that 81 percent of Americans either had never heard of him or had no opinion of him. Ban himself said at the time, "I am known as invisible man."[222]

"His big problem is that he doesn't speak English well and therefore he doesn't project well," said Columbia's Stephen Schlesinger. "Yet if you actually look at the content of what he's said on any number of issues, I think he's the most outspoken secretary-general that I've ever seen.... He does have backbone."[223]

"One doesn't come away from a public lecture [by Ban] in awe, saying that it was brilliant," commented Fletcher's Sung-Yoon Lee, "but in personal conversation, a smaller group, he comes across as an impressively erudite, balanced, and articulate person."[224]

"I've seen so many secretaries-general in the past who are so ego driven," commented Edward Luck. "Ban doesn't need to see his name in lights. His sense of commitment is very, very strong. You can tell pretty easily what he cares about.... If the results don't come, he's all the more determined to keep pushing."[225]

Often, particularly as he travels, the honest emotions of this practiced diplomat do rise to the surface. When visiting a Somali refugee camp near the Kenyan border in December 2011, Ban admitted that he heard firsthand of so many human difficulties that "my heart and mind are crying inside."[226] Similarly, when he flew by helicopter over flooded areas of Thailand the month before, he said he was truly saddened, humbled, and shocked by what he saw.[227]

Ban feels an especially strong commitment to the international community's obligation to help those in need with security, food, and shelter, said Meyer: "And he will tell you that the UN saved...lives in Korea and helped it rebuild."[228]

Some of Ban's best moments with an audience have come when he goes off script, as he did in his speech at Oxford University in February 2011. His focus was the United Nations' responsibility to protect (R2P) civilians.

"We maybe had one sentence in the speech on the role of regional and subregional organizations," recalled Edward Luck, one of the writers. "He sort of read it, and then he stopped and said, 'You know, we really should think about this. How is it that the founders of the UN were so farsighted that they included a whole chapter in the Charter on regional arrangements that didn't exist at the time? They foresaw that someday...these would be integral to everything the UN does.' It was a very important insight, very personal, and people related to it."[229]

Ban has bolstered the United Nations' partnership with regional organizations. Rather than viewing them as marginalizing the United Nations' role, as some critics allege, Ban has actively sought their aid in peace and security efforts.[230] Speaking to leaders at the Association of Southeast Asian Nations (ASEAN) Summit in Bali in the fall of 2011, for instance, he strongly urged them to take the lead on issues from climate change and human rights to helping Myanmar move to more democratic rule. "The world needs your help," he insisted.[231]

Some critics have argued that Ban too often defers to the P5 nations on the Security Council, particularly to the United States.

The Secretary-General "has critics but as far as I know, he has no enemies," noted Fletcher's Sung-Yoon Lee. "It would be very uncharacteristic of Mr. Ban to pick a fight."[232]

Like several of his predecessors, Ban has complained of how long it takes, sometimes six months to two years, to recruit needed peacekeepers when conflicts arise. Like those before him, he would like to see the United Nations have a standing army. Facing the reality that such a move is unlikely, he continues to urge national governments to have their own standby military arrangement.[233]

Ban took on the United Nations' top job in the aftermath of the oil-for-food scandal, a time when many people were accusing the organization of corruption and inefficiency. He promised to do his best to make the United Nations more efficient, transparent, and accountable.

As he knows full well, there is always more to be done. On a table in his residence sits a framed March 5, 2007, *Newsweek* cover (Pacific Edition). It features his picture with the line "Why This Man Will Fail."[234] The article inside stresses the myriad global challenges he faced in taking on the job. Though Ban certainly has not been able to accomplish all that he hoped, it is not for lack of trying. In that sense, the "failure" label is unlikely to stick.

Before Ban first took office, he was described as "a man with a truly global mind at the helm of the world's only universal organization" by his predecessor Kofi Annan. While the first UN secretary-general, Trygve Lie, once called the post "the most impossible job on earth," Annan said that, while that description may be true, he would also call it "the best possible job on earth."[235] Certainly Ban Ki-moon and the other secretaries-general have experienced moments when they shared both views of the job.

LIST OF INTERVIEWS

Arria, Diego

Boutros-Ghali, Boutros

Claude, Inis L., Jr.

Eckhard, Fred

de Soto, Álvaro

Finger, Seymour Maxwell

Finkelstein, Lawrence S.

Franck, Thomas

Gaer, Felice

Gordenker, Leon

Hannum, Hurst

Jacobson, Harold K.

Krasno, Jean

Laurenti, Jeffrey

Lee, Sung-Yoon

Luck, Edward C.

Luers, William J.

Maksoud, Clovis

Malone, David M.

Meyer, Michael R.

Menon, Bhaskar

Okun, Herbert S.

Picco, Giandomenico

Rikhye, Indar

Rivlin, Benjamin

Schlesinger, Stephen C.

Schoettle, Enid

Sherry, George

Sills, Joe

Sutterlin, James

Thornburgh, Richard

Urquhart, Sir Brian

Waldheim, Kurt

Wedgewood, Ruth

Weiss, Thomas

End Notes

Chapter One: Why a United Nations?

1. Stephen C. Schlesinger, *Act of Creation: The Founding of the United Nations* (Boulder, CO: Westview), 292.
2. Sir Brian Urquhart, interview with author.
3. Ibid.
4. Ibid.
5. Cited in Schlesinger, 251.
6. Trygve Lie, *In the Cause of Peace* (New York: Macmillan, 1954), 36–38.
7. Sir Brian Urquhart, *A Life in Peace and War* (New York: W. W. Norton, 1987), 93.

Chapter Two: The World's Most Impossible Job

1. Walter Lippmann, *The New York Herald-Tribune*, November 7, 1961, cited in *The UN Secretary-General: His Role in World Politics,* Commission to Study the Organization of Peace, 14th Report (New York: January 1962), 53.
2. James Holtje, *Divided It Stands: Can the United Nations Work?* (Atlanta: Turner, 1995), 106
3. U Thant, *View from the UN* (New York: Doubleday, 1978), 31.
4. Kurt Waldheim, interview with author.
5. Javier Pérez de Cuéllar, *Pilgrimage for Peace: A Secretary-General's Memoir* (New York: St. Martin's, 1997), 28.
6. Boutros Boutros-Ghali, *Unvanquished: A US–UN Saga* (New York: Random House, 1999), 9.
7. Boutros Boutros-Ghali, "Global Leadership after the Cold War," *Foreign Affairs,* March–April 1996.
8. Kofi Annan, "Remarks at Council on Foreign Relations Inauguration of Peter G. Peterson Center of International Studies," (speech, New York, January 19, 1999).
9. Sir Brian Urquhart, interview with author.
10. Sir Brian Urquhart, *A Life in Peace and War* (New York: W. W. Norton, 1987), 277.
11. Inis L. Claude Jr., interview with author.
12. Edward Newman, *The UN Secretary-General from the Cold War to the New Era: A Global and Peace Security Mandate?* (New York: St. Martin's, 1998), 14.
13. Claude, interview.
14. Waldheim, interview.

15. Herbert Okun, interview with author.
16. Claude, interview.
17. Boutros-Ghali, "Global Leadership," *Foreign Affairs.*
18. Claude, interview.
19. James Sutterlin, interview with author.
20. Claude, interview.
21. Thant, *View,* 43.
22. Sutterlin, interview.
23. Urquhart, interview.
24. Leon Gordenker, interview with author.
25. Paul Kennedy, *The Parliament of Man: The Past, Present, and Future of the United Nations* (New York: Random House, 2006), 60.
26. Hurst Hannum, interview with author.
27. Okun, interview.

Chapter Three: Trygve Lie

1. Trygve Lie, *In the Cause of Peace: Seven Years with the United Nations* (New York: Macmillan, 1954), 17.
2. Ibid., 3.
3. Ibid., 17.
4. Leon Gordenker, *The UN Secretary-General and Secretariat* (New York: Routledge, 2005), 10–11.
5. Sir Brian Urquhart, *A Life in Peace and War* (New York: W. W. Norton, 1987), 99.
6. Ibid., 100.
7. Stephen Schwebel, *The Secretary-General of the United Nations: His Political Powers and Practice* (Cambridge: Harvard University Press, 1952), 54.
8. Urquhart, *A Life,* 100.
9. Lie, *In the Cause of Peace,* 42.
10. Cited in Stanley Meisler, *United Nations: The First Fifty Years* (New York: Atlantic Monthly, 1995), 34.
11. Lie, *In the Cause of Peace,* 30.
12. Urquhart, *A Life,* 102.
13. Cited in Thomas Franck, *Nation against Nation: What Happened to the UN Dream and What the US Can Do about It* (New York: Oxford University Press, 1985), 27.
14. Lie, *In the Cause of Peace,* 79–88.
15. Ibid., 80.
16. Ibid., 83.
17. Ibid.

18. Ibid., 85.
19. Schwebel, *The Secretary-General*, 94.
20. Lie, *In the Cause of Peace*, 75.
21. Ibid.
22. Schwebel, *The Secretary-General*, 90.
23. James Barros, *Trygve Lie and the Cold War: The UN Secretary-General Pursues Peace, 1946–1953* (DeKalb: Northern Illinois University Press, 1989), 105.
24. Ibid., 114.
25. Harry S. Truman, *Memoirs: Years of Trial and Hope, 1946–1952* (Garden City, NY: Doubleday, 1956), 156.
26. Lie, *In the Cause of Peace*, 158.
27. Ibid., 194.
28. Ibid., 168.
29. Ibid., 170–71.
30. Ibid., 175.
31. Leon Gordenker, *The UN Secretary-General and the Maintenance of Peace* (New York: Columbia University Press, 1967), 159.
32. Schwebel, *The Secretary-General*, 32.
33. Lie, *In the Cause of Peace*, 188.
34. Nitza Nachmias, "The Role of the Secretary-General in the Israeli–Arab and the Cyprus Disputes," in *The Challenging Role of the UN Secretary-General: Making the "Most Impossible Job in the World" Possible*, eds. Benjamin Rivlin and Leon Gordenker (Westport, CT: Praeger, 1993), 113.
35. Cited in Nachmias, "The Role of the Secretary-General," 114.
36. Sir Brian Urquhart, interview with the author.
37. James Sutterlin, interview with the author.
38. Urquhart, interview.
39. Barros, *Trygve*, 168.
40. Meisler, *United Nations*, 53.
41. Urquhart, *A Life*, 114.
42. Barros, *Trygve*, 55.
43. Gordenker, *Maintenance of Peace*, 106.
44. Lie, *In the Cause of Peace*, 261.
45. Schwebel, *The Secretary-General*, 158.
46. Franck, *Nation against Nation*, 130.
47. Leon Gordenker, interview with the author.
48. Lie, *In the Cause of Peace*, 328.
49. Franck, *Nation against Nation*, 123.
50. Meisler, *United Nations*, 59.
51. Schwebel, *The Secretary-General*, 106–7.

52. Robert E. Riggs, Jack C. Plano, and Lawrence Ziring, *The United Nations: International Organization and World Politics* (Pacific Grove, CA: Brooks/Cole, 1988), 122.

53. Sir Brian Urquhart, *Hammarskjöld* (New York: W. W. Norton, 1994), 7.

54. Lie, *In the Cause of Peace*, 335.

55. Ibid., 342.

56. Ibid.

57. Ibid., 323.

58. Sutterlin, interview.

59. Ibid.

60. Inis L. Claude Jr., interview with author.

61. Urquhart, interview.

62. Gordenker, interview.

63. Lie, *In the Cause of Peace*, 399.

64. Shirley Hazzard, *Defeat of an Ideal* (Boston: Little, Brown, 1973), 20.

65. Dean Acheson, *Present at the Creation: My Years in the State Department* (New York: W. W. Norton, 1969), 698.

66. Lie, *In the Cause of Peace*, 369.

67. Barros, *Trygve*, 36.

68. Lie, *In the Cause of Peace*, 375–76.

69. Gordenker, *Maintenance of Peace*, 41.

70. Lie, *In the Cause of Peace*, 383.

71. Jeffrey Laurenti, interview with author.

72. Franck, *Nation against Nation*, 153.

73. Lie, *In the Cause of Peace*, 367.

74. Ibid., 418–19.

75. Linda M. Fasulo, *Representing America: Experiences of US Diplomats at the UN* (New York: Facts on File, 1984), 258.

76. Edward C. Luck, interview with the author.

77. Barros, *Trygve*, 347.

78. Julian Huxley, *Memories II* (New York: Harper and Row, 1973), 37.

79. Schwebel, *The Secretary-General*, 165.

80. Thomas Boudreau, *Sheathing the Sword: The UN Secretary-General and the Prevention of International Conflict* (Westport, CT: Greenwood, 1991), 26.

81. Urquhart, *A Life*, 103.

82. Sutterlin, interview.

83. Lie, *In the Cause of Peace*, 418.

84. Barros, *Trygve*, 31.

85. Urquhart, *A Life*, 100.

86. Ibid.

87. Urquhart, interview.
88. Barros, *Trygve*, 347.
89. Ibid., 353.
90. Gordenker, interview.
91. Lie, *In the Cause of Peace*, 418–21.
92. Edward Newman, *The UN Secretary-General from the Cold War to the New Era: . A Global Peace and Security Mandate?* (New York: St. Martin's, 1998), 38–39.

Chapter Four: Dag Hammarskjöld

1. Trygve Lie, In the Cause of Peace: Seven Years with the United Nations (New York: Macmillan, 1954), 417.
2. Sir Brian Urquhart, Hammarskjöld (New York: Alfred A. Knopf, 1972), 12.
3. Remarks on Arrival, UN press release SG/287. (April 9, 1953).
4. Peter B. Heller, *The United Nations under Dag Hammarskjöld, 1953–1961* (Lanham, MD: Scarecrow, 2001), 12.
5. Ibid., 4.
6. Paul Gore-Booth, *With Great Truth and Respect* (London: Constable, 1974), 166–67.
7. Urquhart, *Hammarskjöld*, 13.
8. Seymour Maxwell Finger, interview with the author.
9. Sir Brian Urquhart, interview with the author.
10. Cited in the *Montreal Star*, September 19, 1961.
11. Urquhart, *Hammarskjöld*, 29.
12. Ibid., 28.
13. Leon Gordenker, interview with author.
14. Andrew W. Cordier, "Motivations and Methods of Dag Hammarskjöld," in *Paths to World Order*, eds. Andrew W. Cordier and Kenneth L. Maxwell (New York: Columbia University Press, 1967), 6.
15. Lester B. Pearson and Robert W. Reford, "Dag Hammarskjöld: Strength for Peace," *International Journal* 17 (1961): 6.
16. Urquhart, *Hammarskjöld*, 84–85.
17. Ibid., 31.
18. Inis L. Claude Jr., interview with author.
19. Indar Rikhye, interview with author.
20. Ibid.
21. Heller, *The United Nations*, 3.
22. Ibid, 4.
23. Urquhart, *Hammarskjöld*, 43.
24. Sir Brian Urquhart, *A Life in Peace and War* (New York: W. W. Norton, 1987), 126.

25. Urquhart, *Hammarskjöld*, 27.
26. Urquhart, *A Life*, 126.
27. Urquhart, *Hammarskjöld*, 77.
28. Urquhart, interview.
29. Urquhart, *Hammarskjöld*, 30.
30. Urquhart, interview.
31. Urquhart, *Hammarskjöld*, 51.
32. James Jonah, "Secretariat: Independence and Reform," in *The Oxford Handbook on the United Nations*, eds. Thomas G. Weiss and Sam Daws (New York: Oxford University Press, 2007), 162.
33. Gordenker, interview.
34. Urquhart, *Hammarskjöld*, 51.
35. Urquhart, interview.
36. Kent J. Kille, *From Manager to Visionary: The Secretary-General of the United Nations* (New York: Palgrave Macmillan, 2006), 90–91.
37. Urquhart, *A Life*, 127.
38. Urquhart, *Hammarskjöld*, 117.
39. George Sherry, interview with author.
40. Urquhart, interview.
41. Urquhart, *Hammarskjöld*, 131.
42. Claude, interview.
43. Lawrence Finkelstein, interview with author.
44. Urquhart, *Hammarskjöld*, 145.
45. Leon Gordenker, *The UN Secretary-General and the Maintenance of Peace* (New York: Columbia University Press, 1967), 167.
46. Urquhart, *A Life*, 132.
47. Ibid., 133.
48. James Sutterlin, interview with author.
49. Leon Gordenker, *The UN Secretary-General and Secretariat* (New York: Routledge, 2005), 43.
50. Claude, interview.
51. Urquhart, *A Life*, 133.
52. Urquhart, *Hammarskjöld*, 190.
53. Urquhart, *A Life*, 134.
54. Thomas Franck, *Nation against Nation: What Happened to the UN Dream and What the US Can Do about It* (New York: Oxford University Press, 1985), 43.
55. Urquhart, *A Life*, 138.
56. Linda M. Fasulo, *Representing America: Experiences of US Diplomats at the UN* (New York: Facts on File, 1984), 50–51.
57. Urquhart, *A Life*, 137.

58. Stanley Meisler, *United Nations: The First Fifty Years* (New York: Atlantic Monthly, 1995), 95.

59. Michael Howard, "The Historical Development of the UN's Role in International Security," in *United Nations, Divided World: The United Nations' Roles in International Relations*, eds. Adam Roberts and Benedict Kingsbury, 2nd ed. (New York: Oxford University Press, 1993), 67.

60. Heller, *The United Nations*, 75.

61. Urquhart, *A Life*, 138.

62. Reprinted from the *Washington Post* in 105 Congressional Record, Appendix A23 (January 9, 1959).

63. Urquhart, *Hammarskjöld*, 243.

64. Ibid., 251–52.

65. Gordenker, *Maintenance of Peace*, 76.

66. Paul Kennedy, *The Parliament of Man: The Past, Present and Future of the United Nations* (New York: Random House, 2006), 61.

67. Franck, *Nation against Nation*, 127.

68. Seymour Maxwell Finger, *American Ambassadors at the UN: People, Politics and Bureaucracy in Making Foreign Policy* (New York: UN Institute for Training and Research, UNITAR RR/36, 1988), 101.

69. Franck, *Nation against Nation*, 146.

70. Urquhart, *Hammarskjöld*, 265.

71. Gordenker, interview.

72. Urquhart, *A Life*, 142.

73. Heller, *The United Nations*, 57.

74. Thomas Boudreau, *Sheathing the Sword: The UN Secretary-General and the Prevention of International Conflict* (Westport, CT: Greenwood, 1991), 47.

75. Finger, *American Ambassadors*, 102.

76. Franck, *Nation against Nation*, 146.

77. Heller, *The United Nations*, 82.

78. Ibid., 83.

79. Gordenker, *Maintenance of Peace*, 76.

80. Urquhart, *Hammarskjöld*, 353–54.

81. Urquhart, interview.

82. Jean E. Krasno, *The United Nations: Confronting the Challenges of a Global Society* (Boulder, CO: Lynne Rienner, 2004), 233.

83. Franck, *Nation against Nation*, 125.

84. Urquhart, *A Life*, 156.

85. Finkelstein, interview.

86. Edward C. Luck, interview with author.

87. Urquhart, *Hammarskjöld*, 423–24.

88. James Reston, "United Nations: A Refuge of Sanity in a Silly World," *New York Times*, August 9, 1960.

89. Urquhart, *A Life*, 161.

90. U Thant, *View From the UN* (Garden City, NY: Doubleday, 1978), 109.

91. Sir Brian Urquhart, "The Tragedy of Lumumba," *New York Review of Books* 48, no. 15 (October 4, 2001).

92. Gordenker, interview.

93. Urquhart, interview.

94. Ibid.

95. Jonah, "Secretariat," 162.

96. Urquhart, *Hammarskjöld*, 466.

97. Heller, *The United Nations*, 259.

98. Urquhart, *A Life*, 173.

99. Heller, *The United Nations*, 138.

100. Meisler, *United Nations*, 125.

101. Urquhart, *A Life*, 175.

102. Sherry, interview.

103. Urquhart, interview.

104. Luck, interview.

105. Alan James, "The Secretary-General as an Independent Political Actor," in *The Challenging Role of the UN Secretary-General: Making the "Most Impossible Job in the World" Possible*, eds. Benjamin Rivlin and Leon Gordenker (Westport, CT: Praeger, 1993), 27.

106. Boudreau, *Sheathing the Sword*, 55.

107. Gordenker, interview.

108. Harold Jacobson, interview with the author.

109. Gordenker, *Maintenance of Peace*, 82–83.

110. Sutterlin, interview.

111. Claude, interview.

112. Dag Hammarskjöld, *Markings* (New York: Alfred A. Knopf, 1964), 166.

113. Urquhart, interview.

114. Boudreau, *Sheathing the Sword*, 106–107.

115. Finkelstein, interview.

116. Urquhart, *Hammarskjöld*, 48.

117. Ibid., 496–99.

118. Urquhart, interview.

119. Sherry, interview.

120. Rikhye, interview.

121. Inis L. Claude Jr., *Swords into Plowshares: The Problems and Progress of International Organization*, 3rd ed. (New York: Random House, 1967), 285–86.

122. Claude, interview.
123. Thomas Franck, interview with author.
124. Franck, *Nation against Nation*, 130.
125. Urquhart, *Hammarskjöld*, 51.
126. Gordenker, interview.
127. Claude, interview.
128. Gordenker, *Maintenance of Peace*, 157.
129. Urquhart, *A Life*, 140.
130. Urquhart, *Hammarskjöld*, 28.
131. Urquhart, *A Life*, 124.
132. Urquhart, *Hammarskjöld*, 23.
133. Kennedy, *The Parliament of Man*, 60.
134. Claude, interview.
135. Meisler, *United Nations*, 75.
136. Finger, interview.
137. Gordenker, interview.
138. Urquhart, interview.
139. Gordenker, interview.
140. Benjamin Rivlin, "The Changing International Political Climate and the Secretary-General," in *The Challenging Role of the UN Secretary-General*, eds. Rivlin and Gordenker, 17.
141. Franck, *Nation against Nation*, 127.
142. Urquhart, interview.
143. Ibid.
144. Urquhart, *Hammarskjöld*, 50.
145. Jeffery Laurenti, interview with author.
146. Luck, interview.
147. Sherry, interview.

Chapter Five: U Thant

1. U Thant, *View from the UN* (Garden City, NY: Doubleday, 1978), 3.
2. Ibid.
3. Walter Lippmann, *New York Herald-Tribune*, April 16, 1961, cited in June Bingham, *U Thant: The Search for Peace* (New York: Alfred A. Knopf, 1966), 248.
4. Leon Gordenker, *The UN Secretary-General and the Maintenance of Peace* (New York: Columbia University Press, 1967), 50.
5. Thant, *View*, 15.
6. Cited in Bingham, *U Thant*, 257.
7. Ibid., 281.

8. Plenary Meeting of the United Nations General Assembly, November 3, 1961, cited in Bernard J. Firestone, *The United Nations under U Thant, 1961–1971* (Lanham, MD: Scarecrow, 2001), 114.

9. Firestone, *The United Nations*, xx.

10. Thant, *View*, 36.

11. Ibid., 39.

12. Ibid., 36–37.

13. *London Observer*, September 3, 1961, cited in Thant, *View*, 6.

14. Thant, *View*, 21.

15. Ibid., 20.

16. Bingham, *U Thant*, 11–12.

17. Ibid., 6–7.

18. "Adlai Stevenson Presents," WABC-TV, October 29, 1961.

19. Indar Rikhye, interview with author.

20. Cited in Bingham, *U Thant*, 10.

21. Firestone, *The United Nations*, 63.

22. Sir Brian Urquhart, *A Life in Peace and War* (New York: W. W. Norton, 1987), 193.

23. Thant, *View*, 108.

24. Cited in Firestone, *The United Nations*, 116.

25. Ibid., 7.

26. Thant, *View*, 140.

27. James Dobbins et al., *The United Nations' Role in Nation-Building: From the Congo to Iraq* (Santa Monica, CA: Rand, 2005), 17.

28. Urquhart, *A Life*, 193.

29. Thant, *View*, 143–44.

30. Ibid., 107.

31. Sir Brian Urquhart, interview with author.

32. George Sherry, interview with author.

33. Rikhye, interview.

34. Ibid.

35. Thant, *View*, 144–45.

36. Ibid., 107.

37. Rikhye, interview.

38. Linda M. Fasulo, *Representing America: Experiences of US Diplomats at the UN* (New York: Facts on File, 1984), 60.

39. Firestone, *The United Nations*, 117.

40. Thant, *View*, 158.

41. Ibid., 156–57.

42. Anthony Parsons, "The UN and the National Interests of States," in *United Nations, Divided World: The United Nations' Roles in International Relations*, eds.

Adam Roberts and Benedict Kingsbury (New York: Oxford University Press, 1994), 107.

43. Urquhart, *A Life*, 19.
44. Thant, *View*, 167–68.
45. Firestone, *The United Nations*, 14.
46. Thant, *View*, 182–83.
47. Ibid., 186.
48. Rikhye, interview.
49. Benjamin Rivlin, "The Changing International Political Climate and the Secretary-General," in *The Challenging Role of the Secretary-General*, eds. Benjamin Rivlin and Leon Gordenker (Westport, CT: Praeger, 1993), 7.
50. Thant, *View*, 158.
51. Theodore Sorensen, "The Leader Who Led," *New York Times*, October 18, 1997.
52. Thomas Franck, interview with author.
53. Lawrence Finkelstein, interview with author.
54. Seymour Maxwell Finger, interview with author.
55. Thomas G. Weiss, interview with author.
56. Urquhart, interview.
57. Bingham, *U Thant*, 274.
58. Firestone, *The United Nations*, 15.
59. Edward Newman, *The UN Secretary-General from the Cold War to the New Era: A Global Peace and Security Mandate?* (New York: St. Martin's, 1998), 50.
60. Thomas Boudreau, *Sheathing the Sword: The UN Secretary-General and the Prevention of International Conflict* (Westport, CT: Greenwood, 1991), 70.
61. Thant, *View*, xvi–xvii.
62. Ibid., 58.
63. Ibid.
64. Raymond Daniell, "Thant Deplores Talk of Using Atomic Weapons in Vietnam War," *New York Times*, May 27, 1964.
65. Thomas Franck, *Nation against Nation: What Happened to the UN Dream and What the US Can Do about It* (New York: Oxford University Press, 1985), 154.
66. Thant, *View*, 66.
67. Ibid., 82.
68. Ibid., 67.
69. Dean Rusk and Tom Rusk, *As I Saw It* (New York: W. W. Norton, 1990), 463.
70. Stanley Meisler, *United Nations: The First Fifty Years* (New York: Atlantic Monthly, 1995), 162.
71. Thant, *View*, 67–69.
72. Rusk and Rusk, *As I Saw It*, 462–64.
73. Ibid., 463.

74. Urquhart, interview.
75. Finkelstein, interview.
76. Rikhye, interview.
77. Urquhart, interview.
78. Franck, *Nation against Nation*, 157.
79. Gordenker, *Maintenance of Peace*, 198.
80. Thant, *View*, 403.
81. Urquhart, *A Life*, 205
82. Thant, *View*, 400.
83. Thant, *View*, 408–9.
84. Firestone, *The United Nations*, 41.
85. Thant, *View*, 415.
86. Urquhart, interview.
87. Franck, *Nation against Nation*, 150.
88. Gordenker, *Maintenance of Peace*, 60.
89. Franck, *Nation against Nation*, 125.
90. Indar Rikhye, *The Sinai Blunder* (New Delhi: Oxford & IBH, 1978), 17.
91. Thant, *View*, 222; Firestone, *The United Nations*, 84.
92. Rikhye, interview.
93. Thant, *View*, 225–26.
94. Urquhart, *A Life*, 210.
95. Thant, *View*, 223.
96. Urquhart, *A Life*, 210–11; Thant, *View*, 231.
97. Finger, interview.
98. Ilene R. Prusher, "Forty Years Later, Two Views from the West Bank's Road 60," *Christian Science Monitor,* June 5, 2007.
99. Nitza Nachmias, "The Role of the Secretary-General in the Israeli–Arab and the Cyprus Disputes," in *The Challenging Role of the UN Secretary-General*, eds. Rivlin and Gordenker, 120.
100. Thant, *View*, 232.
101. Cited in Thant, *View*, 230.
102. Alan James, "The Secretary-General as an Independent Political Actor," in *The Challenging Role of the UN Secretary-General*, eds. Rivlin and Gordenker, 27.
103. Paul Gore-Booth, *With Great Truth and Respect* (London: Constable, 1974), 365.
104. Sherry, interview.
105. Cited in Franck, *Nation against Nation*, 90, footnote 75.
106. Inis Claude Jr., interview with author.
107. Newman, *The UN Secretary-General*, 50.
108. Urquhart, interview.

109. Ibid.
110. Rikhye, interview.
111. Kurt Waldheim, interview with author.
112. Thant, *View*, 493–94.
113. Ibid., 27.
114. Leon Gordenker, interview with author.
115. Thant, *View*, 49.
116. Cited in Bingham, *U Thant*, 276.
117. Sir Brian Urquhart, United Nations Correspondents Association press conference, New York, June 7, 1995.
118. Thant, *View*, 50.
119. Ibid., 51.
120. Ibid., 46.
121. Ibid., 27.
122. Urquhart, *A Life*, 190.
123. Bhaskar Menon, interview with author.
124. Weiss, interview.
125. Thant, *View*, 60–61.
126. Claude, interview.
127. Urquhart, *A Life*, 221.
128. Boudreau, *Sheathing the Sword*, 75.
129. Bhaskar Menon, "The Secretary-General," *Undiplomatic Times*, part 3 (New York: Impact Communications Consultants, June 2001).
130. Thant, *View*, 33–34.
131. Ibid., 27.
132. Ibid., 32.
133. Urquhart, *A Life*, 190.
134. Bingham, *U Thant*, 10.
135. Thant, *View*, 27.
136. Bingham, *U Thant*, 117.
137. Ibid., 39.
138. Newman, *The UN Secretary-General*, 49–52.
139. Urquhart, *A Life*, 190.
140. Urquhart, United Nations Correspondents Association press conference.
141. Urquhart, interview.
142. Ibid.
143. Sherry, interview.
144. Bingham, *U Thant*, 20.
145. Thant, *View*, 241.
146. Newman, *The UN Secretary-General*, 49.

Chapter Six: Kurt Waldheim

1. Kurt Waldheim, In the Eye of the Storm: The Memoirs of Kurt Waldheim (Bethesda, MD: Adler & Adler, 1986), 37–38.
2. Ibid., 38.
3. Ibid., 36.
4. Ibid., 35–36.
5. Stanley Meisler, United Nations: The First Fifty Years (New York: Atlantic Monthly, 1995), 185, 194.
6. Seymour Maxwell Finger and Arnold A. Saltzman, Bending with the Winds: Kurt Waldheim and the United Nations (New York: Praeger, 1990), 23.
7. Seymour Maxwell Finger, interview with author.
8. Robert E. Herzstein, Waldheim: The Missing Years (New York: Morrow, 1988), 259–60.
9. Meisler, United Nations, 187–88.
10. Finger and Saltzman, Bending, 29.
11. Waldheim, Eye of the Storm, 38.
12. Ibid., 41.
13. James Daniel Ryan, The United Nations under Kurt Waldheim, 1972–1981 (Lanham, MD: Scarecrow, 2001), 23.
14. Ibid., 24.
15. Finger and Saltzman, Bending, 56.
16. Waldheim, Eye of the Storm, 45–46.
17. Finger and Saltzman, Bending, 71.
18. Ryan, The United Nations, 25.
19. Kurt Waldheim, interview with author.
20. Finger and Saltzman, Bending, 74.
21. Bhaskar Menon, "The Secretary-General," Undiplomatic Times, part 4 (New York: Impact Communications Consultants, June 2001).
22. Bhaskar Menon, interview with author.
23. Clovis Maksoud, interview with author.
24. Ryan, The United Nations, 17.
25. Sir Brian Urquhart, A Life in Peace and War (New York: W. W. Norton, 1987), 229.
26. Ibid.
27. Meisler, United Nations, 200.
28. Waldheim, interview.
29. Waldheim, Eye of the Storm, 39.
30. Thomas Franck, Nation against Nation: What Happened to the UN Dream and What the US Can Do about It (New York: Oxford Press, 1985), 4.
31. Waldheim, interview.

32. Ibid.
33. Ibid.
34. Ryan, *The United Nations*, 21.
35. Waldheim, *Eye of the Storm*,150.
36. Ryan, *The United Nations*, 182.
37. Ryan, *The United Nations*, 27.
38. Waldheim, *Eye of the Storm*, 41.
39. W. Ofuatey-Kodjoe, "The Role of the UN Secretary-General in the Decolonization of Namibia," in *The Challenging Role of the UN Secretary-General*, eds. Benjamin Rivlin and Leon Gordenker (Westport, CT: Praeger, 1993), 134.
40. Ryan, *The United Nations*, 26.
41. Waldheim, interview.
42. Waldheim, *Eye of the Storm*,100.
43. Urquhart, *A Life*, 308.
44. Waldheim, *Eye of the Storm*, 57.
45. Ibid, 58–59.
46. Urquhart, *A Life*, 236.
47. Franck, *Nation against Nation*, 171.
48. Urquhart, *A Life*, 237.
49. Waldheim, *Eye of the Storm*, 61.
50. Waldheim, interview.
51. Franck, *Nation against Nation*, 172.
52. Urquhart, *A Life*, 240.
53. Edward Newman, *The UN Secretary-General from the Cold War to the New Era: A Global Peace and Security Mandate?* (New York: St. Martin's, 1998), 56.
54. Waldheim, interview.
55. Ibid.
56. Newman, *The UN Secretary-General*, 56, and Urquhart, *A Life*, 243–44.
57. Thomas Franck, interview with the author.
58. Urquhart, *A Life*, 245.
59. Waldheim, *Eye of the Storm*, 72.
60. Ryan, *The United Nations*, 203.
61. Urquhart, *A Life*, 260.
62. Ibid., 249.
63. Meisler, *United Nations*, 198.
64. Alan James, "The Secretary-General as an Independent Political Actor," in *The Challenging Role of the UN Secretary-General*, eds. Rivlin and Gordenker, 30.
65. Kurt Waldheim, *The Challenge of Peace* (New York: Rawson, Wade, 1980), 84.
66. Waldheim, *Eye of the Storm*, 55.
67. Waldheim, interview.

68. Ibid.
69. Meisler, *United Nations*, 213.
70. Ibid, 215.
71. Waldheim, *Eye of the Storm*, 44.
72. Finger, interview.
73. Ibid.
74. Waldheim, *Eye of the Storm*, 87.
75. Ibid., 83.
76. Waldheim, interview.
77. Waldheim, *Eye of the Storm*, 85.
78. Ibid.
79. Urquhart, *A Life*, 257.
80. Waldheim, *Eye of the Storm*, 86.
81. Ryan, *The United Nations*, 69, 219.
82. Waldheim, *Eye of the Storm*, 78.
83. Ibid., 92.
84. Franck, *Nation against Nation*, 139.
85. Nitza Nachmias, "The Role of the Secretary-General in the Israeli–Arab and the Cyprus Disputes," in *The Challenging Role of the UN Secretary-General*, eds. Rivlin and Gordenker, 125.
86. Ibid.
87. Ibid.
88. Urquhart, *A Life*, 259.
89. Waldheim, *Eye of the Storm*, 92.
90. George Sherry, interview with author.
91. Urquhart, *A Life*, 268.
92. Ibid., 265.
93. Waldheim, *Eye of the Storm*, 137–38.
94. Ibid.
95. Ibid., 142.
96. Franck, *Nation against Nation*, 141.
97. Ryan, *The United Nations*, 73.
98. Thomas Franck, "The Good Offices Function of the UN," in *United Nations, Divided World: The United Nations' Roles in International Relations*, eds. Adam Roberts and Benedict Kingsbury (New York: Oxford University Press, 1993), 147.
99. Waldheim, interview.
100. Urquhart, *A Life*, 268.
101. Ibid., 270.
102. Ryan, *The United Nations*, 256.
103. Waldheim, *Challenge*, 93; *Eye of the Storm*, 188.

104. Meisler, *United Nations*, 198.
105. Waldheim, *Eye of the Storm*, 187.
106. Ryan, *The United Nations*, 257.
107. Waldheim, *Eye of the Storm*, 191.
108. Ibid., 192.
109. Waldheim, *Challenge*, 97.
110. Ibid.
111. Waldheim, *Eye of the Storm*, 196.
112. Urquhart, *A Life*, 294.
113. Waldheim, *Eye of the Storm*, 196.
114. Ibid., 199.
115. Waldheim, interview.
116. Finger and Saltzman, *Bending*, 62.
117. Franck, *Nation against Nation*, 126.
118. Ryan, *The United Nations*, 277–78.
119. Waldheim, *Eye of the Storm*, 4.
120. Waldheim, interview.
121. Franck, *Nation against Nation*, 141.
122. Waldheim, *Eye of the Storm*, 2.
123. Cameron R. Hume, *The United Nations, Iran and Iraq* (Bloomington: Indiana University Press, 1994), 32.
124. Waldheim, *Eye of the Storm*, 1.
125. Waldheim, interview.
126. Waldheim, *Eye of the Storm*, 5.
127. Ibid., 6.
128. Ayatollah Ruhollah Khomeini, *New York Times*, December 12, 1979, cited in Hume, *The United Nations*, 32.
129. Waldheim, *Eye of the Storm*, 6–7.
130. Ibid., 8–9.
131. Ibid., 9–10.
132. Ibid., 10.
133. Ibid.
134. Ibid., 5.
135. "Waldheim Doubts Early Release of the Hostages," *New York Times*, January 5, 1980.
136. Waldheim, *Eye of the Storm*, 11.
137. Ibid., 164.
138. Hume, *The United Nations*, 34.
139. Waldheim, *Eye of the Storm*, 165.
140. Waldheim, interview.

141. Leon Gordenker, interview with author.
142. Sir Brian Urquhart, interview with author.
143. Ibid.
144. Urquhart, *A Life*, 324.
145. Hume, *The United Nations*, 39.
146. Ibid., 38.
147. Javier Pérez de Cuéllar, *Pilgrimage for Peace: A Secretary-General's Memoir* (New York: St. Martin's, 1997), 131–32.
148. Ibid.
149. Ibid.
150. Franck, *Nation against Nation*, 152.
151. Urquhart, *A Life*, 325.
152. Waldheim, *Eye of the Storm*, 150–51.
153. Franck, *Nation against Nation*, 151.
154. Waldheim, *Eye of the Storm*, 151.
155. Franck, *Nation against Nation*, 143.
156. Waldheim, *Eye of the Storm*, 152–53.
157. T. T. B. Koh, "The United Nations Perception and Reality," (speech to a meeting of Asian media, sponsored by the UN Department of Public Information, Manila, May 12–14, 1983), 1.
158. Waldheim, *Eye of the Storm*, 155.
159. Franck, *Nation against Nation*, 143.
160. Urquhart, *A Life*, 331.
161. Finger, interview.
162. Finger and Saltzman, *Bending*, 79.
163. Meisler, *United Nations*, 201.
164. Waldheim, *Eye of the Storm*, 235.
165. Waldheim, interview.
166. Ibid.
167. Finger, interview.
168. Ibid.
169. Finger and Saltzman, *Bending*, 47.
170. *Secretary-General's Annual Report to the General Assembly*, cited in Franck, *Nation against Nation*, 122.
171. Waldheim, *Eye of the Storm*, 146.
172. Urquhart, interview.
173. Waldheim, *Challenge*, 5.
174. James Sutterlin, interview.
175. Lawrence Finkelstein, interview.
176. Newman, *The UN Secretary-General*, 66.

177. Sutterlin, interview.
178. Meisler, *United Nations*, 198.
179. Ryan, *The United Nations*, 14.
180. Finger, interview.
181. Linda M. Fasulo, *Representing America: Experiences of US Diplomats at the UN* (New York: Facts on File, 1984), 186–87.
182. Newman, *The UN Secretary-General*, 53.
183. Urquhart, *A Life*, 269.
184. Urquhart, interview.
185. Ibid.
186. Finger, interview.
187. Urquhart, *A Life*, 282–83.
188. Ibid., 229.
189. Ryan, *The United Nations*, 16.
190. Finger and Saltzman, *Bending*, 76.
191. Waldheim, *Eye of the Storm*, 40.
192. Finger, interview.
193. Waldheim, interview.
194. Waldheim, *Eye of the Storm*, 189.
195. Finger, interview.
196. Edward C. Luck, interview with the author.
197. Waldheim, interview.
198. Urquhart, *A Life*, 225.
199. Sherry, interview.
200. Finger and Saltzman, *Bending*, 7.

Chapter Seven: Javier Pérez de Cuéllar

1. Javier Pérez de Cuéllar, *Pilgrimage for Peace: A Secretary-General's Memoir* (New York: St. Martin's, 1997), 27.
2. Ibid.
3. George L. Lankevich, *The United Nations under Javier Pérez de Cuéllar, 1982–1991* (Lanham, MD: Scarecrow, 1991), vii.
4. Ibid., 21.
5. Pérez de Cuéllar, *Pilgrimage*, 22.
6. Ibid., 20.
7. Ibid., 24.
8. Ibid., 24.
9. Lankevich, *The United Nations*, 20.

10. Sir Brian Urquhart, *A Life in Peace and War* (New York: W. W. Norton, 1987), 382–83.

11. Jeane J. Kirkpatrick, *Reagan Phenomenon—and Other Speeches on Foreign Policy* (Washington, DC: American Enterprise Institute, 1983), 215.

12. James Sutterlin, interview with author.

13. Pérez de Cuéllar, *Pilgrimage*, ix.

14. Urquhart, *A Life*, 334.

15. Sutterlin, interview.

16. William Luers, interview with author.

17. Earl W. Foell, "Maestro of the Five-Power Lunch" *World Monitor,* August 1991, 28–29.

18. Pérez de Cuéllar, *Pilgrimage*, 20.

19. Urquhart, *A Life*, 352.

20. Pérez de Cuéllar, *Pilgrimage*, 7–8.

21. Sutterlin, interview.

22. Ibid.

23. Giandomenico Picco, interview with author.

24. Joe Sills, interview with author.

25. Sutterlin, interview.

26. Pérez de Cuéllar, *Pilgrimage*, 7.

27. Fred Eckhard, interview with author.

28. Cited in Pérez de Cuéllar, *Pilgrimage*, 8

29. Ibid., 10.

30. Ibid., 23.

31. Edward Newman, *The UN Secretary-General from the Cold War to the New Era: A Global Peace and Security Mandate?* (New York: St. Martin's, 1998), 69.

32. Pérez de Cuéllar, *Pilgrimage*, 13.

33. Ibid.

34. Urquhart, *A Life*, 348.

35. Ibid.

36. Newman, *The UN Secretary-General*, 71.

37. Thomas Boudreau, *Sheathing the Sword: The UN Secretary-General and the Prevention of International Conflict* (Westport, CT: Greenwood, 1991), 85.

38. Newman, *The UN Secretary-General*, 71.

39. Urquhart, *A Life*, 341.

40. Pérez de Cuéllar, *Pilgrimage*, 392–93.

41. Sutterlin, interview.

42. Pérez de Cuéllar, *Pilgrimage*, 392.

43. Boudreau, *Sheathing the Sword*, 85.

44. Álvaro de Soto, interview with author.

45. Pérez de Cuéllar, *Pilgrimage*, 35.
46. Urquhart, *A Life*, 342.
47. Lankevich, *The United Nations*, 135.
48. Ibid., 12.
49. Pérez de Cuéllar, *Pilgrimage*, 65.
50. Lankevich, *The United Nations*, 13.
51. Pérez de Cuéllar, *Pilgrimage*, 31.
52. Ibid., 37.
53. Nitza Nachmias, "The Role of the Secretary-General in the Israeli–Arab and Cyprus Disputes," in *The Challenging Role of the UN Secretary-General: Making the "Most Impossible Job in the World" Possible*, eds. Benjamin Rivlin and Leon Gordenker (Westport, CT: Praeger, 1993), 126.
54. Javier Pérez de Cuéllar, "The Role of the UN Secretary-General" (Cyril Foster Lecture, Oxford University, Oxford, England, May 13, 1986).
55. Thomas Franck and Georg Nolte, "The Good Offices Function of the UN Secretary-General," in *United Nations, Divided World: The United Nations' Roles in International Relations*, 2nd ed., eds. Adam Roberts and Benedict Kingsbury (New York: Oxford University Press, 1993), 166.
56. Lankevich, *The United Nations*, 32.
57. Thomas Franck, *Nation against Nation: What Happened to the UN Dream and What the US Can Do about It* (New York: Oxford University Press, 1985), 152.
58. Pérez de Cuéllar, *Pilgrimage*, 14.
59. Hurst Hannum, interview with author.
60. Boudreau, *Sheathing the Sword*, 115–16.
61. Pérez de Cuéllar, *Pilgrimage*, 23.
62. Franck, *Nation against Nation*, 159.
63. Pérez de Cuéllar, *Pilgrimage*, 10.
64. Boudreau, *Sheathing the Sword*, 97.
65. James Sutterlin, *The United Nations and the Maintenance of International Security: A Challenge to Be Met* (Westport, CT: Praeger, 1995), 54.
66. Pérez de Cuéllar, *Pilgrimage*, 9–10.
67. Ibid., 10.
68. Vladimir Avakov, "The Secretary-General in the Afghanistan Conflict, the Iran–Iraq War, and the Gulf Crisis," in *The Challenging Role of the UN Secretary-General*, eds. Rivlin and Gordenker, 159.
69. Newman, *The UN Secretary-General*, 88.
70. Ibid., 88.
71. Pérez de Cuéllar, *Pilgrimage*, 132, 150.
72. Ibid, 137.
73. Ibid, 134.

74. Boudreau, *Sheathing the Sword*, 91.
75. Picco, interview.
76. Lankevich, *The United Nations*, 41.
77. Boudreau, *Sheathing the Sword*, 92.
78. Pérez de Cuéllar, *Pilgrimage*, 147–48.
79. Ibid., 154.
80. Stanley Meisler, *United Nations: The First Fifty Years* (New York: Atlantic Monthly, 1995), 249–50.
81. George Shultz, *Turmoil and Triumph: Diplomacy, Power, and the Victory of the American Ideal* (New York: Scribners, 1993), 932.
82. Pérez de Cuéllar, *Pilgrimage*, 170.
83. Ibid., 173.
84. Lankevich, *The United Nations*, 70.
85. Pérez de Cuéllar, *Pilgrimage*, 175.
86. Avakov, "The Secretary-General," 164.
87. Pérez de Cuéllar, *Pilgrimage*, 177.
88. Sutterlin, interview.
89. Leon Gordenker, interview with author.
90. Inis L. Claude Jr., interview with author.
91. Pérez de Cuéllar, *Pilgrimage*, 177–78.
92. Seymour Maxwell Finger and Arnold A. Saltzman, *Bending with the Winds: Kurt Waldheim and the United Nations* (New York: Praeger, 1990), 88–89.
93. Meisler, *United Nations*, 247.
94. Ibid., 252.
95. Picco, interview.
96. Pérez de Cuéllar, *Pilgrimage*, 182.
97. Ibid., 186.
98. Ibid., 143–44.
99. Sutterlin, interview.
100. Urquhart, *A Life*, 355.
101. Pérez de Cuéllar, *Pilgrimage*, 192.
102. Newman, *The UN Secretary-General*, 77.
103. Pérez de Cuéllar, *Pilgrimage*, 181.
104. Ibid., 196.
105. Ibid., 198.
106. Ibid., 201.
107. Ibid., 208.
108. Ibid., 212.
109. Sutterlin, interview.
110. Avakov, "The Secretary-General," 158.

111. Pérez de Cuéllar, *Pilgrimage*, 99.
112. Lankevich, *The United Nations*, 120.
113. Pérez de Cuéllar, *Pilgrimage*, 108.
114. Ibid., 105–6.
115. Cited in Terry Anderson, *Den of Lions: A Startling Memoir of Survival and Triumph* (New York: Crown Publishers, 1993), 313–14.
116. Ibid., 315–16.
117. Ibid., 270.
118. Pérez de Cuéllar, *Pilgrimage*, 110.
119. Ibid., 114.
120. Ibid., 126–27.
121. Ibid., 100.
122. Cited in Benjamin Rivlin, "The International Political Climate and the Secretary-General," in *The Challenging Role of the UN Secretary-General*, eds. Rivlin and Gordenker, 15.
123. Pérez de Cuéllar, *Pilgrimage*, 124.
124. Bhaskar Menon, interview with author.
125. Sills, interview.
126. Rivlin, "International Political Climate," 15.
127. Elaine Sciolino, "Tea in Teheran," *New York Times*, December 6, 1991.
128. Picco, interview.
129. W. Ofuatey-Kodjoe, "The Role of the UN Secretary-General in the Decolonization of Namibia," in *The Challenging Role of the UN Secretary-General*, eds. Rivlin and Gordenker, 135.
130. Ralph Wilde, "Trusteeship Council," in *The Oxford Handbook on the United Nations*, eds. Thomas G. Weiss and Sam Daws (New York: Oxford University Press, 2007), 153–54.
131. Pérez de Cuéllar, *Pilgrimage*, 301–2.
132. Ibid., 297.
133. Ibid., 296.
134. Lankevich, *The United Nations*, 92.
135. Pérez de Cuéllar, *Pilgrimage*, 292.
136. Thomas G. Weiss, interview with author.
137. Ofuatey-Kodjoe, "The Role of the UN Secretary-General," 134.
138. Pérez de Cuéllar, *Pilgrimage*, 353.
139. Ibid., 403.
140. Cited in Lankevich, *The United Nations*, 28.
141. Pérez de Cuéllar, *Pilgrimage*, 403.
142. Ibid., 404.
143. Ibid., 409.

144. Ibid.

145. Ibid., 412–13.

146. Ibid., 416.

147. Ibid., 395.

148. Lankevich, *The United Nations*, 103.

149. Pérez de Cuéllar, *Pilgrimage*, 406.

150. Ibid., 419.

151. de Soto, interview.

152. Ibid.

153. Pérez de Cuéllar, *Pilgrimage*, 417.

154. Newman, *The UN Secretary-General*, 92–93.

155. Pérez de Cuéllar, *Pilgrimage*, 425.

156. Ibid., 422, 425.

157. Ibid., 426.

158. Ibid., 431.

159. Ibid.

160. Edward C. Luck, interview with author.

161. Pérez de Cuéllar, *Pilgrimage*, 433–34.

162. Ibid., 435.

163. Ibid.

164. Newman, *The UN Secretary-General*, 94.

165. de Soto, interview.

166. Pérez de Cuéllar, *Pilgrimage*, 435.

167. Rivlin, "International Political Climate," 16.

168. Meisler, *United Nations*, 255.

169. Pérez de Cuéllar, *Pilgrimage*, 419.

170. de Soto, interview.

171. Pérez de Cuéllar, *Pilgrimage*, 448.

172. Sutterlin, interview.

173. Pérez de Cuéllar, *Pilgrimage*, 452.

174. Ibid.

175. Ibid., 453–54.

176. Franck and Nolte, "Good Offices," in Franck and Nolte, *Divided World*, 152.

177. Newman, *The UN Secretary-General*, 99.

178. Lankevich, *The United Nations*, 105, 115.

179. Newman, *The UN Secretary-General*, 99.

180. Pérez de Cuéllar, *Pilgrimage*, 447.

181. Newman, *The UN Secretary-General*, 99.

182. Meisler, *United Nations*, 260–61.

183. Rivlin, "International Political Climate," 14.

184. Meisler, *United Nations*, 267.
185. David M. Malone, interview with author.
186. Newman, *The UN Secretary-General*, 102.
187. Pérez de Cuéllar, *Pilgrimage*, 263.
188. Ibid.
189. Ibid., 265–67.
190. Ibid., 267.
191. Ibid., 270; Meisler, *United Nations*, 268.
192. Pérez de Cuéllar, *Pilgrimage*, 276.
193. Ibid., 268.
194. Rivlin, "International Political Climate," 15.
195. de Soto, interview.
196. Sutterlin, interview.
197. Malone, interview.
198. Pérez de Cuéllar, *Pilgrimage*, 13–14.
199. Ibid., 28–29.
200. Olga Pellicer, "The United Nations in Central America: The Role of the Secretary-General," in *The Challenging Role of the UN Secretary-General*, eds. Rivlin and Gordenker, 185.
201. Phyllis Bennis and Tony Benn, *Calling the Shots: How Washington Dominates Today's UN* (New York: Olive Branch, 1995), 60.
202. Malone, interview.
203. Claude, interview.
204. Sutterlin, interview.
205. Menon, interview.
206. de Soto, interview.
207. Clovis Maksoud, interview with author.
208. Sutterlin, interview.
209. Newman, *The UN Secretary-General*, 64.
210. Giandomenico Picco, *Man without a Gun: One Diplomat's Secret Struggle to Free the Hostages, Fight Terrorism, and End a War* (New York: Times Books, 1999), 160.
211. Picco, interview.
212. de Soto, interview.
213. Sutterlin, interview.
214. Pérez de Cuéllar, *Pilgrimage*, foreword.
215. James Sutterlin, "The UN Secretary-General as Chief Administrator," in *The Challenging Role of the UN Secretary-General*, eds. Rivlin and Gordenker, 57.
216. Pérez de Cuéllar, *Pilgrimage*, foreword.
217. Eckhard, interview.
218. Cited in Foell, "Filling."

219. Pérez de Cuéllar, *Pilgrimage*, 21.
220. Picco, interview.
221. Weiss, interview.
222. Cited in Foell, "Filling."
223. Secretary-General's Address at University of Bordeaux, UN Press Release SG/SM/4560 (April 24, 1991).
224. Pérez de Cuéllar, *Pilgrimage*, 6.
225. Felice Gaer, interview with author.
226. Pérez de Cuéllar, *Pilgrimage*, 4.
227. Foell, "Filling."
228. Pérez de Cuéllar, *Pilgrimage*, 23.
229. Ibid., 28.
230. Sutterlin, interview.
231. Bonnie Angelo, "United Nations: Challenge for the New Boss," *Time*, February 3, 1992.
232. Gordenker, interview.
233. Luck, interview.
234. Pérez de Cuéllar, *Pilgrimage*, 16.
235. Picco, interview.
236. Luck, interview.
237. de Soto, interview.
238. Pérez de Cuéllar, *Pilgrimage*, 29.

Chapter Eight: Boutros Boutros-Ghali

1. Boutros Boutros-Ghali, *Unvanquished: A US–UN Saga* (New York: Random House, 1999), 9.
2. Ibid., 13.
3. Cited in James Holtje, *Divided It Stands: Can the United Nations Work?* (Atlanta: Turner, 1995), 115.
4. Boutros-Ghali, *Unvanquished*, 7.
5. Ibid., 12.
6. Meisler, *United Nations: The First Fifty Years* (New York: Atlantic Monthly, 1995), 279.
7. Rivlin, interview with author.
8. Sherry, interview with author.
9. Meisler, *United Nations*, 280.
10. Richard Thornburgh, interview with author.
11. Boutros-Ghali, *Unvanquished*, 14.
12. Ibid., 12–13.

13. Ibid., 179.
14. Ibid., 157.
15. David M. Malone, interview with author.
16. Boutros-Ghali, *Unvanquished*, 23.
17. Álvaro de Soto, interview with author.
18. Boutros-Ghali, *Unvanquished*, 26.
19. Edward Newman, *The UN Secretary-General from the Cold War to the New Era: A Global and Peace Security Mandate?* (New York: St. Martin's, 1998), 114–15.
20. Leon Gordenker, interview with author.
21. Session of UN Correspondents Association (June 7, 1995).
22. Boutros-Ghali, *Unvanquished*, 15.
23. Paul Lewis, "UN Chief's First Four Months: Red Tape Cut, Feathers Ruffled, Funds Exhausted," *New York Times*, May 3, 1992.
24. Boutros-Ghali, *Unvanquished*, 16.
25. Ibid.
26. Ibid., 21.
27. Bonnie Angelo, "United Nations: Challenge for a New Boss," *Time*, February 3, 1992.
28. Boutros-Ghali, *Unvanquished*, 16, 20.
29. Thornburgh, interview.
30. Fred Eckhard, interview with author.
31. Diego Arria, interview with author.
32. de Soto, interview.
33. Meisler, *United Nations*, 286.
34. Boutros-Ghali, *Unvanquished*, 27.
35. Gordenker, interview.
36. Anonymous staffer, interview with author.
37. Holtje, *Divided It Stands*, 115.
38. Sherry, interview.
39. Bhaskar Menon, interview with author.
40. Thomas Franck, interview with author.
41. Boutros-Ghali, *Unvanquished*, 19, 21.
42. *The David Frost Show*, WETA, April 30, 1993.
43. William Shawcross, *Deliver Us from Evil: Peacekeepers, Warlords, and a World of Endless Conflict* (New York: Simon & Schuster, 2000), 231.
44. Boutros-Ghali, *Unvanquished*, 31.
45. Stephen F. Burgess, *The United Nations under Boutros-Ghali, 1992–1997* (Lanham, MD: Scarecrow, 2001), 23.
46. Boutros-Ghali, *Unvanquished*, 32.
47. Burgess, *United Nations under Boutros-Ghali*, 24.

48. Boutros-Ghali, *Unvanquished*, 43.

49. Ibid., 31.

50. Burgess, *United Nations under Boutros-Ghali*, 23.

51. Boutros-Ghali, *Unvanquished*, 78.

52. Ibid., 79.

53. Ibid., 80–81.

54. Ibid., 81.

55. Burgess, *United Nations under Boutros-Ghali*, 26.

56. Boutros-Ghali, *Unvanquished*, 212.

57. James Sutterlin, *The United Nations and the Maintenance of International Security: A Challenge to Be Met* (Westport, CT: Praeger, 1995), 23.

58. Boutros-Ghali, *Unvanquished*, 37.

59. Ibid., 38.

60. Ibid., 39.

61. Ibid., 45.

62. Ibid., 40.

63. Meisler, *United Nations*, 288.

64. Ibid., 316.

65. Boutros-Ghali, *Unvanquished*, 52, 53.

66. Ibid., 54, 55.

67. Burgess, *United Nations under Boutros-Ghali*, 93.

68. Boutros-Ghali, *Unvanquished*, 70.

69. Ibid., 73.

70. Shawcross, *Deliver Us*, 110.

71. Meisler, *United Nations*, 332.

72. Arria, interview.

73. Boutros-Ghali, *Unvanquished*, 84.

74. Ibid., 86.

75. de Soto, interview.

76. Malone, interview.

77. Thomas G. Weiss, interview with author.

78. Shawcross, *Deliver Us*, 111, 113.

79. Meisler, *United Nations*, 324.

80. Boutros-Ghali, *Unvanquished*, 76.

81. Ibid., 86.

82. Meisler, *United Nations*, 324.

83. Boutros-Ghali, *Unvanquished*, 90.

84. Ibid, 86.

85. de Soto, interview.

86. Edward C. Luck, interview with author.

87. Boutros-Ghali, *Unvanquished*, 143.
88. Meisler, *United Nations*, 325.
89. Ibid., 326.
90. Ibid., 326–27.
91. Ibid., 328.
92. Boutros-Ghali, *Unvanquished*, 235–36.
93. Ibid., 236–37; Newman, *The UN Secretary-General*, 134.
94. Shawcross, *Deliver Us*, 177–78.
95. Ibid., 162–63.
96. Boutros-Ghali, *Unvanquished*, 238.
97. Ibid., 239–40.
98. Ibid.
99. Malone, interview.
100. Boutros-Ghali, *Unvanquished*, 244.
101. Ibid., 240.
102. Ibid., 245–46.
103. Richard Holbrooke, *To End a War* (New York: Random House, 1998), 174–45.
104. Shawcross, *Deliver Us*, 187.
105. Meisler, *United Nations*, 313, 329.
106. Cited in Boutros-Ghali, *Unvanquished*, 41.
107. Newman, *The UN Secretary-General*, 135.
108. de Soto, interview.
109. Sir Brian Urquhart, interview with author.
110. Weiss, interview.
111. Fouad Ajami, "The Mark of Bosnia," *Foreign Affairs*, May–June 1996, 163.
112. Indar Rikhye, interview with author.
113. Boutros-Ghali, *Unvanquished*, 87, 149.
114. Shawcross, *Deliver Us*, 177–78.
115. Boutros-Ghali, *Unvanquished*, 54.
116. Meisler, *United Nations*, 297.
117. Shawcross, *Deliver Us*, 87.
118. de Soto, interview.
119. Boutros-Ghali, *Unvanquished*, 54–55.
120. Burgess, *United Nations under Boutros-Ghali*, 69.
121. Newman, *The UN Secretary-General*, 138.
122. Meisler, *United Nations*, 299.
123. Ibid., 300.
124. Newman, *The UN Secretary-General*, 138.
125. Boutros-Ghali, *Unvanquished*, 60.
126. Burgess, *United Nations under Boutros-Ghali*, 8.

127. Meisler, *United Nations*, 294–95.

128. Shawcross, *Deliver Us*, 119.

129. David Frost, WETA interview.

130. James Joyner, "5 Questions for Robert Oakley," *New Atlanticist*, April 15, 2009, http://www.atlanticcouncil.org/blogs/new-atlanticist/5-questions-for-robert-oakley.

131. Boutros-Ghali, *Unvanquished*, 59.

132. Meisler, *United Nations*, 304.

133. Boutros-Ghali, *Unvanquished*, 96.

134. Meisler, *United Nations*, 306; Shawcross, *Deliver Us*, 120.

135. Boutros-Ghali, *Unvanquished*, 100.

136. Ibid., 100, 101.

137. Edward C. Luck, *Mixed Messages: American Politics and International Organizations, 1919–1999* (Washington, DC: Brookings Institution Press, 1999), 189.

138. Rikhye, interview.

139. Boutros-Ghali, *Unvanquished*, 119.

140. Newman, *The UN Secretary-General*, 141.

141. Boutros-Ghali, *Unvanquished*, 123.

142. Meisler, *United Nations*, 309.

143. Ibid., 310.

144. Shawcross, *Deliver Us*, 122.

145. Boutros-Ghali, *Unvanquished*, 124.

146. Newman, *The UN Secretary-General*, 141.

147. Walter Clarke and Jeffrey Herbst, "Somalia and the Future of Humanitarian Intervention," *Foreign Affairs*, March–April 1996, 76.

148. Sutterlin, interview.

149. Jackson Diehl, "The Somalia Example," *Washington Post Weekly*, November 5–11, 2001, 26.

150. Ibid.

151. Newman, *The UN Secretary-General*, 140.

152. Ibid., 136, 142.

153. Ibid., 141.

154. Lawrence Finkelstein, interview with author.

155. Meisler, *United Nations*, 291.

156. Roméo Dallaire, *Shake Hands with the Devil: The Failure of Humanity in Rwanda* (Cambridge, MA: Da Capo, 2003), 6.

157. Boutros-Ghali, *Unvanquished*, 134.

158. Ibid., 130.

159. Ibid.

160. Burgess, *United Nations under Boutros-Ghali*, 225.

161. Dallaire, *Shake Hands*, 320.
162. Boutros-Ghali, *Unvanquished*, 131, 133.
163. Burgess, *United Nations under Boutros-Ghali*, 226.
164. Meisler, *United Nations*, 291.
165. Burgess, *United Nations under Boutros-Ghali*, 105.
166. Boutros-Ghali, *Unvanquished*, 138.
167. Newman, *The UN Secretary-General*, 150.
168. Boutros-Ghali, *Unvanquished*, 177.
169. Ibid., 135.
170. Ibid., 140.
171. Dallaire, *Shake Hands*, 6.
172. Ibid., 515, 522.
173. Shawcross, *Deliver Us*, 145.
174. Herbert Okun, interview with author.
175. Boutros-Ghali, *Unvanquished*, 162.
176. Sir Brian Urquhart, foreword, in *The Challenging Role of the UN Secretary-General*, eds. Rivlin and Gordenker, viii.
177. Boutros-Ghali, *Unvanquished*, 162, 174.
178. Ibid., 170.
179. Ibid., 167, 171.
180. Ibid., 174, 319.
181. Sutterlin, interview.
182. Boutros-Ghali, *Unvanquished*, 319, 334.
183. Meisler, *United Nations*, 290, 335.
184. Burgess, *United Nations under Boutros-Ghali*, 199.
185. Meisler, *United Nations*, 290, 334.
186. Malone, interview.
187. Boutros-Ghali, *Unvanquished*, 161–62.
188. Ibid., 158, 179.
189. Ibid., 337.
190. Holtje, *Divided It Stands*, 116.
191. Meisler, *United Nations*, 293.
192. Clovis Maksoud, interview with author.
193. Holbrooke, *To End a War*, 202.
194. Boutros-Ghali, *Unvanquished*, 67.
195. Franck, interview.
196. Boutros-Ghali, *Unvanquished*, 302–3.
197. Ruth Wedgwood, interview with author.
198. Luck, *Mixed Messages*, 52.

199. Stanley Meisler, "U.S. Weighs Vetoing UN Chief's 2nd Term," *Los Angeles Times*, February 21, 1996, 8.
200. Hurst Hannum, interview with author.
201. Sutterlin, interview.
202. Okun, interview.
203. Boutros-Ghali, *Unvanquished*, 5, 268.
204. Steven Erlanger, "US Will Oppose Move to Re-Elect Top UN Official," *New York Times*, June 20, 1996.
205. Boutros-Ghali, *Unvanquished*, 3.
206. Luck, *Mixed Messages*, 28.
207. Boutros-Ghali, *Unvanquished*, 68.
208. Ibid., 331; Shawcross, *Deliver Us*, 240–41.
209. de Soto, interview.
210. Boutros-Ghali, *Unvanquished*, 336–37.
211. Shawcross, *Deliver Us*, 48.
212. Boutros-Ghali, *Unvanquished*, 221.
213. Ibid., 251, 337.
214. Urquhart, interview.
215. Joe Sills, interview with author.
216. Malone, interview.
217. Cited in Holtje, *Divided It Stands*, 46.
218. Sills, interview.
219. Rivlin, interview.
220. Boutros-Ghali, *Unvanquished*, 283–84.
221. Burgess, *United Nations under Boutros-Ghali*, xvii.
222. Maksoud, interview.
223. Wedgwood, interview.
224. Boutros-Ghali, *Unvanquished*, 275.
225. Rosemary Righter, *Utopia Lost: The United Nations and World Order* (New York: Twentieth Century Fund Book, 1995), 281–82.
226. Urquhart, interview.
227. Gordenker, interview.
228. Sherry, interview.
229. Sills, interview.
230. Ibid.
231. Giandomenico Picco, interview with author.
232. Hannum, interview.
233. Ibid.
234. Urquhart, interview.
235. Luck, interview.

236. Malone, interview.
237. Urquhart, interview.
238. Arria, interview.
239. Meisler, *United Nations*, 284.
240. Maksoud, interview.
241. Arria, interview.
242. Sutterlin, interview.
243. Urquhart, interview.
244. Luck, interview.
245. Sills, interview.
246. Boutros-Ghali, *Unvanquished*, 299.
247. Hannum, interview.
248. Rivlin, interview.
249. Malone, interview.
250. Hannum, interview.
251. William Luers, interview with author.
252. Lucia Mouat, "Championing UN Causes," *Christian Science Monitor*, October 23, 1995.

Chapter Nine: Kofi Annan

1. *Boutros Boutros-Ghali, Unvanquished: A US–UN Saga (New York: Random House, 1999)*, 298.
2. Cited in William Shawcross, *Deliver Us from Evil: Peacekeepers, Warlords, and a World of Endless Conflict* (New York: Simon & Schuster, 2000), 239.
3. Boutros-Ghali, *Unvanquished*, 322.
4. Shawcross, *Deliver Us*, 240.
5. Barbara Crossette, "A Salesman for Unity: Kofi Annan," *New York Times*, December 14, 1996.
6. Clovis Maksoud, interview with author.
7. Joshua Cooper Ramo, "The Five Virtues of Kofi Annan," *Time*, September 4, 2000.
8. Richard Holbrooke, *To End a War* (New York: Random House, 1998), 103.
9. Shawcross, *Deliver Us*, 239.
10. Sir Brian Urquhart, interview with author.
11. James Traub, *The Best Intentions: Kofi Annan and the UN in the Era of American World Power* (New York: Farrar, Strauss & Giroux, 2006), 73.
12. Barbara Crossette, "Annan's Stratospheric Profile Gives UN a New Cause Célèbre," *New York Times*, June 14, 1998, 5.
13. David M. Malone, interview with author.

14. Thomas G. Weiss, interview with author.

15. Shawcross, *Deliver Us*, 217.

16. Kofi Annan, "Annual Meeting of the Academic Council on the United Nations System," (lecture, June 17, 1999).

17. Traub, *Best Intentions*, 92.

18. Shawcross, *Deliver Us*, 227–8.

19. Edward Mortimer and Richard Lambert, "Unraveling the United Nations," *Financial Times*, October 17, 1997.

20. Kent J. Kille, *From Manager to Visionary: The Secretary-General of the United Nations* (New York: Palgrave Macmillan, 2006), 171.

21. Ibid., 178.

22. Bhaskar Menon, *UNdiplomatic Times*, 2001, no. 4:4.

23. James Sutterlin, interview with author.

24. Álvaro de Soto, interview with author.

25. Malone, interview.

26. Fred Eckhard, interview with author.

27. Marcia Kurop, "UN Reformer Skilled at Art of the Possible," *Christian Science Monitor*, April 3, 1997.

28. Shawcross, *Deliver Us*, 226.

29. Ibid., 240.

30. Stanley Meisler, "Man in the Middle," *Smithsonian*, January 2003, 35.

31. Stanley Meisler, *Kofi Annan: A Man of Peace in a World of War* (Hoboken, NJ: John Wiley & Sons, 2007), 69.

32. Ibid., 150.

33. Ibid., 152.

34. Shawcross, *Deliver Us*, 281.

35. Traub, *Best Intentions*, 73.

36. Shawcross, *Deliver Us*, 280.

37. Ibid., 38–39.

38. Shawcross, *Deliver Us*, 247–8; Meisler, *Kofi Annan*, 151–2.

39. Shawcross, *Deliver Us*, 283–4; Meisler, *Kofi Annan*, 102.

40. Shawcross, *Deliver Us*, 284.

41. Meisler, *Kofi Annan*, 103.

42. Shawcross, *Deliver Us*, 288–9.

43. Eckhard, interview.

44. Shawcross, *Deliver Us*, 289–90.

45. Ibid., 316.

46. Kofi Annan, "Remarks at Council on Foreign Relations Inauguration of Peter G. Peterson Center for International Studies" (speech, New York, January 19, 1999).

47. Barbara Crossette, "Ignoring Critics, Annan Presses Quest for Peace," *New York Times*, December 28, 1998, 6.

48. Gordon Goldstein, "The Middle East," in *A Global Agenda: Issues before the 54th General Assembly of the United Nations: 1999–2000*, eds. John Tessitore and Susan Woolfson (Lanham, MD: Rowman & Littlefield, 1999), 47.

49. Traub, *Best Intentions*, 77–78.

50. Eckhard, interview.

51. Kofi Annan, interview by Yale University for its United Nations Oral History Project, May 10, 2000.

52. Eckhard, interview.

53. Urquhart, interview.

54. Annan, Yale interview.

55. Ibid.

56. Barbara Crossette, "A Testy Hussein Deputy and a Candid UN Chief Fence with the Press," *New York Times*, February 24, 1998, 9.

57. Christopher S. Wren, "Annan Says He Has the Council's Backing," *New York Times*, February 25, 1998, 10.

58. Shawcross, *Deliver Us*, 33.

59. Eckhard, interview.

60. de Soto, interview.

61. Annan, "Remarks at the Council on Foreign Relations," January 19, 1999.

62. Boutros-Ghali, *Unvanquished*, 201.

63. Ibid., 207.

64. Craig Turner, "Challenges Reveal United Nations' Shrinking Clout," *Los Angeles Times*, November 23, 1998.

65. Shawcross, *Deliver Us*, 348.

66. Ibid., 350.

67. Ibid., 351.

68. Annan, "Remarks at the Council on Foreign Relations," January 19, 1999.

69. Shawcross, *Deliver Us*, 360.

70. Traub, *Best Intentions*, 93.

71. Gordon Goldstein, "The Former Yugoslavia," in *A Global Agenda: Issues before the 54th General Assembly of the United Nations: 1999–2000*, eds. Tessitore and Woolfson, 61.

72. Shawcross, *Deliver Us*, 362.

73. Gordon Goldstein, "The Former Yugoslavia," in *A Global Agenda: Issues before the 54th General Assembly of the United Nations: 1999–2000*, eds. John Tessitore and Susan Woolfson (Lanham, MD: Rowman & Littlefield, 1999), 61–2.

74. Shawcross, *Deliver Us*, 362–3.

75. Ibid.

76. Ibid., 37.

77. Ibid., 365.

78. Samantha Power, *Chasing the Flame: Sergio Vieira de Mello and the Fight to Save the World* (New York: Penguin Press, 2008), 241.

79. Kofi Annan, "Secretary-General Profoundly Outraged by Reports of 'Ethnic Cleansing' Conducted by Serbian Forces in Kosovo," United Nations press release SG/SM 6942, March 30, 1999, http://www.un.org/News/Press/docs/1999/19990330.sgsm6942.html.

80. Meisler, *Kofi Annan*, 177–8.

81. Ibid.

82. Kille, *From Manager to Visionary*, 207.

83. Power, *Chasing the Flame*, 241.

84. Shawcross, *Deliver Us*, 372–5.

85. Ibid., 382.

86. Ibid., 383.

87. Traub, *Best Intentions*, 96.

88. Shawcross, *Deliver Us*, 368.

89. *Breakfast with Frost*, British Broadcasting Corp., June 27, 1999.

90. Power, *Chasing the Flame*, 266–7.

91. Ibid., 263–4.

92. Meisler, *Kofi Annan*, 180, 205.

93. Traub, *Best Intentions*, 100–101.

94. Power, *Chasing the Flame*, 284.

95. Ramesh Thakur, "Humanitarian Intervention" and Bertrand Ramcharn, "Norms and Machinery," in *The Oxford Handbook on the United Nations*, eds. Thomas G. Weiss and Sam Daws (New York: Oxford University Press, 2007), 398, 446.

96. Simon Chesterman, "Responsibility to Protect," *UNdiplomatic Times*, 2002, no. 1.

97. Richard J. Goldstone, "Whither Kosovo? Whither Democracy?" *Global Governance* 8 (2002): 143.

98. Traub, *Best Intentions*, 102.

99. Kofi Annan, "The United Nations Will Stay... Your Friends Will Continue to Help," United Nations press release SG/SM 8243, May 20, 2002. http://www.un.org/News/Press/docs/2002/sgsm8243.doc.htm.

100. Meisler, *Kofi Annan*, 181.

101. Shawcross, *Deliver Us*, 371.

102. Ibid.

103. Ibid., 390.

104. Meisler, *Kofi Annan*, 182.

105. Shawcross, *Deliver Us*, 391.
106. Ibid., 392.
107. Meisler, *Kofi Annan*, 182, 184; Shawcross, *Deliver Us*, 393, 394.
108. Shawcross, *Deliver Us*, 395.
109. Ibid., 396.
110. Ibid.
111. Meisler, *Kofi Annan*, 184.
112. Barbara Crossette, "Annan Says UN Must Take Over East Timor Rule," *New York Times*, October 6, 1999.
113. Christopher S. Wren, "UN Creates an Authority to Start Governing East Timor," *New York Times*, October 26, 1999.
114. Dan Murphy, "UN Makes Feeble Timor Midwife," *Christian Science Monitor*, February 14, 2001.
115. Dan Murphy, "East Timor's Avenues to Justice Blocked," *Christian Science Monitor*, December 27, 2000.
116. "A New Nation is Born," editorial, *New York Times*, May 20, 2002.
117. Annan, "The United Nations Will Stay..."
118. Chandra Lekha Sriram, *From Promise to Practice: Strengthening UN Capacities for the Prevention of Violent Conflict*, International Peace Academy Policy Report (March 2002).
119. Thomas Franck and Georg Nolte, "The Good Offices Function of the UN Secretary-General," in *United Nations, Divided World: The United Nations' Roles in International Relations*, 2nd ed., eds. Adam Roberts and Benedict Kingsbury (New York: Oxford University Press, 1993), 179–80.
120. Traub, *Best Intentions*, 111.
121. Ibid., 112–3.
122. Ibid., 50.
123. Sir Brian Urquhart, "In the Name of Humanity," *New York Review of Books*, April 27, 2000, 19–22.
124. Meisler, *Kofi Annan*, 102.
125. Shawcross, *Deliver Us*, 145.
126. Ibid.
127. Traub, *Best Intentions*, 114.
128. Shawcross, *Deliver Us*, 145.
129. Urquhart, "Humanity," 22.
130. Eckhard, interview.
131. Weiss, interview.
132. John Bolton, "Lessons from Annan," *Earth Times*, December 1999.
133. Urquhart, "Humanity," 22.
134. Malone, interview.

135. Barbara Crossette, "UN Chief Issues a Call to Speed Interventions and Halt Civil Wars," *New York Times*, September 21, 1999.

136. Ibid.

137. Traub, *Best Intentions*, 127–8.

138. Ramo, "Five Virtues," 35–40.

139. Meisler, *Kofi Annan*, 203.

140. Traub, *Best Intentions*, 128–9.

141. Roland Paris, "Post-Conflict Peacebuilding," in *The Oxford Handbook on the United Nations*, eds. Weiss and Daws, 420.

142. Jean E. Krasno, "To End the Scourge of War: The Story of UN Peacekeeping," in *The United Nations: Confronting the Challenges of a Global Society*, ed. Jean E. Krasno (Boulder, CO: Lynne Rienner, 2004), 255–6.

143. Paris, "Post-Conflict Peacebuilding," 430.

144. John Bolton, "Kofi Annan's Quiet Coup d'État," *National Post*, September 11, 2000.

145. Barbara Crossette, "Kofi Annan: An Idealist Who Took the Heat, Shook Up the UN, and Keeps Top Post," *New York Times*, June 29, 2001, 1.

146. Traub, *Best Intentions*, 129.

147. Sutterlin, interview.

148. "A New Global Compact?" editorial, *Christian Science Monitor*, September 8, 2000.

149. Barbara Crossette, "Globalization Tops 3-Day UN Agenda for World Leaders," *New York Times*, September 3, 2000, 1.

150. Ibid.

151. John Ruggie, "The Global Compact as Learning Network," *Global Governance* 7, no. 4 (October–December 2001): 371–8.

152. Weiss, interview.

153. Crossette, "Globalization."

154. Traub, *Best Intentions*, 146–7.

155. William Luers, interview with author.

156. Malone, interview.

157. Eckhard, interview.

158. Transcript of Press Conference by Secretary-General Kofi Annan at Headquarters, United Nations press release SG/SM 7342, April 3, 2000, http://unispal.un.org/unispal.nsf/1ce874ab1832a53e852570bb006dfaf6/daa24ab9f0a7e21c85256913004ddbdc?OpenDocument.

159. Traub, *Best Intentions*, 149.

160. Meisler, *Kofi Annan*, 317.

161. "Kofi Annan's Millennial Vision," editorial, *The New York Times*, April 9, 2000.

162. Jeffrey Sachs, "Bubbles Burst and Bursting" (lecture, Chicago Humanities Festival, October 30, 2008).

163. Luers, interview.

164. Malone, interview.

165. Barbara Crossette, "Annan Begins 2nd Term Pledging to Bring UN Closer to People," *New York Times*, June 30, 2001.

166. Traub, *Best Intentions*, 156.

167. Ibid, 167.

168. Shawcross, *Deliver Us*, 45.

169. Meisler, *Kofi Annan*, 206–7.

170. Ibid.

171. Serge Schmemann, "Nobel Peace Prize is Awarded to Annan and the UN," *New York Times*, October 13, 2001, 1.

172. Ibid.

173. Sarah Lyall, "In Nobel Talk, Annan Sees Each Human Life as the Prize," *New York Times*, December 10, 2001, 3.

174. Sarah Lyall, "In Norway, Annan Warns US against Attacking Iraq," *New York Times*, December 10, 2001.

175. Meisler, *Kofi Annan*, 238.

176. Meisler, *Kofi Annan*, 238–9.

177. George Packer, *The Assassins' Gate: America in Iraq* (New York: Farrar, Straus and Giroux, 2005), 45.

178. Meisler, *Kofi Annan*, 239–41.

179. Traub, *Best Intentions*, 179–80.

180. Ibid.

181. Associated Press, "Annan: Give Inspectors More Time in Iraq," *New York Times*, January 27, 2003.

182. Traub, *Best Intentions*, 181.

183. Ibid., 185.

184. Meisler, *Kofi Annan*, 249.

185. Tim McGlone, "Annan Warns Bush Against Unilateral Attack on Iraq," Reuters, February 8, 2003.

186. Traub, *Best Intentions*, 184.

187. McGlone, "Annan Warns Bush."

188. Meisler, *Kofi Annan*, 251.

189. Felicity Barringer, "UN Secretary-General Faces His 'Most Difficult' Moment," *New York Times*, March 30, 2003.

190. Meisler, *Kofi Annan*, 252.

191. Traub, *Best Intentions*, 185–6.

192. Meisler, *Kofi Annan*, 257.

193. Meisler, *Kofi Annan*, 259–60.

194. Traub, *Best Intentions*, 194.

195. Packer, *Assassins' Gate*, 213.

196. Ibid., 215–6.

197. Mark Malloch-Brown, *The Unfinished Global Revolution: The Pursuit of a New International Politics* (New York: Penguin Press, 2011), 162–3.

198. Packer, *Assassins' Gate*, 217.

199. Traub, *Best Intentions*, 196; Meisler, *Kofi Annan*, 262.

200. Meisler, *Kofi Annan*, 263.

201. Packer, *Assassins' Gate*, 217.

202. Felicity Barringer, "Questions Haunt a Saddened Annan," *New York Times*, August 21, 2003.

203. Malloch-Brown, *Unfinished Global Revolution*, 164.

204. Traub, *Best Intentions*, 197.

205. Meisler, *Kofi Annan*, 265.

206. Traub, *Best Intentions*, 199.

207. Ibid., 197.

208. Meisler, *Kofi Annan*, 267–8.

209. Ibid., 269.

210. Ibid., 272.

211. Warren Hoge, "US and UN are Once Again the Odd Couple over Iraq," *New York Times*, November 14, 2004.

212. Patrick E. Tyler, "UN Chief Ignites Firestorm by Calling Iraqi War 'Illegal,'" *New York Times*, September 14, 2004.

213. Malloch-Brown, *Unfinished Global Revolution*, 213.

214. Warren Hoge, "Annan Reiterates His Misgivings about the Legality of War in Iraq," *New York Times*, September 22, 2004.

215. Meisler, *Kofi Annan*, 275–7.

216. Malloch-Brown, *Unfinished Global Revolution*, 165.

217. "Annan Vows to End Sex Abuse Committed by UN Mission Staff in DR of Congo," UN News Centre, November 19, 2004, http://www.un.org/apps/news/story.asp?NewsID=12590&Cr=democratic&Cr1=congo#.UmGfTfk3uSo.

218. Warren Hoge, "Report Calls for Punishing Peacekeepers in Sex Abuse," *New York Times*, March 25, 2005.

219. Reuters, "UN Council Condemns Sex Abuse by Its Troops," *New York Times*, June 1, 2005.

220. Warren Hoge, "UN Official Rejects Calls to Step Down under Fire," *New York Times*, February 19, 2005.

221. Traub, *Best Intentions*, 260.

222. Meisler, *Kofi Annan*, 313.

223. Boutros-Ghali, *Unvanquished*, 327.

224. "Kofi, Kojo, and a Lot of Shredded Documents," *Economist,* April 2, 2005.

225. "UN Will Not Pay for Legal Fees of Official Implicated in Iraq Oil-for-Food Probe," UN News Centre, March 28, 2005, http://www.un.org/apps/news/story.asp?NewsID=13778&Cr=iraq&Cr1=oil#.UmGgMvk3uSo.

226. Warren Hoge, "Annan Failed to Curb Corruption in Iraq's Oil-for-Food Program, Investigators Report," *New York Times*, September 7, 2005, 6.

227. Judith Miller, "UN Fires Aide Who Was Accused in Oil-for-Food Program," *New York Times,* June 2, 2005.

228. "Annan Finds No Grounds for Disciplining Former Aide in Oil-for-Food Probe," UN News Centre, April 28, 2005, http://www.un.org/apps/news/story.asp?NewsID=14114&Cr=iraq&Cr1=oil#.UmGgYfk3uSo.

229. Hoge, "Annan Failed to Curb Corruption."

230. Meisler, *Kofi Annan*, 285.

231. Ibid.

232. "Burden of Proof in Oil-for-Food Probe Shifts to Accusers Now, UN Official Says," UN News Centre, last updated March 29, 2005, http://www.un.org/ (link discontinued).

233. Meisler, *Kofi Annan*, 305–6.

234. Judith Miller, "House Inquiry into UN Aid for the Iraqis is Extended," *New York Times*, February 10, 2005.

235. Agence France-Presse, "Panel Report Points Finger at US in Iraq Oil Scandal," *New York Times*, May 17, 2005.

236. Malloch-Brown, *Unfinished Global Revolution*, 169–70.

237. Meisler, *Kofi Annan*, 284–5.

238. Warren Hoge, "Annan Remark on Oil Sales Draws Nods of Agreement," *New York Times*, April 24, 2005.

239. Malloch-Brown, *Unfinished Global Revolution*, 171.

240. Warren Hoge, "Secret Meeting, Clear Mission: 'Rescue' UN," *New York Times*, January 3, 2005.

241. Traub, *Best Intentions*, 392.

242. "Without Reform of Human Rights Body, UN Credibility at Stake, Annan Says," UN News Centre, April 7, 2005, http://www.un.org/apps/news/story.asp?NewsID=13895#.UmGhUvk3t8E.

243. Mark Malloch-Brown, "The John W. Holmes Lecture: Can the UN Be Reformed?" (speech, Annual Meeting of the Academic Council on the UN System, June 7, 2007).

244. Malloch-Brown, *Unfinished Global Revolution*, 177.

245. Traub, *Best Intentions*, 399.

246. "Voting 120 to 50, UN Assembly Adopts Text Seeking Details on Annan's Reform Plan," UN News Centre, May 10, 2006, http://www.un.org/apps/news/story.asp?NewsID=18423&Cr=#.UmGhhvk3uSo.

247. Traub, *Best Intentions*, 416.

248. Malloch-Brown, *Unfinished Global Revolution*, 174.

249. Traub, *Best Intentions*, 412.

250. Malloch-Brown, *Unfinished Global Revolution*, 167.

251. Meisler, *Kofi Annan*, 309.

252. "Fréchette Unveils UN Reforms Responding to Volcker Panel's Criticism," UN News Centre, May 17, 2005, http://www.un.org/apps/news/story.asp?NewsID=14311&Cr=UN&Cr1=r...#.UmGhtvk3uSo.

253. Edward C. Luck, "Principal Organs," in *The Oxford Handbook on the United Nations*, eds. Weiss and Daws, 655.

254. Kofi Annan, "UN Remains Best Tool to Achieve Key Goals of International Relations" (speech, Truman Library, Independence, MO, December 11, 2006).

255. Felice Gaer, interview with author.

256. Sutterlin, interview.

257. Malone, interview.

258. Luers, interview.

259. Sutterlin, interview.

260. Malloch-Brown, *Unfinished Global Revolution*, 260.

261. Crossette, "Ignoring Critics."

262. Cited in Meisler, *Kofi Annan*, 318.

263. Walter Niederberger, "Kofi Annan: 'A World without the UN Would Be a Disaster—Above All for the USA,'" *Tages-Anzeiger*, December 30, 2006, 6–7.

264. Meisler, *Kofi Annan*, 316–7.

265. Luers, interview.

266. Eckhard, interview.

267. Malone, interview.

268. Luers, interview.

269. Malloch-Brown, *Unfinished Global Revolution*, 229.

270. Thomas Franck, interview with author.

271. "Parting UN Chief Chides US," *Chicago Tribune*, December 12, 2006, 13.

272. Leon Gordenker, interview with author.

273. Richard Thornburgh, interview with author.

274. Jean E. Krasno, interview with author.

275. Luers, interview.

276. Stephen Bosworth, "Introduction of Kofi Annan as Speaker at Fletcher School of Law and Diplomacy Alumni Gathering" (speech, Medford, MA, September 2001).

277. Ramo, "Five Virtues."
278. Gordenker, interview.
279. Bhaskar Menon, interview with author.
280. James Traub, "Kofi Annan's Next Test," *New York Times Magazine*, March 29, 1998, 49.
281. Shawcross, *Deliver Us*, 45.
282. Meisler, *Kofi Annan*, 319.

Chapter Ten: Ban Ki-moon

1. Warren Hoge, "For New UN Chief, a Past Misstep Leads to Opportunity," *New York Times*, December 9, 2006.
2. Ibid.
3. Laurenti, interview with author.
4. Farley, "S. Korean Poised to Succeed Annan," *Los Angeles Times*, October 3, 2006.
5. Keating, "Selecting the World's Diplomat," in *Secretary or General? The UN Secretary-General in World Politics*, ed. Simon Chesterman (Cambridge, England: Cambridge University Press, 2007), 64–65.
6. Fackler, "On His Ancestor's Wings, a Korean Soars to the UN," *New York Times*, December 22, 2006.
7. Sung-Yoon Lee, interview with author.
8. Aldridge, *Ban Ki-moon*, Modern World Leaders series (New York: Chelsea House, 2009), 73.
9. Weymouth, "A Baptism by Fire," *Newsweek*, October 22, 2006.
10. Ibid.
11. Hoge, "For New UN Chief."
12. Aldridge, *Ban Ki-moon*, 48.
13. Hoge, "For New UN Chief."
14. Tom Plate, *Conversations with Ban Ki-moon: What the United Nations Is Really Like: The View from the Top*, Conversation with Giants of Asia series (Singapore: Marshall Cavendish, 2012), 67.
15. Ibid.
16. Aldridge, *Ban Ki-moon*, 44.
17. Plate, *Conversations*, 68.
18. Plate, *Conversations*, 156.
19. Benny Avni, "In Interview, New UN Chief Sets New Path," *New York Sun*, December 26, 2006.
20. Plate, *Conversations*, 34–35.
21. Plate, *Conversations*, 69.

22. Anna Fifield, "Relentless Pursuit Brings a Challenge Close to Home," *Financial Times*, October 10, 2006.

23. Lee, interview.

24. Plate, *Conversations*, 23.

25. "Acceptance Speech by H. E. Ban Ki-moon on Appointment as the 8th Secretary-General of the United Nations," October 3, 2006, http://www.un.org/News/dh/infocus/sg_elect/ban_speech.htm.

26. Hoge, "For New UN Chief."

27. Lee, interview.

28. Howard LaFranchi, "Early Accolades for United Nations' New Chief—with Caveats," *Christian Science Monitor*, January 31, 2007.

29. Plate, *Conversations*, 13, 97.

30. Edward C. Luck, interview with author.

31. Aldridge, *Ban Ki-moon*, 45.

32. Hoge, "For New UN Chief."

33. Aldridge, *Ban Ki-moon*, 45.

34. Warren Hoge, "UN Chief Returns to Headquarters Where Battles Await Him," *New York Times*, February 6, 2007.

35. Barbara Crossette, "Meet Your New Secretary-General," *The Interdependent* (New York: UNA–USA, Winter 2006–2007): 10, 12.

36. Hoge, "UN Chief Returns."

37. Robert C. Orr, "Comments at the Annual Meeting of the Academic Council on the United Nations (ACUNS)" (speech, New York City, June 14, 2012).

38. Louise Fréchette, "A New Global Agenda," *The Interdependent* (New York: UNA–USA, Winter 2006–2007), 13–14.

39. Luck, interview.

40. Julia Preston, "New UN Chief Invites Controversy by Declining to Oppose Hussein Execution," *New York Times*, January 3, 2007.

41. Luck, interview.

42. Thalif Deen, "Standoff: Developing Nations Intensify Challenges to Secretary-General, Rich Nations," *The Interdependent* (New York: UNA–USA, Fall, 2007).

43. Maggie Farley, "New Secretary-General Is Still Finding His Footing at the UN," *Los Angeles Times*, April 9, 2007.

44. Luck, interview.

45. Weymouth, "A Baptism by Fire."

46. William Luers, "My View: Ban Ki-moon's First Month," February 6, 2007, http://www.unausa.org/ (link discontinued).

47. Crossette, "Meet Your New Secretary-General," 10.

48. Maggie Farley, "US Suspicious of Aid to North Korea," *Los Angeles Times*, January 20, 2007.

49. Aldridge, *Ban Ki-moon*, 102.

50. LaFranchi, "Early Accolades."

51. Aldridge, *Ban Ki-moon*, 49–50.

52. Suzanne DiMaggio, "The Ban Ki-moon Era Begins," *The Interdependent* (New York: UNA–USA, Winter 2006–2007), 9–12.

53. Aldridge, *Ban Ki-moon*, 86.

54. Warren Hoge, "UN Chief Isn't Discouraged by His Close Call in Iraq," *New York Times*, March 24, 2007.

55. Howard LaFranchi, "How Much Can the UN Achieve in Iraq?" *Christian Science Monitor*, September 21, 2007.

56. Aldridge, *Ban Ki-moon*, 96.

57. Reuters, "UN Leader Protests Arrests and Beatings of Aid Workers in Darfur," *New York Times*, January 25, 2007.

58. Aldridge, *Ban Ki-moon*, 88.

59. Howard LaFranchi, "First Test for New UN Chief: Darfur," *Christian Science Monitor*, January 26, 2007.

60. Farley, "Still Finding His Footing."

61. Maggie Farley, "UN Mission Urges Charges in Darfur Crisis," *Los Angeles Times*, March 13, 2007.

62. Farley, "Still Finding His Footing."

63. Maggie Farley, "UN to Deploy Peacekeepers to Darfur," *Los Angeles Times*, August 1, 2007.

64. Aldridge, *Ban Ki-moon*, 91.

65. Warren Hoge, "Lack of Donated Copters Harms Darfur Effort, UN Leader Says," *New York Times*, December 7, 2007.

66. Aldridge, *Ban Ki-moon*, 92.

67. "Ban Ki-moon Kicks Off First Visit to Sudan," UN News Centre, September 3, 2007, http://www.un.org/apps/news/story.asp?NewsID=23679&Cr=Sudan&Cr1#.UmGh4vk3t8E.

68. Ban Ki-moon, "A Climate Culprit in Darfur," *Washington Post*, June 16, 2007.

69. DiMaggio, "Ban Ki-moon Era Begins," 9–12.

70. Ibid.

71. Colum Lynch, "UN Secretary-General Calls Global Warming a Priority," *Washington Post*, March 2, 2007.

72. Warren Hoge, "UN Chief Calls for Action on Global Warming," *New York Times*, September 25, 2007.

73. Aldridge, *Ban Ki-moon*, 99.

74. "Secretary-General, in Address to General Assembly, Lays Out Vision of Stronger, More Flexible, Efficient, Accountable United Nations," United Nations press release SG/SM/11182, GA/10622, September 25, 2007, http://www.un.org/News/Press/docs/2007/sgsm11182.doc.htm.

75. Barbara Crossette, "Antarctica to Bali: Ban Becomes the Environmental Secretary-General," *The Interdependent* (New York: UNA–USA, Winter 2007).

76. Ibid.

77. Ban Ki-moon, "Message to the General Assembly on the Algiers Attack Delivered by Videolink from Bali," UN News Centre, December 12, 2007, http://www.un.org/apps/news/infocus/sgspeeches/statments_full.asp?statID=162#.UmGiJ_k3t8E.

78. "Let 2008 Be the Year of the World's Poorest 'Bottom Billion,'" UN News Centre, January 7, 2008, http://www.un.org/apps/news/story.asp?NewsID=25222&Cr1=Ki-moon#.UmGiWPk3t8E.

79. Barbara Crossette, "Midway to the Goals, the UN and the World Bank Are Hopeful but See Disturbing Signs," *The Interdependent* (New York: UNA–USA, Fall 2008).

80. "How to Feed the Hungry Billion," *Christian Science Monitor*, January 29, 2009.

81. Neil MacFarquhar, "Stimulus Sought for Poorest Countries," *New York Times*, March 26, 2009.

82. Neil MacFarquhar, "UN Chief Says Working Poor Still Suffer," *New York Times*, September 18, 2009.

83. Neil MacFarquhar, "UN Chief Set to Announce Sharp Rise in Aid for Health of Women and Children," *New York Times*, September 22, 2010.

84. Luck, interview.

85. MDG Gap Task Force, *2011 Report: The Global Partnership for Development: Time to Deliver,* accessed October 21, 2013, http://www.un.org/millennium-goals/pdf/(2011_E)%20MDG%20Report%202011_Book%20LR.pdf.

86. Peter Grier, "State of the World: UN Poverty Reduction Goals on Track," *Christian Science Monitor*, December 26, 2011.

87. Michael Meyer, interview with author.

88. Helene Gandois, "After the Millennium Development Goals: What Next?" in *A Global Agenda: Issues before the United Nations 2011–2012*, ed. Irwin Arieff (New York: UNA–USA) 134–6.

89. "Secretary-General, in Address to General Assembly...," SG/SM/11182, GA/10622.

90. Warren Hoge and Seth Mydans, "UN Chief Calls Crackdown in Myanmar 'Abhorrent,'" *New York Times*, October 6, 2007.

91. Laurenti, interview.

92. Maggie Farley, "How to Help When Help Is Refused?" *Los Angeles Times,* May 14, 2008.

93. Ella Gudwin, "Policy on Burma Shouldn't Pivot on Aung San Suu Kyi," *Christian Science Monitor,* July 22, 2009.

94. "At Donors' Meeting Ban Ki-moon Says Myanmar Relief Effort to Last at Least Six Months," UN News Centre, May 25, 2008, http://www.un.org/apps/news/story.asp/html/story.asp?NewsID=26793&Cr=myanmar&Cr1=.

95. Bruce Wallace, "UN Secretary-General Defends His Approach to the Job," *Los Angeles Times,* July 4, 2009.

96. "UN Chief Calls for Burma Releases," BBC News, July 3, 2009, http://news.bbc.co.uk/2/hi/asia-pacific/8131869.stm; Neil MacFarquhar, "Myanmar Junta Rebuffs Effort by UN Leader to Meet with Jailed Dissident, *New York Times,* July 4, 2009.

97. Neil MacFarquhar, "With No Clear Path out of Diplomatic Thicket, a Push to Redraw the Map," *New York Times,* July 5, 2009.

98. Thant Myint-U, "In Myanmar, Seize the Moment," *New York Times,* October 5, 2011.

99. *All Things Considered,* National Public Radio, September 11, 2011.

100. Thomas Fuller, "Myanmar Backs Down, Suspending Dam Project," *New York Times,* October 10, 2011.

101. Joseph Alchin, "Burma: A Fake Out—or Real Reform?" *Christian Science Monitor,* October 16, 2011.

102. "Myanmar: Ban Welcomes Reform Measures in Meeting with President Thein," UN News Centre, November 19, 2011, http://www.un.org/apps/news/story.asp//realfile/story.asp?NewsID=40448&Cr=Myanmar&Cr1=#.UmVyM_k3uSo.

103. Steven Lee Myers and Seth Mydans, "US to Renew Myanmar Ties, Citing Reforms," *New York Times,* January 14, 2012.

104. Thomas Fuller, "UN Chief Will Ask West to Lift Myanmar Sanctions," *New York Times,* April 30, 2012.

105. Stephen Schlesinger, interview with author.

106. Nathanial Gronewald, "Haiti Quake Smashed 20 Years' Progress," in *A Global Agenda: Issues before the United Nations 2010–2011,* ed. Irwin Arieff (New York: UNA–USA), 26–28.

107. Neil MacFarquhar, "Haiti's Woes are Top Test for Aid Effort," *New York Times,* March 31, 2009.

108. Ginger Thompson and Neil MacFarquhar, "United Nations Mission's Challenges and Triumphs Reflect Those of Host Country," *New York Times,* January 18, 2010.

109. Randal C. Archibold, "Haitians Train for a Future," *New York Times,* October 26, 2011.

110. Schlesinger, interview.

111. Somini Sengupta, "Ethnic Divide Worsens as Sri Lanka Conflict Escalates," *New York Times*, March 8, 2008.

112. Sarah Trefethen, "A Weak Link in a Chain of Responsibility," in *A Global Agenda: Issues before the United Nations 2010–2011*, ed. Arieff, 32–34.

113. Jacques Fomerand, "A New Human Rights Council?" in *A Global Agenda: Issues before the United Nations 2010–2011*, ed. Arieff, 57.

114. Thomas G. Weiss and Ramesh Thakur, *Global Governance and the UN: An Unfinished Journey* (Bloomington: Indiana University Press, 2010), 333.

115. "Sri Lanka's Failure to Prevent Disruption of UN Work 'Unacceptable'—Ban," UN News Centre, July 8, 2010, http://www.un.org/apps/news/story.asp/story.asp?NewsID=35269&Cr=sri+lanka&Cr1=#.UmVyYPk3t8E.

116. "Ban Stresses Importance of Accountability as Sri Lanka Recovers from Civil War," UN News Centre, October 26, 2011, http://www.un.org/apps/news/story.asp?NewsID=40209&Cr=sri+lanka&Cr1=#.UmVyxvk3uSo.

117. Louise Arbour, "A Next Chapter in Human Rights," in *A Global Agenda: Issues before the United Nations 2011–2012*, eds. Traub, Arbour, and Arieff, 8.

118. Lydia Polgreen, "Report by UN Panel Says Sri Lanka Attacked Civilians near End of War on Rebels," *New York Times*, April 19, 2011.

119. Raj Gonsalkorale, "Ban Ki-moon Publishes His Report on Sri Lanka and Ends His Hopes for a Second Term," *Asian Tribune*, April 26, 2011.

120. Namini Wijedasa, "Sri Lanka's Ghosts of War," *New York Times*, December 31, 2011.

121. Mark Magnier, "Self-Critical UN Report Spurs Calls for Investigation of Sri Lanka War," *Los Angeles Times*, November 16, 2012.

122. Schlesinger, interview.

123. Luck, interview.

124. Weiss and Thakur, *Global Governance*, 319–20.

125. Ibid., 318.

126. Ibid., 329.

127. Luck, interview.

128. Ban Ki-moon, "Human Protection and the 21st Century United Nations," (Cyril Foster Lecture, Oxford University, February 3, 2011.) UN News Centre, February 2, 2011, http://www.un.org/apps/news/infocus/sgspeeches/search_full.asp?statID=1064.

129. Meyer, interview.

130. Luck, interview.

131. Weiss and Thakur, *Global Governance*, 316.

132. Luck, interview.

133. Roger Cohen, "How Kofi Annan Rescued Kenya," *New York Review of Books* 55, no. 13 (August 14, 2008).

134. Elisabeth Lindenmayer and Josie Lianna Kaye, *A Choice for Peace? The Story of Forty-One Days of Mediation in Kenya* (New York: International Peace Institute, August 21, 2009), 23.

135. Adam Nossiter, "Ivory Coast President Orders UN to Leave," *New York Times*, December 19, 2010.

136. Richard Gowan, "UN Intervention Rescues Ivory Coast by a Hair's Breadth," in *A Global Agenda: Issues before the United Nations 2011–2012*, eds. Traub, Arbour, and Arieff, 80.

137. Nossiter, "Ivory Coast President."

138. Dan Bilefsky, "Recent UN Actions Show Policy Shift, Analysts Say," *New York Times*, April 5, 2011.

139. Meyer, interview.

140. David Smith, "UN Evacuates All Staff from Ivory Coast Base," *Guardian*, April 3, 2011.

141. Bilefsky, "Recent UN Actions."

142. Gowan, "UN Intervention," 81.

143. Luck, interview.

144. "UN Chief Urges Syrian President to Stop Killing His Own People," UN News Centre, January 15, 2012, http://www.un.org/apps/news/story.asp/html/story.asp?NewsID=40948&Cr=Syria&Cr1=#.UmVy6Pk3t8E.

145. Laurenti, interview.

146. Meyer, interview.

147. Luck, interview.

148. Arbour, "Next Chapter in Human Rights," 8.

149. Allan Rock, "Libya in Revolt: Testing the Responsibility to Protect," in *A Global Agenda: Issues before the United Nations 2011–2012*, eds. Traub, Arbour, and Arieff, 11–16.

150. Cited in "News Release of the Global Centre for the Responsibility to Protect," part of the Ralph Bunche Institute for International Studies of the City University of New York Graduate Center, March 4, 2011.

151. "Arab Spring Shows New Way of Working Needed at UN," UN News Centre, September 22, 2011, http://www.un.org/apps/news/story.asp?NewsID=39696&Cr=arab+spring&Cr1=#.UmVzF_k3uSo.

152. "In Tripoli, UN Chief and Assembly President Laud Bravery of Libyan People," UN News Centre, November 2, 2011, http://www.un.org/apps/news/story.asp/html/story.asp?NewsID=40287&Cr=libya&Cr1=#.UmVzPPk3uSo.

153. Laurenti, interview.

154. Neil MacFarquhar, "UN Report Faults NATO's Response to Civilian Toll and Libya's Failure to Curb Violence," *New York Times*, March 3, 2012.

155. Arbour, "Next Chapter in Human Rights," 10.

156. Dulcie Leimbach, "The US and Others Support Ban in His Re-Election," *The Interdependent* (New York: UNA–USA), June 8, 2011.

157. "General Assembly Appoints Ban Ki-moon to Second Term as Secretary-General," UN News Centre, June 21, 2011, http://www.un.org/apps/news/story.asp/html/realfile/story.asp?NewsID=38797&Cr=secretary-general&Cr1=#.UmVzYvk3t8E.

158. "Ban Ki-moon Says Syria President Lacks Credibility," Al Arabiya news video, posted June 23, 2011, http://www.alarabiya.net/articles/2011/06/23/154532.html.

159. Edith M. Lederer, "Ban Ki-moon, UN Secretary-General, Accuses Syria of Breaking Promises," *Huffington Post*, September 15, 2011, http://www.huffingtonpost.com/2011/09/15/ban-ki-moon-syria_n_965172.html.

160. Patrick J. McDonnell, "UN Chief to Syria's Bashar Assad: 'This Killing Must Stop,'" *World Now* (blog), *Los Angeles Times*, October 17, 2011, http://latimesblogs.latimes.com/world_now/2011/10/un-syria-bashar-assad-ban-ki-moon.html.

161. "Secretary-General Hopes Syria Will Carry Out Arab League Plan to End Crisis," UN News Centre, November 2, 2011, http://www.un.org/apps/news/story.asp?NewsID=40292#.UmV4Bfk3t8E.

162. Nada Bakri, "King of Jordan Becomes First Arab Leader to Tell Syria's Assad to Quit," *New York Times*, November 15, 2011.

163. Nada Bakri, "UN Human Rights Official Calls for Intervention in Syria," *New York Times*, December 3, 2011.

164. Plate, *Conversations*, 113.

165. Ibid., 134.

166. Nick Bryant, "Syria Chemical Weapons: UN Adopts Binding Resolution," BBC News, September 28, 2013, http://www.bbc.co.uk/news/world-middle-east-24314186.

167. Keith Krause, "Disarmament," in *The Oxford Handbook on the United Nations*, eds. Thomas G. Weiss and Sam Daws (Oxford, England: Oxford University Press, 2007), 287.

168. Weiss and Thakur, *Global Governance*.

169. "UN Chief Outlines Five-Point Nuclear Disarmament Plan," *Agence France Presse*, October 24, 2008.

170. Krause, "Disarmament," 292.

171. Ban Ki-moon, "Dysfunctional Disarmament," *Project Syndicate*, May 18, 2011.

172. Plate, *Conversations*, 218.

173. Joseph Cirincione and Benjamin Loehrke, "Balance and Perseverance: The Case for Continued Engagement with Iran," in *A Global Agenda: Issues before the United Nations 2011–2012*, ed. Arieff (New York: UNA–USA), 27.

174. Rick Gladstone, "Ayatollah Denounces UN Nuclear Report," *New York Times*, November 10, 2011.

175. Greg Thielmann and Benjamin Loehrke, "Chain Reaction: How the Media Has Misread the IAEA's Report on Iran," *Bulletin of Atomic Scientists*, November 23, 2011.

176. Scott Peterson, "Iran Nuclear Report Fizzles," *Christian Science Monitor*, November 21, 2011.

177. Stanley Meisler, *United Nations: A History*, rev. ed. (New York: Grove, 2011), 379.

178. Joe Lauria and Jay Solomon, "UN Slaps Iran with New Curbs," *Wall Street Journal*, June 9, 2010.

179. Michelle Nichols, "UN's Ban Tells Iranian Leaders to Prove Nuclear Program Peaceful," Reuters, August 29, 2012, http://www.reuters.com/article/2012/08/29/us-iran-summit-un-idUSBRE87S0Y020120829.

180. Schlesinger, interview.

181. Plate, *Conversations*, 198, 200.

182. Lee, interview.

183. "'Enormous' Challenges ahead for New State of South Sudan," United Nations Radio News & Media, July 9, 2011, UNmultimedia.org/radio/english/2011/07/09.

184. Luck, interview.

185. Meyer, interview.

186. Richard Gowan, "Floating Down the River of History: Ban Ki-moon and Peacekeeping, 2007–2011," in *Global Governance: A Review of Multilateralism and International Organizations* 17 (Boulder, CO: Lynne Rienner, October–December 2011): 410.

187. "Ban Voices Deep Concern over Worsening Rhetoric between Sudan and South Sudan," UN News Centre, November 14, 2011, http://www.un.org/apps/news/story.asp?NewsID=40387&Cr=sudan&Cr1=.

188. Jeffrey Gettleman, "Mixed Signals in Darfur as Attacks Shadow Progress," *New York Times*, August 19, 2012.

189. Meyer, interview.

190. "Ban Urges Rapid Progress in Negotiations on New Climate Change Pact," UN News Centre, September 3, 2009, http://www.un.org/apps/news/story.asp?NewsID=31926&Cr=climate+change&Cr1=#.Uml5OPk3uSo.

191. Margot Roosevelt, "A Global Warming Star Search," *Los Angeles Times*, February 27, 2011.

192. "The Secretary-General Off-the-Cuff: Secretary-General's Year-End Press Conference," UN News Centre, December 14, 2011, http://www.un.org/sg/offthecuff/index.asp?nid=2137.

193. Emily Gertz, "Durban Climate Talks Not a Total Disaster after All," *TPM*, December 12, 2011, http://talkingpointsmemo.com/idealab/durban-climate-talks-not-a-total-disaster-after-all.

194. Plate, *Conversations*, 222.

195. Neela Banerjee, "Climate Deal Puts Off Any Action," *McClatchy News Service, New Hampshire Sentinel*, December 12, 2011, http://www.sentinelsource.com/mobile/article_e094c95b-68f5-5749-b906-d2e1f50203f2.html.

196. "The Secretary-General Off-the-Cuff."

197. Ban Ki-moon, "The Future We Want," *New York Times*, May 23, 2012.

198. "Ban Kicks Off Beijing Visit with Live Social Media Conversation with Weibo Users," UN News Centre, July 17, 2012, http://www.un.org/apps/news/story.asp?NewsID=42496&Cr=social+media&Cr1#.UmV9xvk3uSp.

199. Simon Romero and John M. Broder, "Progress on the Sidelines as Rio Conference Ends," *New York Times*, June 24, 2012.

200. John Vidal, "Rio+20: Reasons to Be Cheerful," *Poverty Matters Blog, Guardian*, June 27, 2012, http://www.theguardian.com/global-development/poverty-matters/2012/jun/27/rio20-reasons-cheerful.

201. Jacob Scherr, "Measuring the True Reach of the Rio+20 Summit," *Switchboard* (blog), *Natural Resources Defense Council*, August 2, 2012, http://switchboard.nrdc.org/blogs/jscherr/measuring_the_true_reach_of_th.html.

202. Orr, ACUNS meeting, June 2012

203. Isabel Kershner, "UN Chief, Visiting West Bank, Urges Israel to End Settlement Construction," *New York Times*, March 21, 2010.

204. Meisler, *United Nations*, 382.

205. "Palestinians Win Upgraded UN Status by a Wide Margin," BBC News, November 30, 2012, http://www.bbc.co.uk/news/world-middle-east-20550864.

206. Plate, *Conversations*, 135–6.

207. Ethan Bronne and Isabel Kershner, "Head of UN Panel Regrets Saying Israel Intentionally Killed Gazans," *New York Times*, April 3, 2011.

208. Fares Akram, "Protesters in Gaza Throw Shoes and Sticks at UN Chief," *New York Times*, February 3, 2012.

209. Plate, *Conversations*, 113.

210. Joe Lauria, Mark Champion, and Joshua Mitnick, "UN Calls Israeli Force on Flotilla 'Excessive,'" *Wall Street Journal*, September 2, 2011.

211. Schlesinger, interview.

212. Laurenti, interview.

213. Jacob Heilbrunn, "Nowhere Man: Why Ban Ki-moon Is the World's Most Dangerous Korean," *Foreign Policy* 173 (July–August 2009): 23–24.

214. Meyer, interview.

215. Luck, interview.

216. Laurenti, interview.

217. Luck, interview.

218. Meyer, interview.

219. Laurenti, interview.

220. Jason Burke, "India Gang-Rape Victim Cremated as UN Chief Calls for Action to Protect Women," *Guardian*, December 30, 2012.

221. Matthew Russell Lee, "As UN's Ban Says Nobody Follows Him, He's Presiding Over Chaos on Ethics and Disclosure," article and full text of speech in *Inner City Press*, September 2, 2008, http://www.innercitypress.com/ban1turin090208.html.

222. Joe Lauria and Steve Stecklow, "The UN's Invisible Man," *Wall Street Journal*, July 14, 2009.

223. Schlesinger, interview.

224. Lee, interview.

225. Luck, interview.

226. Mohammed Ibrahim and Jeffrey Gettleman, "UN Chief Pays Surprise Visit to Somalia," *New York Times*, December 10, 2011.

227. "Ban Voices UN Solidarity with Thailand after Viewing Flood-Hit Areas," UN News Centre, November 16, 2011, http://www.un.org/apps/news/story.asp/html/story.asp?NewsID=40412&Cr=thailand&Cr1=#.UmV_VPk3t8E.

228. Meyer, interview.

229. Luck, interview.

230. "Ban Ki-moon Outlines Steps to Bolster Collaboration with Regional Organizations," UN News Centre, April 1, 2008, http://www.un.org/apps/news/story.asp?NewsID=26171&Cr=conflict&Cr1=prevention.

231. "UN Chief Urges Asia to Take Up Leadership on Global Issues," UN News Centre, November 19, 2011, http://www.un.org/apps/news/story.asp?NewsID=40450&Cr=ASEAN&Cr1#.UmWAmfk3uSo.

232. Lee, interview.

233. Plate, *Conversations*, 211.

234. Ibid., 176.

235. Warren Hoge, "South Korean Is Appointed Secretary-General of the UN," *New York Times*, October 14, 2006.

Index

Proof

Made in the USA
Charleston, SC
13 February 2014